Home in Hollywood

FILM AND CULTURE / *John Belton, General Editor*

FILM AND CULTURE   *A series of Columbia University Press*   John Belton, General Editor

Elisabeth Bronfen

Home in
Hollywood

The Imaginary Geography
of Cinema

COLUMBIA UNIVERSITY PRESS / NEW YORK

8-05

Columbia University Press
Publishers Since 1893
New York   Chichester, West Sussex
Copyright © 2004 Columbia University Press
All rights reserved

Library of Congress Cataloging-in-Publication Data
Bronfen, Elisabeth.
[Heimweh. English]
Home in Hollywood / Elisabeth Bronfen.
p.   cm.—(Film and culture)
ISBN 0–231–12176–8 (cloth : alk. paper)—ISBN 0–231–12177–6 (pbk. : alk. paper)
1. Motion pictures.   I. Title.   II. Series.
PN1994.B71913 2004
791.43—dc22

2004045530

∞

Columbia University Press books are printed
on permanent and durable acid-free paper.

Designed by Lisa Hamm

Printed in the United States of America
c 10 9 8 7 6 5 4 3 2 1
p 10 9 8 7 6 5 4 3 2 1

Contents

Acknowledgments

Dialogue was very much part of writing this book, and I want to thank Barbara Straumann, Muriel Gerstner, and Linda Zerilli for their untiring comments, criticism, and support. For assistance in putting the manuscript together, I also thank Scott Loren, Daniela Janser, and Mic Milic Frederickx. A preliminary version of my reading of *The Wizard of Oz*, which appeared in *Parallax* 16 (July–September 2000) was initially translated by Eric Baker, while a preliminary version of my reading of *Imitation of Life* appeared, translated by Rebecca J. Davis, in a collection of essays titled *Crossover: Cultural Hybridity in Ethnicity, Gender, Ethics*, edited by Therese Steffen (Tübingen: Stauffenburg Verlag, 2000). While I have completely revised the text of the original German version for this English-language publication, I want to thank both of these translators for the formulations I have kept. For criticism and suggestions that helped me in the process of reworking my text for an English-speaking audience, I also want to thank Slavoj Žižek. Finally, thanks go to Jan McInroy for her thorough editing of my manuscript, and to my editor at Columbia University Press, Jennifer Crewe.

Home in Hollywood

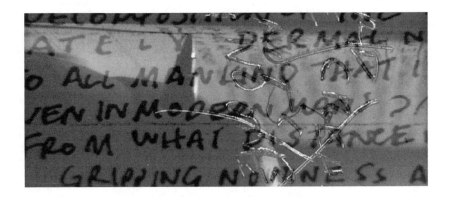

Prologue
Out of the Library: *Seven*

A Nocturnal Journey

On a bleak, rainy evening homicide detective William Somerset (Morgan Freeman) suddenly decides to leave the shelter of his living room. Although he will retire from the police force within a week, he is haunted by his final case, one that he had hoped would allow for a clean break from his past and, concomitant with this, for a new future far removed from the crime-ridden city in which he now resides. On the previous day (Monday) he had been called to a crime scene where an obese man, dressed only in his underwear, was found murdered—sitting at his kitchen table and facedown in a plate of spaghetti. His hands and feet had been tied together with wire to prevent him from getting up, so that he had to eat the food his killer forcibly fed him until his stomach burst. Somerset quickly realizes that because this murder must have taken more than twelve hours to complete, it represents not a random killing but a methodically conceived form of punishment. Not least, the risk of detection the murderer was willing to take convinces Somerset that the enactment of the murder itself is significant, consciously calculated for an intelligent spectator like himself who, because he is knowledgeable in the allegorical imagery of damnation and redemption, is able to decode its message. He is not surprised, then, when in the course of the autopsy the pathologist discovers bits of plastic mixed in with the food the victim had been forced to eat. Upon returning to the crime scene, Somerset notices that these strips of plastic fit scratches found on the floor in front of the refrigerator and correctly surmises that this is a deliberate clue left by the murderer. Upon pushing the refrigerator aside, Somerset discovers the word *GLUTTONY* written on the wall behind it; pinned beneath the word is a piece of paper onto which the murderer has inscribed a quotation from Milton's *Paradise Lost*: "Long is the way and hard that out of hell leads up to light."

When, early Tuesday morning, the police find a prosperous Jewish lawyer murdered in his office—dead because he had been forced to cut a pound of flesh from his left side—Somerset begins to see a pattern. The corpse of prominent lawyer Eli Gould is kneeling before the word *GREED*, written in his own blood—an embodiment of attrition, enacting repentance for past sins and likely motivated by fear that the stranger who had penetrated his office would kill him. During the meeting to which the chief of police calls Somerset and the young man who is about to replace him, David Mills (Brad Pitt), the veteran detective reminds them that gluttony and greed are two of the seven deadly sins and warns that they can expect to see five more crimes carried out with a similar signature. Somerset suspects that these initial deaths are part of a constructed allegorical performance representing the murderer's need for a morally (rather than legally) motivated punishment of sinners.

Because he believes the investigation will linger beyond the week that he has left on the police force, and desperate to leave this soul-crushing urban environment, Somerset initially tries to extricate himself from the case. Increasingly aware of the impotence and futility of law enforcement in the City, he is puzzled by the fact that Mills explicitly requested to be reassigned from upstate to this big-city homicide department. During their first meeting, when he asks his successor about this, the younger man, filled with naive self-confidence, explains that he felt he could do some good here because his years on the police force in a smaller city had sufficiently prepared him to take on the crime of an urban center. Doubtful at the outset, Somerset soon begins to seriously question whether his new partner is really up to the challenge of this assignment; the older man is all too aware of the critical difference between the world David Mills comes from and this infernal city. Here moral values no longer offer protection against the collapse of the community, and the ever-present threat of violence has produced a culture of apathy in which no one is willing to take responsibility for others and disinterest has replaced empathy and trust. Director David Fincher translates this dissolution of urban life into the very architecture of his strife-prone city. In *Seven* (or *Se7en*, per the title sequence), even the walls of rooms and buildings offer no protection against the incursion of evil from the outside. As Richard Dyer notes, "There is a perception that the body is in our times ever less safe from injury and mutilation; in particular, we live in a world whose anonymity and indifference have spawned and facilitated the serial killer."[1] Indeed, in this world in which anonymity rules, a criminal can enter the home of his victim undetected and potentially transform any domestic space into a crime scene. Even those spared from direct contact with crime are unable to keep the sounds of the outside turmoil from invading their private living spaces and are therefore constantly reminded of just how fragile the protection their homes supposedly afford actually is. Only the monotonous tick of a metronome can distract Somerset from the unrelenting street noise around him and allow him to fall asleep at night, while David Mills and his wife, Tracy (Gwyneth Paltrow), have to resign themselves to the fact that their new apartment home reverberates whenever a subway train passes.

Late on Tuesday, the day after they found the first corpse, Somerset decides to get involved after all, perhaps partly out of concern for the blind enthusiasm of his young successor, perhaps partly because he wants to spare the younger man from premature disappointment. Even though he had that very afternoon emphatically declined to continue working on the case, he now embarks upon his journey into the dreary night, hailing a taxi just outside his apartment building to escape the ceaseless rain. From the backseat of the speeding car, he looks mournfully out onto the bleak squalor unfolding beyond the window, where policemen have marked off yet another crime scene and are about to pack a corpse into a plastic body bag. "Where you headed?" the driver asks him, and he quietly answers, "Far away from here," obliquely giving voice to the feeling of fallibility that has come over him at the sight of this nocturnal urban scene. Although he may already have in mind the new home in the country to which he intends to retire, his present journey takes him to a different place, a countersite to the reality of urban crime, which harbors a profusion of representations that might help make sense of it: the public library. Upon entering, he is greeted by the laughter of the night guards sitting at a table on the mezzanine next to a large staircase, a stone balustrade separating them from the open space of the reading room. They are playing cards and eating take-out pizza. Somerset greets his old friends before selecting a table and putting down his briefcase, coat, and hat. He then turns to them once more and, as though the reading room were his stage and they an audience looking down at him from their balcony seats, he gestures grandly toward the walls surrounding them and proclaims, "Gentlemen, I'll never understand. All these books. A world of knowledge at your fingertips. And what do you do? You play poker all night." As though accustomed to his nocturnal visits and his resigned criticism, the guards won't let the reproach stand. Without interrupting their game, they respond in one voice, "We got culture!" To prove this, one of them actually gets up from the table and places his tape deck on the stone balustrade, turning the speakers toward the reading room. "Alright! How's that for culture?" he challenges his critic, as J. S. Bach's "Air" begins to waft solemnly throughout the library—the perfect musical accompaniment for the research into the baroque images and texts pertaining to questions of salvation and damnation that Somerset undertakes for his young partner.

Once the guard has returned to the game, Somerset begins to walk through the stacks, searching for books that will serve as iconographic references for the dramatically staged crime scenes that have unexpectedly appeared in the midst of what he perceives to be a world of gratuitous violence: Chaucer's *Canterbury Tales*, Dante's *Divine Comedy*, and *The Encyclopedia of Catholicism*. The illustrations he finds in these volumes, along with the stories of suffering inflicted upon sinners by a wrathful God, allow him to reconstruct the cultural tradition that the serial killer has appropriated for his own monstrous transformation of the contingency of death into a moral narrative of justified punishment. David Fincher intercuts this sublime visual journey—a repertoire of Western cultural images depicting God's violence toward humankind—with images of David Mills staring helplessly at the photographs taken at the crime scenes, reading the inventory of pieces of evidence found there, unable to make any sense of the data. The difference in the body gestures of the two men forcefully underlines their dissimilarity. While Somerset is serenely absorbed by the familiar texts, clearly at home in the geography of the baroque imagination, Mills grows increasingly irritated by the representations he is confronted with, because the cultural citations the serial killer has employed for his perverse masterpiece are utterly foreign to him. He demonstratively massages his cramped back and neck muscles, finally giving up in frustration and turning his attention to the football game on TV. There he finds a ritually enacted violence that he can enjoy with impunity, because it follows a code he is familiar with. Somerset, however, persistent in his pursuit of meaning, photocopies the images that he finds relevant to the case and puts them, along with Dante's map of the inferno and a list for suggested reading, into a manila envelope, which he eventually leaves on his partner's desk before returning to his noise-infected home.[2]

Somerset has lately been finding it ever more difficult to shield himself from the all-encompassing horror of urban violence in the City by turning it into meaningful case histories. The library, however, still offers him the safe haven he yearns for—a heterotopic countersite to vulnerable homes and dangerous streets, a place in which he feels at ease.[3] The library harbors texts that allow him to come up with an ethical explanation for the presence of cruelty in the world, even when he cannot solve an individual case or when, having found the perpetrator, he cannot detect the motives behind a particular crime—indeed, even in the all too frequent instances when he cannot use his evidence in court. In contrast to the contingent violence reigning on the streets of the City, the library represents for him a familiar geography, one in which he knows his way because of its rich stock of accumulated visual and textual representations; manifested here is proof of the meaningful battle between evil and good as it veers toward a final confrontation with divine justice. Here the complacency he experiences daily can be transformed into the certainty that even the most contingent act takes on meaning in a divinely created universe. Yet the imaginary home of Christian theology offers a satisfying refuge to the weary detective for another reason as well—not by promising the ultimate eradication of evil but, rather, by confirming the emotional and spiritual dichotomy that allows him to oscillate between resignation and hope. He wants to believe that there could be a world from which all traces of evil have been eradicated. In contrast to his naive successor, however, he knows that one can find one's way in the geography of postmodern megapoles only by acknowledging the ineffaceable moral devastation that violence has introduced into these communities. Although he hopes for a better tomorrow, Somerset is only too aware that failure is built into the very heart of his work as a detective, since solving one case does not resolve the presence of evil, cruelty, and vice in the world in any conclusive way.[4] Yet in the midst of all this doubt he still believes in the protective power of images. Indeed, the library, as the repository of traditional Christian images, offers an apotropaic shield against the immutable forces of antagonism inscribed into all social and psychic existence precisely because it translates what is irresolvable into a divinely inspired design of virtue and vice as warring factions. Owing to this translation of concrete acts of violence into a morally imbued narrative, each criminal case takes on a sublime and uplifting aspect, even if the general destructive power it reflects can never be fully dissolved. An untranslatable and irresolvable core shimmers through any representation of the fight for psychic salvation, whether it be the moral battle between virtue and vice, the legal engagement between detective and criminal perpetrator, or the psychoanalytically schooled reader's concern with psychic happiness.[5]

There is, of course, a final reason why Somerset enjoys tarrying in the library. He recognizes a resemblance between himself and the serial killer, insofar as both seek to transform the ubiquity of gratuitous violence in this urban center into a meaningful act. Both approach material bodies and the violence inflicted upon them as though they were meaningful representations. At the same time, they also share a particular genre—the morality play. Within Christian theology, sin was, from the start, conceived by Prudentius as what he called an "induration of evil" pitted against the working of the Holy Ghost (which could never be forgiven), thus bringing with it the loss of grace. However, since the Middle Ages, individual manifestations of ethically disreputable actions have come to be translated into seven personifications, for which the spiritual battle between allegorical figurations of evil and of good, as described by Prudentius in his *Psychomachia*, served as the core text. The cultural survival of this dramatic refiguration of a fundamentally irresolvable kernel of evil into the enactment of an agonistic competition between virtue and sin is, then, the trope to which both the serial killer and Somerset have recourse, as they devise a fantasy scenario befitting their psychic needs—in the case of the perverse killer, a monstrous demonstration of evil; in the case of the veteran detective, an insistence upon sympathy and understanding. Although their motivations are diametrically opposed, the fact that both appropriate the same allegorical language of agonistic strife deployed by Christian iconography opens up familiar territory amid the meaninglessness of gratuitous violence that dominates their world of apathy and complacency; it is here that they will find common ground.

The Detective as Reader and the Killer as Artist

Earlier that same day (Tuesday)—the film's emerging structure covering seven days is clearly meant to resonate with the killer's plan—the chief of police visits Somerset in his office and voices his own doubts as to whether the detective will really give up his work and leave the City. Somerset responds by telling him about a particularly senseless act of violence that took place the night before, a few blocks from the police station, then declares, "I don't understand this place any longer." By the end of the day, however, Somerset actually welcomes the challenge from the serial killer to be the witness and commentator of his monstrous masterpiece. For the detective, now faced with this refiguration of a medieval morality play, the City has suddenly been transformed into a familiar site. He can once again trust his hermeneutic abilities, indeed feel empowered—and not only because the cultural codes underlying the serial killer's enactments are familiar to him, making his ability to decipher them the only tool the police have for solving the case. More significantly, Somerset feels justified in seeking conclusive meaning in the midst of the violence that dominates his everyday reality precisely because the killer is broadcasting so unequivocal a message.

On the one hand, then, Somerset's belief that he can decipher the serial killer's acts of violence by reading them as a postmodern refiguration of Christian iconography emerges as a protective fiction. It reassures him that the contingency of the world can be understood and provides him with a psychic shield against the fragility of his life in this megalopolis by offering him the certainty that infallible knowledge exists, if only one can find the relevant key. On the other hand, as the designated interpreter of the serial killer's lethal morality play, he is also implicated in the very manifestation of cruelty that he seeks to understand. As the investigation progresses, he realizes that the killer cannot complete his monstrous work without a witness who will bear testimony after the event. The detective, who seeks knowledge about the indurate kernel of evil inhabiting any manifestation of the seven deadly sins, and the murderous director, enacting the monstrous representation of those sins, prove to be mutually dependent. However, although the serial killer appropriates Milton's text, his message does not support the Puritan belief that there most definitely is a way that leads out of hell and up to light. Rather, he seeks a merciless revelation of the ubiquitous and ineradicable presence of sin in the world, and thus of an unnegotiable damnation. Like Somerset, he feels at home in the imaginary landscape of Christian theology and resignifies these visual tropes to broadcast a cultural discontent comparable to that of the world-weary detective. Both, after all, are convinced that in urban postmodernity there can be no refuge from a dissolution of social order (much as the gratuitous violence reigning there cannot be understood) because common cultural codes of morality have broken down. In contrast to Somerset, however, whose goal it is to show empathy—while remaining fully cognizant of the failure that any attempt at understanding manifestations of evil entails—the serial killer seeks to construct a devastating monument to the power of evil, a terrifying lesson meant to enlighten his peers about their moral apathy, and he does this by transforming his killings into a ritual of punishment and attrition. Staging his victims' deaths to correspond to allegorical figurations of sin thus explicitly imitates the images of divine wrath that Somerset finds in the library and allows the killer to reenact the battle between virtue and vice so that even the most complacent inhabitants of the City must pay attention.

Indeed, as the investigation progresses, the serial killer proves to be the obscene counterpart to the older detective. Three days after his nocturnal visit to the library, Somerset tries to explain to Mills that he doesn't think he can continue to live in a place that "embraces and nurtures apathy as if it was a virtue." As will be discussed in more detail later, the killer eventually makes a final confession to the two detectives that uncannily resonates with a very similar critique of urban reality. Given that the murderer is driven as much by a desire to fight against the City's indifference as by a desire to reveal the manifestation of evil in the world, the perception of apathy emerges as the enemy for both men, even though their responses to such human callousness are radically different. While the serial killer clandestinely enters the homes of his victims, kills them, and disfigures their bodies in order to proclaim his message to the world, Somerset responds with empathy and sorrow to the scenes of violence he is called to investigate. Although both men inhabit the archive of Christian literature, the serial killer has fashioned himself in the image of an artist creating a masterpiece whose full significance will be revealed in a final scene proving the inevitable victory of evil over virtue. Somerset, in turn, fashions himself as a psychoanalytical reader seeking knowledge about the manifestations of human cruelty in the world, fully aware that these can never be unequivocally explained or ultimately resolved. His interest in the Western cultural archive of divine punishment confirms his belief that even the most monstrous revelation of the triumph of sin misses the traumatic core at the heart of Christian narratives of salvation and damnation. It merely translates the contingence of violence in the world into a morally unambiguous narrative, and in so doing reduces to a simple opposition what must be maintained as an irresolvable antagonism. Most significantly, however, he refuses to read the serial killer himself in relation to allegorical categories, which would mean reducing him either to a demonic figure or to a psychopath.[6] Somerset instead seeks to pit empathy against apathy, and thereby refutes any explanation in which the police, as heroes, are unambiguously good, and the perpetrators of crimes, as villains, are unequivocally bad. He insists on the humanity of the other, not least to assure himself of his own. This goes in tandem with recognizing the limitations of the very archive of knowledge he has recourse to, for as satisfying as he finds the texts stored in the library to be, he realizes that this imaginary landscape, with its clear demarcations between evil and good, offers nothing more than a provisional refuge, one that is itself threatened by the reality of gratuitous violence and indifference taking place outside its walls. His experience as a detective with the police force has forced him to accept that there can be no conclusive explanation, nor any truly comforting solution, for psychic and social antagonisms, and his careful reading of authors such as Prudentius and Milton has taught him that the "induration of evil" is precisely what can never be forgiven and thus also never fully effaced, functioning instead like a repressed kernel of knowledge upon which all subsequent struggles for human salvation or healing feed without ever touching it.

The question of whether, after the conclusion of any individual crime case, a trace of the violence it contained remains proves to lie at the heart of both detective Somerset's contention with the serial killer and also his disagreement with his naively deluded young partner. Unlike Somerset, David Mills is unwilling to acknowledge that there can be no simple, unequivocal solution to any individual manifestation of human cruelty. A conversation that clarifies the difference between them takes place in a bar late in the week (Saturday night) after the discovery of two more corpses—the first a criminal tied to his bed, meant to embody sloth; the second a prostitute, representing lust, killed by a client who was forced to wear a leather suit with a knife in place of the penis. During this conversation in the bar Somerset tries to convince the young man that this case isn't going to have a happy ending. While Mills believes they will catch the perpetrator, the older detective advances his argument: "If we catch John Doe and he turns out to be Satan himself, that might live up to our expectations, but he's not the devil. He's just a man." Somerset's position is that although this killer appropriates the language of morality plays and stages allegorical representations of the battle between good and evil, he remains a human player, not a divine one. Mills, however, needs the security that the man they are looking for can unambiguously be declared insane; he needs to support his own fantasy that he can be the hero in this scenario of urban violence. While

Somerset tries to sustain the contradiction that a criminal can perpetrate a monstrous act and nevertheless be judged as a human being because his transgression is part of everyday reality and not something pathological, Mills wants a world of unambiguous opponents. Having fashioned for himself the role of righteous champion, he refuses to accept the notion of an unresolvable antagonism and instead holds on to the belief that he is justified in deciding who—by reason of insanity—deserves no sympathy.

In so doing, however, he has recourse to the serial killer's own language of vice and will respond in savage grief-stricken wrath (the film's last deadly sin) to the man he considers to be the epitome of evil. In other words, Mills uncannily resembles the serial killer in that, like him, he too ignores the humanity of the victims, casting them instead as allegorical figures in *his* morality play so that he, as heroic representative of the law, is not only morally justified in resorting to violence but also will triumph in the end. By ignoring the humanity of the other so that he or she may fit the fantasy scenario, both men are seeking to enact—whether it be the fantasy of the omnipotent detective who will catch every criminal or that of the omnipotent killer-artist who will expose every sinner—both Mills and the serial killer become guilty of the very apathy they denounce, while at the same time in thrall to their own violence.

Nevertheless, there is a significant difference in how each of the three figures in this crime scenario plays out his part. To the bitter end, the serial killer remains in control of his lethal game, and the two detectives can do little more than follow his lead. Throughout, Somerset, as the empathetic reader (interpreter) of clues, stands in the place of the audience; but Mills will unwittingly be forced to climb onto the stage of this monstrous morality play. As in Milton's *Paradise Lost*, the "indurate kernel of evil" ultimately finds dramatic resignification in the staging of a final battle in which nothing less than the salvation of the hero is at stake. In contrast to Milton's epic, however, Fincher's serial killer, John Doe (Kevin Spacey), has chosen to reenact all seven deadly sins in order to prove that virtue always succumbs to vice. But while he has cast his morbid tableaux in the symbolic language of classic theological texts and designed everything so that on the seventh day his masterpiece will reach its destined end in a final horrific revelation, his refiguration also proves to be irretrievably enmeshed with the power of the sinful violence he seeks to disclose as yet one more sin—envy—becomes a stunning catalyst in the outcome to his plan. The two privileged observers, Mills and Somerset, are then confronted with a choice that is actually forced upon them. They can side with heroic virtue and take up the battle against this representative of vice—thus becoming helplessly and inevitably implicated in the very violence they seek to thwart. Or they can assume the position of a witness who is involved in the events but makes no claims to righteous actions and, instead, simply administrates all evidence that violence has taken place.

Administrating Evidence

While Somerset and Mills are sitting in the corridor of the police station (late Wednesday), waiting for a technician to process the fingerprints found at the crime scene of the murdered lawyer, the older detective voices doubts that they will come to a meaningful solution to the case. He explains that after all these years on the police force he can no longer believe that his work is about catching the criminal. Asked by Mills what he thinks they are actually doing, he replies: "Picking up the pieces. We're collecting all the evidence. Taking all the pictures and samples, writing everything down, noting the time things happen. Putting everything into neat little piles and filing it away on the off-chance it will ever be needed in the courtroom." To Mills's angry rebuttal he offers a dictum that will prove to be the ruling logic of their investigation and of the film itself: "Even the most promising clues usually only lead to others." Mills, unwilling to listen to this sober scenario, turns away from the other detective and, resting his head on the arm of the couch, falls asleep. Somerset stares silently into the empty space of the corridor before he, too, falls asleep. Although he has come to terms with the fact that failure is written into any criminal investigation, he still insists on nurturing the ambivalence inscribed in this resignation. While he humbly accepts his own insignificance, given that as an administrator of evidence he can only collect, regulate, and survey information pertaining to a crime, he is not yet ready to give up believing in the value of this knowledge. The individual pieces of evidence, piled up and locked away in filing cabinets, may initially be useless, but he nonetheless compares them with diamonds, which, if fate turns, may suddenly acquire enormous value. Still, Somerset recognizes that some significant piece will always recede from their grasp—because clues lead only to other clues—while his young partner, who has cast for himself the role of champion, maintains that clues ultimately lead to a final revelation and a decisive battle between the hero and his opponent, the pathological villain.

As the hours stretch into early Thursday morning, they are roused from their disparate dreams by the chief of police, who, like David Mills, continues to trust in an unequivocal conclusion to this case. He tells them that fingerprints found in the lawyer's office match those of a known criminal. But when the police squad enters the man's home, Somerset's uneasy intuition proves to have been right, for what they find is a lethal and grotesque enactment of sloth: the criminal—tied to his bed, his tongue bitten off in pain, with one hand severed by the serial killer in order to leave fingerprints at the crime scene of the lawyer representing greed—turns out to be yet another victim. Real progress, however, is made when Somerset comes up with the idea that the killer, like himself, might be a user of the public library system. Following a hunch that it might be possible to detect the killer's identity based on books he has been borrowing, he returns to the library and there procures a list of books that have been checked out recently and could relate to the case. A friend at the FBI, in charge of a clandestine security program monitoring flagged books in the public library system, runs a trace for Somerset, whose intuition proves once more to be right. Among the possible candidates on the list provided by the FBI's computer search is one "John Doe." As Somerset and Mills wait in front of his apartment, they finally run into luck—their surprised suspect, returning home with a bag of groceries, is indeed the man they have been looking for. Dropping the bag, John Doe fires several shots before bolting; in the pursuit that follows, Mills is ambushed from behind in an alley and held at gunpoint. For reasons ultimately made clear at the film's climax, the murderer decides not to kill the young detective and instead gives him a violent blow to the head before escaping.

Provoked by this demeaning gesture, and skirting the law, Mills gains access to his assailant's apartment. There he and Somerset discover the obscene countersite to the public library—the storage space for an arsenal of instruments for torture, burglary, and killing; a variety of medications; objects connected to crime scenes they have already found, and others possibly heralding atrocities yet to come. In a darkroom at the back of the apartment, they also find conclusive photo-documentation of the murders, piles of library books, and, most important, more than two thousand notebook-diaries. In each notebook, undated and apparently placed on the shelf "in no discernible order," John Doe has minutely recorded his thoughts on the moral depravity of society. Yet all this evidence leads not to the serial killer's identity but only to further clues. As the police search every corner of the apartment, they find no bank statements, no address books, and inexplicably, not a single fingerprint. Once again the detectives are forced to accept that they can merely administrate the evidence; they can collect, label, order, evaluate, sift through, and file away all the uncannily damning materials John Doe has accumulated, even discern the killer's mental geography—his religious fanaticism, his delusions of grandeur—without coming any closer to actually finding him.

While they are still in the apartment, John Doe calls them, nominally to express his admiration for getting so close, yet actually to taunt them with their own impotence. As he explains, leaving no doubt that he is still in control, their discovery of his apartment has forced him to "readjust my schedule in light of today's little setback." After committing two additional murders—in one case (as noted above) a prostitute representing lust, in the other a rich woman representing vanity—he finally gives himself up to the police, with the objective of making a pact with the two detectives. As his lawyer explains to the chief of police, there are yet two more corpses, whose whereabouts his client is willing to reveal along with making a full confession—but only under the condition that the law enforcement agents follow his specific directions. At dusk on the seventh day of the investigation, John Doe instructs Somerset and Mills to drive him to a deserted area outside the City, in order to have them witness the final episode of his morality play. He needs both—Somerset, because he will understand the meaning of the last two corpses and thus transmit John Doe's message to the world, and Mills, because in the course of the investigation the serial killer has correctly recognized in him a perfect representative of wrath. The detectives accept the pact, but wire themselves with hidden microphones and organize several helicopters to monitor their actions. Ironically, this surveillance will ultimately prove to be the final coup in John Doe's plan, for Mills, as eager as the serial killer to bring this case to its definitive conclusion, unwittingly enacts the part designed for him with the police squad tuned in, thus also proving Somerset right—that, as he had maintained all along, there would be no happy ending to this case.

During the ride, the three players once more debate whether psychic and social antagonisms can be negotiated as a simple opposition between good and evil, between the allegedly normal and the pathological, or whether an irresolvable trace of the "induration of evil" necessarily remains over and beyond any moral and psychic combat between virtue and vice, much as it always also recedes from the jurisdiction of the law. John Doe supports Somerset's diatribe against the apathy of the postmodern urban dweller. As he explains, he is, after all, only trying to wake his fellow men from their moral stupor. Upon being asked what his work consists of, he defends his radical mode by arguing that "wanting people to listen, you can't just tap them on the shoulder anymore. You have to hit them with a sledgehammer. Then you'll notice you've got their strict attention." Mills refuses, however, to recognize any moral or aesthetic significance in his crimes and instead accuses him of having killed innocent people. John Doe defends his work in a manner that sounds uncannily like the toxic counterpart to Somerset's earlier lecture on apathy. Only in a world so riddled with indifference and complacency, he proclaims, "could you say these were innocent people and keep a straight face." He then proceeds to argue: "We see a deadly sin on every street corner, in every home, and we tolerate it, because it's common, it's trivial." It is against this blindness that he seeks to pit his monstrous warning, a work that, he is convinced, will be puzzled over, studied, and imitated.

Even as John Doe thus denounces the moral complacency of his fellow men, he also admits that he has himself not been able to resist the temptation to sin. In this he has found a perfect collateral in David Mills. During the drive the latter adamantly maintains that there is a radical difference between John Doe's psychopathology and his own will to enforce the law, even if it requires the use of force. He thus rejects John Doe's objection that it is more comfortable for him to label his adversary insane than to admit that he, too, would enjoy inflicting his wrath upon others.

Once they reach their final destination, the two detectives initially simply stare perplexed at the bleak open landscape. In the distance, as a delivery van arrives from the direction of the City, Somerset runs toward it, fearful that the killer may be attempting to escape their custody after all. Mills remains with John Doe, forcing him to kneel on the ground, his hands still handcuffed behind his back. Upon reaching the van, Somerset is given a package by the driver, who explains that he has been paid to deliver it to David Mills. With a sense of mounting dread, Somerset opens it and discovers, to his horror, that it contains the head of the only truly innocent figure in the story: Tracy Mills. He is forced too late to recognize that the final scene of this morality play will be a battle for the soul of his young colleague.

As Somerset leaves the package and rushes back toward the two men, John Doe begins his last and cruelest act of torture. He calmly informs the clueless Mills about how he entered his home that morning, tried to enjoy the pleasures of domestic bliss in his stead, only to discover that he couldn't succeed and thus took the head of his wife as a token of this failure. When Somerset finally reaches them, an anguished David Mills is already pointing his weapon at the head of the man defenselessly kneeling before him. Somerset pleads with Mills to drop the gun, as John Doe continues with his fateful speech. He confesses that he had coveted Mills's normal life, making envy his sin, and calls out to the detective to take his vengeance for the death of his wife and his unborn child and thus turn himself into the figure of wrath. For a moment his face shines with delight, for he knows that his seduction is infallible and that the very agent who had resisted his doctrine most adamantly will prove, by his own actions, the validity of his belief in the supremacy of vice over virtue. Somerset's sober warning ("If you kill him he will have won") remains unheard. Against his hope that there might, after all, be an exit from the infernal circuit of violence, Somerset is forced to accept what he always knew to be the case—that it is easier to succumb to one's blind passion than to undertake the difficult task of understanding another human being, as it is easier to conceive of the antagonism underwriting all social relations as a simple battle (even if this requires a transgression of the law) than to accept the irresolvable contradiction inscribed in all manifestations of violence and psychic torment. As he himself had predicted, Mills does ultimately make a difference in this investigation, yet in a manner unforeseen by him. He shoots his adversary, only to find that before the law there is no difference between them anymore. In the police car, now returning to the City, he finds himself sitting in the backseat behind an iron grate—which is to say, precisely in the position John Doe had occupied when Mills called him a psychopath and insisted on a radical difference between them. But by shooting John Doe, he becomes inextricably caught up in the very violence he sought to combat, and so confirms the message his adversary had proclaimed all along: familiarity with human cruelty is everywhere, and complacency leads to blind contempt for the humanity of everyone; in the end, we must all live with the knowledge that at any time any one of us could succumb to his or her sins.

In David Fincher's postmodern morality play, no one can escape unscathed by the "induration of evil," even as this traumatic core subtending all psychic and social relations cannot be settled as a simple opposition fought out in the open. John Doe sought to give material shape to this fundamental antagonism in the form of his allegorical refigurations of the seven deadly sins, while David Mills tried, naively, to believe that by catching the perpetrator he could eradicate such manifestations of evil in the world; ultimately, however, both become engulfed and consumed in the battle.

Yet within this conflict a third possible position emerges—namely, that of the witness, who not only comments on the motivations and intentions behind the events, determining how they are to be interpreted but also insists to the end that he can do nothing other than administrate the evidence. Because he can recognize the allegorical meaning of the crime, he is able to explain to those remaining that John Doe had intended all along to impose a moral matrix onto the map of urban crime and depravity. At the same time, he pits against John Doe's claim to having perpetrated a unique masterpiece his own sober evaluation of the serial killer's work. He sees in this particular case yet another example of how he can only collect the evidence and store it away without having really solved the case; indeed, not only has he not been able to end the violence, he has also been forced to watch helplessly as his partner is inextricably drawn into the relentless circuit of crime and transgression. As Richard Dyer notes, Somerset represents how "our desire to know is sinful," so that "the fulfillment of the film's structure is the consummation of deadly desire," leaving the audience with "a feeling that the world is beyond both redemption and remedy."[7] Nonetheless, one must add that by resisting all conclusive and final revelations, Somerset also represents the gesture of humanity, which alone can serve as a protective fiction against the contingencies disintegrating the postmodern urban world. He gives voice to a patience and humility that tarry with the violence that manifests itself daily, so as to understand it, even though he knows that this is an undertaking in which he can only lose. In the end, the chief of police proves to have been right after all. Called to this final crime scene a week after the case began, he asks his longtime colleague, whose duty is about to end on this Sunday evening, where he is going to be in the near future. Somerset answers quietly, looking at the ground beneath his feet, "Around. I'll be around."

The Title Sequence

With this cinematic demonstration of how the postmodern subject can have recourse to allegorical figurations of the range of medieval Christian images, so as to endow a world marked by indifference and apathy with moral meaning (yet not overlooking how the unequivocal representation of spiritual strife inscribed in subjectivity and aimed toward a conclusive solution of psychic and social contradictions misses its subject), David Fincher's *Seven* is more than a humanistic morality play. He consciously refers to his own medium, the language of narrative film, and locates therein another way to negotiate the antagonistic core that lies at the heart of early Christian images revolving around salvation and damnation. Fincher appropriates these already existing images for his enactment of the battle between virtue and vice, yet understands that his own role as director is analogous to the one Somerset claims for himself—presenting his narrative in a manner that displays how clues ultimately lead to other clues, while at the same time rejecting any single conclusive explanatory visual matrix, preferring instead to sustain the contradictions and incommensurabilities that are part and parcel of any complex description of an event of social or psychic strife. This self-reflexive comment on his own medium becomes most clear when *Seven* is read in relation to its opening titles, designed by the video artist Kyle Cooper. Here we are shown a sequence of images pertaining to the genesis of the journals, in which John Doe documents his murderous aesthetics. The way the images are staged, however, also comments on what the director is doing himself. Initially we see a close-up of one of John Doe's notebooks, while a hand that flickers like a shadow across the screen turns the pages. This is followed by an image of two hands drawn in charcoal and pasted onto squared paper, as though the background grid was meant to serve as a matrix. But because the two hands have been drawn in a naturalist mode, one also has the sense that they are pressing down on the paper, as though leaving an imprint on it. With the next cut we are again shown the hands of the serial killer, this time, however, to illustrate his attempt to eradicate his fingerprints. In extreme close-up, we see a razor blade gliding between the fingertips of one hand, as well as blood emerging from a cut. (The film makes clear that John Doe regularly cuts the skin off his fingertips to make sure he leaves no fingerprints.) The credit sequence—which is, ironically, all about naming (identifying) those who took part in the film's creation—then reverts to an image of the notebook, which we now see from the front, before we are once again shown an opened page and a hand writing minute sentences onto the paper.

It is significant that representations of the genesis of the notebooks are incessantly interrupted by images that refer not to the work of the serial killer but to that of the director David Fincher and his crew—specifically, his name and function as well as the names of his collaborators and their functions. These are scrawled in raw white letters on a black background, as though etched into the film stock itself. Sometimes they are blurred, sometimes they are double-exposed (creating the impression of spectral doublings), sometimes they are superimposed on used or exposed film, next to scratches leaving arbitrary meaningless traces. As the title sequence alternates between the names being credited and images representing the author of the notebooks, we see the serial killer's meticulous methodology: how he develops his photographs, cuts a row of negatives into single images, trims a photograph, pastes the photograph onto pages already covered with his cramped handwriting, uses a felt-tipped pen to cross out fragments of sentences or strike through the eyes of a drawn face, and so on. Repeatedly, Cooper superimposes these various modes of representation—the writing, the drawn images, the photographic negatives, the prints—onto each other. He also rapidly interpolates frequent images of empty notebook pages into the sequence, suggesting that the entire enterprise is an ongoing project. To illustrate how the notebooks are held together, he at one point shows us a hand carefully threading twine through the eye of a needle and sewing together a bundle of pages completely covered with tiny writing. Because the entire process is filmed in extreme close-ups, with each action lasting for only a few seconds in what appears to be a random order, the viewer begins to feel a growing sense of almost subliminal disquiet. One can't easily find his or her way around this uncanny process of visual production. One feels estranged, disoriented, and yet at the same time jolted out of one's familiar way of seeing. Finally, turning away from the actual fabrication process, the camera starts to pan the spines of the hundreds of notebooks already lining John Doe's shelves, then returns one last time to a close-up of the two hands drawn in charcoal. This is followed by another close-up of the killer's hands as he cuts the word GOD from the IN GOD WE TRUST motto of a one-dollar bill and carefully picks it up with a pair of tweezers. At last, as the camera once more pans the shelves of notebooks, director David Fincher's name emerges, blurred and hardly legible, heralding the end of the title sequence.

Significantly, however, the title sequence does not occur at the beginning of the film; rather, it appears after a brief opening prologue during which detective Somerset is introduced, along with his insomnia—as inferred by a close-up of the metronome he puts into motion to help him fall asleep. The title sequence is then followed by the start of a Monday morning in the City, which brings the discovery of the first corpse. Because of this diegetic framing device, therefore, one could surmise that the title sequence, which visualizes the analogy between the medium of film and the serial killer's mode of representation, not only refers to the primal scene for the planning of the crimes that will culminate in the serial killer's execution on the following Sunday but also can stand as a representation of Somerset's dream.

Introduction
Not Master in His Own House

Given that what follows after the disquieting title sequence in *Seven* (1995) is the unfolding of a fantasy scenario involving a serial killer's appropriation of cultural texts that both he and his witnesses (Somerset—and of course the film's viewers) are at home in, it is productive to read David Fincher's movie as a self-conscious comment on the workings of cinematic narration in general. The film obliquely invokes the long-held position of Hollywood as the place where stories were created and brought into circulation to deal with our personal anxieties and desires as well as those of our culture. Analogous to the traditional texts that Somerset finds in the public library, Hollywood functions as one of the most salient archives we have of our visual culture of nightmares and dreams. One might claim, then, that in *Seven* not only is the analogy between a serial killer and a literate detective at stake but there is also a second analogy at work—one involving the similarity between Somerset's and John Doe's appropriations of the visual culture that has informed Hollywood's refiguration of the repertoire of traditional Western images; an appropriation that cites previous visual and narrative representations and transforms them in order to adjust them to the demands of contemporary culture.

One might further surmise that—like detective Somerset—the director and his team, as well as the reader (interpreter) of cinematic narratives, are all concerned with meaning, notably the matter of rendering culturally relevant desires and anxieties visible, decipherable, and negotiable. After all, when one speaks of the "dream factory" that is Hollywood, one does so not least because the film scenarios produced there are analogous to our own private fantasies, except that Hollywood's are realized on the screen and made public.[1] And because fantasy is our most powerful tool for organizing personal desires into coherent narratives, cinema has emerged as particularly prominent in the representation of psychic processes—notably the ciphered and fragmentary representation of unconscious knowledge.[2] The film screen, in other words, can be thought of as functioning like an externalized *mind screen* on which both personal and collective desires can be transformed and reconfigured, much along the lines of what Freud calls the hallucinatory return of repressed psychic material.[3] Indeed, following those rules that, according to Freud, regulate both our daydreams and our nocturnal dreams, Hollywood stars represent sublime figures whose stories take place in heterotopias more magical and more perilous than the sites we inhabit in everyday reality—even as the images represented there consist of refigurations of actual lived realities as well as genuine pressing cultural concerns. While in the work of dreams the censorship required by psychic considerations for what can and cannot be represented takes the shape of displacements and condensations, the language of Hollywood cinema is in part dictated by laws of censorship that were prevalent particularly during the Studio System, but also in part by the constraints of movie genres.[4] Ultimately, our enjoyment of Hollywood cinema is contingent upon a welcome familiarity with the imaginary geography it produces (its characters, its stories), much as Somerset feels comfortable in the archive of theological texts because it represents an imaginary home for him. At the same time, comparing the film screen with a mind screen, one must remember that Hollywood cinema is always also the result of a complex production apparatus meant to serve its producers' economic interests as well as the entertainment interests of a highly heterogeneous audience. These film scenarios thus form a murky interface between personal and public enjoyment, even though one can also see them as embodying the way in which all intimate fantasy work is inscribed by and refigured along the lines of culturally preestablished visual and narrative codes.

Yet, with respect to its unsettling title sequence, David Fincher's *Seven* invokes still another aspect of the fascinating power of Hollywood cinema—namely, the fact that while its visual language recycles familiar narratives and figurations, it is nevertheless also uncanny (in the Freudian sense) because it presents in bold relief the failure written into the very process of substitution underlying, as psychoanalysis argues, all forms of representation.

Desire, deferral, and the enjoyment of one's fantasies emerge, after all, precisely because any representation of familiarity provokes a soothing sense of stability and articulates the provisional status of one's sense of being at home. Indeed, I want to claim that cinematic representation can fruitfully be seen as a reference to a fundamental aporia inscribed in psychic existence, namely the desire to recoup an allegedly originary state of plenitude, whose loss is the foundation for all desire. Or put another way, cinematic narratives, particularly when they are concerned with concepts of home, are inscribed by a nostalgia for an untainted sense of belonging, and the impossibility of achieving that is also the catalyst for fantasies about recuperation and healing. Psychoanalytic discourse can thus inform the way we approach the enjoyment that Hollywood cinema affords, since it offers a resilient tropic language to describe how the psychic apparatus is inhabited by a foreign body (the primal repression of psychic material), to which the conscious subject can never have direct access except through symptoms and fantasy work. It is this notion of fundamental dislocation subtending subjectivity that will serve as the resilient trope for the following discussion of Hollywood's visual and narrative configurations of home.

My central claim for the individual readings that follow is that a knowledge of the uncanniness of existence haunts all attempts at devising protective fictions that will allow us to make sense of the contradictions and contingencies of our reality—and this is true not only for cinematic narrative but for other types as well. The films discussed here give voice to why we need stories about the successful achievement of a sense of being at home and at the same time obliquely articulate that even while their fantasy scenarios fill an originary sense of lack in plenitude, the traumatic core of dislocation can never be fully erased.

Seeking to deconstruct the opposition between the notion of home and that of dislocation, I also make a second claim: The ambivalences and unresolvable antagonism written into any conception of home may well be one of the cultural energies at the heart of the connection between Hollywood cinema and psychoanalytic discourse. Both share a set of visual and theoretical tropes that revolve around the relation that the subject entertains toward his or her desire for protection and plenitude on the one hand and the symbolic codes dictating a constraint of narcissistic pleasure on the other—but they do so by casting the notion of home, and the enjoyment of familiarity that it promises, as the common nexus of these two modes of producing meaning. The tropic figurations of psychic dislocation illustrated by the films I will discuss are thus to be thought of as analogous to concrete experiences of the loss of home, and to a nostalgic desire to return home. In crossmapping psychoanalytic terminology onto cinematic language, what is at stake is the metaphoric equivalency that emerges as Freud introduces tropes such as "psychic apparatus," "other scene," or "private theater" to describe the site of fantasy work. If, in so doing, he has recourse to a cultural image repertoire that is similar to the stories on which Hollywood cinema is based, that repertoire in turn appropriates the figural language of psychoanalytic texts and transforms it into cinematic language, which in turn seeks not only to thematize psychic processes and dream work but also to impregnate the fantasy work of the spectator. Taking as a working premise that we dream in dialogue with visual and narrative texts familiar to us, I propose this crossmapping of cinematic and psychoanalytic engagement with questions of dislocation, of home, and of nostalgia so as to trace the exchange of highly charged metaphors that has informed both discourses.

Freud significantly links the discovery of the unconscious as an "other scene," from which symptoms and affects, as well as all fantasy work, emerge, to an insistence that the subject is split between psychic material consciously available to it and repressed material to which it has no direct access. The psychoanalytic cure thus consists in making the subject take notice of traumatic knowledge that it seeks to repress and more generally making it acknowledge that "the ego is not even master in its own house, but must content itself with scanty information of what is going on unconsciously in its mind."[5]

In the following seven chapters, I read seven individual films under the aegis of this psychoanalytic dictum. My aim is to explore different configurations of psychic dislocation as it becomes embedded with situations of exile and displacement, regardless of whether *home* refers to an imaginary place of belonging, to a concrete house that affords protection and comfort, or to a particular geocultural community.[6] Indeed, part of my claim for the resilience of the concept of home in Hollywood cinema is that the psychic situation of not being master in one's own house and the concrete experience of a loss of home prove to be mutually implicated in these fantasy scenarios, often standing in for each other.[7]

At the same time, at stake in this proposed analogy is the question of whether a successful inhabitation of, or an untarnished sense of belonging to, a particular place isn't a belated nostalgic fantasy meant to shield the subject from a more originary displacement. For by casting the unconscious as a site of alterity within the psychic apparatus, Freud insists on its disturbing, liminal, and hybrid quality. In his article "The Uncanny," he highlights psychic situations in which the subject is forced to confront its own internal difference. He insists that the experience of discomfort provoked by a seemingly unintended return to a place of origin—the family, a familiar home, or one's homeland—does not, in fact, have recourse to any originary intactness. Rather, what the uncanny articulates is an originary fissure in what is believed to be familiar. The uncanny, he concludes, "is that class of the frightening which leads back to what is known of old and long familiar."[8] Far from referring to something new or strange, it gives voice to the return of repressed material: "The *unheimlich* is what was once *heimisch*, familiar; the prefix 'un' is the token of repression."[9] Having recourse to a semantic analysis of the German word *heimlich*, he claims to discover that "*heimlich* is a word the meaning of which develops in the direction of ambivalence, until it finally coincides with its opposite, *unheimlich*. *Unheimlich* is in some way or other a sub-species of *heimlich*."[10] While in German the adjective *heimlich* refers either to something familiar or to something secret, the word *unheimlich* collapses these two meanings into one to articulate the presence of a secret at the core of the familiar. Any imaginary notion of home, referring to a familiar haven of safety, could then be understood, from the start, to be inscribed by something foreign, and the articulation of this fundamental dislocation at the heart of the home is at stake in any experience of the uncanny. Because it compels the subject to recognize that he or she never was and never will fully be master of his or her own house, the uncanny emerges as the privileged trope for psychic dislocation.

But insofar as the rhetorical gesture of the uncanny provokes an acknowledgment of the fissure subtending all identity constructions, it also proclaims the impossibility of externalizing what is considered to be foreign, insisting instead on the intimate quality of the unfamiliar.[11] This means that a safe withdrawal from the uncanny is equally impossible. Instead, as Heidegger notes, the uncanny articulates an indefiniteness of anxiety, giving expression to what makes existence authentic, namely a combination of the utterly familiar with the totally strange: "In anxiety one feels 'uncanny.' . . . As *Dasein* falls, anxiety brings it back from its absorption in the 'world.' Everyday familiarity collapses. *Dasein* has been individualized."[12] Fundamental to both Freud's and Heidegger's definitions of the uncanny—as a cipher for the dislocation inscribed in any sense of being at home in the world—is thus their mutual insistence that the foreign can never be extricated from any experience or conceptualization of the familiar; traces of dislocation inextricably inhabit any configuration of home.

For the readings that I am proposing, it is equally significant that as Freud theorizes fantasy work, he has recourse to another trope, one that emphasizes the liminal status of the workings of the unconscious. Fantasies, he explains, are derivatives of the unconscious. Although they can often hardly be distinguished from formations of the conscious, they oscillate between belonging qualitatively to the preconscious and belonging factually to the unconscious. Crucial for my own discussion of cinematic configurations of home is, however, the particular trope he uses to compare this uncanny indeterminacy of fantasies:

> Their origin is what decides their fate. We may compare them with individuals of mixed race [*Mischlinge*] who, taken all round, resemble white men, but who betray their colored descent by some striking feature or other, and on that account are excluded from society and enjoy none of the privileges of white people. Of such a nature are those fantasies of normal people as well as of neurotics which we have recognized as preliminary stages in the formation both of dreams and of symptoms, and which, in spite of their high degree of organization, remain repressed and therefore cannot become conscious.[13]

For Freud, daydreams represent the most important expression of fantasy work. Here the subject fashions for him- or herself scenes, episodes, or entire scripts that, like nocturnal dreams, correct a dissatisfying reality even as they offer a ciphered rendition of traumatic knowledge that the subject seeks to deny or repress. Most fantasies, Freud claims, revolve around "ambitious wishes, which serve to elevate the subject's personality."[14] Although each daydream tells its own story, Freud believed that he could identify a common denominator in the fantasies related to him by his patients. In the imagined scenario, the daydreamer designs a situation in which he has "regained what he possessed in his happy childhood—the

protecting house, the loving parents and the first objects of his affection-
ate feelings."[15] Freud significantly calls this paradigmatic scenario a family romance, to be thought of primarily as the liberation of an individual
from the authority of his parents. Such a scenario allows the subject to
voice a discontent with his or her current family situation by translating
that dissatisfaction into the fantasy of being an orphan and casting the
parents one wants to get rid of as adoptive parents who belong to a lower
social class. Freud, however, locates a second function in this fantasy
transformation: Denigrating one's parents not only makes the necessary
separation easier, it also harbors a nostalgic recollection of the alleged happiness of childhood. "The whole effort at replacing the real father by a superior one is only an expression of the child's longing for the happy, vanished days when his father seemed to him the noblest and strongest of
men and his mother the dearest and loveliest of women."[16] Freud recognizes that this memory of lost happiness actually represents a protective
fiction, because the father that the dreamer has exalted in fantasy is a repetition of the actual father, "in whom he believed in the earlier years of his
childhood." The completely satisfying family recuperated in fantasy "is no
more than the expression of a regret that those happy days have gone."

Family romances do more than articulate the lack inscribed in the sense of
happiness and belonging, which all fantasy work seeks to overcome; they also
refer belatedly to the fallible judgment of the child, who serves as the central
figure in this nostalgic scenario. Freud concludes by noting that "in these
fantasies the overvaluation that characterizes a child's earliest years comes
into its own again." If, in the following readings, I extend the notion of the
family romance to include what I will call the home romance, I do so in
order to emphasize that fantasy work satisfies precisely because it produces
protective fictions to ward off traumatic knowledge about the uncanniness
that lies at the heart of all worldly emplacement. However, the happiness
achieved at the end of a cinematic narrative—notably the return to a familiar place, to the protection of the family or the successful couple building—
as well as the pleasure that such resolution affords the spectator, remains
aporic, for these narratives inevitably also render visible the fissure written
into any notion of recuperation of home. Indeed, while Hollywood cinema
on the manifest level tends to translate psychic and concrete dislocation into
a successful resolution of conflict and the restitution of order, on a latent
level Hollywood's happy endings are often fragile, infected by a disturbing

reminder of what can never be. Fantasies shaped by notions of home thus preserve the uncanniness that inextricably resides in the familiar to the end and point out that any conceptualization of origins is always already displaced, even as they nostalgically produce protective fictions in response to this ineradicable fissure.

Do films acknowledge the fallibility of any sense of home, or do they instead devise scenarios of empowerment or control? Do we enjoy the law of displacement or do we pit fantasies of consistency against its contingency? These are the questions to be explored in the following chapters. I will begin my journey by turning to Hitchcock's first American film, *Rebecca* (1940), in which the director, a stranger to Hollywood, and his unnamed heroine, a stranger to Manderley, appear to mirror each other. Both, after all, have to confront a harsh representative of the foreign law reigning over the fascinating place they have chosen as their new home—in the case of the unnamed heroine, the spirit of Rebecca, represented by Mrs. Danvers; in the case of Hitchcock, the demands of the female audience, represented by the producer David O. Selznick. While Hitchcock's heroine will never become mistress of her house, but instead becomes mistress of her dreams about Manderley, the director will become master of the horror genre, after appropriating the cinematic codes of his new home. In the second chapter I will turn to the arch cinematic myth of home—Victor Fleming's *Wizard of Oz* (1939). Ruled by the ideological dictum "There's no place like home," Fleming's world of Oz emerges as a hallucinatory distortion of Dorothy's imaginary relation to her dissatisfying home in Kansas, only to render visible the core antagonism of any home romance: the film proclaims the need to believe in the notion of home, even while it illustrates that this place of happiness is ultimately an ideological construction that can be maintained only in fantasy.

With the third chapter I will turn to the first of three Hollywood genres shaped in relation to home, namely the issue of culture trouble underwriting the western. Focusing on John Ford's *The Searchers* (1956), I will explore the gendering of the provisional homes of the settlers, on the basis that the classic western hero flees into the prairie and the seemingly simple race trouble he finds there, in order to avoid confronting the unsolvable gender trouble waiting for him at the heart of the home. In the fourth chapter I read John Sayles's *Lone Star* (1996) as a countertext, which I claim explores what confronting the antagonism of gender and of race at home might look like. In the fifth chapter I will turn to Fritz Lang's *Secret Beyond the Door* (1948), making the claim that this film noir negotiates the cultural anxiety surrounding the homecoming of war veterans at the end of World War II. By telling a postwar bluebeard story, Lang translates any explicit discussion of trauma experienced on the battlefield to another scene and performs instead the trauma inhabiting the home romance of his protagonist as a horrific refiguration of the abjection of the mother prescribed by the Oedipus complex. If Lang offers a troubled representation of homecoming, Douglas Sirk's melodrama *Imitation of Life* (1959) renders visible the impossibility of returning home. In the sixth chapter I will read this film in conjunction with his claim that his troubled existence as an exile in Hollywood began when he decided to change his German name, because in so doing he turned himself into one of the split and ambivalent characters who feature in his films. I will argue that Sirk's last American film can be understood as a performance of the psychic and social dislocation resulting from a split symbolic interpellation. The reading of Sirk's heroine Sarah Jane can go beyond viewing her as a foil for the German director, who was about to leave the provisional home Hollywood had served for him since World War II. Torn between the black culture she was born into and the white culture she can only pretend to belong to, she also poses a crisis in symbolic interpellation that complicates notions of belonging to only one cultural home. I will conclude in the seventh chapter with a reading of a film that maps aspects of the western, the film noir, and the melodrama genres onto the imaginary geography of the cartoon—*Batman Returns* (1992). Explicitly prefiguring the story of Moses' return from exile, director Tim Burton also resignifies the gender trouble residing at the heart of so many Hollywood performances of home by presenting Gotham City as the battleground for his dislocated heroes. Yet in contrast to classic Hollywood narratives, his heroine, Selina Kyle, is the most radical of the three players in her embrace of homelessness, destroying her own home so as to intervene in the battle between the Penguin and Batman, and insisting to the end that any notion of a happy home is only an untenable illusion. I have chosen *Batman Returns* (1992) as my final example (although home continues to be a resilient trope in many recent Hollywood productions) because it contains the three figurations of nostalgia for home in relation to which all the films I discuss are shaped. Returning home can be concomitant either with death (the Penguin) or with accepting that one will never be master of one's house (Batman). Or home represents that which must be abjected so that one can inhabit a dream geography (Catwoman). Yet as the figure who roams the nocturnal rooftops of Gotham City, the feline Selina Kyle is also the object of Bruce Wayne's dream, shaping his nostalgic yearning for a new fantasy scenario of strife to commence so that he can leave the boredom of his castle. As such, she is also the object of our own desire for escape into the fantasy world of cinema.

David Fincher's wise detective goes to the library in order to find confirmed there a moral geography that will serve as a matrix for interpreting the horrific morality play John Doe has asked him to bear testimony to, but he knows full well that he will not be able to avert the inevitable unhappy ending and can make a difference only as a reader. The wager of this book is that we, like him, return to the familiar archive of Hollywood cinema to find the stories that will allow us to sustain and live with the contradictions and contingencies of our everyday reality. We, too, are guided by our wish to understand what puzzles us, and we, too, must recognize that as readers, all we can do is administrate the visual materials that these cinematic narratives offer us. Entering into this archive allows us to rediscover visual narratives that maintain a minimal symbolic consistency and thus protect us, as Freud argues all fantasy work does, from a fundamental antagonism subtending all psychic and social existence, even while organizing our enjoyment of it. Like the detective Somerset, we embark upon this journey fully cognizant that some kernel of meaning inevitably recedes from our interpretation. Reading cinematic scenes in conjunction with tropes proposed by psychoanalysis allows us to decipher the desires and anxieties that have been refigured in the language of film. Yet a quality that I am inclined to call the charismatic core of cinema can never conclusively and unequivocally be defined, and therefore any reading of the cultural energies that are circulated by Hollywood films never fully explains why we are drawn to what is already a familiar imaginary geography. What, I continue to ask in my own readings, keeps fascinating us, even after a theoretically informed explanation has been found? Which is to say, what remains uncanny?

In the following revisitation of classic Hollywood films that explore different aspects of what home has come to mean in twentieth-century culture, what is at stake, then, is the manner in which the antagonism, subtending all symbolic communities and all psychic processes, finds a correlative in this charismatic core of cinematic representation. Like any other library, the image repertoire of Hollywood—being a finite and, indeed, a heterotopic experience—performs the failure written into our desire for an untainted safe haven that we might inhabit forever and at the same time discloses this impossibility to be the very precondition of fantasy work. The pact that we enter into as we pass over the threshold into the virtual home of cinema provides nothing more, but also nothing less, than the promise of provisional happiness, which is, perhaps, the only one we can really hope for.

Rebecca—Between a paternal object of desire and a maternal one

Chapter 1

Uncanny Appropriations
Rebecca

Alfred Hitchcock: A Stranger in Hollywood

In response to François Truffaut's suggestion that it was only after Alfred Hitchcock's arrival in the United States that he reached his creative peak as the master of the horror thriller, Hitchcock insists that it was his work for the British film industry that helped him develop his natural instincts, his directorial techniques, and his camera precepts, even though he did develop new and offbeat ideas once he left for Hollywood. In contrast to his mature American phase, which he considers "the period when the ideas were fertilized," Hitchcock calls his early British phase "the period of the sensation of cinema," in order to emphasize that his cinematic perceptions had already been fully awakened while he was employed by British film studios at Islington. At the same time, he is only too eager to point out that the films he made in the 1930s belong to a period of great expectations rather than to the perfectionism of his later work.[1] As he explains during interviews with his young French colleague, the producer David O. Selznick had called him to Selznick International Studios in 1939 to make a film about the destruction of the *Titanic*. Upon arriving in Hollywood, however, Hitchcock discovered that he was to be entrusted with an entirely different project, namely Daphne du Maurier's best-selling novel *Rebecca*, for which he had tried to procure the rights himself one year earlier, only to find that they were too expensive.[2]

My argument in this chapter is that the first American film Hitchcock made after leaving his British home can fruitfully be read as a cinematic negotiation of Freud's dictum that the ego must learn that it isn't master of its own home. The proposed crossmapping of Hitchcock's cinematic language onto Freud's critical vocabulary is in part supported by the fact that the master of the psychothriller repeatedly appropriated psychoanalytic thinking in his films of the 1940s and 1950s to help him stage the delusions, aberrations, and perversions of his heroes and heroines. In *Suspicion, Spellbound,* and *Marnie* we find explicit references to Freud's work in the form of characters reading psychoanalytic texts, while *Rear Window, Vertigo,* and *Psycho* offer cinematic refigurations of psychic disturbances such as voyeurism, necrophilia, and matricide. At the same time, the trajectory of the detective plot of *Rebecca,* in the course of which the unnamed heroine (Joan Fontaine) discovers the terrible secret of her husband (Laurence Olivier), is explicitly designed along the lines of the psychoanalytic process. In order to bring the repression of traumatic material out into the open, "I" (as she is called in the film script) insists that her melancholic husband relate his memories of the terrible death of his first wife, so that, having made his confession, he can overcome the ghost that has been haunting him. Yet I choose to focus on Hitchcock's cinematic translation of Freud's conviction that mature subjectivity requires an acknowledgment of psychic dislocation in my reading of *Rebecca* because of the biographical resonance this entails. It is, after all, not only the first film of his rich and productive American period but also the first that he made after having chosen the cultural dislocation of Hollywood, and with it Selznick Studios, where he was continually reminded by the producer himself that he was not the master there.

What is indeed striking about *Rebecca* is the analogy that can be drawn between the young British director, who chooses to work as an exile in the foreign world of Hollywood's Studio System, and his heroine, who chooses to marry a mysterious man and live in a world completely foreign to her.[3] On the one hand we have Hitchcock, moving to an unfamiliar place, onto which he has projected his own fantasies of filmmaking and his expectations of international success. Having arrived there he discovers, however, that he will have to assert himself against the omniscient gaze of his powerful producer, David O. Selznick. As the representative of what one might call the paternal authority of Hollywood aesthetic codes, Selznick chose to surveil every aspect of the production of *Rebecca,* forcing the young British director to accept all his decisions. As Hitchcock would write many years later, he experienced Selznick at the time as "an *éminence grise* whispering in my ear, 'Don't you think, &tc., &tc.?'"[4] On the other hand we have the film's diegesis involving a nameless heroine, who must acquaint herself with an unfamiliar world—Manderley—onto which, like her director, she has projected fantasies of grandeur and expectations of happiness. She, too, must learn to assert herself against the punitive gaze of a figure of authority who seeks to thwart her sense of mastery. The housekeeper, Mrs. Danvers (Judith Anderson), proves herself to be an éminence grise, whispering into "I's" ear that, as the representative of the dead Rebecca, she will keep the memory of her deceased mistress alive, subverting the command of both the second Mrs. de Winter and her husband, and in so doing making it perfectly clear to both of them that they are not the actual masters of Manderley.

In proposing this analogy, I take my cue from Hitchcock himself, who, in his discussions with Truffaut, lavishly describes the way in which he took possession of America in his imagination long before he decided to emigrate there. In response to Truffaut's question as to why he never attempted to imitate the British type of film while he was in Hollywood, Hitchcock points out that he had always been interested in American films and had primarily worked for American companies, so that his training in film was from the start a foreign education. Even when the British film studios came to Islington, he explains, the cameras, the lights, the Kodak film they used were American. He concludes with a description of how, as a young man, he had always had a precise idea of what America looked like, much as "I" harbors a detailed fantasy about what Manderley looks like long before she actually gets there. "Later on," Hitchcock recalls, "I often wondered about the fact that I made no attempt to visit America until 1937; I'm still puzzled about that. I was meeting Americans all the time and was completely familiar with the map of New York. I used to send away for train schedules—that was my hobby—and I knew many of the timetables by heart. Years before I ever came here, I could describe New York, tell you where the theaters and stores were located. When I had a conversation with Americans, they would ask, 'When were you over there last?' and I'd answer, 'I've never been there at all. Strange, isn't it?'"[5]

My argument is that his own experience of being forced to recognize that in Hollywood he was everything *but* master of the home afforded him by the Selznick studio implicitly underwrites his mise-en-scène of an orphaned heroine, who by marriage hopes to gain a new home and thereby overcome her own dislocation, only to discover that once one has lost one's home the gap can never be filled without leaving a scar. Although Hitchcock insisted in a statement to *Newsweek*, once the production of *Rebecca* was over, that "his first film would reflect no personality other than his own," Leonard J. Leff has minutely traced the many concessions the British director actually had to make as Selznick forced him to subjugate himself to the laws governing the expectations of Hollywood audiences.[6] The film itself, in turn, plays through this confrontation with the big Other as a battle between "I" and the first Mrs. de Winter, whose stringent authority is maintained through her devoted servant Mrs. Danvers. Hitchcock, of course, never admitted to an identification between himself and his filmic "I," although he does confess in his conversations with Truffaut that he insisted on casting Joan Fontaine in his first American films because she, like him, was a stranger in Hollywood.

Manderley: A Phantasmatic Site

Chronologically, Hitchcock's *Rebecca* begins in Monte Carlo, where "I," whose mother has been dead for years and whose father died recently, works as a paid companion for the vulgar American millionaire Mrs. Van Hopper.[7] There she meets the rich and attractive but melancholic Maxim de Winter, who is clearly harboring a traumatic secret in relation to the death of his first wife, Rebecca, who drowned the year before. Their respective states of mourning make both of them feel alienated from the sparkle of this city of gambling and luck, yet their romantic attachment evolves not only because they are in a state of psychic liminality but also because they share a sense of geographic displacement. "I's" lack of a name signals her lack of a clear symbolic position within society, and her wish to regain social position through marriage. Maxim, in turn, has fled from Manderley after his wife's fatal sailing accident, thus disengaging himself from the estate he has inherited from his father.

He decides to court the young, innocent, and seemingly clueless woman, and when he discovers that she is about to leave for New York with her employer, he proposes to her. Mrs. Van Hopper rightly calls this unexpected turn of events a "whirlwind romance"—and indeed, Hitchcock presents the entire marriage as an improvised affair. The bride wears a simple frock without a wedding veil, and no one gives her away. Only after "I" has already sat down in her husband's car does Maxim run to a flower vendor to buy the traditional wedding bouquet. But there are no bridesmaids for her to toss it to, and besides, it is so huge that, as he hands it to her, it seems to smother her seated figure completely.

Hitchcock had already signaled the fact that this union wasn't fully authorized by having the couple forget to take with them the actual marriage license when they left the registrar's office. The judge was forced to call to the groom, who was already standing on the street with his bride, and ask him to catch the document, which he threw out the window at them. As the plot progresses, we discover that this is indeed an "improper" marriage, insofar as Maxim is still emotionally tied to Rebecca, even though not in love with her, as "I" believes. Rather, he knows he is responsible for her death. As though to further render visible the fragile ground on which the marriage contract is based, Hitchcock offers images of the honeymoon only as a belated representation—the home movies, which the couple watch in a darkened parlor of Manderley. The seeming happiness they find depicted on film stands in stark contrast to the mistrust that has affected them since their return to Maxim's home.[8]

The most visible evidence that the marriage between "I" and Maxim is from the start tainted by unshared secret desires occurs in the scene when the new couple arrives at Manderley. In radiant sunlight Maxim drives through the iron gates of his estate and proceeds along the winding path that leads through an enormous park and up to the mansion. The heroine is clearly nervous, unsure what to expect of her new home, and even Maxim's soothing reassurance that she need not be frightened or worried about anything, since Danvers has everything under control, does not alleviate her anxiety. Suddenly it begins to rain, and to protect his young bride Maxim covers her head with a raincoat that had been lying on the backseat. Yet Hitchcock is not particularly using this detail to establish his hero as a solicitous protector. Rather, as the cheerful music imitating the sound of chirping birds quickly changes to the somber dramatic tones of the film's leitmotif, we find that the change in weather serves a different purpose. In "I's" face we see her initial fear transformed into a moment of confused ecstasy, while the sound track culminates in an exuberant tonal apex. She lets out a heavy sigh, as though to voice a clandestinely harbored desire. As

Maxim proclaims, "That's it. That's Manderley," Hitchcock presents an image of her new home from her subjective perspective, rising powerfully from amid the trees, then cuts back to a close-up of her face as she stares, openmouthed, at the spectacle before her. Hitchcock's mise-en-scène poignantly highlights the phantasmatic quality of Manderley, for not only does he stage "I's" first view of her new home as a gaze through the windshield of Maxim's car but he uses the sudden rain shower to have this gaze emerge as the windshield wiper clears her field of vision. In other words, the new bride's first view of Manderley is explicitly framed, as though this were her own private film screen.

The camera then disengages itself from "I's" subjective gaze and pans along the facade of the house, while the dramatic music dies away. Although the heroine's short, ecstatic exclamation subsides before she actually crosses the threshold into her new home, we can assume that she will take on her symbolic mandate as the second Mrs. de Winter under the auspices of this quasi-erotic enjoyment of a phantasmatic site as image. As Slavoj Žižek notes, Hitchcock often stages an arrival at an unfamiliar home in such a way that the spectator has the uncanny impression that the house itself is returning his or her gaze. This disembodied gaze, which according to Jacques Lacan constitutes the subject, is effectively a missing gaze, in the sense that it is purely phantasmatic.[9]

The phantasmatic value of Manderley has in fact been foreshadowed by an earlier scene in Monte Carlo, in which "I" confesses to Maxim that she has been dreaming about his estate for a long time.[10] In response to his question as to whether she has ever been in Cornwall, she explains that once, while vacationing there with her father, she bought a postcard of a beautiful house by the sea, which the shopkeeper explained was called Manderley. She adds that she felt embarrassed at the time because she did not know this. One could speculate that buying this postcard stands as the primal scene of "I's" home romance, for after her conversation with the shopkeeper she comes to use the image of Manderley as the focal point for her daydreams about ascending to a more distinguished and elegant life, while equally feeding her masochistic notions of her own inferiority. As Maxim— the rightful master of Manderley—begins to court her, he gives material body to the phantom place, haunting her imagination, as well as to the ambivalence of feelings she has invested it with.

The actual mansion Manderley, then, emerges in "I's" field of vision as the materialization of an image she had incorporated into her psychic apparatus much earlier. Furthermore, having the heroine perceive Manderley through the window of her husband's car only after the windshield wiper has cleared her field of vision allows Hitchcock to highlight the shift of her psychic predisposition into a different register. Crossing the threshold of her new home is tantamount to entering a fantasy site; it blurs the boundary between concrete and psychic reality. While fantasies about Manderley as an unreachable home were safe, the actual proximity of this long-wished-for home turns her daydream into a paranoid hallucination. And if the master of the house had initially served to reactivate her long-harbored romance with upper-class status, he now transforms into an inscrutable master, signaling to her the inadequacy of her fantasy that she might become mistress of his stately house.

Hitchcock's inclusion of the windshield wiper detail provokes further speculation that the actual object of "I's" desire is not really the man but his house. Their improvised marriage clearly does not fully satisfy her desire, for if getting a wealthy husband was all she wanted, the rest of the film—thriving off her phantasmatic investment in his home—would be unnecessary. The uncanny fault line written into this marriage from the start leads one to consider whether, insofar as Manderley came to be "I's" object of desire in what one might call an enmeshment of a family and a home romance long before she actually married Maxim, her desire now encompasses both the symbolic master of the house and the feminine spirit that has taken hold of this alluring mansion—the homeless, dislocated, revenant Rebecca, who will not stay in place.

Indeed, following the numerical logic of fairy tales, Mrs. Van Hopper mentions Maxim de Winter and his estate three times, and in each case she refers to its deceased first mistress. The first instance occurs after "I's" employer unexpectedly meets Maxim in the lobby of the hotel in Monte Carlo. Seeking an explanation as to why he left them so abruptly, Mrs. Van Hopper assures her bewildered companion that he is a bereaved man, unable to overcome the death of the woman he adored. Later, after Mrs. Van Hopper has fallen ill, leaving "I" free to go on clandestine outings with Maxim, Hitchcock has his heroine enter her employer's bedroom unnoticed, thereby becoming privy to a conversation in which Mrs. Van Hopper explains to a nurse that she knew Rebecca before her marriage to Maxim. She then describes the fatal boating accident and its effect on the husband, declaring that everyone says he is a grieving, broken man. To emphasize the importance of these words for "I's" fantasy life, Hitchcock cuts to a scene depicting "I" restlessly tossing about in her hotel bed, repeating Mrs. Van Hopper's words while a shadow covers her face. The third time, Mrs. Van Hopper, outraged at the sudden turn of events, warns her paid companion that she isn't up to the tasks that lie before her as mistress of a grand estate. Casting a critical eye one last time upon her former employee, the woman gives a short, derisive laugh and mockingly calls her "Mrs. de Winter," before turning away and grudgingly wishing her good luck. A similar maternal superego, reminding the heroine of her own inadequacy, will reappear in the figure of Mrs. Danvers to allow "I" to explore what Maxim, impatiently waiting in the hotel lobby, forbids at this point in the story, namely the enjoyment of submitting not only to the commands of one's husband but also to the far more lethal dictates of a forbidding maternal figure of authority.

One must not, however, overlook that in the scene in which "I" confesses to buying a postcard image of Manderley, Maxim calls it the place where he was born and where he has lived all his life. To be the master of Manderley thus means to be in possession of precisely that which "I" lacks—the material and psychic protection of a place one can call home. By marrying Maxim de Winter, "I" not only acquires a name but—and more important—she overcomes the handicap of belonging nowhere. The logic of her daydream can be summarized as follows: if she properly fills her role as the second Mrs. de Winter, she will finally be able to realize her dream of being the mistress of her own home. Yet in the course of their courtship, she also comes to recognize the fallibility of the home romance that Maxim promises to satisfy, for he concludes his description of what makes his home most precious to him on a mysterious note of trepidation: "But now I don't suppose I shall ever see it again." If we take into account that Maxim may be voicing a latent desire, not just a premonition, we could surmise that while "I," on a manifest level, identifies with the notions of belonging that her husband connects with Manderley, on a latent level she identifies with his fantasies of irrevocable displacement. Indeed, his emotional ambivalence toward his home opens up a different solution to her own romance with Manderley, a solution that, as will be discussed in greater detail further on, Hitchcock privileges with the narrative framing of *Rebecca*—the nostalgic bliss of the dislocated exile, who, having lost the actual mansion, can finally fully possess Manderley in her dreams.

The proposal scene itself also explicitly plays with the murky interface of the double encodings that Manderley has for "I." Maxim significantly prefaces his proposal by sketching the two options open to her: "Which would you prefer, New York or Manderley? . . . Either you go to America with Mrs. Van Hopper or you come home to Manderley, with me." Only after she has shyly asked him whether he wants a secretary does he make his proposal explicit: "I'm asking you to marry me, you little fool." As he sits down to have his breakfast, he notices her bewilderment. "I" explains that she is hesitating because she doesn't belong to his sort of world, which is to say, to Manderley. Though "I" ultimately declares her unconditional love for Maxim, what becomes clear from this dialogue is that she has melded in her fantasies a desire for the fascinating Manderley, where she fears she cannot fit, with what is only seemingly its opposite, namely an equally strong desire for the sense of belonging and security that marriage to its owner would afford her. While "I" believes that by going to Manderley with Maxim, she will be able to heal the sense of dislocation she has felt as Mrs. Van Hopper's paid companion, Maxim hopes to vanquish the spirit of the deceased Rebecca that has rendered his home uncanny. He is deeply attracted to this young orphaned woman precisely because her spirit is so different from the deceit, mistrust, and strife represented by Rebecca. Her cluelessness is to serve as an apotropaic charm to protect him from the spectral feminine spirit that continues to make him feel he is no longer master of Manderley. In Hitchcock's enactment, however, the couple's return to Cornwall thrives on the fact that "I's" innocence is itself threatened. Too late, Maxim is forced to admit his own ambivalence. If he had initially told himself that he chose his second wife as an antidote to the deceased Rebecca, he is ultimately forced to recognize that this choice may also have emerged from a sadistic desire. As "I" is drawn ever more strongly into the force field of her predecessor, she appears to be bait in the battle between him and his first wife rather than a healing agent.

Hitchcock's film thus revolves around the following aporia: though Maxim went into temporary exile in the south of France to flee from the power of his deceased wife, he discovers that he cannot obliterate Rebecca's traces—and it's not only because this subversive feminine spirit has taken possession of his home. Rather, Rebecca, invisible yet omnipresent, emerges as the dark core of "I's" unconditional love for him. Given that the unnamed heroine's romance from the start enmeshes her love for Maxim, exiled from his home, with her fantasy about Manderley, a place that is currently possessed by a beautiful deceased woman, she must traverse several fantasy scenarios before reaching the position of the mature woman who is fit to be called Mrs. de Winter: first, her fantasy that she might attain a secure place where she belongs, along with a rise in class and romantic happiness, which in her imagination has come to be connected with the postcard image of a stately mansion; second, Maxim de Winter's fantasy that she has embraced, namely that by returning home together they might exorcise all traces of the uncanny power the dead Rebecca now holds over his family estate; and third, the fantasy called forth by Mrs. Van Hopper's warning, namely that Manderley will prove to be the battleground between "I" and a female rival, allowing her to displace any fear she has of her husband's destructive urges onto his dead first wife. All three scenarios ultimately modulate what Jean Laplanche and Jean-Bertrand Pontalis call the primal scene of fantasy, revolving around the three questions that the daughter, torn between paternal and maternal figures of authority, must answer if she is to successfully negotiate her desire in relation to the symbolic law: "Where do I come from and what is my home?" "Who is the object of my desire?" and finally "What must I accept and what must I relinquish in order to become mistress of my desires and thus, accepting a symbolic mandate assigned to me, assume a proper place within a family genealogy?"[11]

The Second Mrs. de Winter: A Stranger at Manderley

After arriving at the place she has so extensively fantasized about, "I" experiences Manderley as a disempowering crypt, at whose center lies the mysterious bedroom of her feared predecessor. Hitchcock uses his reflexive camera to stage her subjection to the overwhelming architectural design of this mansion and to the equally overwhelming presence of her rival. Before the first dinner in her new home, Mrs. Danvers accompanies her new mistress along the halls of the ancient house, which, given their enormous height and massive expanse, make "I" look like a child. They stop a few feet from the door to Rebecca's room in the west wing, which is still guarded by her old dog. This, Danvers whispers to "I," who has frozen in awe, is the most beautiful room in the house, the only one with a view of the sea. Then she turns away slowly, walking quietly out of the frame and taking the heroine with her, while Hitchcock's camera instead moves forward, until the door of the mysterious room completely fills the frame.[12]

His message is unequivocally clear. It is not the path the heroine takes that fascinates us, but rather the clandestine presence of a dead woman on the other side of the door. With the help of a superimposition that combines the image of this door and Rebecca's initials on the napkin that "I" is about to unfold and place on her lap, Hitchcock proceeds to the scene of her first dinner at Manderley. Once more "I" seems lost, sitting opposite Maxim at one end of a huge, festively decorated dining table, nodding insecurely to him at the other end. In the following scenes Hitchcock repeatedly visualizes his heroine's foreignness in this phantasmatic place by showing her wandering helplessly along corridors and halls whose massive size dwarfs her, clearly lost and unable to find her way, entering the wrong room and thus forced again and again to ask the butler for help.[13]

Hitchcock is particularly careful to stage details illustrating that Rebecca's inescapable spectral presence is responsible for "I's" inability to feel that she is mistress of her new home, for example focusing on objects that carry Rebecca's initials, "RdeW." "I," disturbed by the way these marked objects leave her no room of her own, finally decides to penetrate the source of this uncanny power, her predecessor's bedroom. Fearful, but at the same time excited, she opens the door and enters the darkened room, where she discovers that a long, semitransparent curtain divides the sleeping and the sitting areas. She crosses the suite as though she is an actress on the stage of her private theater, walks with determination to the windows at the very end of the room, pulls apart the heavy, dark curtain, and opens the window so that light can fill this magnificent room. Her first glance falls upon a photograph of Maxim on the dressing table. Quickly turning away from this image, which clearly disturbs her, she slowly approaches Rebecca's bed, only to be startled by the sound of the open window banging against the window frame.

As Hitchcock shows us the curtains blowing in the breeze, as if their movement is an indication that Rebecca's spirit has awakened, we hear Danvers asking "I" whether she has any wishes. She, too, has passed beyond the transparent curtains into the innermost part of Rebecca's suite, as though to direct the fantasy scenario that is to be played out there. Confronting "I" with her forbidden wishes, Danvers tells her that she has known all along that she wanted to see this room, and, after drawing apart the second curtain, she proceeds to show her Rebecca's intimate possessions, which she has preserved as relics and placed on display. Within the walls of this room, in which nothing has been changed since the night of the accident, these objects attest that though Rebecca's body is dead, her spirit remains alive and present here forever.

At the same time, Rebecca's bedroom emerges as the architectural materialization of the very kernel of "I's" forbidden and unacknowledged homoerotic desires. This heterotopic countersite confirms "I's" fantasy that there is a place within the master's house where an all-possessing, phallic woman reigns. Yet this bedroom is above all a place in which her fantasy is confronted by that of the other woman who also fashions herself in relation to the deceased Rebecca.[14] As though to signal the intimacy of their rapport, Danvers recalls how Rebecca would come home at night and tell her about the magnificent parties she had been to. As Danvers speaks about the past, she forces "I" to sit on Rebecca's chair, and without actually touching "I's" hair, Danvers pantomimes brushing it, the spectral body of Rebecca now encompassing that of the unnamed heroine. If Danvers thus uses the living body of the second Mrs. de Winter to give new life to the body of the dead woman, she does so to reinforce her point that the second Mrs. de Winter can never fill the symbolic position inhabited by the late Rebecca.

Hitchcock's ironic appropriation of the Oedipal configuration hinges once more on the use of a detail. As "I" sits at the dressing table, watching Danvers move toward Rebecca's bed, her glance again falls on the photograph of Maxim, on the table next to the hairbrushes. She is thus visually positioned like a child, between the two parental figures who compete for her identification: on her right, the silent image of Maxim, the figure of paternal authority; on her left, Danvers's voice, invoking an omnipotent figure of maternal authority.

Suddenly the heroine turns away from the image of her husband and follows Danvers, who has picked up the case she embroidered for her mistress's sleeping garment. Like all Rebecca's other possessions, it carries an insignia of her name, though not the "RdeW" that the nameless heroine found in the rooms her predecessor shared with her husband; this is the solitary letter "R." As Danvers takes out the transparent lace nightgown, "I" initially tries to resist the image of the seductive, barely clad Rebecca that is evoked by Danvers's suggestive voice. As Hitchcock's camera moves around the bed, facing "I," and in so doing implicitly taking on the position Rebecca might have had, had she been sitting on the bed, Danvers once more forces her new mistress to vicariously take part in the nocturnal spectacle she is evoking. Now no longer in the position of the child usurping the place of her mother at her dressing table, but rather in that of the voyeur enjoying a clandestine scene, "I" watches Danvers drape the lace gown over her hand and exclaim, "Look, you can see my hand through it." At this point "I" has clearly reached the acme of her forbidden *jouissance*, for she slowly moves away from the bed and, panting softly, tries to flee from the room. As John Fletcher notes, "The musical crescendo that marks Fontaine's recoil and withdrawal from the hand in the negligee also marks her grief and exclusion from the imaginary sexual scene memorialized in Rebecca's bedroom," namely the scene of parental coitus.[15]

Given, however, that Danvers has been emphasizing that this room was Rebecca's haven, allowing her to escape both her friends and her social obligation as Mrs. de Winter—which is to say it was a site in which she lived only under the sign of her first name, "R," a further interpretation suggests itself. "I" flees from Rebecca's bedroom because the sight of Danvers's hand beneath the transparent lace of the nightgown evokes an enjoyment forbidden by the allegedly healthy solution to the Oedipal conflict. At stake is less her voyeuristic enjoyment of Danvers's love for a dead woman than her own identification with this desire for a forbidden feminine body. In this short moment of recognition, the fantasy that she might usurp the position of the previous mistress of Manderley is displaced in favor of one far more disturbing, namely that she might enter into and merge with the irresistibly seductive body of the other woman.

The traumatic impact of this anagnorisis at the bed of the deceased Rebecca results in "I's" vehement resistance to the dictates of the maternal superego, which she continues to find represented by Danvers's reprimanding gaze. For the first time she refuses to let her housekeeper take care of everything—which is to say she refuses to let Danvers manage the household in the way Rebecca would have wanted it. Sitting at the desk in the morning room, where up to this point she had felt so helpless and inadequate amid the stationery carrying the initials "RdeW," she calls for Danvers. Filled with new confidence, she explains that she wants all the possessions of her predecessor removed, and as the housekeeper indignantly retorts that they belong to Mrs. de Winter, she has recourse for the first time to the symbolic mandate bestowed upon her by virtue of her marriage: "I am Mrs. de Winter," she replies.

Yet the heroine is still incapable of completely detaching herself from her powerful maternal predecessor; instead, she unwittingly chooses a different mode of identification—an uncanny appropriation of the appearance of the very figure she seeks to undermine. Having convinced Maxim that she wants to have a costume ball at Manderley so she can publicly prove the legitimacy of her claim to being the mistress of the de Winter estate, she lets Danvers help her choose a costume, a replica of the dress worn by Lady Caroline de Winter in a painting that hangs in the portrait gallery. Danvers leads "I" to this portrait of a woman wearing a large straw hat and a dress with a full white skirt and a low-cut neckline. In the painting Lady Caroline is holding a fan in both hands as though seeking to cover her sex. On a more suggestive note, this fan could also be seen as a phallic object that she is pointing toward her sex—the mark of the woman's bisexuality—while the decorative silk flowers on the front right side of her skirt, between her breasts, and behind her left ear seem to accentuate her femininity. Although this is an explicit staging of feminine charms utterly opposed to the body gestures and dresses of "I," Danvers suggests that it might have been designed for her; then the housekeeper walks out of the frame and "I," dwarfed by the huge painting, obediently follows her.

As in the scene where Danvers first pointed out Rebecca's room to her new mistress, only to lead her out of the frame, the camera once again does not follow the two women but tarries with their object of fascination, moving closer to the portrait. For a few moments the shadow of "I" walking away passes over it, until its image almost completely fills the frame. Hitchcock's interpolation of a short superimposition of the mansion between this scene and the one that opens with the fatal costume ball serves once more to visually cement the analogy between seductive feminine body and the de Winter home, and since we are about to find out that Rebecca had worn exactly this dress at the last costume ball, it also renders visible how a dead woman has enveloped Manderley, having first assumed the costume of one of its ancestors. At the same time, Hitchcock uses the costume ball scene to illustrate that appropriating the appearance of another in order to usurp her symbolic position can be a dangerous undertaking. As Judith Butler notes, "There is a cost in every identification, the loss of some other set of identifications, the forcible approximation of a norm one never chooses, a norm that chooses us, but which we occupy, reverse, resignify to the extent that the norm fails to determine us completely."[16] By choosing this costume, which Danvers has actually chosen for her, "I" seeks to prove she is now the rightful mistress of Manderley, yet in so doing she unwittingly effaces herself. In a gesture of empowerment, she appropriates the costume of someone whose title to the de Winter heritage is uncontested, identifying herself with Lady Caroline, as a representative of the masculine lineage of her husband. Yet she finds that in so doing she has instead re-animated Rebecca. If she fled from the bedroom because the image of Rebecca in her nightgown evoked by Danvers flooded her with desire, she now literally transforms herself into this forbidden body. Like her new home, Manderley, she, too, has come to be engulfed by the spectral body of her predecessor.

Initially unaware of the uncanny heritage she has thus appropriated, "I" has her maid help her dress behind the locked door of her own bedroom and will let no one see her costume before the ball begins. On her way to joining the others in the entrance hall, she hesitates once more before the portrait, to reassure herself that the similarity is perfect. Now it is her body that fills the frame, while we can only see the bottom part of the full white skirt in the portrait. Pleased with the resemblance, "I" pulls at her skirt one last time, checks her posture, and proudly begins descending the stairs toward her husband, his sister, and her brother-in-law, who have their backs to her. Expecting their approval, she is already wearing the smile of a woman assured of her seductive charm, even though a trace of insecurity and doubt remains. Only when she calls her husband by his last name, does Maxim finally turn around, and in the rapid change of his facial expression we recognize the uncanny horror underlying her beautiful attire.[17] Hitchcock cuts to a close-up of his heroine, who initially tries to defend herself against the harsh rebuff of her husband, but then, in confusion, flees up the stairs to obey his command to take the dress off. For a moment she stops in front of the portrait of Lady Caroline, then she follows Danvers, whom she sees entering Rebecca's room. Only there does she discover the horrible meaning of her appropriation of this costume.

"I's" descent down the stairs, her hopes of finally establishing herself as mistress of Manderley, and the subsequent rejection, which forces her to recognize that this is impossible, thus signify the ambivalent feelings she has for the two figures of authority she must choose between if she is to reach the full status of Mrs. de Winter. On the one hand, Hitchcock poignantly illustrates his heroine's vanity, as she enjoys imagining how she has transformed herself into a ravishing and irresistible object of her husband's approval. But her flight from the public space of the ball offers a counterimage to the way she had literally fallen into Maxim's arms in the same entrance hall after fleeing from Rebecca's bedchamber in the earlier scene.

Now, rather than vanquishing her rival, she seeks solace with that rival's faithful representative, not least because she has been forced to accept that while she can have all of her predecessor's possessions removed, she cannot appropriate the position formerly held by her.

A crucial aspect of Hitchcock's mise-en-scène, then, is the manner in which it highlights "I's" ambivalent feelings. While manifestly seeking to disengage from this castrative figure of maternal authority, she is actually drawn ever more into the vortex of Rebecca's force field. At the same time, Hitchcock asks us to read the entire scene—her flight from the costume ball, ending with an image of her, still dressed in Rebecca's costume, sitting on the windowsill of her predecessor's bedroom, looking down at the sea, while Danvers whispers fantasies of suicide into her ear—in conjunction with her first encounter of Maxim. Hitchcock cannily introduced that earlier scene with a depiction of waves beating against the cliffs of a beach in Monte Carlo. His camera slowly pans up the mountain, finally coming to rest in a close-up of Maxim staring, as if in a trance, at the violent sea below. The camera then cuts to Maxim's feet, as they move forward to the edge of the cliff he is precariously standing on. As Tania Modleski notes, he is "staring out at the ocean but clearly 'seeing' something that we don't see," so that the effect is unsettling.[18] Indeed, one could surmise that this subjective point of view marks Maxim's suicide fantasy. In the vortex of the water he imagines the dead Rebecca, beckoning him to follow her.

It is at this moment that "I" takes the place of the absent woman—emerging both in Maxim's field of vision and in ours as she calls out to him to be careful, and thus interrupts his death fantasy. Bearing this scene in mind as we think through the resolution of the costume ball sequence, we discover a significant reversal, for now, several months after this ominous meeting, she, who displaced the absent body in the previous scene and drew the camera's focus onto herself, has used her own body to bring the absent woman back into his—and implicitly our—field of vision. And she has done so in a manner that replaces the whirlpool (a metonymy for Rebecca's corpse) with his first wife's spectral resuscitation in her ("I's") own body.

That a complete identification with her predecessor is concomitant with "I's" self-distinction was, furthermore, already played through in an earlier scene, where the unnamed heroine, sitting at her desk in the morning room, had answered a phone call for Mrs. de Winter by explaining, "Mrs. de Winter is dead." Now, standing once more in Rebecca's room, "I" helplessly listens to Danvers assuring her that she can never become the mistress of Manderley, because she can't fight Rebecca. While the housekeeper goes on to explain that if Rebecca was beaten in the end, it wasn't because of a man or a woman, but because of the sea, "I" breaks down in despair on the bed of her predecessor.

Danvers suddenly opens the window, asks "I" to come sit there, and proceeds, with a firm but compelling voice, to tell her new mistress whom she will never acknowledge, to leave Manderley. Then, shifting into the register of a lover, she begins to whisper into "I's" left ear a death wish that would be tantamount to consummating her passion for the dead woman, whose lure she can't seem to resist: "You have nothing to live for really, have you?" she says enticingly, as the sound track imitates the panting of a lover about to reach an orgasm. Prodding the young woman, who has begun to lean over the windowsill and look into the deadly space below, she adds, "It's easy. Why don't you? Go on, don't be afraid." Like Maxim, drawn to the whirlpool beneath his feet in the scene of their first encounter in Monte Carlo, "I" now seems fatally drawn to the fog cloud covering the tiles of the terrace beneath this window. Hitchcock films the alluring object, which the two women see although it is invisible to us, by placing his camera behind them and including their shoulders in the frame, much as he filmed Maxim's feet edging toward the cliff's precipice, by including his shoulders in the frame.

The visual analogy between these two scenes is further cemented by the fact that "I," like Maxim, is awakened from her trance by a sudden noise, though in her case it is the fire signals in the sky and the shot heralding a boating accident. In contrast to Maxim's return to the living, however, Hitchcock depicts this waking up as the acme of "I's" orgiastic enjoyment. The sound of the gun literally seems to penetrate the heroine, and as she straightens her upper body, moving away from the window, she is frozen for a moment, as if rigid in ecstasy, staring at the fireworks in the sky above her. The sigh with which she finally awakens denotes that her gaze is no longer directed at the enjoyment of her imagined fatal embrace with her alluring rival, but is now focused on the concrete world around her. Saddened and relieved, she can leave the scene of her necrophilic fantasy, only to discover, once she has reached the others at the beach, that it is Rebecca's boat that has been washed ashore, with a female corpse in its cabin. The logic of the fantasy played through in the failed costume ball can thus be summarized as follows: the unnamed heroine's initial desire to take Rebecca's place, by unwittingly appropriating her costume, transforms into a desire to be consumed by her, which finds its acme in the erotically encoded representation of "I's" suicide attempt. Interrupted by the phallic shot heralding a real death, this fantasy finds closure in the actual appearance of the dead woman whom the three main players have been keeping alive in their imagination.

The counterfantasy, which will allow "I" to psychically relinquish her desire for the maternal body and thus become a mature subject, sets in with Maxim's confession. He assures his second wife that he had always been consumed by hatred for the woman who dared live out her unrestricted sexuality behind the masquerade of the devoted wife and mistress of Manderley. Long before he fled Manderley, and with it her ghost, she had already made him feel how little he was master of his own home, reducing him instead to a mere pawn in the deceit she performed in public, while he privately witnessed a complete subversion of his authority and the values he stood for. In the course of his confession, Maxim describes the accidental death of his first wife, and as in the scene where Danvers remembers her nocturnal meetings with Rebecca, this rendition of a commemorative recreation of the past works because Rebecca's absent body is depicted in such a manner as to seem phantasmatically present.[19] Pascal Bonizer has suggested that in cinema, offscreen space, which we don't actually see, though we are nevertheless aware of it, is the space of horror par excellence: "Specular space is on-screen space; it is everything we see on the screen. Offscreen space, blind space, is everything that moves (or wriggles) outside or under the surface of things, like the shark in *Jaws*. If such films 'work,' it is because we are more or less held in the sway of these two spaces. . . . The point of horror resides in the blind space."[20]

Using this concept of offscreen space, Tania Modleski suggests that the scene in which Maxim confesses his involvement in Rebecca's death is uncanny because Hitchcock superimposes the offscreen space of Maxim's memory onto the onscreen space of the beach house. The absent Rebecca thus takes on a horrific presence, both for the couple and for the spectators. Maxim mentally retraces the details of that night—how Rebecca told him about her pregnancy, so as to torture him with the thought that she would give birth to the son of another, yet claim this was the rightful heir to the de Winter name; how he had slapped her after she taunted him by telling him he could do nothing about her deception and asking him whether he would now kill her; how she had smiled at him triumphantly before suddenly stumbling and falling to the ground, hitting her head on a heavy piece of ship's tackle, her horrific smile now frozen on her face. Rather than inserting a flashback of the scene—and with it finally a concrete image of Rebecca—Hitchcock instead has the camera follow the body movements Maxim invokes from his subjective perspective. Hitchcock thus presents us with the disembodied voice-over of the male hero that was to become a standard narrative technique in film noir in the 1940s and 1950s, even while Maxim's absence from the screen ironically gives more force to Rebecca's spectral presence.

Indeed, the horror effect of the confession scene feeds off the fact that Rebecca is never actually shown, yet is incessantly invoked, thus straddling onscreen and offscreen space. At the same time, this spectral force writes itself into the very mode of representation, for, as Mary Ann Doane has noted, equally uncanny is the fact that Hitchcock allows his camera to move into the position taken by the dead woman. "In tracing Rebecca's path as Maxim narrates," she explains, "the camera pans more than 180 degrees. In effect, what was marked very clearly as Maxim's point of view, simply transferred to Fontaine as narratee, comes to include him."[21] Much as in the scene where Danvers showed Rebecca's nightgown to "I," while the camera surreptitiously took on the position of the dead woman sitting on her bed, Hitchcock's camera now has come around full circle to include Maxim in the frame. The result is a blurring of the boundary between the past and the present, between the invoked and the actual, to such a degree that we have the impression that the gaze represented by the camera is that of the dead Rebecca herself, resuscitated by his voice.

This shift in perspective, which effaces Maxim by the very feminine force that his narrative evokes, is significant, furthermore, because it allows "I" to identify with his sadistic desire, wanting her dead even if he didn't actually kill her. It is easier for her to accept that Maxim could have been a killer than to live with her jealousy of a seemingly invincible rival. In imitation of his willingness to use violence to get rid of the forceful woman challenging his authority, she is finally able to abject this maternal figure of authority, and with it her pose of the clueless child, and fully appropriate her position as the second Mrs. de Winter. Of course, to comply with Hollywood's Hays Code, Selznick had to change Du Maurier's ending. Rather than Rebecca being pregnant, as in the novel, with Maxim unequivocally responsible for her death, the film's script resolves matricide into the required happy ending by having Rebecca discover on the day of her death that she has incurable cancer. Maxim now proves to be nothing more than the catalyst for a fatal accident that Rebecca consciously provoked. Yet one could argue that there is more than moral compunction involved in this alteration of Du Maurier's text, namely a massive jettisoning of the very figure whose spectral body haunts the film that carries her name. Hitchcock visually cements this ousting of Rebecca's power, and with it the shift in "I's" sense of self-empowerment, by staging the next dialogue between her and Maxim not in the boathouse (clearly encoded as Rebecca's territory) but next to a lit fireplace in one of Manderley's salons, i.e., at the hearth of the conventional home of the master.[22] Here a different form of castration is played through; rather than the lethal embrace with a feminine figure of authority, this is the curtailment of a multiplicity of identity positions open to the subject. As Hitchcock's camera moves into a close-up of Maxim, holding his wife's head firmly between his hands, he visualizes what maturity will cost his heroine. Their embrace is framed in such a manner that, while she is now almost as tall as he, her head seems to be severed from her body, as though it were a trophy lying in his hands, while he explains: "It's gone forever, that funny, young lost look I loved. It will never come back. I killed that when I told you about Rebecca. It's gone. In a few hours you've grown so much older." "I's" position of Mrs. de Winter is now uncontested, but this symbolic status is bought at the price of what Judith Butler calls "the forcible approximation of a norm one never chooses," even while one can resignify it "to the extent that the norm fails to determine us completely."[23] "I's" loss of innocence proves to be her gain because she has finally been able to exorcise the feminine power that had marred the completion of her home romance.

And yet uncanniness remains, because in this gothic appropriation of Freud's Oedipus story, mature subjectivity means acknowledging that though the ghost of Rebecca can be laid to rest, the couple can never be masters of the house. Indeed, it seems to be the price they must pay for the happy ending to their whirlwind romance. Danvers burns down the estate, because she doesn't want to see them living there. While the destruction of the space haunted by Rebecca confirms the psychic need of the daughter to destroy the maternal superego before fully committing herself to a heterosexual marriage, it also confirms the rule of homelessness underwriting the entire film. As Thomas M. Leitch notes, "Rebecca will now be eternally misremembered, de Winter separated from his ancestral home, and the heroine without any home at all."[24]

Daphne du Maurier's Feminine Novelette and Hitchcock's Birth as Master of Horror

Turning once more to Hitchcock's own preoccupation with homelessness, we also discover the logic of the family romance cropping up in the manner in which he presents *Rebecca* not as his proper child but as an orphan that he adopted. In his conversations with Truffaut he explains, "Well, it's not a Hitchcock picture; it's a novelette, really. The story is old-fashioned; there was a whole school of feminine literature at the period, and though I'm not against it, the fact is that the story is lacking in humor."[25] It is, then, precisely the feminine encoding that renders the novel *Rebecca* foreign to the British director, seeking to establish himself in his new home, Hollywood. Yet it is also a familiar but rejected text, insofar as he had wanted to film it in England but couldn't do so for financial reasons; in this respect it marks an uncanny moment of the past coming to haunt him after he had already crossed the ocean to America. One can only surmise that while a filming of Du Maurier's novel in England would have allowed him to transpose the feminine novelette into his distinctive visual sense, the omnipotence of his producer in Hollywood forced him to comply with an American influence, which, as he would later explain to critics, became most noticeable in the requirement that he adhere to the script by Robert Sherwood. What most made Hitchcock recognize how far he was from the position of master in the Hollywood Studio System was, however, Selznick's compunction to defend the feminine spirit of the original novel, representing Du Maurier's intentions in a way that uncannily recalls Danvers's insistence in representing the dead Rebecca's wishes. A memo from Selznick to Hitchcock shortly after he had arrived from England illustrates how the American producer put pressure on his British director to subject himself to the feminine style of the text, much as the unnamed heroine initially has to subject herself to all the possessions bearing her predecessor's initials before she can finally assert her own command. Against Hitchcock's efforts to impose his own visual sense on the text, Selznick forcefully intervened:

> Every little thing that the girl does in the book, her reactions of running away from the guests, and the tiny things that indicate her nervousness and her self-consciousness and her gaucherie are all so brilliant in the book that every woman who has read it has adored the girl and

has understood her psychology, has cringed with embarrassment for her, yet has understood exactly what was going through her mind. . . . We have removed all the subtleties and substituted big broad strokes, which in outline would betray just how ordinary the plot is and just how bad a picture it would make without the little feminine things which are so recognizable and which make every woman say, "I know just how she feels. . . . I know just what she's going through."[26]

What is significant about this filmic treatment of the home fantasy of an orphaned woman haunted by her dead predecessor, then, is not only that Hitchcock should make it at the onset of his American career but that he should treat it as a *Mischling*, for which he was ultimately to take full credit in the press, all the while confessing to critics like Truffaut that he didn't want to fully acknowledge his parentage. At the same time, he concedes to Truffaut in hindsight that making this film inspired him to enrich many of his later films with the psychological elements he found in Daphne du Maurier's novel. In retrospect one can surmise that it was exactly this encounter with a decidedly feminine novel that marked the turning point in his handling of the psychothriller genre, for which he—and not his American producer—would ultimately find a secure place in our film archive.

Reading *Rebecca* as the peripeteia in Hitchcock's own Oedipal development toward the established position of successful Hollywood director allows one to further note the analogy between the way Hitchcock speaks about his own sense of aesthetic dislocation on the Selznick set while making a film about dispossession which he doesn't quite want to call his own. Both, after all, follow what Freud called the family romance—a fantasy scenario in which the liberation of the maturing subject from the authority of his parents finds a psychically satisfying reenactment.

As already discussed in the introduction, the structure of this fantasy revolves around the idea of being an orphan, or an adopted child, unjustly punished by its parents. It can serve as a wish fulfillment because the figure of authority, whose harsh law the daydreamer seeks to resist in actual life, is degraded in fantasy and replaced by someone grander—an imaginary figure whose attributes are derived from nostalgic recollections of the vanished days of lost childhood. Significant in the oblique, though never directly named ties between Hitchcock's biographical situation and the plot of *Rebecca* is that his fictional "I," the unnamed heroine, replaces the father and the home she has lost with a grander man and a more magnificent house. Yet what she encounters as she embarks on a fantasy meant to support her nostalgic idealization of childhood is certainly not protection and security but rather a violent battle between the two figures of authority that replace her lost parents, ending in the abjection of the maternal figure, the irrevocable loss of the new home, and a sober de-idealization of the paternal figure she has married. Analogously, Hitchcock's Hollywood romance lived off the fantasy that America would be a grander site for developing his cinematic vision than his place of birth, but upon arrival, he found that he, too, would have to battle the figure of authority who reigned over his new home. In his case, though, the grander figure substituting for any real parents was the composite David O. Selznick—the harsh, paternal producer seeking to preserve the authorial voice of the woman who had written the novel *Rebecca*.

For both Hitchcock and his unnamed heroine, violent encounters with harsh figures of parental authority reveal that what had seemed a familiar site in fantasy proves fundamentally uncanny once it is actually experienced. The apparently omnipotent, inescapable, yet also invisible feminine figure that "I" discovers at the heart of the home gives voice to the foreign body always already inherent in our psychic apparatus—the alterity that Freud locates as the ground and vanishing point of the psychic split between conscious and unconscious. The gothic transcription of the family romance in *Rebecca* gives body to the intangible alterity in the ghost of the first mistress, allowing the daydreamer to negotiate her relationship with this uncanny entity and forcing her to recognize that arriving at a home, whether it is a concrete geographical place or a position within the symbolic order, is inevitably marked by the loss of full empowerment. As Julia Kristeva has compellingly shown in her study of the powers of horror, although jettisoning the maternal body is the prerequisite for psychic maturation, that body continues to reside in the psychic apparatus of each individual, and even if it doesn't erupt in bouts of psychic delusions, its oblique presence reminds one of the fragility of any habitation—be it in a place, in a social position, or in the happiness afforded by successful couple building.[27]

It is thus only logical that in a novel emerging from a feminine school of literature, a fantasy scenario should be played through, in which the feminine subject, hoping to rediscover her lost home, instead has to confront another lost emotion—the initial bisexuality of the little girl, which continues to haunt her long after she has seemingly given it up in favor of heterosexual identity. It is also only logical that this twofold resurgence of uncanniness—of the difference written into heterosexual identity and the difference written into any sense of belonging—should be negotiated in relation to a maternal spirit that won't be contained, rather than a paternal figure seeking to assert his masculine authority.[28]

After all, identity formation involves a process in which the subject initially assimilates traits, gestures, and indeed the appearance of an idealized other. The implicit danger in this necessary act of appropriation is that the subject runs the risk of being completely consumed by the object of her or his identification. The possibility of this outcome explains the violence with which the maternal body, as site of identification par excellence, must be abjected in *Rebecca*. As Tania Modleski compellingly notes, *Rebecca* isn't simply a film "about a woman's problems of 'overidentification' with another woman," leading to the vilification of the latter in response to the threat of self-annihilation. Rather, Hitchcock's desire to repudiate Rebecca also draws our attention to "that feminine element in the textual body that is unassimilatable by patriarchal culture." This feminine foreign body can, however, not be completely jettisoned, since Selznick insists that Hitchcock adhere to the feminine voice of Du Maurier's text and preserve the inescapable presence of Rebecca's unseen body, which haunts the film to the very last image. "Such are the paradoxes of auteurship," Modleski argues. "By being forced to maintain a close identification with du Maurier's 'feminine' text to the point where he felt that the picture could not be considered his own, Hitchcock found one of his 'proper' subjects—the potential terror and loss of self involved *in* identification, especially identification with a woman."[29]

The experience of psychic as well as concrete homelessness as the primal force behind all fantasy work is thus negotiated in *Rebecca* as a question of the fascinating as well as endangering identification with an explicitly feminine interpellation, which one hasn't necessarily chosen but to which one must acquiesce even though one can resignify it: for Hitchcock it's the feminine spirit of the novel, haunting his filming of it; for his cinematic "I," it's the spirit of her predecessor, haunting her new home. In one aspect, however, Hitchcock and his unnamed heroine differ dramatically. The home romance that she begins to unfold, as her voice-over accompanies the dream images of Manderley at the beginning of *Rebecca*, marks how this fantasy is contingent upon her having been forced to give up all hope of experiencing the safety and protection of the home she has been yearning for. In other words, if relinquishing any identification with the powerful but dangerous Rebecca is the precondition for her fully accepting her symbolic mandate as Maxim de Winter's second wife—which is to say her psychic position as a mature female subject—relinquishing Manderley is the prerequisite for her position as narrator. Precisely because she has no home, she can return to the Manderley of her dreams with no restraints imposed on her fantasy work. Dreaming about Manderley and Rebecca is her way of resignifying the approximation of the heterosexual norm that has been forced upon her as a norm she never chose.

Multiple Framings

As we turn to the actual beginning of the film, we notice that while "I's" voice-over functions as the narrative framing of the story that is about to unfold, the film *Rebecca* is itself framed by a title sequence, which commences after we have been shown a close-up of a huge white sign bearing the name "The Selznick Studios" and then a long shot of a stately white mansion. The names of all the people who worked on the film are superimposed on a painted image of Manderley's park, shrouded in fog. Thus from the start, the supremacy of Selznick's authority is not only visually stated but rendered in relation to the question of place. In contrast to the homeless director, whose name is superimposed on the painted image along with all the others, the producer's power is represented architecturally, his ownership signified by the white mansion, his symbolic home.

Only with this image firmly in place does Hitchcock cut to the moon, as it suddenly appears from behind a cloud, while Joan Fontaine's voice-over explains that last night she had dreamed she had gone again to Manderley.[30] The moonlit iron gate leading to the drive is shown in the next frame, as "I's" voice-over continues to recall her dream. It had seemed for a while, she explains, that she could not enter because the way was barred to her. Then suddenly, like all dreamers, she found herself possessed with supernatural powers "and passed like a spirit through the barrier" before her. As Hitchcock's camera begins to imitate this spectral path, slipping effortlessly through the iron rods of the gate and meandering along the path leading up to the mansion, we continue to hear the heroine's disembodied voice. She has become aware that a change has come upon her old home: "Nature had come into her own again and little by little had encroached upon the drive with long, tenacious fingers." The gaze of the heroine slowly moves along the overgrown, unfamiliar path, until Manderley appears, not suddenly and powerfully, as it had on the day of her initial arrival there, but rather as the last step in her furtive approach to the alluring house: "There it was, Manderley, secretive and silent." As Hitchcock shows us the mansion rising against a nocturnal sky, the heroine explicitly refers to the phantasmatic effect of this dream vision. "Moonlight," she explains, "can play odd tricks upon the fancy." For a moment the entire scene grows dark, as though a shadow had been cast; then, as the heroine remarks that it suddenly seemed to her as though light were coming from the windows, we see an image of Manderley, lit from within. A cloud once more covers the moon, while the heroine notes that with it the illusion of reanimation has gone. As the camera now drives directly toward Manderley, we discover along with the heroine that the object of her spectral eye is in fact the forlorn skeleton of a house, "a desolate shell with no whisper of the past about its staring walls." Sighing, she recognizes that "we can never go back to Manderley again, that much is certain," only to add an afterthought commemorating the power of her own fantasy work: "But sometimes, in my dreams, I do go back to those strange days of my life, which began for me in the south of France." After his camera has driven directly into the darkness of one of Manderley's walls, Hitchcock cuts to the scene of "I's" first encounter with Maxim—the whirlpool at the bottom of a cliff in Monte Carlo.

The disembodied heroine's tone is clearly nostalgic, recalling Maxim's anticipation of loss, yet installing this as the frame for the home romance about to unfold. However, while her nostalgia invokes the traumatic destruction of Manderley, it actually mitigates this loss by enabling her imagination to overcome actual homelessness, even while her own disempowerment is accentuated. As a nocturnal dreamer she has no body, nor does she occupy any clear location in the world outside the tale she is about to tell. Indeed, unlike the male voice-overs deployed in classic film noir, Hitchcock offers us no indication of where she is. Rather, as a spectral visitor of Manderley, she takes on the attitude of her predecessor, Rebecca, and like her, uses her willpower to resist the iron gate barring her way. Hitchcock thus visualizes from the start that Manderley isn't simply a phantasmatic site but, more crucially, is a secret one, comparable to a crypt, which is barred from any conscious entry, even though in fantasy the gate can be trespassed with impunity. The image of the burnt-out shell of the house that we find at the end of the narrative frame haunts all subsequent depictions of this stately mansion, suggesting, before the actual home romance even begins, that "I's" desire to arrive at an infallibly stable protective home is an impossibility.[31] Yet, although she knows that she will never be able to return to Manderley, the dreamer successfully uses her powers of fantasy to overcome the homelessness that is her reality.

Thus Hitchcock's cinematic language, by enmeshing a frame narrative that asserts the heroine's loss of home with an inserted story that allows her to return to this phantasmatic site from which she is barred in reality, undercuts the very narrative of homelessness that it also appropriates. The dangerous alterity that must be abjected in the course of the heroine's Oedipal trajectory can be regained in fantasy. Hitchcock's heroine thus acquiesces to the paternal law, requiring the renunciation of a dangerous proximity between the daughter and the mother, and with it a phantasmatic home, even while preserving this alluring bond as a cipher for the lethal fulfillment that a true homecoming would entail. With her cheerful assurance that in her dreams she is able to return to the home she has irrevocably lost, the heroine calls upon us to identify with her situation of homelessness, even though in the course of the story she unfolds for us, she will have us identify with her desire for the uncanny spectral presence of her predecessor.[32] Her voice thus initially functions as a counterpoint to the voiceless, absent body of Rebecca that takes over as spectral presence once "I's" voice-over breaks off, in the scene at the cliff in Monte Carlo. At the same time, given its prominence in the film's frame, "I's" voice-over serves as a counterpoint to the two voices dominating the actual story: Danvers's seductive yet firm one, remembering her own intimate clandestine moments with Rebecca and calling upon the heroine to take her own life, and Maxim's sober one, in one scene anticipating the irrevocable loss of his home, while in a later one confessing his own fateful implication in the death of his wife. Like an uncanny, hybrid body, "I's" voice-over actually combines these opposing positions. In her dreams she overcomes the iron barrier, returns to the site of lethal allure—and thus to her fascination with Manderley's first mistress—all the while self-consciously reflecting that this transgression is possible only as a dream and keeping fully intact the iron gate that protects her from all dangerous enjoyment.

On the one hand, then, the happy ending of this strange romance that revolves around the reappropriation of a home—a project that is doomed to fail from the start—veers toward an unconditional acknowledgment of homelessness. The last image Hitchcock offers of his fated couple is that of their desperate embrace as they watch Manderley burn. On the other hand, Hitchcock pits two feminine dreams against the condition of dislocation. The first is the sober fantasy of the nocturnal dreamer, who has come to accept that she can never be mistress of her own home. Owing to the power of her imagination, however, she now fully owns Manderley in the way she has always desired it—as a representation. That the attitude of nostalgic dreamer perfectly corresponds to "I's" notions of happiness was, after all, a point she made during one of her outings in Monte Carlo with Maxim. She told him that she wished there could be an invention that bottled up memory like perfume, so it would never fade and never get stale. Then whenever she wanted to, she could uncork the bottle and live the memory all over again. "I" is keen on preserving memories of happy moments, even if they are marred, and she sets this wholesome *ars memoria* against both Maxim's desire to obliterate all the demons of the past and Danvers's desire to preserve the deceased Rebecca as a materially embodied memory. If in the film's diegesis "I" comes to stand in for Rebecca, to the point of appropriating her appearance, in the film's narrative frame it is her psychic apparatus, and the manner in which it converts her desires into memory scenes, that emerges as the location of the uncanny spectacle. Here she is no longer an actress in a scenario exploring her masochistic enjoyment of disempowerment and its matricidal turn. Rather, her mind emerges as the cryptophoric chamber/camera through which a representation of the clandestinely alluring but now utterly destroyed Manderley, and the feminine power reigning there, can be preserved with impunity.

As the source for this phantasmagoric resuscitation of memory scenes, she above all emerges as a mirror of the director himself. For isn't the core around which Hitchcock's later Hollywood psychothrillers revolve the maintenance of precisely such an uncanny dialogue with lost, absent, or dead objects of desire? Indeed, one might ask whether Hitchcock doesn't employ this feminine dreamer—who is able to pass through the iron bars toward a mysterious site and to re-create there the memories that give meaning to her condition of homelessness—to point to the power of his own cinematic apparatus. After all, his camera will become most famous for penetrating into locked rooms.

To the end, however, this nostalgic dreamer has a rival, and it is to the rival that the second dream scenario clings. Hitchcock's film closes neither with an image of the happily united couple nor with the disembodied voice that led us so surreptitiously into the story that began in Monte Carlo.

Rather, his camera turns away from the couple staring in horror at the destruction of their home and pans along the facade of the wing leading to Rebecca's room until it catches sight of Danvers, trapped inside and moving frantically about her beloved mistress's bedroom in an effort to escape the flames. Suddenly she stops in front of the big window, but rather than looking out at the crowd gathered below, she looks up, almost piously. Hitchcock then switches the perspective of the camera to her subjective point of view and shows us the burning planks falling on her. Once Danvers has disappeared from the field of vision, the camera remains in the heart of the fire, seemingly immune to all danger, for it begins to move around the burning room, now clearly no longer tied to the perspective of any of the film's characters. Taking the same route that Danvers did when she first led "I" to Rebecca's bed, Hitchcock's camera once again approaches the precious case containing the rival's lace nightgown. The camera comes to rest only after it has reached a close-up of the embroidered letter "R," now framed by flames, where it remains even while two further inscriptions are superimposed over this monogram—"The End" and "A Production of the Selznick Studios"—seeking closure for the resilient feminine spirit it represents.

As John Fletcher astutely notes, while the film's conclusion suggests that "the price paid for possession of the Master, and the elimination of the older woman, is the loss of the House," the completion of the feminine Oedipal trajectory that it drives toward is in part diverted and qualified, with Mrs. de Winter sleeping with Maxim but dreaming of Manderley: "Both the film's opening and closing moments, its voice-over dream sequence and its final image of the flames devouring the embroidered cover and its hidden negligee, reveal the persistence and repetition of a scene and a fantasy that—in defiance of its Oedipal plot—can never finally be laid to rest."[33] While Fletcher argues that in this final scene the camera moves as the spectral presence of Rebecca herself, one could equally surmise that the position reflected by the camera is that of "I," who, locked in the arms of her husband and barred from the burning house, has begun to dream. The camera performs a dream image of the hidden site of a dangerous and forbidden feminine enjoyment that will now burn in her memory forever. The inevitable mark of narrative closure—"The End"—is significantly not superimposed over a view of the ruined mansion shown at the onset of the film. Rather, it competes with the resilient letter "R" that will not fade. It is as though Hitchcock wants to visualize one last time that the film's entire diegesis had been determined all along by two laws, of which neither has to do with the legitimate master of Manderley: the one was the law of Rebecca's undefeatable feminine desire; the other, the producer Selznick's law, which sanctioned the persistence of the feminine spirit of Du Maurier's novel in Hitchcock's film.

Slavoj Žižek argues that "narrative as such emerges in order to resolve some fundamental antagonism by rearranging its terms into a temporal succession. It is thus the very form of narrative which bears witness to some repressed antagonism."[34] If we apply this to *Rebecca*, we could surmise that what is negotiated in "I's" fantasy is the fundamental incommensurability between an enjoyment that the subject must relinquish (most notably its identification with the maternal body) in order to fully accept its symbolic interpellation, and the transgression of this law, which may occur through forbidden forms of erotic pleasure (adultery, lesbian love) or forbidden forms of aggression (suicide, murder, arson). As Hitchcock appropriates the Oedipal trajectory that Freud prescribes for the tales of horror he seeks to stage, he insists that the psychic material the mature subject is forced to give up leaves traces behind, so that all protective fictions seeking to constrain forbidden desires maintain an uncanny core of transgression. One must, then, ask what repressed antagonism "I's" home romance bears witness to. Within the model proposed by Žižek, the antagonism that narrative sublates and bears witness to ultimately refers to the fact that enjoyment in general is properly traumatic, "the disturbed balance . . . which accounts for the passage from Nothing to Something." As such, *jouissance* refers to "the place of the subject—one is tempted to say: his 'impossible' Being-there, *Da-Sein*; and, for that very reason, the subject is always-already displaced, out-of-joint, with regard to it." If one accepts that the most elemental experience of dislocation occurs in relation to this traumatic enjoyment, which the subject can never fully assume, appropriate, or integrate into its symbolic existence, the relinquished enjoyment emerges as coterminous with "that notorious *heimliche* which is simultaneously the most *unheimliche*, always-already here and, precisely as such, always-already lost." The home romance of Hitchcock's "I"—thus my own claim—allows his heroine to reformulate this traumatic knowledge into a narrative about the fateful loss of home preserved in memory. Located in a liminal site, somewhere between home and exile, Manderley is where she can enjoy the situation of being fully at home in a place that is always already lost, as something that was always already in her possession. Within the logic of her narrative she had appropriated this "home" in fantasy, and though upon actually arriving there she discovers that it was lost to her, she takes possession of Manderley again after it is actually and irrevocably lost—namely as a dream image.

Thus the battle between a maternal and a paternal law, staged on the mind screen of the heroine after she has crossed the threshold of Manderley, doesn't simply articulate the way a relinquished homoerotic desire disturbs "I's" marriage to Maxim. Rather her encounter with the dead woman negotiates the insurmountable contingency of human existence—a knowledge that disturbs all sexual bonds, be it the heterosexual romance between the heroine and Maxim or the homoerotic one between her and the omnipresent Rebecca. Indeed, like the law of symbolic heritage, this knowledge about the uncanniness of human existence functions as the third element that disturbs all narcissistically informed love dyads. By visualizing how one can never fully escape this law of uncanniness—his camera's enjoyment of the flames that have burnt down the master's house—Hitchcock pits the open ending of a dislocation that will never end against the closure represented by the double insignia that names the conventional conclusion to any narrative ("The End") and the man under whose auspices it was produced. The horror articulated in *Rebecca* thus perhaps refers less to the fact that Maxim could have been a murderer than to the knowledge that the home we believe we possess is always already burning from inside—and that we, furthermore, enjoy this dangerous fire. Hitchcock releases us with a hybrid ending: we have the heroine's transformation of existential dislocation into a narrative about the fatal circumstances leading to her actual homelessness, and we also have a celebration of the home consumed by the fire of the traumatic *jouissance* that inhabits all protective narratives about a safe emplacement in the world—be it psychic or material. Thus Hitchcock's sober message: only the actual loss of one's home can safely distance one from the dangerous vortex at the heart of the home, even while in fantasy one can enjoy its traumatic resilience.

In his conversations with Hitchcock, Truffaut also harps on the significance of the concept of home in *Rebecca*. "Whenever home is mentioned, it's as the Manderley mansion or the estate. Whenever it is shown there is an aura of magic about it, with mists, and the musical score heightens that haunting impression." Hitchcock agrees: "That's right, because in a sense the picture is the story of a house. The house was one of the three key characters of the picture."[35] Hitchcock refuses to name the other two, leaving us to guess whether he means Maxim and his second wife or the absent Rebecca and her servant. Instead he declares Manderley to be the trope for the lack of any concrete location, obliquely referring both to the disembodied voice of the heroine at the beginning of the film and to his own dislocation in his new American home:

> In *Rebecca* the mansion is so far away from anything that you don't even know what town it's near. Now, it's entirely possible that this abstraction, which you've described as American stylization, is partly accidental, and to some extent due to the fact that the picture was made in the United States. Let us assume that we'd made *Rebecca* in England. The house would not have been so isolated because we'd have been tempted to show the countryside and the lanes leading to the house. But if the scene had been more realistic, and the place of arrival geographically situated, we would have lost the sense of isolation.[36]

One could call this "sense of isolation" in *Rebecca* the point of emergence for Hitchcock's mature cinematic language, given that it allowed him to explore the psychological components of the thriller genre, for which he was to become famous in the following decades. His compounded visualization of dislocation—Manderley grown strange to its owner, the couple meeting in exile and returning to exile, a dead woman without a proper grave—articulates the knowledge of the uncanniness of human existence. While Hitchcock's heroine discovers the power of her fantasy only after losing the home she has always yearned for, the British director came to discover his own inimitable style in the strange world of Selznick Studios. Significantly, he did so by appropriating a compound of feminine modes of expression—the feminine novelette by Daphne du Maurier, the disembodied voice of his heroine, the relentless will to remember of the faithful servant Danvers, and finally the suggestive power of a disembodied, yet omnipresent, feminine desire.

And like his heroine, Hitchcock comes out as the winner in the end. That is the point of the protective fiction he spins with his confederate Truffaut. He willingly admits that only in his new American home could he fully exploit his own creativity and thus become the unquestioned master of the psychothriller. Yet to the end the issue of the Oedipal restrictions imposed on his narcissistic fantasy work by the punitive law of a paternal authority figure remains. The bond between the two directors, celebrated in their interviews, can't exist without a reference to a third entity that troubles their happy union. In response to Truffaut's comment that *Rebecca* had, after all, won an Oscar, Hitchcock responds by admitting that his first American film had been voted the best picture of the year 1940. As Truffaut persists by asking whether it is true that this was the only Oscar he had ever won, Hitchcock staunchly replies, "I've never received an Oscar," then explains to his confused interviewer, "The award went to Selznick, the producer."[37]

The Wizard of Oz—Between Oz and Kansas

Chapter 2

Home—There's No Place Like It
The Wizard of Oz

Happiness: Somewhere Over the Rainbow

Ted Sennett explains the lasting influence of Victor Fleming's legendary musical *The Wizard of Oz* by noting that "the movie appeals to a common need: the need to belong, to have a home that offers warmth and shelter after the world's witches have been conquered."[1] Fleming's heroine, the orphaned *everygirl* Dorothy (Judy Garland), is dissatisfied with her life on her Uncle Henry (Charley Grapewin) and Aunt Em's (Clara Blandick) farm in Kansas. She dreams of a place somewhere over the rainbow, which would be more exciting than home, where there would be no worries, no calamity, and no strife. Plagued by an indefinable sense of dissatisfaction with her actual home, by a sense that something is lacking in her familiar world, Dorothy takes her dog, Toto, and sets out upon a journey in search of this fantasy place.

Initially, her attempt at escape fails, for on the way she meets the magician Professor Marvel (Frank Morgan) and asks him to take her and Toto along on his travels. The older man, however, immediately recognizes that she has run away from home, and on the pretext that he cannot make such an important decision without consulting his crystal ball, he dissuades her from her plan. Asking the girl to close her eyes, he surreptitiously searches her basket for clues to her identity and finds a photograph of her standing next to her aunt in front of their farmhouse. As he explains to Dorothy that in his crystal ball he sees a woman with a broken heart, she is overcome by a sense of guilt that proves stronger than her desire to travel to unknown places, and she realizes that she must return home. As she and Toto head back, however, a tornado descends upon the little frontier town, thus enabling Dorothy to embark on her quest for happiness somewhere beyond her home turf after all, albeit in a manner she hadn't expected.

Fully in accordance with Freud's definition of the uncanny as the experience of something that terrifies one not because it is completely unfamiliar but rather because it represents something familiar that was repressed and has now resurfaced, this outbreak of a natural catastrophe can be read as an example of Dorothy's belief in the omnipotence of her own thoughts. The tornado can be seen as a hallucinatory materialization of her desire for a violent separation from the home she is dissatisfied with, dislodging her from the structures she can't break free of on her own. Upon entering the deserted home of her aunt and uncle, who, together with the farmhands, have sought shelter in the cellar of the house, Dorothy, not knowing where the others have gone, believes that she and Toto are entirely alone. She goes to her bedroom, hoping that she might be protected there, but a window frame comes loose from the wall, hitting her on the head and causing her to collapse, unconscious, on her bed.

Dorothy's journey begins, as will be analyzed in greater detail further on, when, in what is clearly marked as a dream state, she witnesses through the open window the transformation of various characters from her everyday reality into uncanny fairy-tale figures. After the house, which she believes has carried her through the skies to the other side of the rainbow, is once again on firm ground, Dorothy opens the familiar door and discovers beyond its threshold the place that she has so ardently imagined: a phantasmagoric heterotopia that seems to have risen, like a phantom, out of the lack of adventure and magic she had felt at home. The black-and-white sepia tone chosen by Victor Fleming to visually represent the desolate life on the Kansas frontier farm, has now been exchanged for a saturated Technicolor, and Dorothy, astonished and delighted at once, declares to her companion: "Toto, I don't think we're in Kansas anymore."

As her adventures in this foreign land begin, she first encounters Glinda, a good witch (Billie Burke), who informs her that upon landing, her flying house killed the Wicked Witch of the East, so that she has been declared the liberator of the Munchkins. Shortly thereafter, however, the sister of the slain despot, the Wicked Witch of the West (Margaret Hamilton), makes her entrance. She is an uncanny transformation of the schoolteacher Miss Gulch, who, back in Kansas, had precipitated Dorothy's desire to run away in the first place. When the Wicked Witch of the West threatens to destroy the girl out of revenge for her dead sister, Glinda protects Dorothy by giving her the ruby slippers that the Wicked Witch of the East had worn. As long as Dorothy keeps them on, Glinda explains, she is armed against the destructive powers of her adversary. She nonetheless strongly advises the girl to go to Emerald City and seek out the Wizard of Oz, so that he might help her to leave the land of Oz.[2]

In search of her lost home, Dorothy meets three hybrid male figures, each, like herself, convinced that he lacks something essential and is thus doomed to being dissatisfied—the cunning Scarecrow (Ray Bolger) who longs for intelligence, the sentimental Tin Woodsman (Jack Haley) who longs for a heart, and the Cowardly Lion (Bert Lahr) who longs for courage in order to be the king of the forest. These figures are uncanny not only because they blur the boundary between the animate and the inanimate, the animal and the human, but also because Dorothy recognizes in each of the unfamiliar magical beings traces of the familiar faces of her uncle's farmhands. Together the four embark on their journey along the yellow brick road, hoping that the Wizard will provide each of them with what is lacking. The Wicked Witch of the West, of course, attempts to subvert this undertaking, at one point even capturing Dorothy, but with the help of her valiant companions, the Kansas *everygirl* succeeds in destroying her adversary and liberating Oz of all evil powers.

Having finally arrived at Emerald City, however, Dorothy is forced to realize that she cannot rely on paternal authority as a source of infallible knowledge, for the mysterious Wizard proves to be a con man. Conversely, however, she can rely on the maternal protection of the good witch to the end. Glinda offers her the advice that she needs in order to come to terms with the dissatisfaction she felt at home and thereby to resolve her fantasy that the happiness she thought was lacking there could be found in a foreign place. The world of Oz, initially conceived as an ideal place where all sense of strife was absent, has proved to be just as strife-ridden as the Kansas she left behind; it is nothing other than an uncanny refiguration of the frontier farm she was seeking to abandon. It is as though Fleming wanted to signal to the *Wizard of Oz* audience that any attempt to escape inevitably carries with it traces of the home left behind. Indeed, Dorothy discovers in this magical place that she had always possessed the home she thought she lacked—or, to put it in more sinister terms, she discovers that home is the place from which there is no escape, the place that follows one wherever one goes. As Glinda asks her to tell her friends what she has learned on her romance quest through Oz, Dorothy finally articulates the catechism that will let her return home and will also prevent her from wanting to leave again: "If I ever go looking for my heart's desire again, I won't look any further than my own backyard. Because if it isn't there, I never really lost it to begin with."

This recognition, of course, does not represent any new insight; it is simply a familiar, albeit previously repressed, piece of knowledge that she had always possessed, though she needed the detour of her quest for happiness for this curtailment of her desire to become recognizable and acceptable. We, as the audience, may wonder along with Dorothy's three companions why Glinda didn't tell her from the outset that to return to her family she need only state the supremacy of the familiar over the unknown by declaring, "There's no place like home," and instead offered this advice only after the Wicked Witch of the West had been destroyed and the Wizard unmasked and debunked. It may have been because, on a latent level, Fleming was concerned with a much less pristine notion of homecoming than the simple homilies he manifestly offers as the ideological message of the film. Knowledge that attainment of a viable sense of belonging requires relinquishing, as Ted Sennett puts it, the general "longing to move beyond one narrow corner of the world" and thus leave "worlds undiscovered and lives unlived"[3] may be inherent in the very act of daydreaming. Yet the detour into the land of fantasy is not merely a prerequisite for coming up with a story about the loss and recuperation of a happy home that can then help one live with one's sense of discontent about the boredom of everyday reality. Rather, one might fruitfully speculate that Dorothy's return to her Uncle Henry and her Aunt Em is also accompanied by a far more disturbing insight, namely that to be at home means acknowledging the sense of unease and dissatisfaction that inhabits the familiar at its very core.[4]

Dorothy enthusiastically follows Glinda's instructions. She closes her eyes, holds Toto tightly in her arms, clicks the heels of her magic red slippers together three times, and repeats the sentence "There's no place like home," as though she has fallen into a trance. With this speech act providing the link between Oz and Kansas, Fleming cuts from Technicolor Oz back to the sepia tone of the Kansas frontier farm, where Aunt Em and Uncle Henry look with concern upon the girl tossing and turning in her bed and mumbling to herself as she begins to regain consciousness. Once she is fully awake,

Dorothy recognizes in the familiar faces of her family and friends—the farmhands Hank, Zeke, and Hickory, as well as the magician Professor Marvel—the fantasy figures she has left behind, and she immediately tries to tell them about her adventures. After she realizes that they do not believe that her incredible journey through Oz actually took place, she finally accepts her aunt's sober explanation that she had only had a foolish dream.

She knows full well, however, that this dream has led her to formulate the script of her own home romance, which will allow her to accept the limited position ascribed to her within the symbolic community of this Kansas farm. She can now translate constraint into a protective fiction declaring that happiness resides in the curtailment of one's desires. In a close-up shot we see Judy Garland, in sentimental rapture, assuring her relatives that she will never again desire to leave the farm, for she has come to understand how much she loves her foster family and their friends. While on the sound track we hear the tune of the song she sang to give voice to her desire for a place over the rainbow, we see her on the screen turning to Aunt Em, at first looking directly at her, then shifting her gaze to some undefined point slightly above her right shoulder and behind her. She declares one last time, "There's no place like home," but now her eyes are wide open. We are, in fact, dealing with a double prohibition here: Dorothy recognizes, for us all, that if we want to fulfill our desires, we must not look beyond our own backyard, but if we do not find the object of desire there, we cannot cast ourselves as desiring subjects. We must instead deny the feeling of dissatisfaction that causes us to desire, that spurs us to go in search of the object of desire.

Thus Fleming's plot faithfully follows Freud's notion that at the end of the subject's Oedipal journey through a phantasmatic world, a journey that enables his *everygirl* to organize her contradictory desire for self-aggrandizement, she ultimately realizes that she can be at home in her symbolic community—the farm owned by her aunt and uncle—although she is never fully mistress of the only place of belonging she can actually call her own, because being satisfied there means curtailing all fantasies of being in other, more exciting places. As I have argued in previous chapters, Freud equates reaching maturity with the recognition that insofar as "home" serves as the trope for the desire to achieve an infallible condition of belonging—of being perfectly at one with oneself, one's community, one's geographical habitation, one's culture—failure is always written into the project. Accordingly, the point of psychoanalysis is not to obliterate all dissatisfaction, but rather to enable the subject to transform unbearable suffering into normal unhappiness. It is precisely the familiar but repressed knowledge of an ineluctable displacement—the general uncanniness of human existence—that calls upon the mature subject to acknowledge that any fulfillment of the desire for a fully satisfying home must be abandoned in reality, even though it can be played out incessantly in fantasy.

But at the same time, Fleming's *Wizard of Oz* also propagates the opposite message: the desire for home is structured in such a way that its radical affirmation goes hand in hand with the annihilation of all work of fantasy. To remain at home, and to pay no attention to that which disturbs domestic familiarity, is tantamount to eradicating all longing for what is other, different, foreign—for all fantasy work, in other words. We are thus dealing with the aporetic rhetoric of the *pharmakon*. Only by having recourse to the dangerous desire for a better home can one learn to live with the home that one feels is inadequate.[5] Home—which Dorothy claims there is no place like—is just as much a drug as the fantasy place beyond the rainbow, and the unconditional belief in this home in Kansas is just as phantasmatic as the dream of her journey through Oz.

Accordingly, the circularity underlying the film's plot is such that Dorothy not only discovers the foreign in the familiar—on the bed right in the middle of her foster parents' home—nor does she simply learn to accept the curtailment of her desire as dictated by everyday reality and her position as a foster daughter. Rather, she also realizes that it was only her insistence on holding on to a concept of home that she had in fact created for herself that allowed her to return to her actual home in Kansas and continue living there in a less dissatisfied state. Indeed, having returned, she longs for no further trips, for, owing to her power of memory, she now carries the heterotopia Oz within her as a site to be revisited in fantasy—much like the nameless heroine in Hitchcock's *Rebecca* does with Manderley. Dorothy does not need to return to Oz because this dream site is now located at the heart of her psychic apparatus, constituting that nexus from which she can organize her pleasure as well as negotiate her relationship to the symbolic laws that define her—the law of self-curtailment and the responsibility toward her fellow human beings.[6]

Ideology: A Dream Produced in Hollywood

One might, of course, simply dismiss the ideological message of *The Wizard of Oz*—that one must unconditionally accept one's affiliation with one's home, along with the living conditions that dominate this allegedly familiar haven—as a mystification of the true reality of the American farmer and worker, and read in the sentimental ending of the film nothing more than Hollywood's dream machine perpetrating the repression of all the social injustices that characterize Dorothy's everyday life.[7] A considerably more chatoyant reading of *The Wizard of Oz* emerges, however, if one follows Louis Althusser's suggestion that the ideology expressed in the film be understood in analogy to Freud's notion of the dream—that is, as a pure dream that is as timeless as the unconscious, for ideology is always already there, a transhistorical present from which there can be no escape, through either thoughts or actions, and that forms the individual as a cultural subject. According to Althusser, ideology is an imaginary construct, whose status is exactly like the status of dream work and fantasy work. Ideology never fully corresponds to reality, instead representing an illusion that serves, at the same time, as an allusion to reality. Put succinctly, "ideology represents the imaginary relationship of individuals to their real conditions of existence."[8] Conceived as a dream, and representing the relationship of the subject to the cultural laws that determine it, ideology indeed found a perfect materialization in the Hollywood dream machine, since from the start Hollywood cinema developed fantasy scenarios that produce and propagate, through home and family romances, the relationship that the American subject maintains with the cultural codes and prohibitions that define it.

This seminal analogy—ideology is a pure dream, while the dreams produced in Hollywood are pure ideology—is visualized in Fleming's film by the way the dream episode in Oz functions as a *mise en abyme* of the entire dream narrative that proclaims, "There's no place like home," for Dorothy's dream of Oz serves as both the primal scene of ideology and the ideology of origins. Indeed, it performs the imaginary relationship that enables Fleming's *everygirl* to reconfigure her specific geographical locatedness (as ascribed in her in a purely accidental manner by virtue of birthplace and family genealogy) into a protective fiction she can live by. This story, furthermore, is one in which contingency is transformed into fate, in order to declare that cultural and geographical emplacement in a specific home is a question of necessity, not choice. At stake, then, is more than the imaginary character of the relationship that Dorothy entertains in relation to her home. Also at issue is the fact that it is not the cultural laws and real conditions of human existence that constitute the core of her dream work, but rather the place occupied by her in relation to the symbolic law that regulates her real living conditions.

Fleming's reconfiguration of a general American ideology revolving around the centrality of home into the story of a Kansas farm girl who leaves home only to discover in the end that there is no place like it can, furthermore, also be read as an allusion to Freud's definition of dream work, notably his claim that all dreams represent a wish fulfillment of sorts. Indeed, pursuing such an analogy, one might speculate that both ideology as pure dream and the specific ideology transported by Dorothy's dream of Oz satisfy the ambivalent feelings that the implied audience shares with the heroine, namely the desire for adventures as this is shaped in relation to an equally strong desire for home. At the end of the film Dorothy has, after all, not only enjoyed a journey to a heterotopic site where she could emerge as the heroic liberator of a suppressed people but also returned home with impunity. Seminal to Freud's discussion of dream and fantasy work, however, is that the modes of representation that dictate these imaginary refigurations of reality—condensation, distortion, displacement, and substitution—bring an ambivalence of meaning into play. According to Freud, even if the dream represents a wish fulfillment, it does so only by performing the unresolved unconscious conflict that led to the work of dreaming in the first place. As Freud insists, "A happy person never fantasizes, only an unsatisfied one. The motive forces of fantasies are unsatisfied wishes, and every single fantasy is the fulfillment of a wish, a correction of unsatisfying reality."[9] One can thus surmise that dream work, in the same way that it offers an antidote to dissatisfaction, recognizes that the kernel of discontent will never be completely eradicated so long as the subject continues to desire and to dream.

Along these lines, one could argue further that a cinematic fantasy like *The Wizard of Oz* has recourse to a highly equivocal mode of representation. While one can readily isolate the manifest ideological message proclaiming that one should be content with conditions culturally and socially prescribed to one and not strive for anything better, this appeal to an unconditional accommodation of cultural laws is visibly undermined, since it can be transmitted only through the rhetoric of redundancy. Dorothy is, after all, required to continually repeat the same sentence, as though possessed by it, if she is to return home again. In so doing, she does more than give voice to the fact that there is no place as familiar to her as the home she left behind; she also obliquely articulates her awareness of the lack at the heart of the home and uses her repeated invocation of the simple homily to repress that uncanny knowledge. Apodictically put, it is only because the knowledge of the lack inscribed in any familiar notion of "homely" happiness is overwhelmingly strong that she has to proclaim the singularity of her familiar home with such vehemence. But if one is compelled to claim constantly that there is no place like home, the uncanniness of the proclamation comes to the fore, with the implied figural meaning inadvertently collapsing into its opposite, namely the literal. Spoken redundantly, the magic formula implicitly suggests that there is no place one could call home. Home as a place does not exist. The concept *home* refers to an impossible place, a utopia—but also to an extimate place, a notion of belonging as a possibility that one carries around with oneself in fantasy to help mitigate the lack of satisfaction in one's real living conditions, to a symbolic fiction that makes one's actual place of habitation bearable. As is so often the case with the products of Hollywood's dream factory, it is up to us to decide which reading we privilege in the end—an ideological reading, whose force consists in pitting the law of curtailment in respect to where one is allowed to feel one belongs against any sense of discontent with one's real living conditions, or a psychoanalytic reading, which, as Mladen Dolar argues, is profoundly anti-ideological, because it tries to put asunder what ideology has united: "The remedy that analysis has to offer is not a promise of some other happy union or another harmony. It only shows that no such harmony is possible (or desirable)." Indeed, the aporia of homecoming, around which so many of the film narratives discussed in this book revolve, consists in rendering visible the psychoanalytic claim that "the disease that the subject suffers from is incurable—yet analysis shows that this incurable disease is another name for the subject, that it founds the very possibility of human experience."[10]

An astonishing point about Fleming's *Wizard of Oz*, furthermore, is that unlike most of the musicals of the thirties—and although its premiere made little money—this film has not been forgotten. Instead, over the decades it has become a cultural icon, broadcast every Christmas on American television. In his study of the musical genre, Ted Sennett claims that one must question the simple homilies offered by *The Wizard of Oz* because while the final message may be comforting, it also curtails all experiences of unfamiliar places and lives and thereby contradicts the American Dream of unlimited self-fashioning. In answer to the question of why this musical still glows while so many other films of the same period have faded from our cultural memory, he suggests: "It may be that when Dorothy steps from black-and-white Kansas into the bright colors of Munchkinland, she is taking everyone's first voyage of discovery. With the universality of the best fables, *The Wizard of Oz* has her learning about evil (the Wicked Witch), friendship (her companions on the road to Oz), and fallibility (the Wizard). And somehow children—and the child in all of us—like to see this voyage made repeatedly, every year on television." He concludes, "*The Wizard of Oz* has gone beyond popularity to become a ritual."[11] Yet the ritualized return to the dreams of childhood evoked by the film can also be thought of fruitfully in terms of Althusser's description of how ideology is culturally represented and cemented. He claims that the practices defined by a given ideology are regulated through the performance of a concrete ritual, even though these practices can subsist only through a self-consciously performed belief in the ideological message they contain.

An anecdote told to me by a U.S. soldier stationed in Berlin in the mid-1980s illustrates how the ritual viewing of Fleming's film has come to regulate its ideological message—that there is no place like home—not only by presupposing a community of people who fully believe in this pure dream but also by reproducing and authorizing this ideology at regular intervals through collective action. My friend had invited the members of her unit to a backyard barbecue. All at once, the party moved to her living room because these Americans, living in a foreign land, wanted to gather around the TV and watch *The Wizard of Oz*. Since the guests had already seen the film many times and thus knew it by heart, the boundary between the dream unfolding on the screen and their own childhood memories, as well as the boundary between foreign Germany and familiar Hollywood, began to dissolve. The guests sang along with all the musical numbers and repeated aloud the purple passages of the text. Through the ritual participation in this very explicitly ideologically informed cinematic dream scenario, these GIs stationed in a foreign country were able to sustain the illusion that there was a home for them to which they could return when their assignment was over. At least for the duration of the film they allowed themselves to forget all the conflicts with which the real conditions of their existence at home were actually inscribed, by turning away from any references to their concrete family situations or their real places of origin and concentrating instead on their relationship to the virtual home produced by Hollywood—a relationship that could be described along the lines of Freud's family romance as a universal longing for a secure abode in the world and for a return to the allegedly happy time of childhood.[12]

One must, however, bear in mind that the wish fulfillment promised by the film never completely succeeds; otherwise, there would be no need for the repeated viewing of it. As Freud has argued, the repetition compulsion feeds off the subject's need to return to past experiences that primarily refer to situations of discomfort that have not been fully abreacted and instead have left traces in the psychic apparatus. With this in mind, one might speculate that neither the childhood nor the home evoked by the annual viewing of Fleming's *Wizard of Oz* represents a situation of untarnished happiness. Is it not rather a knowledge of the foreignness at the core of any dream ideology promising an infallible sheltering home or a perfectly intact childhood that calls forth the desire to watch this story of homecoming every year? Does the ritual not function precisely because its audience fully recognizes it to be a dream and consciously pits the satisfying illusion against an all too sobering knowledge of their real conditions of existence? And does the astonishingly resilient survival of the film perhaps lie less in its transparent ideological message than in its ability, by virtue of its repeated viewing, to create a home for its devoted public, in the sense of an affiliation with a familiar imaginary world? What can actually be regained through this ritual viewing of *The Wizard of Oz* is a home in the sense of a cultural space shared with others, in the sense of a feeling of belonging and recognition based on self-conscious participation in a repertoire of images that one has in common with like-minded others. My wager is that it isn't just the reference to childhood as a situation of happy security that accounts for the astonishing survival of *The Wizard of Oz*. Its resilience can also be located in the film's orchestration of our already imaginary relationship to any sense of security—be this in a family or in a familiar geocultural place. What is at stake isn't so much the real conditions of family and home life as the vision of a home that one can inhabit through the power of one's imagination. Perhaps this Technicolor musical has enchanted audiences for more than half a century because of the feeling of familiarity it invokes—a feeling that can be incessantly reinvoked and, like all fairy-tale geographies, can always be counted on to give one the same pleasure as the last time it was viewed.

As Richard Selcer has noted, *home* is "the one word the idea of which I cannot explain. . . . It must be depicted rather than defined."[13] Along these lines one could reformulate Fleming's dictum as follows: "Home is what I have to sing along with, because I cannot speak of it." The ritual performance called forth by his cinematic myth of home works because it doesn't answer the question of where the desire for a satisfying sense of belonging might be fulfilled with any real location. Instead, it places the object of this desire in the virtual locality of familiar signs, explicitly marked as an illusion. As we sit in front of the television screen, we follow Dorothy, who, after the window frame has fallen on her head, perceives through her bedroom window a dream world informed more by the reading of children's books than by her actual living conditions. This dream world superimposes itself completely upon her actual world, allowing her to enter the hallucination as though it were real. Like us, she sits before a screen on which she sees not her real-life circumstances but a film depicting her imaginary relationship to her aunt and uncle, to the teacher Miss Gulch, whom she hates—in fact, to everything she would call home. By staging Dorothy's crossing from Kansas to Oz and back again explicitly as the transgression into and the exit from an imaginary world of uncanny distortions and artful disfigurations, Fleming presents us with a mirror image of our own position as spectators. We feel ourselves at home in the world of cinema because it represents such an unequivocally illusionary world, defamiliarizing our everyday reality by using the image repertoire of familiar fairy-tale and adventure stories. In so doing, this illusory world offers us precisely the sense of belonging that we seek to negotiate through notions like home.

It is not the message of the film—namely that one should be content with the limitations of one's real home—that is responsible for the function of the ritual viewing of *The Wizard of Oz* as wish fulfillment. My claim is that the charm lies much more in the suggestion that there is no real place that would completely fulfill the conditions for what one imagines home to be. By contrast, the ideology of home can find a thoroughly satisfying visual materialization in the fully artificial, virtual world of cinema. Accordingly, one could further speculate that the reason this film has succeeded in fascinating cinema and television audiences for more than half a century lies less in our willingness to identify with the *everygirl* Dorothy and her journey into fantastic lands, year in and year out, than in the way Fleming inextricably enmeshes the failure inherent in the dream of home with the journey of discovery and homecoming of his heroine. The notion of home that *The Wizard of Oz* offers is as fragile for the moviegoer as it is for the heroine; it is nothing but a pure illusion, but that is exactly how it is perceived. This purely cinematic home offers pleasure in part because it superimposes itself onto the differences, the discontent, and the strife of any real conditions of existence, and in so doing it becomes itself a condition of existence, albeit an imaginary one. This virtual home, however, also satisfies us because it is staged as an illusion that explicitly distances itself from any awareness of the radical displacement and unremitting discontent that inhabits all human existence, even while it recognizes this awareness as the ground and vanishing point of its ideological effect. We are able to recognize ourselves repeatedly in Fleming's musical dream because it imparts to us a reliable sense of belonging by virtue of familiar images. Yet the force behind these "homey" images that incessantly draws us into the film in fact consists in nothing other than the knowledge that it is a pure dream.

Michael Wood has convincingly argued that in contrast to other periods, the 1940s and 1950s were an era of big stars, big studios, and big audiences. The films produced by Hollywood during this period were based on a system of assumptions and beliefs and preoccupations informed by "a moral and physical geography of its own: a definite landscape." These films, he suggests, are to be thought of as "a world, a country of familiar faces, a mythology made up of a limited number of stories," with the moviegoers as the inhabitants of this familiar world.[14] Acknowledging that the business of films is a business of dreams, Wood further claims that this cinematic world should not be thought of as an accurate reflection of any social or cultural reality of the time, nor as the portrait of "an anxious nation pretending to be confident"; rather it should be viewed as an oblique reflection on "the anxieties of a still confident nation; of a confidence that was cracking but still substantial." These movies are less a mirror than "a sort of historical stethoscope. We hear heart murmurs through them; some already heard, some pretty unexpected."[15]

Wood thus correctly insists that any reading of the Hollywood films of this period is concerned less with the myths that they stage than with a collective unconscious, with shared fears that have recourse to mythic modes of expression. "These movies did not describe or explore America," he concludes.

> They invented it, dreamed up an America all their own, and persuaded us to share the dream. We shared it happily, because the dream was true in its fashion—true to a variety of American desires—and because there weren't all that many other dreams around. But given this unreality at the heart of the business, we should perhaps reverse our questions and our doubts, and ask, not how so many interesting meanings crept into flawed and ephemeral films, but how these films could possibly have kept such meanings out. Even trivial lies are a form of confession; even thin and calculated dreams have secrets to give away.[16]

Wood refers directly to Althusser's notion of ideology as a structure, as images and concepts that are lived by human beings as perceived, accepted, and suffered cultural objects "not at all as a form of consciousness, but as an object of their 'world'—as their 'world' itself," and he does so in order to argue that these overwhelmingly successful Hollywood films of the 1940s and 1950s take up "wishes, dreads, and preoccupations that are loosely . . . scattered about ordinary life and give them a lodging in fiction." In so doing they "purvey myths that exist outside the movies, but that also feed on their movie career."[17]

Interpellation: An Ambivalent Cure for Unhappiness

With Dorothy's dream functioning as a *mise en abyme* for the entire narrative, a further explanation for the resilient fascination of the *Wizard of Oz* emerges. The film negotiates both our conception of Hollywood as a world apart from any real living conditions and the desires and anxieties connected to the question of what one can call one's home, an issue that had come to occupy the American public in the second half of the twentieth century. We return again and again to this film, one might say, because, owing to the identification with the *everygirl* Dorothy, it shows us that our desire for a reliable home must be understood as a symptom that shields us by endowing our contingent world with meaning and structure. As Slavoj Žižek has noted, one is well advised to love one's symptom as one loves oneself, for by not doing so one runs the risk of becoming insane. The symptom, which arises where the word fails, is more than merely a ciphered message about unconscious desires. It is also "a way for the subject to organize his/her enjoyment," with the fantasy formation masking or filling a certain void in the symbolic order. Every symptom, he suggests, has "a radical ontological status" in that it functions as the only substance available to the subject. The symptom allows the subject to avoid madness by presenting it with the possibility of choosing something (a symptom formation) instead of nothing (the radical destruction of the symbolic universe). This life-sustaining choice occurs "through the binding of enjoyment to a certain symbolic formation which assures a minimum of consistency to being-in-the-world. This binding, which is to be understood as the corporeal materialization of certain psychically protecting concepts, assures the subject that her or his existence is endowed with at least a minimum of meaningful consistency."[18] In this view, one could surmise that our heroine, Dorothy, achieves the only stability accessible to her once she has learned to identify herself with her symptom, namely the fantasy of home as a unique condition. Understood as a materialized psychic reality, this symptom—the unconditional belief that there is no place like home—allows her to graft a meaningful consistency onto what was initially perceived as an inconsistent world. Don't the first scenes of the film contradict this symptom by showing her aunt and uncle's lack of interest in her, as well as their inability to defend themselves against Miss Gulch's harsh demands? And doesn't this lack of solidarity at home then take material form as the destructive tornado that threatens to fully take apart this seemingly treacherous place? Only Dorothy's firm belief at the end of the film in the idea of home as a symbolic fiction allows the harmonious resolution of an antagonism that is, strictly speaking, unresolvable—namely the difference between the desire for belonging and the knowledge that any real conditions of habitation can never fully fulfill this desire.

If *The Wizard of Oz* enmeshes a universal ideology (negotiating the relationship that an individual has to his or her home) with the private dream of its *everygirl* (allowing Dorothy to negotiate her relationship to the concrete place where she lives with her aunt and uncle), it does so by alluding to one of the fundamental fantasy structures isolated by Freud—the family romance. Dorothy clearly sees her uncle and aunt as inferior parents and their Kansas farm as an undesirable abode, and in her Oz fantasy she elevates the drab sepia-toned Kansas into the magnificent Technicolor Munchkinland, even while her companions on the farm are transformed into powerful magical creatures that are far more unpredictable and wicked, but also far more fallible and kind, than in reality. Yet as Freud points out, this particular fantasy, revolving around the necessary severing of the child from its parents, allows the daydreamer not only to turn away from her real conditions of living and exchange them for more noble ones but also to preserve an image of the parents that has been lost forever in reality: "an expression of the child's longing for the happy, vanished days when his father seemed to him the noblest and strongest of men and his mother the dearest and loveliest of women. . . . His fantasy is no more than the expression of a regret that those happy days have gone. Thus in these fantasies the overvaluation that characterizes a child's earliest years comes into its own again."[19] In Dorothy's home romance, what comes into its own again isn't, however, any correspondence between her longing for a protective abode and infallible foster parents in her everyday life on a Kansas frontier farm. At issue instead is the overvaluation of a lost home, which was always a fictional refiguration of lived reality, an overestimation that, according to Freud, is typical in the daydreams of adults and, one might add, in those of the cinema addict.

If, however, in the process of analysis, the normal neurotic learns nothing other than to exchange his particular psychic distress for the unhappiness shared by all human beings, this common unhappiness is made bearable only through a happy identification with and a belief in one's symptoms. Fleming pits his *everygirl* Dorothy's home romance against an unremittingly harsh symbolic law, but also conceives her fantasy of home as a protection against the equally threatening danger that if one relinquishes all laws that forbid one's desire but are necessary for social reality to hold, one risks being consumed by a lethal whirlwind of desire, concomitant with the destruction of the symbolic world. Her home romance, one might surmise, serves as an apotropaic gesture both against the curtailment of desire dictated by symbolic law and against the self-expenditure that goes along with a relinquishing of that law. In the film's frame Dorothy sings about a virtual place, where "the dreams that you dare to dream really do come true," and then she experiences this virtual place as a hallucination in the real, only to conclude by exchanging her dream of the beyond for a more viable symptom, her dream of home. Given the way her journey through Oz ends, it is significant that she begins to sing about a place where there isn't any trouble only after Aunt Em has reprimanded her about disturbing the farmhands at work and told her to find a place where she won't get herself into any trouble. Her daydream about this desired happy place that she once heard of in a lullaby clearly conforms to the home romance that Freud called an overestimation of the happiness of childhood. At the same time, this fantasy is structured by an ideological code imposed upon our dreaming *everygirl* from outside. Functioning like a remembered cultural site, this land beyond the rainbow actually belongs to a familiar image repertoire that has become strange to her. It serves as a remainder of archaic knowledge that she once possessed in childhood and that she has preserved as a memory trace, and also to a completely artificial place, the text of a lullaby that a person whom she leaves unnamed once sang to her.

Given Freud's implicit allusions to the work of unconscious processes, notably the way in which repressed material resurfaces in fantasy work, it is no coincidence that Fleming explicitly engages with Freud's claim that at night the dreamer refigures memory traces of the previous day that couldn't be abreacted. For example, as Dorothy moves from the sepia-toned Kansas to the Technicolor Oz, details from her everyday world accompany her. The most significant non-abreacted memory trace of the world she has left behind is, of course, Aunt Em's suggestion that she find herself a place where she won't get into trouble. Her aunt's dictum calls forth her dream song about a place somewhere over the rainbow and also provides the catalyst for the dream scenario she enters once she falls unconscious on her bed. Having arrived in Oz, she will do nothing other than get into trouble, as well as cause trouble for the witches who get in the way of her desire. Yet in Oz she is not reprimanded for her tendency to get into trouble; she is instead hailed as a national hero. Her journey through Oz thus allows her to abreact her aunt's reproach in such a way that the rebuke uncannily coincides with its opposite—recognition—and the threat of punishment transforms into praise. Other significant memory traces from the previous day that Dorothy now confronts in Oz refer to Miss Gulch's threat that she will punish Toto for chasing her cats and to the three farmhands, who offer advice on how to avoid getting into trouble in the future. In response to her story about how Miss Gulch is threatening to take Toto away, Hank reproaches her that her head isn't made of straw and that she should have enough brains to know not to go past the schoolmistress's place on her way home from school. In the heterotopic counterworld Hank reappears as the Scarecrow, suffering from the lack of a brain.

One could surmise that in her dream Dorothy punishes her friend for his rebuke by assigning to him the very deficiency that he accuses her of. Zeke, who advises Dorothy to "have a little courage, that's all" and to simply tell the wicked schoolmistress off, and who almost has a heart attack after Dorothy falls into the pigsty, is refigured by the dreaming *everygirl* into a timid lion who truly lacks courage. This again could be read as a psychic gesture of retribution. Finally, Hickory, who defends her against the reprimands of her aunt, only to be chastised by Aunt Em and threatened that if the farmhands don't work they will soon be out of a job, warns his friends that someday they will erect a statue to him in this town. For a moment he assumes the pose of the statue that he imagines for himself, and it is in this frozen gesture that he will reappear, several scenes later, as the tin man in Dorothy's dream world. In response to her sense of being unable to protect herself against the threat posed by Miss Gulch, Dorothy receives three pieces of advice—"use your brain," "have a little courage," and "become famous"—which she takes with her on her voyage to Oz. There she transforms the three ordinary farmhands into magical creatures, who now themselves desire exactly what they told her she was lacking, notably when they each sing in turn: "If I only had a brain," "If I only had a heart," "If I only had courage."

In the course of their mutual quest, however, it becomes clear that while this sense of fallibility can be mitigated with the help of surrogate objects, it can never be fully eradicated, for the objects that the Wizard gives them at the end of their journey are as much pure illusion as the notion of home that Dorothy carries with her back to Kansas. Furthermore, even though Fleming closely follows Freud's definition of the family romance in the sense that in the fantasy scenario taking place in Oz, figures belonging to the dreamer's everyday reality appear more grand than they actually are, this elevated refiguration of Kansas lives off a significant exclusion: Dorothy's uncle and aunt, who are everything but protective, loving parents, do not appear as marvelous figures. This doesn't mean, however, that they take on no position in Dorothy's fantasy life, for the image and the voice of the harsh maternal law, which calls upon the farmhands to work and upon Dorothy to stay out of trouble, do gain access to the hallucination of the daughter who has fled from home. Significantly, this figure of authority is not distorted by the language of dreams; indeed, Aunt Em is the only figure (apart from Toto) whose appearance hasn't changed when Dorothy encounters her in Oz, evoking in both places a sense of guilt and responsibility, but also one of reason.

The fantasy world of Oz thus allows Dorothy to organize her lethal pleasure, aimed at punishing those who chastise her and, indeed, aimed at destroying the home that she feels is inadequate. In so doing she is able to channel her pleasure in such a way that it actually sustains the symbolic authority that it is aimed against. But her fantasy scenario also plays through modalities of her imaginary relationship to the representatives of the symbolic law who are responsible for curtailing her desires. Slavoj Žižek has argued that in many Hollywood films we find a twofold figuration of symbolic authority. He calls the first part of this a fallible paternal figure, who is himself inconsistent, even while he lends a minimum of consistency to a symbolic order—in Dorothy's case, the magician, Professor Marvel. The second figure is, by contrast, an obscene and destructive representative of symbolic authority, who ruthlessly enjoys her own power—namely Miss Gulch.[20] Along with the foster parents and the farmhands, these two figures of authority are introduced into the frame, only to undergo an uncanny distortion in Oz.

While Dorothy requires no dream representation of the actual Uncle Henry, she uses her dream distortion of these other two figures of authority to negotiate her imaginary relationship to the symbolic law they represent, and does so, significantly, by seemingly transcending their power (dismantling the first by proving he is a con man and killing the second, albeit accidentally). Fleming's introduction of the representative of obscene ruthlessness in the frame narrative before he turns to the fallible figure of paternal authority might well be read as a further indication of how Dorothy's home actually functions as a protective haven. We initially see the schoolteacher, Miss Gulch, grimly pedaling along on her bicycle. Because she owns half of the village, she has been able to persuade the sheriff to sign a warrant against Dorothy's dog, Toto. With a basket firmly in hand, in which she intends to take the dog to the sheriff, she confronts Dorothy's aunt and uncle with her cruel demand. The haughty Miss Gulch will not accede to Dorothy's plea that mercy be shown, and Uncle Henry and Aunt Em are unwilling to oppose what is clearly an arbitrary command, explaining to Dorothy that they can't go against the law.

Dorothy, deeply hurt because she is about to be separated from her beloved dog and because her aunt and uncle will not stand up for her, abruptly leaves the living room, where this confrontation has been taking place. Toto must submit to being imprisoned in Miss Gulch's basket, but as the determined schoolmistress doggedly bicycles toward the sheriff's office, he jumps out unnoticed and runs back to Dorothy. If Miss Gulch, and the obscene law she represents, returns in the shape of the Wicked Witch once Dorothy has entered the dream space of Oz, this, too, indicates the survival of a non-abreacted memory trace from Dorothy's diurnal life. Before she had allowed her aunt and uncle to lock Toto into Miss Gulch's straw basket, she told the schoolmistress to go away, "or I'll bite you myself, you wicked old witch." The dream distortion allows her to perform her imaginary relationship to this representative of an obscenely arbitrary law by transforming its harshness into two scenes of destruction. Following Freud's dictum that all dreams are wish fulfillments, the danger that Dorothy experienced in her everyday reality becomes a scene in which it is the figure threatening her who is endangered. With the omnipotence that Freud attributes to the daydreamer, Dorothy punishes Miss Gulch, who had forced her to recognize how fragile the protection afforded by her home actually was. It will be the house whose harmony the woman so forcefully disturbed by taking Toto away that will crush the sister of the Wicked Witch as it lands in Munchkinland, much as the theft of the dead witch's ruby slippers can be read as retribution for the theft of the dog. Dorothy will also take revenge on the cruel law of the schoolmistress by literally liquidating her and appropriating her broomstick, the distorted dream representation of the bicycle that Miss Gulch used in her failed effort to deport Toto.

Set against this obscene law, which seeks primarily to enjoy its own power, we find the benevolent if fallible magician, Professor Marvel. It is to him that Dorothy flees, hoping that he will take her with him on his travels to foreign places. Though he admits to being a charlatan as a magician, he—unlike Miss Gulch, who imposes her power even if it means separating family members from each other—actually insists on preserving the family unit. His message to Dorothy is that she should return to her aunt immediately, and he succeeds because he is able to change her anger at having been betrayed by her foster parents into a concern for her aunt's wellbeing and a sense of guilt about being the cause of her distress. She is willing to accept the law that Professor Marvel represents, because she doesn't perceive the curtailment of her desires as a lethal danger. Instead, it is clearly accompanied by sympathy for the willingness of the foster mother to suffer for the daughter she is also forced to admonish. One might surmise that Dorothy always knew that her aunt's reprimands were a mirror image of maternal care, analogous to the good witch's claim that she always knew how to return home. Yet Dorothy requires an external figure of authority in order to recognize and accept this clandestine knowledge, just as she will be able to return home to the fallible law reigning there only after having undertaken the detour into the hallucinatory realm of Oz. It is significant that the figure who represents the symbolic codes that Dorothy will ultimately fully subscribe to should be explicitly marked as being both fallible and fraudulent. Professor Marvel and his distorted dream refiguration, the Wizard, can resort only to the illusory power of phantasmagoria in their effort to offer a minimum of consistency to the world of symbolic laws that they represent.

The transition from Dorothy's everyday reality, informed by her feeling of helplessness before the arbitrariness of a merciless law, to a fantastic world that fulfills her desire to appear as a self-empowered subject whose agency is uncontested is staged as a sudden break with the entire system of symbolic codes regulating her real living conditions. Slavoj Žižek has called such a radical psychic withdrawal from any negotiation of the law "the end of the world," because it is tantamount to the unbinding of symptom formations and fantasy work: "The only alternative to the symptom is nothing: pure autism, a psychic suicide, surrender to the death drive up to the total destruction of the symbolic universe."[21] As though Dorothy had to experience the lethal core subtending the fallible protective fiction of a caring aunt and her responsibility toward her, as this was broadcast to her by Professor Marvel, before literally returning to the position of curtailment that she had already verbally acknowledged in the presence of his crystal ball, she must experience the end of her world. The tornado can, then, be read as a manifestation of all the archaic enjoyment that resists symbolic authority and seeks retribution for narcissistic wounds. Within her psychic reality it is as though she is forcing the family members and friends she deems unreliable to find shelter underground, so that she can now literally experience what she has been reproaching them for all along—abandoning her.

It is also significant, however, that at precisely the moment in the film's narrative frame when the tornado, by threatening to destroy Dorothy's frontier farm, traumatically renders visible the lacunae on which this fallible home is erected, the power of pure imagination should emerge as a viable protective force. Here, too, Fleming skillfully employs the rhetoric of the uncanny, for at the center of Dorothy's terrifying experience of a defamiliarized home, her bedroom, where even the window frame turns into an aggressive agent, threat suddenly transforms into pleasure. The window to the external world becomes a window to an inner world, indeed comes to function as the threshold to a world informed by memories of childhood fairy tales, in which familiar faces now become phantasmatic figures. On her private screen she initially sees benign figures such as a grandmother knitting in her rocking chair, a mooing cow, two men in a rowboat who greet her as they fly past. Once she has looked down, however, Dorothy realizes that the house carrying her and Toto is actually at the top of the cyclone's eye, and this recognition triggers a new tone in the film that she's seeing screened in her window frame. Suddenly Miss Gulch appears as our dreaming *everygirl* had last seen her, doggedly pedaling her bicycle against the force of the wind, only to transform seamlessly into a wicked witch riding a broomstick and screeching in obscene enjoyment at the storm's violence. Fleming then cuts from Dorothy, who has turned her face away from the window frame in horror and buried it in the sheets of her bed, to a close-up of the cyclone, from which the flying house slowly disengages and turns around its own axis several times as it descends and then finally lands.

In Oz, the third figure of authority, added to the fallible representative of the symbolic law and its obscene counterpart, is the good witch, Glinda. Hovering over this magical world, and repeatedly intervening with her good magic at just the right moment, she is the only representative of the law whose protection proves to be reliable. She is, moreover, the one figure of authority for whom there is no equivalent in Kansas, as though Fleming wanted to signal that any notion of an utterly infallible law could only be a dream. In this world beyond the rainbow, however, Dorothy finds her relation to representatives of the law in the world she has left behind reduplicated, and the fantasy scenario that unfolds there offers satisfaction because she is able to transcend their curtailing and punishing power. The self-aggrandizement so typical to the work of fantasy, according to Freud, is evident in the first sequence in Munchkinland, with Dorothy's elevation to the status of national heroine. While her journey along the yellow brick road and her arrival in Emerald City nominally sustain her desire to return home, the obstacles she meets along the way must also be read as moments of wish fulfillment, for the logic of dreams dictates that if any dream representation is truly unbearable the dreamer will awake. One could thus surmise that Dorothy remains asleep because these obstacles allow her to play through her imaginary relation to various modalities of the law. The Wicked Witch's repeated attempts to keep Dorothy away from Emerald City help Fleming's *everygirl* to imagine what permanent exile would mean. This traumatic ossification of displacement, emerging as it does under the auspices of what remains of Miss Gulch in Oz, is in fact given an architectural materialization in the shape of the dark castle inhabited by the Wicked Witch. Dorothy's meeting with the Wizard, in turn, whose power is contingent upon no one actually being allowed to see him, lets Dorothy literally encounter the empty space around which those symbolic codes that make for a minimum of consistency in the social reality revolve.

Throughout Dorothy's journey the tension between too much destructive authority (the Wicked Witch) and a fallible authority (the Wizard) is ultimately thwarted by a figure of authority utterly foreign to the magic world of Oz, namely Aunt Em's interpellation. Dorothy has so thoroughly internalized this call that she has taken it with her, like her dog, Toto. Aunt Em's fragile health and Dorothy's conviction that she is responsible for her aunt's anguish are repeatedly mentioned as the central motives for her desire to return home, and at the acme of her distress, when all other protective powers seem to have deserted her, it is significantly her aunt's voice that calls to her to believe in her return home.

As Althusser argues, individuals come to experience themselves as subjects of a given ideology when, having been interpellated along the lines "of the most commonplace everyday police (or other) hailing: 'hey, you there!' . . the hailed individuals turn around, and by the one-hundred-and-eighty-degree physical conversion" indicate that they have recognized that the hail was "really" addressed to them (and not someone else). By responding in the sense of "Yes, it is really me!" these subjects, Althusser claims, indicate the "recognition that they really do occupy the place it designates for them as theirs in the world, a fixed residence."[22] To answer to the interpellation of a given ideology requires that the subject actually accept the place that has been assigned to it by one of its representatives of authority, even if ideology is recognized as being a pure illusion. Yet it is crucial for Althusser that interpellation seems to come to the subject only from the outside, for every concrete individual is, in fact, always already a subject, "and as such constantly practices the rituals of ideological recognition."[23] The process of maturation, which Freud claimed entails the assumption of culturally codified prohibition, can thus be supplemented by a further aspect. To become a mature subject also means to become subject to the ideology that was all along fundamentally inscribed in the concrete position one has been occupying in the world, even if this hadn't been self-evident. Within the language of Fleming's musical, one might say that Dorothy has always possessed the knowledge that she is already interpellated by the ideology of home as a subject, but she needs to traverse her fantasy before she can fully accept this clandestine truth. What she learns is that no one can escape being a subject of ideology, but one can design for oneself the scenario of being hailed by a figure of authority that seems best to accommodate one's desires.

That Dorothy's aunt is the sole viable authority for her and that through her aunt's interpellation she is able to achieve a fixed residence in ideology that allows her to bear the inconsistency of her real living conditions in Kansas are visualized most poignantly in the scene where the Wicked Witch holds Dorothy captive in her dark castle. This scene functions as the counterscene to Dorothy's encounter with Professor Marvel, for here she quite literally experiences her aunt's interpellation, which the magician had merely feigned. After the Wicked Witch has placed an hourglass filled with red sand before Dorothy, announcing that her life will come to an end when the last grains have fallen to the bottom, she leaves the distraught girl alone in the room. Dorothy then sits down on the stone staircase, with her back to an oversized crystal ball, and calls out to her aunt in despair: "I'm frightened, Auntie Em, I'm frightened." Suddenly the image of her aunt appears on the surface of the crystal ball, as though she were searching for her lost niece, and in this interpellation Dorothy comes to fully recognize that it is she who is being hailed. In response to the question "Dorothy, where are you?" Dorothy turns around one hundred eighty degrees to directly face the apparition that has appeared on the circular screen and says, "I am here in Oz, Auntie Em. I'm locked up in the witch's castle and I am trying to get home to you."

With this outcry she signals that she is finally able to accept with complete conviction the symbolic place that was ascribed to her by her aunt. Because this apparition alludes to Professor Marvel's trickery, Fleming's *mise-en-scène* of course underscores the fact that this interpellation merely represents the imaginary (spectral) relationship that Dorothy entertains toward her aunt's authority, even though it calls upon a belief that is utterly necessary for the constitution of the subject. At the same time, the fragility of this ideological bond is illustrated when Auntie Em's reflection seamlessly transforms into a second apparition, clearly the result of the Wicked Witch's sorcery. In the place of Auntie Em, calling out to her niece, an apparition of the Wicked Witch herself appears, mockingly imitating Dorothy's calling to her aunt to come back, before her obscene laughter once again reminds Fleming's *everygirl* that her time is perilously close to running out.

Nonetheless, Dorothy, now secure in her symbolic mandate, can successfully overcome both the destructive law of the Wicked Witch and the fallible law of the Wizard. Once her three comrades have liberated her from her imprisonment, she decides to confront the agent of destructive enjoyment directly. The showdown takes place in the entrance hall of the castle. After the Wicked Witch has set the left arm of the Scarecrow on fire, Dorothy accidentally dumps a bucket of water, which she had intended to use to save her friend from burning completely, onto her adversary. As does any symptom that the subject no longer needs because the piece of repressed knowledge it was articulating has been recognized, the Wicked Witch begins to dissolve. "You cursed brat, look what you've done! I'm melting," she calls out, and as she collapses to the floor, she wails, "Oh, what a world. Who would have thought that a good little girl like you could destroy my beautiful wickedness?" In the end only her black cape, her pointed black hat, and her broomstick remain, empty paraphernalia of her ideology of beautiful wickedness.

The Wizard and his phantasmagoria meet a similar fate. After Dorothy and her three friends have brought him the Wicked Witch's broomstick, he still tries to avoid honoring the promise he had made to help Dorothy get home. Toto, however, simply walks toward the booth at the side of the room where the Wizard is receiving them and pulls aside the green curtain that hides its interior. There the four astonished friends find an old gray-haired man speaking into his microphone and pulling the levers on his machines to produce the terrifying voice and the awe-inspiring reflection of the Wizard's face framed by fire that they had encountered during their previous visits. Hoping to divert their attention from this dismantling of his power, he calls into the microphone, "Pay no attention to that man behind the curtain," but the four petitioners have already averted their gaze from his illusory interpellation and turned to question him directly as to who he is. While he is willing to accept the Scarecrow calling him a humbug, he decidedly contradicts Dorothy, who claims he is a very bad man: "No, my dear, I am a very good man. I am just a very bad wizard."

In contrast to the representative of an obscene law, of whom nothing remains but the paraphernalia of her wicked power once she has literally dissolved, this representative of a benign but fallible law himself remains after his illusory authority has been unmasked to show his all-too-human face. Even though the Wizard confesses his fallibility, however, he can still give to Dorothy's friends surrogate objects that represent the attributes they lack, thereby assuring them of a limited satisfaction of their desire. The Scarecrow receives a university diploma instead of a brain, documenting his intelligence. In lieu of the courage he desires, the Cowardly Lion is given a medal declaring him to be a hero of the city. To the Tin Woodsman the Wizard gives a big artificial heart as evidence that he has done good deeds.

Thus to the end, the Wizard continues to provide at least a minimum consistency in the symbolic world of Oz, against all contingencies and antagonisms. The ideology of a fallible law resists resiliently, for awarding the surrogate objects to Dorothy's friends confirms that identification with a given role can be represented only through symbols. The alternative, a complete destruction of all symbolic fictions, has been effectively warded off. The Wizard cannot, however, help Dorothy return home because the ideology of home, which alone will allow Dorothy to wake up from her dream of Oz, cannot be structured by a rhetoric of substitution, which would permit a surrogate object to stand in for a trait that is lacking. Only Glinda can help her, by directly naming the circularity of her desire, thereby fully satisfying Dorothy's belief in the omnipotence of her thoughts, which proves to be the clandestine core of the fantasy journey beyond the rainbow. She requires no external law—thus the secret ideology of Fleming's magical fantasy scenario—for she has been carrying the ideology that will guarantee her a stable residence in her symbolic world within herself all along. This intimate but so far unrecognized and thus uncanny piece of knowledge, this alien kernel, has been inherent to her from birth, and it has enabled her to already be a subject of ideology long before she consciously crossed the threshold between the desiring individual (who dreams of escape) and the mature subject (who accepts curtailment of her desire). What Dorothy has learned is that she needs only her imagination, which is to say her willingness to believe unconditionally in the ideology of home while at the same time being fully aware of the fictionality of this belief.

As Mladen Dolar emphasizes in his critical reading of Althusser, however, the transition from an individual to a subject interpellated by ideology can never fully succeed. Though Althusser's formula implies a clean cut, this sudden passage "is never complete—the clean cut always produces a remainder. There is a part of the individual that cannot successfully pass into the subject, an element of 'pre-ideological' and 'pre-subjective' *materia prima* that comes to haunt subjectivity once it is constituted as such."[24] This inevitable incompleteness of the process of becoming a subject constitutes the point of departure for psychoanalysis. The subject posited by psychoanalysis is one that has subscribed of its own free will to the cultural laws interpellating it, while at the same time being haunted by a desire for forbidden pleasures, which it furtively fosters in the intimacy of its psychic reality yet which find an oblique utterance in the distorted articulations afforded by symptom formation and dream work. As Dolar insists, while for Althusser "the subject is what makes ideology work[,] for psychoanalysis the subject emerges where ideology fails." Given that "all the formations of the unconscious have this in common, they are accompanied by a 'this is not me,' 'I was not there,' although they were produced by this subject. They depend on the emergence of an 'alien kernel' within subjectivity, an automatism beyond control, the break-down, in certain points, of the constituted horizon of recognition and sense."[25] So, ultimately subjectivity marks precisely the failure to fully become a subject of a given ideology. Even if the last image in Fleming's fantasy of home shows us the *everygirl* Dorothy, who as interpellated subject has returned to claim mastery over her home in Kansas, in the sense of feeling that she fully belongs there, a trace of unease remains. The foreign may have become "homely" (*heimlich*) again and the marvelous figures mundane. But that is also why they suddenly appear to be so uncanny. Against Aunt Em's appeal to reason, seeking to convince Dorothy that we often dream foolish things, the daughter who has suddenly awakened from her coma will never be free of her self-fashioned specters, even if she accepts the curtailment to her fantasy spoken by her aunt. For if memory traces of the day can find their way into the nocturnal world of dreams, then traces of the dream world can find entrance into everyday reality as well, and in so doing remind Dorothy—and implicitly us, the spectators—of their doubles in Oz.

Desire for Homecoming: An Infinite Cycle

As Salman Rushdie has remarked in his compelling homage to *The Wizard of Oz*, the film's initial lack of success might well have had to do with the timing of its premier, just days before the outbreak of the Second World War.[26] In 1939 thousands of European refugees had already taken flight; five years later, the dictum "There's no place like home" had literally become their destiny, for the homelands from which they had fled had been utterly destroyed.[27] But if the ideology of national affiliation promulgated by Fleming's film had less appeal for moviegoers during the war period than the antifascist propaganda produced at the same time in Hollywood, Dorothy's dream was destined to become that much more effective after the notion of home as a unique state of mind worth fighting for had, in the course of the postwar reconstruction of Europe, become the new ideological force installed to sustain the Cold War to support the presence of American armed forces in Europe and the Far East, as well as encourage the later reunification of Germany and the civil wars in the Balkans. The extent to which the desire for a stable dream of home, capable of lending a minimum of consistency to a world increasingly characterized by unresolvable ethnic and class conflicts, lives on as a resilient ideology has been exemplified again and again by allusions to *The Wizard of Oz*—notably the multitude of Hollywood films that iconographically cite Fleming's fantasy of home: George Lukas's *Star Wars* trilogy (1977–1983), in which a princess succeeds in thwarting a figure of evil with the help of robots and a farmer; David Lynch's *Wild at Heart* (1990), where two lovers imagine their world inhabited by benevolent and wicked witches in order to find their way to each other;[28] Barry Levinson's *Good Morning, Vietnam* (1987) in which the Far Eastern theater of war is transformed into a magical world. Here the radio speaker, Robin Williams, calls upon his comrades to follow the Ho Chi Minh Trail, alluding to Fleming's yellow brick road. When he is about to be transferred back to the United States, he refers to Dorothy's magic formula in his last radio broadcast, telling the comrades he is about to leave behind, "There's no place like home, and I wish you could all come back with me." Finally, one inevitably recalls Steven Spielberg's family epic *E. T.* (1985), in which an alien wanders through a California that is for him at once foreign and marvelous, as though he were a Dorothy of the 1980s, unable to decipher its mysteries. He, too, finds help through newly won friends, as his sister had in Oz, yet unlike Dorothy he has only one goal from the start—to return home. And after he has left the people of Earth, whose sympathy he has won during his short stay with them, the home he returns to leads one to dream of a place way up high in the sky, beyond the stars. Both the ritual of an annual watching of *The Wizard of Oz* and the compulsion of Hollywood directors to reverentially cite it over and over again reveal how readily cinematic fantasy epics revolving around an exaggerated sense of the happiness and plenitude of childhood can serve the purpose of an equally exaggerated notion of home as a national and cultural place of belonging.

That the belated appeal of Fleming's musical is evidenced primarily in a world characterized by global migration also means that the notion of belonging to a symbolic community in which one must not look beyond one's own clearly demarcated backyard has explicitly become pure illusion for the majority of the film's viewers. It is perhaps no coincidence that Salman Rushdie, living in exile, locates this film's resilient effect in its colorful celebration of what he considers to be an archetype: "the human dream of *leaving*, a dream at least as powerful as its countervailing dream of roots."[29] Although Fleming's *Wizard of Oz* feeds off the tension between these two dreams, it is beyond dispute for Rushdie that this musical, in its compelling, sentimental scenes, deals unequivocally with the joy of leaving behind all drab living conditions and entering into colorful new ones, with the hope of starting a new life in a place not ridden with strife. "Over the rainbow," he claims, "ought to be the anthem of all the world's migrants, all those who go in search of the place where 'the dreams that you dare to dream really do come true.' It is a celebration of Escape, a grand paean to the Uprooted Self, a hymn—*the* hymn—to Elsewhere."[30] Against the simplistic and reductive moral, with which Fleming and his producer, Mervyn LeRoy, seek to privilege the ideology of homecoming by having Dorothy ecstatically praise the hearth of her home, Rushdie insists on a reading that corresponds more adequately to his real living conditions of exile. Just because those who have stayed at home do not want to believe Dorothy when she says that Oz is no dream, but rather a place where one can really live, does not mean that we, as viewers, have to subscribe to their lack of imagination. Those of us who prefer to privilege the canny wisdom embedded, like a cryptonym, in Dorothy's last utterance, can rest assured that at the end of the film Oz has finally become home. As Rushdie forcefully claims, in this final sequence of *The Wizard of Oz*, "the imagined world became the actual world, as it does for us all, because the truth is that once we have left our childhood places and started out to make up our lives, armed only with what we have and are, we understand that the real secret of the ruby slippers is not that 'there's no place like home,' but rather that there is no longer any such place *as* home: except, of course, for the home we make, or the homes that are made for us, in Oz: which is anywhere, and everywhere, except the place from which we began."[31]

The Searchers—Final departure

Chapter 3
Seduction of Departing
The Searchers

Turn His Back on Home

In their homage to the director who has become coterminous with the western genre, Joseph McBride and Michael Wilmington suggest that there always existed two John Fords, for on closer perusal the man who was initially named Sean Aloysius O'Feeney emerges as a hybrid of iconographer and iconoclast.[1] His cinematic refiguration of the founding legend of America articulates a desire to prove his love for the culture his parents had chosen as their new home, while, at the same time, the cinematic American legends he became famous for also give voice to the disappointment he felt at discovering flaws in the culture he wanted to idealize. His effort at fashioning his personal version of the American Dream is thus fundamentally inscribed by a contradiction. All the films he directed—whether war films, westerns, or historical epics—thrive on the tension between a prominent urge to belong to a community and an equally pronounced desire for solitude. Indeed, they repeatedly articulate his heroes' radical rejection of the unsolvable gender and race antagonisms inhabiting any notion of an American home in the mid-twentieth century. For this reason McBride and Wilmington offer an analogy between the director and the radically solitary men he preferred to portray: "Like his heroes, he often seemed torn between a love for the *idea* of the community and an estrangement from the *fact* of the community which could lead to contempt and even open revolt."[2]

This oscillation between a desire to commemorate the founding myth of America and a drive to disclose the contradictions and shortcomings of that myth finds its acme in two of his acclaimed late westerns—*The Searchers* (1956) and *The Man Who Shot Liberty Valance* (1962). In both, Ford has recourse to nostalgic stories recalling a western frontier that had long since been superseded by its own legend. Ford's turn to the past was, however, always also an iconoclastic move, since his interest lay in depicting the rotten core at the heart of the doctrine of Manifest Destiny. Concerned with the way the project of civilizing the prairie by turning it into a garden had come to be ideologically invoked as an example for cultural progress even though it actually served to defend both the genocide of the indigenous population and the exploitation of the region's natural resources, Ford focuses on the provisional and fragile quality of the frontier homestead as well as on the tragic sacrifice required for its construction. These homes, exposed to a wide array of destructive forces—the attacks of hostile Indians, the random violence of roaming bandits and outlaws, the threat of natural catastrophes—had to be incessantly defended or, after a defeat, quickly rebuilt at a new location. Indeed, as Edward Buscombe argues, "All Ford's films are about home: finding it, building it, losing it," while the classic lone hero remains homeless, because there is no place for him within the communities of the settlers, meant to represent the inevitable march of progress.[3]

However, along with its heroic representative, the lonely cowboy who is alien to the very home he defends, the kernel of erosion endemic to the western genre's celebration of civilizing the prairie also came to be represented as a tension between two forms of community. On the one hand are the settlers, who put down roots knowing full well that these can be only provisional. They engage with the contingencies harbored by the prairie by constantly renegotiating their claims to this fragile home and modifying them according to the ever-changing circumstances. On the other hand are the indigenous Native Americans, who have been displaced from their homeland. They literally perform the contingency of the prairie, because, as nomadic communities, they offer a second rendition of the lack of stability that this contested geography had come to be known for. The western hero, oscillating between these two communities, thus assumes a third, hybrid position; he does not fully belong to either the world of the settlers or that of the indigenous population, though he serves as the intermediary between the two. At home in the open landscape of the prairie and the mountains surrounding it, these solitary figures are obsessed with a nostalgic memory of home. At the same time, these heroes who, as Ford so poignantly shows in his late westerns, become obsolete as the West is successfully civilized, are exactly the ones who live on as mythic figures in our repertoire of cultural images. As such, they inhabit what Michel Foucault calls heterotopic sites, countersites to everyday localities, "designed into the very institution of society, which are sorts of actually realized utopias in which all the other real emplacements that can be found within the culture are, at the same time, represented, contested, and reversed, sorts of places that are outside all places, although they are actually localizable."[4] Indeed, the geography of the prairie perfectly accommodates the western hero's proclivity toward solitude, offering him a site of unconditional roaming—a wide, seemingly unrestrained space in which he can escape the unsolvable contradictions inherent in any life in a community and circle endlessly on the periphery, and in our collective imaginary.

Critics have repeatedly commented that in his films John Ford endows Monument Valley with a mythic quality, staging it like a static dream landscape.[5] Yet as Richard Hutson notes, Ford's landscape corresponds to his deployment of narrative as memorial and mourning, which is to say as a "way of possessing the United States—of *re*possessing it," because the prairie "represents an immense loss even as it refuses to lose all."[6] Indeed, one could argue that the metaphoric quality with which Monument Valley comes to be endowed can be read as another aspect of Ford's iconoclasm. It spatially visualizes his disappointment that the American Dream of unrestricted self-development leads to a dead end. Ironically, any real escape from the restrictions that society imposes on the individual is an impossibility in the West, for here the project of civilization is to succeed at any cost. There is, however, a further analogy at work between Ford's landscape, standing as it does for the only remaining site of illusion and imagination, and the psychic state of his hero once the West has been won. In the same manner that the staunchly solitary Ethan Edwards prefers (and is willing to fight for) the idea of home over actually inhabiting a home with a hearth, John Ford stages the western landscape self-consciously as a heterotopic countersite that stands in opposition to the provisional homes of the settlers but actually proves to be more than any real place. McBride and Wilmington astutely counter all criticism of the fact that during the five-year search for the young woman captured by the Indians, Ethan and his companions—on the story level—wander all the way from Canada to New Mexico, though on the level of the actual setting they never actually leave Monument Valley, since the entire film was shot there: "Monument Valley is more than a real place to Ford. It is a state of mind. . . . It is both a dead end and an ultimate value . . . a moral battleground, stripped down and rendered more perfect by the absence of organic life within its boundaries. . . . The horizons of Monument Valley, both primeval and beyond society, point towards eternity."[7]

Given that John Ford's westerns repeatedly perform the opposition between an ideology of progress, which insists on its civilizing project at all costs, and the desire of the individual to jettison himself from the laws of the community, this chapter will explore the fruitful tension between the homestead and the prairie. In the following chapter I will turn to John Sayles's *Lone Star* (1995) and argue that under the auspices of multiculturalism he consciously transposes what in Ford's late western had become a highly fissured legend. This comparative reading will continue to address the question of a successful inhabitation of home, but will also treat the fault lines inevitably inscribed in the promise of homely satisfaction. At the same time, the fantasy I have been exploring in the previous chapters, namely that the happiness of home is to be found in a place that one never inhabits in reality, finds a radical figuration in *The Searchers*. Here, the home for which the hero is willing to sacrifice everything is not only a place that he cannot be master of but one that he has no intention of possessing, except in fantasy. Because the logic of the western ideology is based on the idea that to fight for the notion of protection that the home is to afford precludes any real belonging to this place of comfort and security, Ethan's enjoyment actually resides in his exclusion from any actualization of home.

As Michael Wood argues, the western can be viewed as a particularly pronounced expression of the dark spot inscribed in the American dream of freedom, in which selfishness is an ideal and individualism proves to be tantamount to stubbornness. While the American hero is repeatedly told that home is what he ought to want, it is also precisely what he can't bear: "America is not so much a home for anyone as a universal dream of home, a wish whose attraction depends upon its remaining at the level of a wish. The movies bring the boys back but stop as soon as they get them back; for home, that vaunted, all-American ideal, is a sort of death, and an oblique justification for all the wandering that kept you away from it for so long." This fantasy of masculine solitude and wanderlust, Wood continues, is fundamentally gendered, for it feeds off the counterimage, namely that it is the women "who assert the myth of community in the movies, who propose a world of children and homes and porches and kitchens and neighbors and gossip and schools—everything the American hero is on the run from."[8] The western genre may insist that the price of civilization must be paid, regardless of the cost, yet Ford's westerns also thrive on a nostalgic sympathy for the characters who refuse to pay up. If, then, on a manifest level, his films seem to support the feminine proposition of a civilized world that one might call home, he pits against this notion the wide, empty space of the undomesticated prairie. The wilderness, as Wood notes, is a clear invitation to solitude, for "in these solitary spaces neither self nor society has any claims on you. The plain and the prairie and the mountain, enlarged and depopulated by the movie camera, offer a life without others, a life with no one, a pacified life in which even your own ego scarcely lifts its voice above a whisper."[9]

By staging the virulent opposition between the feminized provisional homestead and the masculinized prairie, where a battle can be fought against all threats to the world of the settlers, John Ford's film scenarios uncannily resonate with G. W. F. Hegel's theory on the necessity of war. The German Romantic philosopher claims that by exteriorizing all strife— which is to say transferring it to a battle occurring at some distant place— we can preserve a state of peace at home or, rather, we can prohibit internal unrest. He also genders the opposition in a manner analogous to that employed by the western. Womankind, Hegel claims, "changes by intrigue the universal end of the government into a private end, transforms its universal activity into a work of some particular individual, and perverts the universal property of the state into a possession and ornament for the Family, because interested only in private pleasures and enjoyments, Womankind remains indifferent to the cares of the universal."[10] While "the manhood of the community," he continues, resides in the activity in general of the community, women preside over the separatism introduced into the community as a whole, once individual claims for happiness are brought into play. For Hegel, then, the gender strife can be described as follows: the community "*is, moves,* and *maintains* itself by consuming and absorbing into itself the very separation into independent families presided over by womankind . . . by keeping them dissolved in the fluid continuity of its own nature." From this he deduces that "since the community only gets an existence through its interference with the happiness of the Family, and by dissolving individual self-consciousness into the universal, it creates for itself in what it suppresses and what is at the same time essential to it an internal enemy— womankind in general."[11]

Taking Hegel's claim a step further, one could propose the following wager: the world of women, standing in for the proposition of family and home, but doing so in such a way that all claims to universality fall apart into individual, particular, and private interests, embodies an unsolvable antagonism. One might say it harbors an "internal enemy," against which the masculine hero, representing the universal principle of the community, must struggle. If men go to war, one might continue to speculate, they do so to flee the antagonism inscribed in hearth and home, to flee the internal enemy by embracing the simple opposition between equal partners as this is negotiated on the battlefield. War gives focus to the unresolved antagonism subtending the everyday reality of any community in the form of gender trouble. The battle occurring at a location clearly removed from the familiar home—regardless of whether it is a battle between the lone cowboy and indigenous Indians threatening the home or a battle between the lone sheriff and outlaws threatening the symbolic law of the homestead—offers the American hero an escape from the internal difference (in the sense of strife), as it is represented by women. Apodictically put, the simple opposition between two enemies, clearly distinguished as such, which is fought out on a battlefield external to the home, guarantees a secure distance from the too close real antagonism that permanently haunts the community, in the figure of the familiar feminine with its claims on individual homes.[12]

As in Hitchcock's *Rebecca*, home in John Ford's late western is a site imbued with antagonism, in which the hero feels alien because it is occupied by the unbearable overproximity of a feminine principle. In *The Searchers*, however, the destructive power does not reside with the representative of a dead woman who will not relinquish her claim to being mistress of the house. Rather, destructive desires are harbored by the hero himself, who must destroy the actual home so that he can wander forever under its ideological auspices. This leads one to inquire about the enjoyment contained in Ethan Edwards's fantasies of a place he really can't tolerate, given that Ford self-consciously stages the burned and ruined homestead of the Edwards family as though it were a crypt where his lonely cowboy can cherish the lost site of happiness with impunity because it has been so irrevocably turned into a site of memory. In my reading of *The Searchers* I will, however, highlight another aspect of Ford's iconography that is radically different from Hitchcock's psycho horror: in John Ford's western a return home is actually possible, though significantly not for the hero. This, of course, raises the questions of why certain characters, in contrast to the solitary hero, are able to successfully inhabit the provisional homes the settlers have built in the wilderness and of why we continue to dream nostalgically about those who can find no home, rather than those who have learned to negotiate the unsolvable internal antagonism proposed by gender trouble.

The Framing

As the opening credits of *The Searchers* roll across the screen we hear the first stanza of Stan Jones's title song: "What makes a man to wander? / What makes a man to roam? / What makes a man leave bed and board and turn his back on home? / Ride away. Ride away. Ride away." A black screen, on which we see the inscription "Texas 1868" written in white letters, replaces the initial background, which had shown us a segment of a painted brick wall but no clear outlines of a house. For a moment the screen turns completely black, then a door opens from the inside. Over the shoulders of a woman, whom we see only from the back and only in silhouette, we gaze out onto a prairie landscape framed by the open door.[13] Briefly the woman hovers in the door frame, then the camera moves forward from the dark depth of the house's interior toward the back of the woman, while she, in turn, moves forward, stepping over the threshold. As her body begins slowly to take on contours, lit by the glaring sunlight that falls onto the veranda, we follow her gaze, directed toward the wide-open space before her, and with her we spot a male rider, as yet only barely discernible, approaching the house.

Thus, within the first seconds of his film, John Ford leaves no doubt that the landscape, from which his solitary hero returns home and into which, as we can guess from the title song, he will ultimately escape again, is the private film screen of this woman and of the viewer. Entrance into the cinematic fantasy scenario that is about to unfold is explicitly staged as a step across the threshold of the house onto the veranda—that is, onto an intermediary space joining the security of the dark interior and the bright exterior of the wilderness. There the woman stands, her right arm leaning against one of the posts that hold up the roof, waiting, as we are, for something to happen. Her dream of what must remain outside and excluded from the familiarity of her everyday existence sets in at this point, and we identify with this feminine figure—who, like the audience sitting in front of us in the cinema—we continue to see only from the back. With her we, too, enter into a fantasy scenario revolving around the solitary figure, who must sacrifice himself for the project of civilization. The American dream of conquering the wilderness is thus, from the start, presented as a framed image.[14]

Only then does Ford cut to her face, and we see explicitly what until now we could only surmise. With a mixture of desire, fear, and anticipation she is looking out into the empty space at the approaching stranger, while shielding her eyes with her left hand from the bright sunlight. Suddenly a man appears behind her to the left, nods to her, and, as he asks her the name—"Ethan?"—passes her on the right and walks down the steps of the veranda toward the stranger, stopping at the bottom. Now Ford's camera leaves the face of the woman to show the veranda from the left side. Two girls, a boy carrying firewood, and a dog have come to join their parents in front of the house, and we get the tableau of the happily united settler family, as though onstage. At the head of the group, marking the boundary between the home and the open landscape, the father; behind him, still standing on the veranda and both on the same level, the mother and the son; closest to the wall of the house, the two daughters. Arrested in their clearly demarcated positions they await the homecoming wanderer, the prodigal brother Ethan (John Wayne), who, upon reaching the homestead, gets off his horse, extends his hand to Aaron Edwards (Walter Coy) while preserving an almost formal distance, then turns almost immediately to Aaron's wife, Martha (Dorothy Jordan), who embraces him with open arms. "Welcome home," she declares, as he gently kisses her on the forehead. Martha's eyes never leave him as she walks backward toward the door of her home and beckons him to follow. With her at the head, all the other figures return to the dark interior of the house, having been introduced to us as the characters of Ford's cinematic narrative. In the cut that separates the family tableau on the veranda and the "welcome home" dinner about to take place in Martha's kitchen, a 180-degree turn has clearly taken place. Ford shows the hearth of this frontier home, which in contrast to the beginning is now fully lit. We see Ethan lovingly picking up the younger daughter, Debbie (Lana Wood), holding her above his head for a moment, and then protectively cradling her in his arms before putting her down and walking toward the other children, Lucy (Pippa Scott) and Ben (Robert Lyden), to greet them. The story of Ethan Edwards's odyssey has begun. Within hours he will once again leave this home. When next he returns he will find it burnt to ashes, its occupants killed or taken captive, and he will feel compelled to spend five years searching for his only surviving relative, Debbie, whom he has seen for the first time this evening.

In the scenes following this strange homecoming we discover that Ethan, who is still wearing the uniform of the Confederate Army and has only now decided to return to his brother's ranch, three years after the Civil War ended, harbors two secrets. Ford explicitly suggests a clandestine love between Martha and her brother-in-law—in the way she takes his cape and secretly strokes it the next morning before he rides away again and the way the grim Ethan casts gentle looks at the dainty figure of Martha.[15] On the other hand, Ethan steadfastly keeps to himself his whereabouts during the last three years, never answering the question directly; in so doing, he supports his brother's suspicion that the freshly minted gold he is willing to offer as a prepayment for his share of the rent at the ranch has been illegally procured. After the family has already sat down at the dinner table, Ford introduces the last family member, Martin Pawley (Jeffrey Hunter), who, like Ethan before him, rides in on his horse. His arrival is also shot from the inside of the house, so that he, too, initially appears to be a figure belonging to the prairie outside, framed by the open door, before he cautiously steps over the threshold, approaches the table, and warmly welcomes his Uncle Ethan. The stern reticence and unfriendly looks with which Ethan greets the young man, as well as the way he humbles him by suggesting that he might be mistaken for a half-breed—thereby denying all family bonds to the boy even though Ethan had been the one to find him after his parents had been massacred—introduces Ethan's racism at the outset.

As Edward Buscombe notes, Ford, concerned with the perennial American problem of race, shows Ethan "for what he is, a murderous racist, and yet draws out our pity for him. . . . The contradictions of Ethan's character, his compelling strength matched only by his repellent bigotry, cannot be easily resolved."[16] At the same time, Ethan's rejection of a person he considers to be racially inferior allows Ford to introduce the notion of geocultural belonging that is inscribed in his ideology of home, for the adopted son, Martin, who has successfully appropriated the codes of the Edwards household, functions as the counterfigure to the blood-related prodigal brother, who will never be at home in this family because he cannot accommodate himself to its laws.

This reluctant and fragile reconciliation between the two brothers is disrupted the next morning with the appearance of Reverend Captain Samuel Johnston Clayton (Ward Bond), who, as head of the Texas Rangers, has come to swear in Aaron and Martin. The herd of neighboring rancher Lars Jorgensen (John Qualen) was stolen the night before, and

Clayton, along with the men he has brought with him, have put together a search party. Ethan is the last one to join the group of men gathered around Martha Edwards's dinner table, yet he insists on taking his brother's place, astutely warning Aaron to "stay close" to his home. Like Mose Harper (Hank Worden), who has taken on the role of the fool in this group of Texas Rangers but clearly possesses a keen knowledge of Indian customs, Ethan suspects that the stolen herd may simply be a ploy on the part of a group of marauding Comanche, seeking to draw the men into the wide-open prairie. While one can only surmise that Ethan wants his brother to stay with his wife and children so that, like them, he will fall prey to the Indian attack that he anticipates, one thing is uncontested: Ethan is only too willing to flee from the antagonism he finds at the homely hearth of his brother—namely his ambivalence about his forbidden love for his sister-in-law, Martha—into the simple opposition that a battle with the Indians will afford.

Thus, while Ford's hero is portrayed from the start as a conflicted man, his ambivalent feelings result from an unequivocal question of allegiance. Though in the course of the story he will repeatedly prove to be a person who can oscillate between the cultural codes of the Indians and those of the settlers, he is willing to accept only one symbolic interpellation. He refuses to be sworn in by the captain of the Texas Rangers, explaining that it wouldn't be legal. While Clayton challenges him with the question of whether he is being sought for a crime, he responds: "I figure a man is only good for one oath at a time, and I took mine to the Confederate States of America." What is significant about this staunch loyalty, one might say, is less the gesture of nostalgia than the refusal to reformulate his affiliation to a symbolic community based on a change in circumstances—much as he can justify his tenuous position within his brother's family only because Martha repeatedly answers for him in an effort to prevent the eruption of violence. Ethan, occupying an unequivocal position in relation to both his brother and the representatives of Texas law, insists on being loyal only to the one symbolic mandate he has chosen. Unable, but also unwilling, to go with the change in times, he lives by a long-obsolete oath. For him, living in a world of past loyalties and alliances, there has been no capitulation of the Confederate Army. Incapable of all compromises, because he staunchly holds on to the world of clearly defined battlegrounds and simple contradictions, he will not reformulate his position in relation to the law of the settlers, or in relation to the Edwards family. The emotional conflict imposed upon him by his love for Martha can neither be sustained nor worked through; it can only present an impetus for escape. Once more we see Martha, who, handing Ethan's hat and cape to him, lovingly stretches her arms out to him, and he gently kisses her forehead before wordlessly walking past her as she follows him with a longing gaze.

Only when the search party finds Jorgensen's herd slaughtered do they realize that they have indeed fallen into a Comanche trap. They have ridden too far into the prairie, and they can't get back in time to help Aaron Edwards and his family. Thus they unwittingly allow the Comanche chief Scar (Henry Brandon), who is seeking revenge for the death of his own family, to destroy the homestead and kill or take captive its inhabitants. Ethan returns to a burning ranch, the furniture of Martha's living room strewn in front of the veranda, the corpses of the family hidden in the dark interior of the house. Calling out the name of his forbidden beloved, he rushes toward the ruins of the living quarters, yet is unable to pass over the threshold, instead falling to his knees within the door frame. The traces of carnage he glimpses in the darkness before him will remain secret, because he refuses to enter and also holds Martin back from plunging toward the corpse of his beloved Aunt Martha. The manner in which Ford visually introduces the scene of the Indian attack echoes the ambivalence of Ethan's feelings toward his home, in that it remains undecided whether the scene Ford presents is to be read as a mimetic rendition of the destruction of the Edwards family or Ethan's fantasy about what is about to happen because he is not there to help his brother defend his home. One might also ask whether Ford's depiction of the Indian attack is to be regarded as a horrific scenario or a horrific wish fulfillment.

The narrative framing of this traumatic scene of destruction is, thus, significant because of the ambivalence it evokes. Earlier, after the Texas Rangers leave the Edwards family, Ford initially follows the search party into the prairie, where they soon realize they have been fooled by the Indians and decide to split up into two groups. The first group rides on immediately to the Jorgensens', leaving Ethan, Martin, and Mose Harper behind. Ethan insists that the horses must rest and feed before they ride the forty miles back to his brother's ranch. In showing Ethan taking off the saddle and drying the back of his horse, John Ford positions him in such a way that he is framed by the mountains behind him. In the noonday sun he stands in the right corner of the frame, leaning on his horse and gazing with resigned anticipation, at a slight left angle, out into the distance.[17]

Ford then cuts to the next scene, showing Aaron's farm at dusk, the reddish brown light of the sunset making it look like an artificially illuminated fantasy site. Aaron and Martha anxiously barricade the windows and doors of their house, having realized that they are encircled by hostile Indians. First, however, they send their younger daughter, Debbie, out through one of the kitchen windows to hide in the nearby family cemetery, hoping that she will thus escape the attack and survive. As she sits by the grave of her grandmother, lit only by moonlight, Debbie suddenly realizes that she isn't alone. Chief Scar, an imposing figure dressed and painted for battle, has moved out of the emptiness of the prairie into the left part of the frame, his shadow covering her figure. More curious than frightened, Debbie stares at him, while he hesitates briefly, examining her appearance, then gazes into the dark space to the right of him; an instant later he blows his buffalo horn, thus signaling the beginning of the attack. John Ford's *mise-en-scène* suggests a conscious choice to avoid any direct representation of the destruction of the Edwards family. This traumatic blow to their home is instead performed as a compelling lacuna between scenes of anticipation and those of a belated deciphering of the traces of violence that remain after the attack. At the same time, this occluded violence emerges in Ford's *mise-en-scène* as the blind spot that lies at the center of two crossed gazes—the close-up shot of Ethan, gazing toward the left as he stands under the midday sun in the prairie, and the close-up shot of Scar, gazing to the right into a nocturnal landscape. The rhetoric of ellipses, by which Ford obliquely articulates the violent destruction of the homestead, significantly includes another visual element—the figure of Debbie, overshadowed and then replaced by the awe-inspiring figure of the master of the attack. Visually, she is the bond between the two opposed male figures, for she will prove to be the reason for their conflict at the end of the narrative.

From the way John Ford introduces Chief Scar, one readily surmises that he is not only Ethan Edwards's antagonist but also—and perhaps this is more important—his symptom. After all, he enjoys the violence against the family, whereas Ethan avoids violence with respect to the family, even though he evokes it by telling Aaron to stay close to his family and then abandoning him there. Edward Buscombe suggests that Scar "is in some sense Ethan's unconscious. . . . In raping Martha, Scar has acted out in brutal fashion the illicit sexual desire which Ethan harbored in his heart," which, of course, also means that for him "there is no place in the home, no family he can be integrated into."[18] Indeed, fully conforming to the rhetoric of the symptom, Scar broadcasts to Ethan his obscene and violent desire in the form of an encrypted message that is embodied in the corpses of the two people to whom he could never fully clarify his relationship, as well as the doll and the cape that Debbie leaves behind at her grandmother's grave—all metonymies for the violent destruction of the family and the home. If Ethan has waited three years before returning home, the view of the burnt-down ranch satisfies another unconscious desire: it assures him that he will never have to return to this site of unresolvable conflict, because it has literally been consumed.

Scar can be read as Ethan's symptom in yet another way as well, for Ethan allows the chief to translate his conflicted feelings about home and the family into a battle scenario with a clear battleground. Like a fetishist, he can now partake of the result of his destructive feelings toward the family of his brother and at the same time sacrifice himself for an abstract notion of home that he must restore. Thanks to Scar, he can reformulate the unbearable antagonism he had found at the hearth of Martha's home into a satisfying (because it's simple) opposition between himself and his designated enemy. Having burnt down the home in which Ethan could never feel comfortable, Chief Scar has allowed that battleground to be replaced by one on which Ethan can successfully avoid the internal enemy of the community—the gender trouble embodied by women and racially mixed family members.

Furthermore, by designating Scar as his enemy, Ethan can resignify all the ambivalence he felt for his brother and his sister-in-law—his illicit aggression and his illicit desire—into the unequivocal hatred of his family's murderer, who, as Ethan will discover in the course of his search, has committed miscegenation by taking his niece Debbie as one of his wives. Within the parameters of this psychic battleground, the fantasy analogy to the prairie, where it will be played out, Ethan's claim to an unlimited expression of his individualism is not hampered by any internal enemy. Here he has a simple goal—initially to find the captive girl and later, after discovering that she has become one of Scar's wives, to kill her. Once more he can turn his back on home in good faith, much as three years earlier he had chosen not to return home after the surrender of the Confederate Army. As Buscombe notes, "Ethan's assumption of the role of justified avenger, wreaking upon Scar the punishment he deserves, allows him to assume the high moral ground. But his self-righteousness . . . can be seen as an attempt to blot out his own guilt."[19]

At the beginning of the five-year search, Ethan is initially accompanied by the Texas Rangers under the leadership of Reverend Captain Clayton. Even before the funeral ceremony for the Edwardses has ended, Ethan insists on leaving the mourners behind, demonstratively rejecting Mrs. Jorgensen's plea that he not let her two sons waste their lives in vengeance as retribution for murdered parents and captured daughters. After the first hostile confrontation between the small group of Texas Rangers and Scar's band of warriors, the search party realizes that it is far outnumbered. What also becomes apparent is the insurmountable difference between the solitary fighter Ethan and the laws of the community as represented by Reverend Captain Clayton; the former will rebel against all constraints, while the latter will insist on compromise and accommodation. Once more the Rangers divide into two groups, and Ethan, unwilling to turn back until he has avenged the murder of Martha, rides on, accompanied by the two youngest members of the search troop, Martin Pawley and Brad Jorgensen (Harry Carey Jr.), Lucy's beau. Initially Ford uses these characters to underscore how his hero, who can never feel at ease in the family home, is fully comfortable with the laws of the prairie and the customs of its indigenous population and is able to decode the traces that they leave behind. The contrast between Ethan, who waits before acting, and Brad, who, blinded by rage after discovering the rape and murder of Lucy, charges into the Indian village alone and is immediately shot, further highlights the difference between a calculated revenge, based on perseverance, and an imprudent one. Along the lines proposed by Hegel, the resilience of Ethan's hatred feeds off the conviction that the simple opposition of war, fought in the name of the community, is in all cases to be preferred over the unsolvable difference posed by the "internal enemy of the community," which he would have to confront if he returned to the surviving settlers. After one year of searching, Ethan and Martin are forced to turn back because they lose all traces of the Comanche during a heavy snowfall.

As at the beginning of the film, Ethan returns to a homestead, but this time it is not the ranch of his family; rather it is that of their neighbors, the Jorgensens. Again a woman initially steps onto the veranda from the dark interior of her house, her back to us, with a man immediately behind her. In contrast to the first scene of arrival, however, she does not linger on the threshold of her home, but walks directly out into the barren landscape, where she, too, is forced to shield her eyes against the bright sunlight as she looks more closely at the two riders who have appeared on the horizon of the wide space before her. And once more Ford offers us the tableau of a settler family. In a scene shot from the front, we see Lars Jorgensen with his wife by his side and his daughter, Laurie (Vera Miles), who has quickly joined her parents, hovering a few feet behind him. Then, as the riders dismount, Mrs. Jorgensen runs to embrace Martin, and Lars Jorgensen slowly approaches Ethan, extending his hand in greeting after acknowledging receipt of Ethan's letter of a year ago that informed him of the senseless death of his son. Laurie launches herself at Martin, kisses him, and leads him across the threshold into the home, while Mrs. Jorgensen stops Ethan on the veranda, which once again functions as the architectural threshold between wilderness and civilization, to ask about Debbie. Ethan can only voicelessly shake his head. Then he and the two Jorgensens follow the others into the house.

Ford's lonely ranger will not tarry in the family home for long, however. A letter sent there for him by a trader named Fetterman, claiming to have a piece of Debbie's apron and to be able to tell him the whereabouts of the girl, compels him to set out again early the next morning, leaving his young companion behind. Even though Ethan tried to convince Martin the previous evening that, although the Edwards family had given him shelter and raised him after he lost his own parents, he was not a relative of Debbie's, the young man's emotional attachment is invincible. Laurie has been hoping that he will stay and finally marry her, but when she tells him of Ethan's departure, he, too, abruptly flees the Jorgensen home, nominally to prevent Ethan from killing Debbie once he finds her. Yet to a degree his flight is analogous to Ethan's, for he, too, seeks to avoid the gender trouble that Laurie embodies with her proposition of marriage and domesticity, and he privileges the simple opposition to be found in the conflict with Scar.[20]

Two factors, however, affect his decision to follow Ethan and turn his back on Laurie. His actual opponent isn't the Comanche chief Scar but rather his "Uncle Ethan," whose racist notions of miscegenation are all too familiar to him. Furthermore, unlike Ethan, he does not seek to jettison the feminine realm of the family forever. His current actions are aimed at renegotiating cultural codes about interracial exchange that will replace a no longer viable notion of racial purity and assure the survival of the community.[21] Therefore, Martin's decision to return to the battlefield is a provisional one, and he clearly intends to ultimately come back home, rather than wandering forever in the wild prairie. His decision to continue with the search is, furthermore, not fed by a stubborn sense of retaliation, but rather thrives on his love for the young woman he regards as his sister, because they have a shared past. In other words, for him, affiliation with a family and a home is something that one renegotiates as needed in order to address changes in one's actual living situation, even while it is always supported by a fundamental attitude of sympathy for those one feels at home with, regardless of whether through a blood bond or a bond of circumstance. As Peter Wollen notes, for Martin "the period of nomadism is only an episode, which has meaning as the restitution of the family, a necessary link between his old home and his new home."[22]

Of Settlers and Vagabonds

The battle over the captured girl Debbie thus becomes a competition between the philosophies of those who think of themselves as perennial vagabonds of the prairie, positing a threat to all rooted existence, and those who seek to defend their fragile homesteads, and the individual family. The latter set their claims on individual happiness against both the wilderness's force of dissolution and the violence of those who, like Ethan, fight in the name of universal notions of justice.[23] As perhaps the most seminal representative of the settlers, held together under the auspices of a feminine authority that, as John Ford repeatedly shows, is responsible for keeping the husbands and sons from leaving their provisional homes and fleeing into the prairie, Mrs. Jorgensen (Olive Carey) explains her resilience with the following trope: "Just so happens we be Texicans. Texican is nothing but a human man. Way out on a limb. This year and next. And maybe for a hundred more." She confidently adds, "But I don't think it will be forever. Someday this country is going to be a fine good place to be. Maybe it needs our bones in the ground before that time can come."

Ethan, by contrast, is radically opposed to such an attitude of approximation with the main interest being the survival of the community. On the very first day of the search, he had shot out the eyes of a dead Comanche found buried beneath a large stone close to the Edwards ranch. Asked his reason for this gratuitous act of violence, he explained that according to Comanche custom, deceased warriors without eyes cannot enter the realm of the dead and must therefore wander wherever the wind carries them. With this explanation, of course, he implicitly points out an analogy between his own vagabonding and that of the dead Indian. Thus the connection between death and regeneration that he embodies is diametrically opposed to that proposed by Mrs. Jorgensen. Her notion of sacrifice, which includes the death of her oldest son, consists in the belief in a community whose codes and values can be renegotiated according to circumstances, even though it encompasses many different, individual homes. The community she is willing to sacrifice her life for is one to which all those belong who believe in the project of progress as their mutual cause. Ethan, embodying an externalized and, indeed, excluded extremity, functions as the frame for the construction of cities in the wilderness. Though his position is necessary for progress to take place, he nevertheless remains a foreign body within the community, even while his exclusion is the precondition for the feminized gesture of domesticating the wilderness to win the upper hand.

Given the fundamental tension between these two gendered positions— a womanhood proposing individual family happiness against the solitary ranger fighting for universal ideals—it is, significantly, the hybrid figures who become increasingly important as the story progresses. Among these are men who, unlike Ethan, have no difficulty in crossing the threshold into the home dominated by women. Charlie McCorry (Ken Curtis), for example, comfortably courts Laurie while his rival, Martin, wanders around the wide prairie and, rather than returning, sends home a report about the futility of their search for Debbie. In the scene in which Laurie, angered by Martin's continued absence from her home, is for the first time willing to pay attention to Charlie's wooing, John Ford shows us the two lovers framed by the front door of her parents' home, leading out to the veranda. Leaning against the right side of the door frame, Laurie is gazing out into the empty space, dreaming about an absent man, much as Martha had done at the very beginning of the film. Charlie moves forward from behind to join her, strumming his guitar and singing. As he walks toward her from the interior of her parents' home, the camera, positioned outside the door, moves toward the two figures. At the same moment that Charlie stands directly next to her on the threshold, the film frame and the door frame seem to collapse. Slowly Laurie turns her head away from the wide prairie beyond the veranda of her home, with this symbolic gesture giving up her dream of the prodigal lover in order to gaze instead at the man standing next to her on the threshold. The successful proposal scene proves to be—like the American dream of conquering the wilderness—a framed image. Before John Ford cuts to the next scene, he overlaps the tune Charlie had been singing, "Skip to my Lou, my darling," with a scenic shot showing Ethan and Martin riding along a mountain range, lit by an overly artificial sunset.

The romance between Charlie and Laurie will, of course, not be consummated. On the eve before their wedding, the two wanderers return to the Jorgensen homestead a second time. This time there is no woman standing on the veranda in anticipation of their arrival. Rather they are the unwelcome guests at a party already in full swing. Lars Jorgensen, in fact, tries to prevent Ethan from entering the house, where the wedding ceremony is about to begin, explaining that he is wanted for the murder of a tradesman called Fetterman. While Ethan isn't worried about confronting Reverend Captain Clayton (who at present is dressed not as a Texas Ranger but as a minister) and thus briskly passes over the threshold, Martin stays outside. Laurie, who has just descended from her room by an outside staircase, intercepts him, and, rather than joining the groom, leads her lost lover to the fireplace in the main part of the Jorgensen ranch—the very spot where they parted three years earlier. Here they can finally be reconciled, even though they are once again disrupted in their proposal scene, this time by the angry groom, who seeks to chase his rival away. In the courtyard in front of the house the two men enact a fight scene, in which their antagonism, proposed by "womanhood" as the internal enemy of the community, can be fought through as a simple competition before the eyes of the gathered group of friends. This, however, is a battleground contained by the laws of the community, taking place in a liminal space between home and prairie, and not the grand battle Ethan stands for as he roams the wilderness beyond all domesticating constraints. At the same time, the fight with his rival allows Martin to recognize his love for Laurie and for the home she stands for. Nevertheless, even though his fists declare his allegiance to her, the wedding must be postponed. Only after Martin has liberated his sister Debbie from her alleged captivity and brought her home, can all the negotiations required by the gender trouble proposed by woman at the hearth of the home be addressed—which is to say all that remains unsolved after the simple combat between men has been fought and decided.

Even more compellingly than Laurie's lover Martin, who straddles the masculine urge to go to battle in the wilderness and the feminine proposition of home, Mose Harper represents a masculine position that promises a successful affiliation with several cultural communities. The wild speech and strange body language of this man disturb the homogeneity of the settlers' world partly because he introduces into this community aspects of the alien indigenous culture. Significantly, though, he is fully integrated into the community despite his seemingly mad behavior, while Ethan, who is

clearly their hero, elicits mistrust. Mose is also more successful at understanding the hostile Comanche culture than the racist Ethan because, he has
been able to fit in when in captivity as well, using his unconventional behavior as a shield of sorts. He, in fact, is the one who actually finds Debbie.

Most important, however, is that what characterizes Mose from the start
is a desire for home. In the scene in Martha's kitchen, when he warns the
other men that they can expect a Comanche attack, he is, significantly, sitting in her rocking chair, and before leaving with the other men, he explicitly thanks her for the use of this piece of furniture that represents the security and emotional warmth of the hearth. Later, when he is finally able to
give Ethan definitive information about Debbie's whereabouts, he explains
that he wants no money as a reward, "just a roof over old Mose's head and
my own rocking chair by the fire." And only after Ethan has sworn that he
will get his desired home does Mose point out the man who will actually
lead Ethan to Scar. Then, after Ethan has finally met his lost niece and decided to reject her because she has been living in miscegenation as Scar's
wife, he returns to the Jorgensens' with Marty and Mose Harper reappears,
in the company of cavalry soldiers. Having escaped Comanche captivity, he
had tried unsuccessfully to explain to them the location of Chief Scar's
camp, but they brought him to the Jorgensens' instead, because the one utterance they were able to understand was his claim that a rocking chair was
waiting for him there. Sitting in Mrs. Jorgensen's rocking chair, much as he
had been sitting in Martha's just before the chain of fatal events began, he
tells Ethan, in a language that only the latter can understand, where they
can find Scar. At the end of the film Mose's wish will actually come true.
Accepted by the Jorgensen family, much as the Edwards family had taken
Marty in, he sits in a rocking chair on the veranda, positioned there by Ford
as a witness to the homecoming of the captured girl. One can surmise that
he, who can make anyone's rocking chair his own, regardless of where it
may be, is the figure of appropriation par excellence. He can adapt to any
given cultural home, for he is able to combine constant movement with
protective rootedness. He doesn't have to flee from home and endlessly circle the prairie, because he will never experience the roof over his head and
the fireplace at his feet as unbearably constraining. Rocking away peacefully without ever moving from his place, he remains in constant motion.

Apart from the men, oscillating between front line and family, Ford uses
the figure of the mature Debbie (Natalie Wood) to depict a different aspect
of what a viable appropriation of a foreign home might look like. She stands

in stark contrast to the more tragic cases of captured women—mentally deranged and unable to remember their white identity—whom Ethan and Marty discover in an earlier scene at an army post after the cavalry has attacked a Noyaka Comanche village. In contrast to these traumatized white women, she is living peacefully in the Comanche community and initially sits silently next to the other women in the tent of Chief Scar, her back turned to the two visitors who have been seeking her. Once her master commands her to rise, she moves toward them, carrying a wooden lance on which are hung the scalps Scar has taken in revenge for the death of his two sons. Debbie is thus staged as a contested object of exchange, over whose body the hostility between the men is negotiated. Scar draws the attention of the two searchers to himself by showing them the medal he is wearing around his neck, knowing full well that Ethan will recognize it as his own. The Confederate soldier had given this medal of honor to his little niece Debbie early on in the film, during the "welcome home" dinner at Martha's kitchen table. So as to introduce the unsolvable complexity of gender trouble into both Scar's and Ethan's simple logic of aggression and retribution, Debbie then tries to transform the open prairie into a space of negotiation. As a representative of cultural hybridity, who in her sexual alliance with a man of a different race has gained an insight into his way of thinking, she seeks to prevent the final battle between these two revengeful men.

After Ethan and Marty have left the tent of Chief Scar in order to camp at a nearby river, she suddenly appears from behind the sand hills, running toward the two men. She seems to have succeeded in living her two cultural interpellations without having to deny her origin. Dressed in the gowns of the chieftain's wife, she initially speaks to Martin, who has run toward her, calling her by her given name. In the language of the Comanche, she warns him that he must leave this place immediately. In response to his question of whether she doesn't remember the childhood scenes they shared, she seamlessly moves to her mother tongue, which she—unlike the tragic captives at the army post—has not forgotten, much as she has retained all memories of her lost home. "I remember, for always," she assures him. Martin thus articulates one of the happy aporias of the situation of the *Mischling* by calling her his sister. In so doing he illustrates that one's affiliation with a family can be negotiated on the basis of shared experiences in the past, rather than being exclusively an issue of blood relation.[24] Debbie, in turn, addresses an impossible cultural hybridity, which can be lived only as a psychic reality. She assures him that initially she had prayed that he might come to get her and take her home, although he never did. At the same time she also assures him that the Comanche are now her people. She can accommodate both her memories of an original, lost home and her affiliation with a cultural community that had initially been foreign to her.

Ethan, however, can see in Debbie only the embodiment of an antagonistic hybridity, for he can understand her only within the categories of a simple racist opposition between white and Indian, so his response to her appearance is the wish to reassert a clear front line of battle. As wife to Chief Scar, she is not only no longer white to him, she is nothing more than an extension of the designated enemy. Calling upon Martin to stand aside, he points his loaded revolver at her, hoping, by means of her dead body, to fatally wound his enemy. With this violent exchange, Ford recalls an ambivalence that had already implicitly subtended the murder of Debbie's parents. In the open landscape, Ethan is able to give free rein to the destructive desires he harbors toward his own family, which he had to curtail while residing at his brother's homestead. This, too, involves a simplification of the unsolvable antagonism posed by his love for Martha. In his psychic landscape, of which the open prairie is a materialization, Debbie is anything but an ambivalent figure; she is precisely not the hybrid representative of a happy enmeshment between white and Comanche. At the foot of the sand hills she is simply his enemy, guilty of miscegenation, and thus—given his racist moral codes—a woman whom he is justified in killing.

Martin's position proves to be pivotal in Ford's depiction of Ethan's racism, offering a counterbalance to any simple solution of violence, and in so doing recognizing the legitimacy and viability of Debbie's proposition of hybridity. Even though he has downplayed his own interracial heritage in the previous scenes and, indeed, has cultivated a certain illiteracy when it came to reading the signs of what he wanted to designate as a culture foreign to him, he now emerges as the figure who literally stands in for a third space between the two sides of the front line Ethan has declared. One might say he inhabits a site of reconciliation rather than retribution—a claim for understanding the crossover between two incompatible psychic realities, namely the niece's hybridity and the uncle's racism. He literally places himself before Debbie, shielding her body with his, and thus prevents Ethan from killing his own kin. With Hegel, one might describe this act as an attempt to introduce into the open wilderness of the prairie the feminine proposition of individual happiness, and with it the gender and race trouble from which Ethan repeatedly tries to flee. By shielding Debbie with his own body, Martin seeks to transform a battleground where a simple opposition between clearly demarcated opponents is to be fought into a site where antagonisms are negotiated but also sustained because they can never be fully resolved. By personally embodying the demarcation line that separates uncle from niece, he renders tangibly visible the aporia to which Ethan wishes to remain blind—that one and the same woman can be both his beloved sister and the loyal wife of the hated Comanche chief. Neither Ethan, who continues to approach the two with his gun drawn, nor Scar, who has sent his warriors to the two white men, will relinquish his insistence on the logic of simple oppositions that can be resolved only through violence. Ironically, this unremittingly racist attitude is precisely what Ethan shares with his opponent. The prairie must remain a battlefield with clearly demarcated sides. Ultimately, it isn't Martin who prevents the shooting of Debbie, but the arrow of one of Scar's men, which wounds Ethan in his right shoulder. While Debbie simply vanishes from the dunes that have once again become a battleground, the two searchers find themselves encircled by riding horsemen and run to seek shelter from their attackers in a nearby cave.

As McBride and Wilmington note, "Miscegenation, next to war itself, is probably the most dramatic form of collision between two cultures, and by exploring a community's reaction to it Ford is testing its degree of internal tension."[25] One could add that in *The Searchers* the situation is complicated by the fact that Scar's miscegenation transforms the tent he shares with Debbie into a battleground, so that the internal enemy to his community, the captive girl turned chieftain's wife, far from proposing gender and race trouble at the heart of his home, is for him the privileged object of exchange in the collision between two cultures, just as her uncle declares her to be. From this, one might surmise that whenever the internal trouble performed by gender and race difference becomes unbearable, a phobic concept like miscegenation is invoked, so that the sexual contention between men and women can be declared as a state of war. Ford stages the second meeting between Ethan and his niece much along the lines of such an externalization of internal tensions. Having radically denied any further blood bond to Debbie by declaring Martin Pawley to be his only surviving heir, Ethan is able to convince Reverend Captain Clayton one last time to put together a search party.

With the help of information gleaned from Mose Harper on the night of the failed wedding between Laurie and Charlie McCorry, this band of

Texas Rangers decides to attack the Comanche camp at sunrise. Ford once more emphasizes Scar's function as Ethan's symptom, by staging this attack as a reversal of the scene of destruction of the Edwards family at the beginning of the film. Whereas in the earlier episode Ford had chosen the subjective perspective of Aaron, showing us brief flashes of light emerging from the dark prairie as an indication of the clandestine presence of the hostile Comanche, he now visualizes the perspective of the aggressors. Ethan and Clayton use the protection of the dark prairie to surveil the lights of the Indian camp, much as they imitate the Comanche by using animal sounds to communicate with each other about when the attack is to begin. Declaring that he is no longer concerned with saving Debbie but simply wants to destroy his opponent, Ethan one last time invokes the logic of simple combat. Indeed, he hopes that in the course of this surprise attack Debbie, too, will fall victim to the violence he is about to unleash. As he explains to Martin, at stake for him are the allegedly universal concerns of the community—revenge, retribution, and punishment—while the young man continues to think within the categories of an individual family's pursuit of happiness. Indeed, Martin staunchly refuses to suppress the women's proposition—be this Mrs. Jorgensen, Laurie, or Debbie herself—calling upon him to privilege the survival of individual communities over any abstract notions of rightful vengeance. Refusing to let his sister be treated as though she were nothing other than the prize in a simple opposition between Texas Rangers and Comanche, he asks Clayton for permission to steal into the camp and save her before the troop actually starts its attack.

As though he had entered a fairy tale, he finds Debbie sleeping peacefully in one of the tents. Before the two can flee, however, an Oedipal contest must be won. As Chief Scar suddenly appears at the opening of his tent, dressed in full war regalia, Martin shoots without hesitating—not because in so doing he executes the enemy in the name of an abstract law but because, with the happiness of the individual family in sight, he will tolerate no further separation from his long-lost sister. When Ethan arrives at the Comanche chief's tent he finds that Scar is already dead, and so his only recourse for revenge is taking his enemy's scalp. At this moment the two representatives of extremist racist law have become identical. Having arrived at this zero point of cultural collision, Ford can turn one last time to the core question around which the entire search has revolved: What is to be done with the unsolvable gender (and race) trouble embodied by all the women, whether they stay at home or are captured and dislocated to a foreign home in the middle of the prairie? After leaving Scar's tent, Ethan sees Debbie fleeing into the prairie and immediately rides after her. Like Martin, who is unsuccessful in stopping him, we, too, are asked by Ford to fear that he will finally succeed in killing his niece. Debbie breaks down in front of the entrance to a cave and, with his camera positioned inside the dark interior of the cavern, Ford offers us yet another framed image that is as much a part of the American Dream as the happy settler couple and the dream of the women staying behind—the radically racist lone cowboy about to jump off his horse to slay the woman he has been chasing like an animal, because she literally embodies the collision of cultures that his racial fundamentalism sustains. Ford cuts to Martin, his drawn gun in his hand, wild with anger, running toward the cave, clearly ready to kill this paternal figure of authority if Ethan insists on implementing his abstract notions of retribution against Martin's proposition that he be reunited with his only surviving family member, regardless of the cost.

Yet the force of Ford's peripeteia feeds off the fact that, for no apparent reason, a 180-degree reversal has occurred in Ethan's feelings toward his niece. He grasps Debbie under both arms and thrusts her high above his head—just as he had done five years earlier in Martha's kitchen when he saw her for the first time since returning from the war—but now her fists are clenched and she is ready to fight. Visually doubling the scene with which he first led us into the interior of the Edwards ranch home, John Ford has Ethan hold his niece above his head for a few seconds before gently lowering her and enfolding her in his arms, cradling the astonished but relieved young woman with unexpected tenderness, as he declares to her, "Let's go home, Debbie." As she suddenly leans forward to place her arms around his neck, tucking her head against his right shoulder, he softly kisses her on the neck, and with her in his arms, he turns away from the cave to walk back into the prairie, toward Martin and toward his horse. As David Thomson notes, this is "one shot—utterly beautiful, deeply moving, and a way in which the harsh Ethan learns to understand 'family' or 'race' or 'sex' or 'strangeness.'"[26]

Ethan and Debbie's mutual recollection of a shared scene of tenderness encroaches upon the present and allows for the emergence of an impossible emotional site—as though uncle and niece had arrived at the navel of the heterotopic prairie. Owing to his gesture of embrace, Martha's kitchen, forever destroyed in reality, has been superimposed on the prairie landscape, and for a moment the tension between the family hearth inside the home and the battleground outside is suspended as well. The collision between two cultures that was negotiated over Debbie's body has transformed into the understanding of an affective bond, lying beyond all wars fought in the name of universal codes of community but also beyond all individual family happiness. What we recognize is that, for Ethan, any acceptance of the unsolvable gender and race trouble, defining the home, is possible only in the heterotopic geography of the wilderness—which is to say between the entrance to a dark cavern and the wide-open hills. After all, he can say to her, "Let's go home" only in an abstract sense, not in the more particular sentence, "Let's go home and restore a place that will allow us to live together." Home remains a place of anticipation, a possibility, a goal to achieve, without becoming an actual condition of cohabitation.

Thus the two wanderers return home one last time, now accompanied by a woman. Rather than beginning this final scene as he had all other scenes of homecoming, by positioning his camera inside the frame of the door opening to the outside, Ford immediately shows us the right side of the Jorgensen veranda. In the place of a woman gazing out into the open space of the prairie we find Mose Harper sitting in his rocking chair, peacefully watching the homecomers. Both Mrs. Jorgensen and her husband are, however, also already standing on the veranda, and they witness the spectacle of homecoming from this outermost piece of the wooden platform they call home. Laurie, who is the last to appear on this home stage, remains there for only a moment before, like Aaron Edwards in the very first scene of the film, she descends the stairs and runs toward Martin, who, unlike Ethan in the earlier scene, reaches out his hand to her even before getting off his horse. She thus literally leads her groom home. Before him rides Ethan, with Debbie on his lap, as though she were his child bride. For even after they have both dismounted from his horse, he continues to cradle her in his arms as he carries her to the front of the Jorgensen veranda. Ford cuts to Mose Harper's face, beaming with joy at this reunion, as he still calmly rocks in his chair, as though Ford is presenting Mose to us as the figure of identification, before offering us one last tableau—that of the reunited settler family.

Now the camera has once again moved into the dark interior of the home—not the home from which Debbie departed, but the one that will receive her as a lost daughter nonetheless. Framed by the posts of the veranda (far more ornamental than those of the Edwards veranda, as though to show the progress that has taken place in the course of five years), as well as by the two Jorgensens, whose backs are turned to us, we see Ethan walking directly toward the camera so as to instigate the exchange. Both Jorgensens stretch their arms out toward the young woman, who, having arrived at the veranda, slowly disengages herself from her uncle's embrace and looks at them in bewildered awe. Mrs. Jorgensen embraces her and, followed by her husband, leads her into her new home.

In perfect symmetry with the beginning of the film, Ford's camera now moves backward into the dark interior of the house and, as Debbie and her surrogate parents cross the threshold, all three become silhouettes. As they pass the camera on the right, and thereby once again open up our view of the people still outside the door's frame, we see that Ethan has stepped onto the veranda, as though to be the next one to pass from the prairie landscape into the house. But he steps aside to allow Laurie and Martin to enter first, and they, too, become silhouettes, like shadows, also passing the camera on the right side. For a moment Ethan, now framed all by himself by the opened door, stands on the sunlit veranda and hesitates. In contrast to the other figures, he continues to be fully visible. Suddenly he turns around shyly and walks back, still hesitatingly, into the prairie, returning to the virtual landscape from which he had so unexpectedly emerged.

But, one might add, he returns to the impossible depth of the cinema screen as well, on which the heterotopic world of the western had so suddenly appeared because a door had been opened to it. The door closes from the left, and the screen becomes black. Like Mose Harper on his rocking chair, we are now excluded from both worlds—from the family reunion taking place inside the home, for which at the end of *The Searchers* Ford chooses to offer no cinematic representation, and from the wanderings of his lonely hero, who once more turns his back on home and rides away.[27]

The Prairie: A Virtual Geography

One could speak of an optimistic tone breaking through at the end of *The Searchers*. After all, at the end of this five-year period of odyssey, captivity, and waiting, some of Ford's protagonists are able to return home. Yet what is perhaps significant about this happy ending is that it involves those who can live with a hybrid cultural interpellation—the woman who has spent her early adulthood in a foreign culture and the *Mischling*, born of the violent collision of two cultures. Apparently, homecoming is possible for those who know that affiliation with a community must be negotiated, since because of their hybridity, which makes dwelling in any one place fraught with ambivalence, they can be at home in more than one place. In their homecoming Debbie and Martin are supported by those who know how fragile homes at the outer margin of an allegedly civilized world can be and who therefore pit against the contingency of their abodes a ritualized performance of what the individual family consists of—the repeated congregation of the family as tableau on the veranda and with it a negotiation of who can be included and who must be excluded. Because they neither try to escape the unsolvable antagonism inherent in the erection of communities in the wilderness nor wander perennially in the open prairie, these figures are willing to accommodate themselves to all contingencies. In Ford's version of the western, home is a place directed toward the future, caught in a state of transformation and following a movement that is diametrically opposed to that of the solitary hero, who wanders in circles through the prairie. Home is a place one can return to even though one didn't start out there, a substitute that, because these settlers know only too well that they will never fully be masters of their homesteads, does not particularly emphasize the lack of an original, lost home. Rather, they embrace the notion that one can make oneself at home, again and again, in whatever provisional place of abode becomes available.

Yet a nostalgic note remains to accompany any optimism, recognizing that the man who defends universal claims to progress should remain excluded from the home that is erected under the auspices of women's claim to a right to pursue individual family happiness. Ethan's way of thinking and acting according to simple oppositions between friends and enemies makes up the ideological precondition for the conquest of the West by white settlers, given that only a battle staged along clearly demarcated lines can allow a culture to emerge as the dominant one. At the same time, heroes like Ethan have to be relinquished after what in the name of progress was considered the hostile zone of battle is transformed into a public space where claims on individual happiness are brought forward and the unresolvable antagonism at the heart of gender and race trouble moves to the fore of community life. John Ford's hybrid attitudes of iconographer and iconoclast thus overlap most poignantly in the resolution he offers for the tragedy of the solitary hero, as he liked to call *The Searchers*. Fully in accordance with the rules of the genre, his hero must flee all provisional homes, because he neither understands nor acknowledges the laws of the community. Yet this exclusion marks him less as an idealistic rebel than as a figure whose function has become obsolete.

McBride and Wilmington correctly observe that "in transferring the actual heroic deeds, the killing of Scar and the finding of Debbie, to Martin and to Mose, the fool, Ford is destroying the myth of the heroic loner." Ethan's search must include the participation of the community, in whose name it is undertaken, and whose preservation is its aim. "It would never have taken place if the outsider had not initiated it," they conclude, "but it is fundamentally a communal action."[28] However, although all are part of this project, it also requires the tension between center and periphery, between exclusion and inclusion. The tragic solitary hero not only flees into battle so as to prevent the outbreak of internal trouble in the family or the community but the community also requires that certain individuals be clearly marked as non-integratable. By so doing, the community establishes a well-defined distinction between it and its outer enemy that will allow it to sustain the internal antagonism that it can never fully obliterate—a position so ambivalently shared by Ethan and Scar even if Scar performs the forbidden sexual act and violence that Ethan only fantasizes. For those who have learned to stay at home, this clearly marked outsider also embodies the dream that if the internal trouble were to become truly unbearable, he would once again appear and translate the unsolvable difference into a simple battle that could be fought outside the door of the home, in the wide-open prairie landscape.

Put another way, this virtual landscape—already mythical—serves to sustain fantasies about the possibility of war, so that all internal animosity harbored within the provisional homes of the settlers, and threatening to disturb the happiness of individual families, can be held at bay. Thus, even though Ethan Edwards's feelings toward the community and the family may be fraught with ambivalence, what all western heroes cannot escape is the simple opposition between the tendency toward negotiating rules of conventions on the part of the settlers and their perennial wandering among the winds of the prairie. By choosing a nostalgic happy ending Ford refuses to stage what would happen if the solitary hero were actually to live out his ambivalent feelings toward the family by moving into the home, much as he also refuses to offer us any representation of what will happen when the members of the Jorgensen family will, owing to the presence of Debbie in their midst, be unable to avoid the race and gender trouble that she quite literally embodies. He remains silent about whether they will be able to accommodate this unresolvable antagonism within the home or will turn the home into a domestic battle zone.

Insofar as the tragedy at the end of *The Searchers* lies not with the *Mischling* but with the figure who violently opposes all cultural hybridity, Ford opens up the possibility of a second spiritual home—the western genre as one of the privileged imaginary homes that Hollywood's image repertoire has to offer. Ford's nostalgic image of the tragic loner who must be sacrificed so that civilization can progress is obviously neither a realistic rendition of the historic events leading to a conquest of the West nor a realistic refiguration of the cultural climate of Eisenhower's America. Rather, the monumental landscape and its mythic hero clearly belong to a reel world, emerging from our imaginary relation to the real conditions of American history in the form of western ideology. As Andrew Sarris notes, after World War II, Hollywood "seems to have taken to westerns in a glib way . . . as if the themes of power and conquest and empire-building had resonated from the fighting fronts in the world arena to the Hollywood backlots and nearby locations."[29] In the heterotopia of the western genre, with its monumental landscape, cinematic allusions to the real living conditions of 1950s America could be played through obliquely, dislocated to a different historical postwar period—that of the backwash of the Civil War—and translated into the realm of mythic signs, which, according to Roland Barthes, function by depleting history of all context and raising it instead to the level of a universal, essential, forever valid, and all-inclusive story.[30]

The return to the door frame as the visual frame for the story he has to tell allows John Ford to stage this move into the realm of the mythic at the end of *The Searchers* explicitly as the move into the heterotopia of cinema's image repertoire. If Ethan, after a moment of hesitation, ultimately turns his back on home, he does so in order to decidedly turn his back on the future as well, and to wander forever in the world between the present and the past, between the living and the dead; like the dead Indian whose eyes have been shot out, he is now a shadow tossed by the wind. Far from returning to any historical past, however, he once more enters into the impossible geography of mythic and monumental history, in which the cultural difference of white and Indian is fought out forever as a simple battle of opposites, even though in this reel world, depleted of all real history, as McBride and Wilmington note, Scar and Ethan are "blood-brothers in their commitment to primitive justice," sacrificing themselves to make civilization possible. "This is the meaning of the door opening and closing on the wilderness," they conclude. "It is the story of America."[31] Here we find no temporal progression. Here all historical progress is arrested, frozen into familiar images—the western genre, with its reliable character and plot resolutions, another viable home.

But at the end of *The Searchers* Monument Valley also emerges as a mythic countersite, comparable to the world of Oz in Fleming's fairy tale about the pointlessness of looking for home anywhere other than in a dream landscape. The story of this conflicted, lonely hero—who, like Dorothy, would contend that there is no place like home, even though it is precisely the place he can't tolerate—is to be read as a dream scene as well. Comparable to the window in Dorothy's bedroom, where the frontier *everygirl* first watches the transformation of familiar people into fairy-tale characters and then crosses over into this magical world herself, Ford's explicit staging of the opening door at the beginning and the closing door at the end marks both our entrance into and our exit from his dreamscape. The world that supports our dream of America is on the other side of the door, clearly severed from the dark interior of the Edwards and the Jorgensen ranch. Our hope as film audience resides with the figure who has turned his back on us. He is allowed to remain on the film screen, to tarry forever in this virtual space, while we are the ones who are really excluded. The fact that Ford, like Hitchcock at the end of *Rebecca,* offers no images of the reunited family could be read as a gesture of iconoclasm. While a successful homecoming is alluded to, the characters who represent this viable social realm become two-dimensional silhouettes. For the time after, which is to say for the future, Ford chooses not to find images, much as he chose not to represent the destruction of the Edwards family. Analogous to the traumatic core scene, around which Ethan's entire search for Debbie revolved, the interior of the home after Debbie's homecoming remains a dark spot.

Thus, with the end of *The Searchers* we have ironically returned to a simple contradiction. Our real life and the mythic reel legend are mutually exclusive. Though Ethan Edwards may be excluded from the Jorgensen home and the community of the settlers, he has the last cinematic image. But in this aporia also resides the force of Ford's nostalgic iconoclasm. The impossible geography of a monumental past was always already nothing other than cinema. Which is why these stories of wandering heroes and their vengeful nemesis are so much more familiar and so much more satisfying than the real historical events of a violent collision of incompatible cultures that the conquest of the West engendered. Of course, like Dorothy, we know that our real living conditions will always be inscribed by internal trouble—be it class, gender, race, or simply the difference that emerges because the desires of individuals are not necessarily compatible with those of the community. Yet not unlike her, we, as lovers of the western genre, can sustain our knowledge of the troubling difference subtending the family and the home, for we can dream of heroes who can enjoy the freedom of simple contradictions in our stead in a world beyond the darkened movie screen. Fleeing into a battle with clear front lines, they do away with the murky zones of difference that riddle our everyday reality. Ford not only knows about the dark core inhabiting his own cinematic rendition of the western myth but also stages this vanishing point as the position his camera assumes in relation to the optimistic nostalgia he has fashioned, the dark interiors from which his camera captures images of the impossible geography of the prairie and its mythical inhabitants that will haunt our dreams.

Lone Star—Arrival

Chapter 4

Hybrid Home
Lone Star

History Lessons

In *Lone Star*, John Sayles makes explicit reference to John Ford's refiguration of the western tradition, with his narrative oscillating between two time frames, 1957 and the present. In an interview with Gavin Smith, he explained that he chose Texas as the stage for his history lesson because it "has a compressed history that is like a metaphor for the history of the United States" and also because it offers a geographical analogy to the psychic development of his hero. Sheriff Sam Deeds (Chris Cooper) is very much the classic loner, "trying to bring justice to the situation, as far as he has been concerned," because "a wrong has been done and he's going to right it, even if it costs his father's reputation." Driven by a fanatic urge to implement a universal law of truth and justice, Sam Deeds initially antagonizes the members of the city council of the border town Frontero, in Rio County, who privilege their belatedly fabricated version of the past over and against all facts. At the end of his own odyssey, aimed not—as in *The Searchers*—at liberating a relative but at discovering the truth about his father, who was the sheriff before him, he, unlike Ford's Ethan Edwards, is able to return home. He can integrate himself into his community because he decides to allow the legend about his father to persist despite the facts he has discovered. For Sayles, the analogy between this self-righteous loner and the geo-cultural place he inhabits is particularly poignant because, as he explains to

Gavin Smith, since Texans "had their eye on becoming part of the United States, they said, 'We'll be the Lone Star. We're the individual who is eventually going to join the society.'"[1]

What is crucial for this iconoclastic student of John Ford, however, is the way in which both the history of Texas and the loner of the western tradition support the American ideology of integration and assimilation of contradictory—indeed, even incompatible—interests. In contrast to the classic master of the western, the postmodern revisionist John Sayles allows his hero to explore what a return to the gender and race trouble at the heart of the individual home might entail. Furthermore, he does not permit the unsolvable antagonism resulting from a collision of different cultural prejudices to disappear within the dark interior of the home. Rather, he explicitly fashions sites for this conflict, in the form of public spaces—a classroom in Frontero High School, bars and restaurants, and the town square, where the council members wish to erect a statue in memory of the late sheriff Buddy Deeds. These public sites are comparable to the verandas in *The Searchers*, for they, too, function as places for the public debate of differences about how to translate divergent conceptions about the past into a story that is viable for the entire community, and how to articulate and negotiate race and gender differences.

By crossmapping Sayles's *Lone Star* onto John Ford's late westerns, I assert that his narrative begins where a film like *The Searchers* leaves off—at the question of what has become of the West since the Second World War and the Cold War. More precisely, my claim is that John Sayles directly addresses the issue that though in the course of the alleged civilization of the West, the simple contradiction between a hostile wilderness and the provisional homes of the settlers may have been successfully resolved, it has been replaced by a new point of contention—the debate about how cultural hybridity, introduced into individual families and homes in such a manner that it cannot be eradicated, can be put to productive use for a community in general. Indeed, one might claim that in the late-twentieth-century Texas depicted by Sayles, a synthesis has been effected between the homely hearth and the uncanny prairie. The world outside the home has been fully domesticated, and a sense of public space has emerged, in which the claim to happiness proposed by individual families can no longer be considered apart from the universal interests of the community. After the allegedly "successful" campaign of white civilization, the inhabitants of Frontero can turn their backs on a battlefield inscribed by a clearly defined ethnic divide. In its stead, however, they are forced to confront a line of demarcation within the community itself. In this public space what collides is no longer individual members of hostile racial camps but divergent legends. The battle for anglicization of Texas ended when the Texans threw the Mexicans out and drew the boundary between the United States and Mexico. In the hybrid public space of late-twentieth-century Texas, however, all debate about how one is to commemorate the cultural legacy of this region inevitably suggests that the precise definition of what the "correct" representation of the past might be remains unfinished business. As the simple opposition between racial groups—Anglos, Indians, Mexicans, Hispanics, African Americans—has been transformed into the question of how the violent legends of the West's foundation are to be represented, what emerges is not merely a more differentiated picture but an unresolvable antagonism. There can be no history of the West that will harmoniously unite all the discordant versions representing the separate racial interest groups. At the same time, Sayles's film feeds off the recognition that we need legends in order to transform the antagonism at the heart of a Texan town like Frontero—or, one might claim, any American community—into a coherent story by which the community at large can live.

In one of the first scenes in *Lone Star*, an Anglo mother vehemently takes issue with the Hispanic teacher Pilar Cruz (Elizabeth Peña), whose history lessons she finds an offensive demontage of her cultural inheritance. "You're just tearin' everything down!" she shouts. "Tearin' down our heritage, tearin' down our history, tearin' down the memory of people that fought and died for this land." But before she can finish speaking, she is interrupted by an equally irate Chicano father, who yells, "We fought and died for this land, too!"—against the U.S. Army and against the Texas Rangers. Any claim that only the white settlers be credited with the founding of Texas must be emphatically rejected, he argues, because that version of the past radically excludes the actual hybridity of their contemporary reality. In response to an Anglo father's interpolation that the Chicanos lost their battle and should therefore accept the interpretation of those who won, which would amount to an exclusion of all divergent voices, the principal of the school suggests that it might be best "not to put things in terms of winners and losers." Once more the Anglo mother enters the debate, pointing out that in her history classes Pilar "has got everything switched around" and thus does not hold herself to the standard set by the textbook committee. Once more, the principal tries to calm her, arguing that textbooks are guides, "not an absolute." Yet the Anglo mother continues to hold out, insisting that anyone can believe what they want, but when it comes to what her children are taught, she must protest against what she perceives to be alien propaganda. She is once more interrupted, this time by a Chicana mother, who points out that even the category "our children" is hybrid: "They're our children, too!" she exclaims. "And as the cultural majority of this community we have the right."

At this point the battle of the living turns into a question about the claims the dead have in determining how events of the past are to be culturally recorded and commemorated. The Anglo father contends that the interests of those living in Frontero today should not be the measure of how history is taught. Instead, he says, the men who founded this state have a right to have their story told from their perspective, not in the version that the other side wishes to perpetuate. The aporia that Sayles's *mise-en-scène* highlights, of course, is that any representation of history inevitably mirrors the interests of those who are recounting it, and therefore any claim to one single version held as the only true account of the past represents an impossible reduction of different, indeed incompatible, descriptions of reality. Sayles has Danny, a Chicano journalist, bring up the pecuniary interests of the cotton business, which led the Anglo settlers to break with Texas, and an Anglo father immediately takes issue with Danny's comment, insisting—in the spirit of Althusser—that the ideologically dominant version of the imaginary relation that the citizens of this border town entertain toward their past is determined by the position from which this mythic story of the past is formulated: "You may call it history, but I call it propaganda. I'm sure they got their own account of the Alamo on the other side, but we're not *on* the other side, so we're not about to have it taught in our schools!"

Only now does the history teacher, Pilar, decide to take an active part in this battle over interpretation, defending herself against the accusation of being a propagandist by pointing out that assuming a simple opposition between those on this side of the border and those on the other side is untenable, because after generations of cultural interaction in this border region between Texas and Mexico, any clear demarcation between the white settlers and all the other racial groups that now make up the population of Texas is no longer possible. "I've only been trying to get across some of the complexity of our situation down here—cultures coming together in both negative and positive ways." The Anglo mother, however, fights for cultural hegemony to the end, trying to promote an ideologically simplistic founding legend of the world that she calls home: "If you mean like music and food and all, I have no problems with that, but when you start changing who did what to who." Another teacher supports Pilar in her plea for complexity against any attempt at simplification, noting, as if in appeasement, "We're not changing anything. We're presenting a more complete picture," yet the Anglo mother remains incorrigible. With angry determination she retorts, "And that's what's got to stop!"

In John Sayles's *mise-en-scène* she has the last word, not because he privileges her desire for an unambiguous representation of history but because he seeks to render visible the impossibility of arbitrating the question of which version of history is the one true and legitimate one once legends have become porous. Engaging the controversy that emerges as children begin to take issue with the family legacy they have inherited from their parents, Sayles in part portrays an altercation between iconoclasts, seeking an alleged truth, and iconologues, seeking to preserve the established story about the past. He also, however, depicts figures who want to turn their backs on the complex antagonism that arises on the battlefield between these incompatible representations. They stand for an impossible ground of convergence, a peaceful harmony beyond geocultural differences, regardless of whether it is articulated as the dream of romantic love (as Pilar will do at the end of the film) or as the dream of public fame (which will be preserved for Sam's father).

A few sequences after the battle over the history textbook, John Sayles shows Pilar teaching her students the impossibility of reducing to a simple story the disputes that emerged between the various ethnic inhabitants of Texas since its foundation, asking the class what one can deduce from all these parallel battles. Chet Payne (Eddie Robinson I) replies, "Everybody is killing everybody else?" He had been listening with only one ear, being absorbed with the particular battle he fights with his father every evening at home. Yet, because his own family is a site of altercation, he succinctly captures the essence of Pilar's argument for a complex rendition of the past against the Anglo mother's wish for an unequivocal, simple version of who did what to whom. In doing so, however, he also illustrates that in the course of a history lesson that takes into account racial difference, a search for complexity inevitably turns into a simple description of events. Too many points of view alienate him from the sequence of events presented to him, and because this complexity makes it impossible for him to identify with the general stories about the community he is part of, he can detect only what is diametrically opposed to the simple legend the Anglo mother wants—namely a meaningless stringing together of violent actions (the many dates that Pilar writes on the blackboard), even though that also is a simplification, a reduction of complexity.

As a synthesis of these two equally untenable positions—i.e., too much information or a reduction of information—that transforms a plethora of historical events to a mythic narrative, which necessarily excludes some of these events and the unsolvable contradiction they entail, John Sayles presents his cinematic engagement with the history of America, which takes the shape of an iconoclastic gesture on the part of the children that is aimed at reformulating the family and home romance they have inherited from their parents. In Sayles's view, to tell a viable narrative about the past, one must move away from both a radical complexity and an unequivocal simplification, regardless of whether this shift to a different mode of narrating the past involves the interests subtending a particular individual's version of the past or those of the community at large. I have already invoked Slavoj Žižek's argument that narrative emerges "in order to resolve some fundamental antagonism by rearranging its terms into a temporal succession." Narrative bears witness to some repressed antagonism precisely because, as Žižek explains, narrative resolution "silently presupposes as already given what it purports to reproduce."[2] Along the lines of the temporal loop he thus proposes, John Sayles's protagonists—the loner Sam Deeds, his childhood sweetheart Pilar Cruz, and her student Chet Payne—must formulate a sequence of past events that will result in a story by which they can live. They must construct from the shards of the past, from the pieces of family secrets that have been made available to them, a workable scenario for their lives.

In *Lone Star* both the location Texas and the quarrel over the way its history is to be taught serve as a metaphor to illustrate how any engagement with the past on the part of the next generation is tantamount to entering a battle zone. In his interview with Mick Frogley and Matt Symonds, Sayles argues that it is easier for most people to simply accept legends or to entirely rebel against them, rather "than really looking into the facts of it and realizing it was more complex."[3] If, in *Lone Star*, he renders this battleground visible, he does so in order to emphasize how all geocultural identity confronts the individual with an imposed choice. Each of his characters is compelled to explore her or his relation to the family legend because if they don't, the aftereffects of the past they seek to repress inevitably haunt them. And of course, this inquiry, from which no responsible person can escape, has a price. "We have to recognize that it is a battleground. We are never going to know the facts," Sayles explains. "What we are going to know is that there are many different ways to present this legend." In other words, legends, both cultural and familial, need to be reexamined by each generation in order to avoid a renewed outbreak of physical and emotional violence between ethnic groups and between individual family members. For Sayles, to live with contradictions at the very heart of the home as well as the community means consciously shifting the battleground from an abstract space outside the home to the intimate space within the home. In so doing, it is necessary to recognize that once the battle is fought at this site of interiority and intimacy, no one side can hope to win. Yet because the antagonism in which all narrative is grounded can never actually be resolved, the stories that emerge from the home front allow each of the combatants to redefine their imaginary relation to their real living conditions. To do so, they must acknowledge that, far from entirely discovering the facts, they can only learn that there are different ways to present the past.

"History," John Sayles explains in his interview with Eric Foner, "especially the stories we like to believe or know about ourselves, is part of the ammunition we take with us into the everyday battle of how we define ourselves and how we act toward other people."[4] Recalling John Ford's explicitly monumental gesture of framing his version of the American founding myth of the West, one might characterize the aesthetic dictum underlying Sayles's iconoclastic reformulation of this legend as a shift from the monumental to the multiperspectival. At the same time, Sayles insists that while the history one presents is a point of view—a framed picture—historical evidence imposes limits on the subjectivity of any one version. What is, however, particularly crucial for Sayles's notion of one's engagement with history as a battleground, in which past events receive new interpretations even while legends are preserved, is that the equation between subjective perspective and storytelling also raises the question of responsibility. The battle involves more than the collision of different ethnic groups in their efforts to resignify the legend of the West; any effort at redefining our imaginary relationship to the events of the past also inevitably enmeshes general history with personal family stories.

While Sam Deeds's search for the true reasons why his father became the most popular sheriff of Frontero allows him to rewrite his particular family romance, it is also embedded in the public debate over whether history in general can be rewritten, such that who did what to whom in the past is reformulated as well. This allows John Sayles to offer a synthesis between trying to shield oneself from the irreconcilable complexity of past events and wishing to confront this contradiction as the dark kernel subtending all home and family identity. Sober about the amount of agency that any individual can claim, Sayles explains, "There's nothing we can do about history. We can learn what really happened, but we can't change it."[5] Nevertheless, as a nostalgic believer in enlightenment, like Ford, he holds on to the possibility of escaping the fatality that history dictates—at least when it comes to the resolution of his own film narrative. At the end of his odyssey into the past, his lonely hero Sam Deeds finds a way back to the community, by finally returning to his first love, Pilar. In contrast to Ethan Edwards, he is ultimately able to cross the threshold and enter a home in which he will be able to claim a mastery of sorts. Yet paradoxically, he can do so because, in contrast to John Ford's obsolete hero, he can turn his back on the past. Sometimes, John Sayles notes, "what you have to do is just forget history, you have to escape it."[6]

Of Facts and Legends

Claiming to lay bare the hidden facts behind a founding myth, while also seeking to preserve the legend that has succeeded precisely because those facts have remained concealed, Sayles not only pays tribute to the ambivalent oscillation between iconography and iconoclasm that subtends John Ford's own cinematic work on the legend of the West but also explicitly rewrites Ford's staging—in *The Man Who Shot Liberty Valance* (1962)— of both individual and communal efforts to put to rest a past that has not yet been resolved.[7]

Ford's film opens with Senator Ransom Stoddard (James Stewart) returning to Shinbone with his wife, Hallie (Vera Miles), for the funeral of their old friend Tom Doniphon (John Wayne). The local reporters immediately recognize Stoddard as the man who became a legend because he shot Liberty Valance (Lee Marvin) and thus liberated the town from the outlaw's violence, and so they pressure him to tell them why he came all the way out west from the capital to bury a man so insignificant that the younger reporters can discover nothing about him in the newspaper archive and so poor that he died without his boots on and without his gun. While Stoddard initially refuses to tell his story, the journalists insist it is their right to know the truth. Ford uses a flashback to reveal the mysterious circumstances that led to the killing of the outlaw and the founding of the civilized community of Shinbone, yet insists in the final scenes of the film that this more accurate version can never replace the legend everyone has come to live with. After the reporters have discovered that the man lying in the coffin was the actual killer of Liberty Valance, they refuse to print the story, explaining to the astonished senator that, this being the West, "when the legend becomes fact, print the legend." As Peter Bogdanovich notes, this is perhaps John Ford's most mournful, tragic film, because it illustrates not only the monumental power of legend but also the sacrifice that it inevitably entails. The man epitomizing the Old West dies a pauper, while the man of the New West "has ridden to success on the achievement of the first, who was discarded, forgotten." And while there is nothing wrong with the New West, it becomes clear that Ford's love remains with the wilderness now lost to the inevitable march of progress.[8]

In *Lone Star*, John Sayles self-consciously exploits this privileging of legend over fact. From the mayor, Hollis Pogue (Clifton James), who was deputy sheriff at the time of the mysterious disappearance of the violent and cruel sheriff Charlie Wade (Kris Kristofferson), Sam Deeds discovers that, contrary to what he wishes to believe, it wasn't his father, Buddy Deeds (Matthew McConaughey), who killed his predecessor, Sheriff Wade; it was the honorable mayor, Hollis Pogue, himself the deputy sheriff. During a dispute in a bar he had pulled the trigger on his boss, Sheriff Wade, because the sheriff had threatened to kill the African American bar boy, Otis Payne (Gabriel Casseus). Hollis ultimately confesses to Sam because he fears that the son's investigation will mean the other members of the Frontero community will trust Sam's suspicion of his father's guilt more than the story they have been told about Sheriff Buddy Deeds. Once he has heard the facts of the story, Sam, who had initially been so eager to make the truth public, responds the same way the reporters did in Ford's film: "Buddy's a goddamn legend. He can handle it." Here John Sayles critically dismantles Ford's trust in the myth of the West but then respectfully reinstalls it with his own cinematic tribute to legend, all the while, of course, having recourse to his predecessor's staging of the division between a legitimate law and an obscene one that was as big a threat to the project of civilization as any Indian hostility.

The primal scene of violence in Stoddard's narrative occurs at a time before the railroads had been completed, when a law of open violence still reigned in the West. The young lawyer Stoddard, who has come to Shinbone to open a law office there and has brought with him the code of laws sanctioned by Washington, D.C., is attacked by Liberty Valance before he reaches the town, robbed of all his money, and humiliated before the other passengers of the stagecoach. Liberty Valance rips up his legal books and, with a whip in his hand, explains to the young lawyer, crouching before him on the ground, "I'll teach you the law. Western law." Thus from the start, Ford intertwines the controversy between two diametrically opposed representatives of the law with a controversy between two diametrically opposed versions of the past. As James McBride and Michael Wilmington note, "What we are really seeing is not the building of a legend but a gradual stripping away of Stoddard's illusions."[9] Although he remains in Shinbone and ultimately succeeds in pushing through his version of the law—his political career begins with his election as the city's representative at the state assembly—Stoddard is also made to recognize the fallibility of his moral rejection of violent solutions to legal problems. For in this world where the marshal of the town has the right but not the power to arrest the outlaw Liberty Valance, only the most simple course of action—a duel with clearly demarcated sides—can settle the dispute. Furthermore, the double disillusionment played through in the film—stripping Stoddard of his illusions about the feasibility of official law and at the same time stripping the reporters of their belief in the founding legend of civilized Shinbone—feeds off a second contradiction: Stoddard learns to accept that only an illegal act of violence can successfully combat the outlaw, but he discovers that even on the battleground of simple oppositions he is impotent. Only a third party—Tom, who has repeatedly saved Stoddard by threatening to use his gun against Liberty Valance—can effectively fight the lawyer's battle, yet he must do it clandestinely and be sacrificed for it to boot. When Stoddard and Valance finally meet one night for the showdown, Tom waits in a side alley and shoots the outlaw in the back, then recedes into the shadows.

Ford's inclusion of this ambivalently encoded figure, who upholds the official law by means of its obscene underbelly—namely the illegitimate violence that authorities have banned from the community—inspires John Sayles to develop a more complex legend of the Old West. Tom Doniphon serves as a model for Sayles's Sheriff Buddy Deeds precisely because he is willing to defend the official law, even though his means are as obscene as those of his adversary. As J. A. Place notes, Tom and Liberty represent the two sides of the Old West in its proposition of freedom and passion for the individual, rendering Liberty as a mythic figure of evil and Tom as a mythic hero.[10] By killing Liberty for Stoddard, Tom enacts the ritual of progress through his own body, destroying not only the adversary of the official law but also himself. Only he and Stoddard know that the decisive shot was fired by him, and he will die preserving this secret, while the public is happy to ascribe it to the man who will subsequently represent them in Washington.

Yet in his film, Ford includes both versions—the official one and the clandestine one—to perform the incompatibility between fact and legend on which the successful civilization of the West is based. In the official version, he shows Stoddard with a drawn revolver in his right hand, staggering toward Liberty Valance, who is waiting for him on the empty nocturnal main street. After his opponent has shot him in the right arm, forcing him to drop his gun, Stoddard reaches for it with his left hand and fires his one shot. Liberty Valance falls dead to the ground. Tom will prove this to be an inaccurate account of the facts, yet, significantly, he does so not in order to procure his own fame or the love of Hallie (who ends up marrying Stoddard instead of him). Rather, Ford presents Tom's version as part of the confession he makes to Stoddard to convince him that he must accept the symbolic mandate of representing the interests of the small farmers of Shinbone in Washington. It is, of course, impossible to prove that Tom is being absolutely truthful in his claim that he fired the fatal shot from a side street at exactly the same moment that Stoddard fired, so that only one shot was heard. It is more significant that the narrative of Tom's killing Valance in cold blood convinces Stoddard that he has a duty toward the community. Tom is able to live with the guilt and the lack of public recognition because he understands that to be the sacrifice that has to be made in order for Stoddard's civilizing law to replace that of the outlaw in the New West.

Equally crucial to the success of legend with regard to this killing, however, is that the actual truth must remain a secret shared by the two men who were there, and this secret informs all of their subsequent actions. This subterfuge is preserved as a lacuna in the public knowledge of the community—whose members prefer to believe the rumors about what happened that night rather than seeking out the truth. At the same time, since Tom Doniphon, like the lonely Ethan Edwards played by John Wayne six years earlier, decides to clandestinely take the law into his own hands, he will be unable to fulfill his dream of home. Seeing Ransom emerge from his duel with Liberty wounded but alive, Hallie chooses him over Tom and decides to turn her back on her hometown and follow him to Washington. After Tom finds Hallie in the arms of the man whose life he has just saved, he burns down the home he had hoped to share with her. Ford uses Tom's destruction of the home to illustrate how, in destroying his adversary, the hero of the Old West has actually destroyed his own existential space. He is sacrificed along with the obscene representative of "western law" because by taking the law into his own hands in the name of the "official" law designed in Washington he helped pave the way for a destruction of the lawless world—but that was the only world in which he could exist. In contrast to Ethan, who can wander the prairie forever and who will be remembered forever by his relatives and friends, Tom disappears into oblivion, forgotten by the community of Shinbone.[11] Of course, Ford's own juxtaposition of legend and fact feeds off the contradiction that while the newspaper editor is not willing to print the corrected version he has heard from Stoddard, his own cinematic narrative makes these clandestine facts public. Seminal to Sayles's transposition of the plot developed by Ford in *The Man Who Shot Liberty Valance* is that although we discover the truth in the end, we know it only as clandestine knowledge, as a secret shared by a happy few. Or, as Slavoj Žižek argues, what makes the anagnorisis of this film so subversive is that Ford, "while endorsing the myth, simultaneously renders visible the mechanism of its fabrication."[12]

Shared Secrets

In *Lone Star*, John Sayles resignifies the narrative that is seminal to the founding myth of the West—that civilization can succeed only if a law of radical extremes is overcome. At the heart of his journey into the past, Sam Deeds discovers that the jurisdiction legitimated by the community can triumph over the anachronistic lawlessness of the Old West only by virtue of a collectively sanctioned ritual of killing. The sacrifice of the obscene law, so fundamental to the emergence of a New West, however, inflicts a double bind on the very legality it is meant to install. The death sentence executed by Tom renders visible the rottenness in the law, even as it can succeed in cementing the jurisdiction of the community only by virtue of the second crime—that of keeping secret the cold-blooded murder he has committed.

Ford's own ambivalence toward progress allows him to insist that while the transformation of the prairie into a garden may require the ritual killing of those who, owing to their illegal actions, cannot be integrated into the community, the traces of this sacrifice can never be totally eradicated. The secret may be buried along with the corpses of the outlaw and his real killer, yet it is preserved in the collective memory of those involved, as though it shared a crypt with them. While Liberty Valance's corpse decomposes in its grave, the clandestine yet true version of his death continues to affect the community of survivors, obliquely giving voice to the "illegitimate" side of its jurisdiction and leading members of the next generation to suspect a clandestine breach in legality at the heart of all legends about progress and civilization. For John Ford, history was always a question of taking a subjective point of view. At the end of this narrative about secrets and sacrifices, Stoddard and his wife are again in a train car, turning their backs on Shinbone. As the conductor assures the senator that nothing is too good for the man who shot Liberty Valance, Stoddard pensively looks at his feet. Like Tom, he can live with the lie that has become official truth; preserving the secret is his ammunition in the battle he fights in Washington for the community of farmers out West.

The psychoanalysts Nicolas Abraham and Maria Torok have suggested that in a metapsychological sense, the reality of fantasy work can be compared to a secret, with the daydreamer a cryptophore of sorts. "Just as desire is born along with prohibition," they assert, "reality too, at least in the metapsychological sense, is born of the necessity of remaining concealed, unspoken." This leads them to suggest that the primal scene of psychic reality "is comparable to an offense, a crime. The crime's name is not identical with prohibition. . . . Its name is genuinely affirmative, therefore unutterable." At the same time, if this inception is to be thought of along the lines of founding myths, it must necessarily be a collective affair; "All secrets are shared at the start," they continue. "Hence the 'crime' under consideration cannot be a solitary one, since it was turned into a secret. The 'crime' points to an accomplice, the locus of undue enjoyment, as well as to others who are excluded and, by dint of this enjoyment, eliminated."[13]

My interest in crossmapping *Lone Star* onto John Ford's late westerns is that both illustrate this notion that psychic reality produces an affective bond between members of a community on the basis of the shared yet clandestine knowledge of a crime. For both, the inaugural crime must remain covered up. As a shared secret, however, it means that a fulfilled desire lies buried in the initial transgressive act. That desire cannot be brought out into the open, but it will not disappear either. The resilient survival of a bond forged on the basis of clandestine knowledge thus also consists in the fact that it haunts those who are in on the secret. At the same time, those in the know are also fully aware that their bond precludes revelation of this secret knowledge, not least because it thrives on the cryptophoric desire that holds it together.

What Ford stages only indirectly by choosing the dark interiors as the position for his camera and as the vanishing point for his characters, Sayles uses as the starting point for his engagement with the history of America. In legends of the West, the notion of home always harbors a crypt, in which lies buried the clandestine knowledge of a crime that proved to be constitutive for the emergence of the community. This is a knowledge passed on to subsequent generations along with the architectural signs of progress—the house fronts, the verandas, the streets, and the railway tracks. But it is passed on as a kept secret, resulting in what Abraham and Torok call transgenerational haunting. One might therefore surmise the following: The imaginary relationship that the Texans entertain to their real-life conditions by virtue of the legends about the West contains not only a nostalgia for the lost world of archaic, lawless enjoyment. It is also inscribed by an internal disquiet, which feeds off the conviction that the objective and active existence of a secret is the prerequisite for home as an existential category. Each concretely lived psychic reality of home straddles the consciously shared repression of an inaugural secret and the publicly acclaimed founding legend of the community. In order to emphasize that this secrecy informs both those who were initially directly involved and the generations who follow, Abraham and Torok introduce a further term—the phantom. This spectral apparition refers to an invention, brought into circulation by the living, which allows them to give body to the cryptic knowledge that has emerged from the unwittingly inherited legacy of family secrets.[14]

Returning to Slavoj Žižek's claim that we tell ourselves stories about the family or the community in order to resolve some fundamental antagonism, one might now offer the following speculation: whether conceived as an individual family romance or as a collectively shared ideology, the stories we tell about our origins translate this irresolvable contradiction into a protective fiction, imposing it on what Žižek calls "the traumatic kernel" that threatens to disintegrate the individual, the family, or the community. Symbolic fictions thus function as a tempering symbolic structure. Žižek concedes that within the dispute over the most accurate representation of historical events, objective facts might well be presented in the sense of an undistorted view of social reality. For example, Pilar writes on her blackboard the dates of all the battles that were fought around the Mexican American border after the founding of Texas. According to Žižek, however, such a non-narrational representation misses the actual social antagonism that is at stake, while the non-symbolizable traumatic kernel finds articulation precisely in the subjective distortions of the rendition of facts. This non-symbolizable traumatic kernel surfaces in the stories or legends we choose to tell about who is the winner and who the loser, not just in a particular battle but in the more general struggle for the dominant interpretation. The psychic reality of a community is regulated through symbolic fictions that emerge from a founding antagonism, even while that issue is kept as a shared secret. When protective fictions fail, however, the shared secret returns in the form of a phantom, insisting on a renegotiation of currently dominant narrations.

Two points need to be stressed here. After the event, each inaugurating crime already belongs to the realm of symbolic fictions at the same time that they are complemented by phantomatic fictions. Regardless of whether the residents of Frontero know the exact conditions that led to the mysterious disappearance of Sheriff Charlie Wade, the man whom Sam believes his father to have killed, the fantasy that a crime occurred is in itself enough to guarantee a harmonious coexistence. While the crime clandestinely committed by some of the older members of the city points to the non-symbolizable traumatic kernel at the heart of each community, the fundamental antagonism at stake is already negotiated as a social antagonism. The unexplained disappearance of Sheriff Wade is a particular event, a representation of an individual case, that renders visible how the coherence of community depends upon the violent exclusion of a figure that can't be integrated into its social reality. The fundamental antagonism at the heart of symbolic fictions is thus rendered visible as a belated, spatially and temporally displaced representation, relocated on the level of signs. At the same time, the actuality of such an antagonism becomes accessible when, owing to an accident, symbolic fictions divide into two groups—official symbolic fictions (the versions of history sanctioned by different interest groups in a community or the family romances that individuals have fashioned for themselves) and the phantomatic fantasies, which, according to Žižek, fill the fissures left open in official symbolic fictions. Symbolic fictions and phantomatic fantasies thus function as mirror inversions of each other. Because of the former, a community can fashion for itself an image of harmonious social coexistence by repressing fundamental incompatibilities at its heart—which is to say, by functioning as an imaginary, albeit provisional, home. The phantomatic fiction, in turn, gives body to this repression and makes the mechanisms of denial visible.

What returns with the phantom is a message about the rottenness at the heart of the official law, which had initially been used to combat the archaic obscene enjoyment of violence. This also supports the iconoclasm of the children who, without this revelation, would remain helpless against the secrets they have inherited from their parents. Responding to the call of such a phantom, Sam Deeds embarks upon a journey into the past, searching in this heterotopic geography for information that will allow him to unconditionally accept his father's legacy, even while his discoveries will also allow him finally to relinquish this dead family member, who has been haunting him throughout his adult life. He can ultimately return home, because he has laid the ghost of his father to rest by accepting the symbolic mandate that his father represents—that is, by accepting the resilience of shared secrets.

So as to visually foreground the question of transgenerational haunting from the start, John Sayles begins *Lone Star* with a scene of uncanny discovery. Two soldiers, Cliff (Stephen Mendillo) and Mickey (Stephen J. Lang), find a skull while looking for bullet shells in the former rifle range of the army post Fort McKenzie, on the periphery of Frontero. Shortly after arriving at the scene, Sheriff Sam Deeds is given a rusty sheriff's badge by Mickey, who found it lying close to the skeleton. As the soldier suggests that this is the scene of a crime, Sam replies, "No telling yet if there's been a crime," adding, however, "This country's seen a good number of disagreements over the years." In other words, *Lone Star* begins where *The Man Who Shot Liberty Valance* does: with a dead body, returned to the living and posing a hermeneutic task. In contrast to Ford's film, however, the man who insists he has a right to discover the truth behind this death is not a disinterested reporter but rather the representative of the official law himself, who all his life has resisted the legends revolving around his father and their declarations that there "won't be another like him." In the skeleton that has accidentally come into his field of vision he recognizes the phantom that will allow him to uncover the family secret he has inherited, although he cannot name what it contains.

As in Ford's film, the return of this excluded dead person, who has been lying for many years in an unmarked grave on the border between Texas and Mexico, puts the legend about the foundation of Frontero at risk. Sam, suspecting immediately that the corpse is that of his father's predecessor, who suddenly disappeared in 1957, returns to the city to report the macabre finding to the mayor, Hollis Pogue, and to question him about the night he saw Sheriff Charlie Wade for the last time. In the restaurant of Mercedes Cruz (Miriam Colon), the mother of his childhood sweetheart, Pilar, and one of the oldest members of the city council, a debate unfolds between the son, seeking to call the legitimacy of his father's fame into question, and his father's longtime friend, who, along with the other members of the city council, has decided to erect a Buddy Deeds memorial in front of the courthouse. With this statue, they wish to commemorate the law represented by the young man who had returned as a war hero from Korea and had successfully served as sheriff of Frontero for thirty years.

In Sayles's version of the murder that founded this social community, however, a significant transformation has occurred with respect to the figures involved. In answer to Sam's request that he describe the last dispute between Buddy Deeds and Charlie Wade, Hollis has recourse to the opposition between an obscene and a legitimate representative of the law, as this had been elaborated by Ford in his late westerns. However, the official representative of the community's law, Sheriff Charlie Wade, described by Hollis as one of the old-fashioned "bash and bribe or bullets kind of sheriffs," is the one who occupies the position of the outlaw in Ford's story. Insisting on his share of all of the illegal businesses operating in Frontero during the 1950s, he had become known as someone who had no problem with blurring the boundary between the official law of the court and the law of open violence.

As in Ford's late westerns, the primal scene of violence in *Lone Star* has been displaced into an earlier, obsolete period, in which an archaic enjoyment of violence was considered acceptable. Sayles has the witnesses of the past relate scenes in which Sheriff Wade beat up or killed in cold blood those subjected to his obscene misuse of power, notably the African American and Chicano members of the community, to whom he gave bar privileges only if he got his share of the profits, and the Mexican wetbacks whom he discovered illegally crossing the border. The scene described by Hollis is thus paradigmatic. He remembers how Wade explained this blackmail to his new deputy sheriff, Buddy Deeds, as they sat in the restaurant run at the time by the Mexican Jimmy Herrera (one of the men he was blackmailing). Wade ordered his deputy to pick up his share at the beginning of each month, but Buddy refused to participate in this illegal transaction and threatened to bring his superior before the law, suggesting that the sheriff put his shield on the table and vanish. Charlie, who had already walked toward the exit of the restaurant, at this point turned—as we see in the flashback that Sayles inserts into his cinematic narrative—toward his opponent. For a second the two men tarry in the pose of a combat about to begin—Charlie already touching his revolver, while Buddy slowly places his gun on the table, next to his plate. Asking the sheriff, "You ever shoot anybody was looking you in the eye? Whole different story, isn't it?" Buddy actually succeeds in psychically disarming his opponent. Charlie moves toward Buddy and, leaning over the table, uses words rather than bullets to intimidate him: "You're a dead man." All the while the other deputy sheriff, Hollis, has been watching the scene silently. After the sheriff has turned his back on his opponent, Hollis furtively gives Buddy his hat, then both leave the restaurant. In all the testimonies that Sam forces out of those who repeatedly witnessed Sheriff Wade's arbitrary use of violence, Hollis emerges as the one who is unsettled by the breach of the law taking place before his eyes, yet he is also the one who remains silent—an unwilling accomplice. In so doing, he resembles Ford's marshal far more than he does Ransom Stoddard, who, after all, resiliently pits his books of law against the outlaw's dreaded revolver. Hollis ends this first report to the present sheriff of Frontero by explaining that Wade disappeared the next day with $10,000 dollars of county funds from the safe at the jail. Although he is sympathetic toward Sam because he recognizes that Sam has had some problems with his dead father, he nevertheless ends his recollection of the past events by insisting on the legend. "Buddy Deeds," he assures the doubtful son, "was my salvation."

In contrast to *The Man Who Shot Liberty Valance*, in Sayles's film the dead body of the representative of an obscene violent law functions as the catalyst for his story—not the dead body of his opponent, the cowboy who died in oblivion. Thereby Sayles seems to say that what haunts the later generations is less the morally ambivalent, lonely hero of the western legend, who may take the law into his own hands but does so in the name of an official moral code, than the obscene representative of the law. The corpse of Charlie Wade, hidden from sight yet remembered, stands for a point at which the rotten core of the law and the official law collapse, rendering the difference between the two no longer clear. As a result, the ambivalent hero of the western legend—Buddy Deeds—undergoes a double transformation. He returns home from the Korean War and becomes a successful representative of law and order, first as deputy sheriff and then as sheriff of Frontero, because he is able to resignify Wade's insistence on having a part in the transgressive businesses taking place within his jurisdiction. As his son discovers in the course of his investigation, Buddy Deeds did not turn down dubious propositions made to him by those in power. In contrast to his predecessor, however, who in the spirit of the outlaw tried to advance his individual hunger for power, Buddy Deeds understood his own interests as being part of the political machinery of the public. He used his position as sheriff to erect a public space within which the differences between the diverse ethnic groups were not necessarily eradicated but no longer had to be fought out by means of open confrontation.

Sam also finds that the sheriff's public display of violence could be eliminated because the psychic reality of the community of Frontero operated on the principle of a shared secret—the murder of his predecessor—and this came to subtend an unspoken political agreement between the leaders of the diverse ethnic groups. After the disappearance of Charlie Wade, payment of illegal money to the legal authority was no longer at stake; rather, the task became the securing of common political interests, which required that any fundamental incommensurability in this community be buried so that mutual interests could prevail. At the same time, Sayles also rewrites the western hero's ambivalence toward the home and the happiness of individual families that it makes a claim to. In contrast to Ethan, who can only wander in the prairie, and in contrast to Tom, who inhabits the part of the home that survived the fire he set to it, Buddy Deeds came to have two homes. The social and the private aspects of the legend about him are poignantly intertwined, for during more than fifteen years of his marriage to Sam's mother, he had carried on a clandestine affair with Mercedes Cruz—an alliance that the members of the city council were fully aware of. Indeed, as Sam learns at the very end of his journey into the past, the result of this doubly transgressive affair—merging adultery with miscegenation—was his childhood sweetheart, Pilar, whom he has begun to court again. Discovering the truth about his father proves to be coterminous with discovering the truth about his love.

The second rendition of the dispute between Charlie Wade and his insubordinate deputy sheriff finally allows Sam to comprehend the real meaning of Hollis Pogue's declaration that Buddy had been his salvation. As in Ford's film, the confession uncovering the truth of past events is a forced one. Only because Sam's investigation threatens to bring their authority into question are his father's friends willing to reveal what actually happened the night Charlie Wade disappeared. This time it isn't the mayor, but rather Otis Payne (Ron Canada), the owner of the only African American bar in Frontero, who recounts the past. He remembers that, still a bar boy then, he had been running a game of cards on the side in the back, trying not to let his superior or Charlie Wade know about it, because he didn't want to cut them in. That night, Charlie Wade suddenly appeared and caught him in the act. He first beat the young man, then dragged him back to the front part of the bar, where he demanded that Otis take down the cigarette box containing a gun that was hidden next to some bottles behind the counter. Hollis, once again standing silent next to Wade, realizes that he means to shoot the young man and declare after the fact that Otis had violently resisted arrest. As in *The Man Who Shot Liberty Valance*, it is an unequal duel, for Otis, unaware of the fateful turn of events taking place behind his back, has—like Stoddard—no chance to defend himself against the shot the obscene representative of the law is about to fire.

Although Sayles takes from Ford's narrative the murky meetings ground of heroism and cold-blooded murder, his killer Hollis is not someone who would ever have taken the law into his own hands before this; rather, he used to be the accomplice of a corrupt law, in that he silently stood by, watching as Wade abused his victims. While in Sayles's narrative about a foundational murder a third figure also intervenes in a fatal quarrel, Hollis—in contrast to Tom—does so not clandestinely but demonstratively. At the same time, he isn't the only one to fire a significant shot. Before Charlie Wade is able to fire at Otis Payne, Buddy, who has just entered the bar, calls to him, demanding that he drop his gun. Two shots are fired almost simultaneously, hitting Charlie, who is still aiming his gun at Otis's back. Sayles follows Ford's story in that it isn't the man who became a legend who fired the deadly shots but the one who initially stood in the shadow of the sheriff—and will continue to do so once Buddy Deeds takes Charlie Wade's place. In contrast to Ford's Tom Doniphon, however, the man who destroys the representative of an obscene law doesn't fall into oblivion; he himself becomes the powerful politician.

What Sam thus discovers is not only that in suspecting his father he had ascribed the murder to the wrong man. He discovers also that the facts were a well-kept, though shared, secret that had forged a bond between his father, Mayor Hollis Pogue, and the two most powerful leaders of the town's ethnic groups, Otis Payne and Mercedes Cruz. The three men had decided to bury the corpse out by the post and to steal money from the county to make it appear that Charlie Wade had run off with it. They would actually give the money to Mercedes Cruz to set up her restaurant. In closing, Otis explains, "Time went on, people liked the story that we told better than anything the truth might have been." Sam proves to have been uncannily astute when, at the beginning, he cautioned the soldiers who had found the skeleton that there was no telling yet whether there had been a crime. In the act of violence at the heart of his father's fame the distinction between good and evil has become unrecognizable, for the killing of one man saved the life of another.

Hollis Pogue thus is modeled partly on Senator Ransom Stoddard, since he will become the politician of the group, and partly on Tom Doniphon. Yet in contrast to Ford's obsolete hero he kills not in cold blood but to defend someone else, thus committing manslaughter and not murder. By structuring the killing in this way, Sayles has the two deputy sheriffs, Deeds and Pogue, share the heroic gesture of resorting to the archaic law of violence in the name of civilization. More significantly, in contrast to Tom Doniphon, neither of them has to be sacrificed along with the outlaw for the project of multicultural integration to succeed. Even the figure who becomes a successful politician as a result of his role in this killing occupies several positions. Hollis Pogue becomes mayor, and Otis Payne, the accomplice of the two deputy sheriffs, soon takes over the bar and thus becomes the unofficial mayor of the African American section of Frontero, called Blacktown.

As in Ford's film, uncovering the truth of the past renders visible the fissures of the western legend. Here, however, the director's intent is not to voice nostalgia for the world that had to be sacrificed but to celebrate how a chain of accidental events of transgression can serve to install a law of survival. The man who didn't shoot becomes a legend (Buddy Deeds), while the two friends who have survived him and are seeking to build a memorial to him (Otis Payne and Hollis Pogue) have no problem living with their clandestine deeds, since those deeds gave rise to their political authority. Because the story Otis has told under extortion is morally too complex for any simple resolution, Sam himself ultimately enters into an alliance with the men who are bound together by the secret they share. In the course of Otis's confession Sam has shifted his view 180 degrees and is now willing to accept the official version of the sudden disappearance of Charlie Wade: it was simply one of those unsolved cases of violence for which Texas is famous. His father's legend has finally become, for him, a viable imaginary reworking of reality, a home he can emotionally inhabit with impunity.

Forget the Alamo

As in *The Searchers*, the lone hero Sam, before he can look into the future, must traverse the heterotopic space of the past as though it were a countersite to his present, knowing that remnants of the events that he will discard after he closes his investigation will continue to haunt him as memory traces. In order to render visible throughout the film that Sam is living in the shadow of his deceased father, Sayles includes flashbacks that are not distinguished from the present by cuts or superimpositions. As Sam asks his father's peers to recall scenes from the past, for example, the camera simply pans to one side of the film frame, thereby moving in one continuous shot into a different time, the heterotopia of a remembered past juxtaposed with the present. "The purpose of a cut or a dissolve," Sayles explains in his interview with Dennis and Joan West, "is to say this is a border, and the things on opposite sides of the border are meant to be different in some way, and I wanted to erase that border and show that these people are still reacting to things in the past."[15] Indeed, as Philip Kemp notes, for Sayles, "the past isn't another country; it's still here and people like Sam are living it, carrying it with them."[16] Along these lines, Sayles stages the peripeteia of Sam's renewed romance with his childhood sweetheart as a spatialization of time. For the first time since his return to his hometown two years ago, Sam is able to engage Pilar in an intimate conversation, using the occasion to remind her of their clandestine love. As they walk along the river, which is the border between Mexico and Texas, his own distinction between past and present becomes blurred.[17] Pilar suddenly leaves him, overwhelmed by the intensity of their mutual desire for each other, and Sam continues to tarry at the border, which for the wetbacks illegally fleeing Mexico represents freedom. Sheriff Wade, in contrast, viewed the river as a line of demarcation that no one was allowed to pass with impunity; if anyone did, he was justified in killing that person.

At this border, so violently contested in the history of this part of America, Sam isn't after a testimony from his lost beloved Pilar, as he will be in the many places he seeks out later. Rather, with the help of a camera panning along the riverbank, Sayles introduces the conversation that Sam has preserved in his memory, the moment when, sitting on the riverbank, he and Pilar confessed to each other that they felt their love was no sin. Like Ethan at the navel of his heterotopic prairie, Sam now recognizes that the confession of a shared affection for the woman whom he has rediscovered will allow him now to emotionally and symbolically return to his hometown by accepting his part in the community, rather than excluding himself from it. The family romance he has been nourishing, in which he takes on the role of the narcissistically wounded son resisting the authority of his father, can be resignified in the name of a different family romance, one in which his past love for Pilar can overcome their present separation in order to fashion a utopian vision of how this past happiness might be carried into the future. At stake in this sublation of the tacit antagonism underlying the love between Sam and Pilar is more than the obliteration of past psychic wounds and differences. At issue instead is how to psychically sustain the murky interface between right and wrong that becomes evident once Sam discovers that their love quite literally involves transgressing cultural taboos, not just miscegenation between the son of an Anglo sheriff and the daughter of a Mexican restaurateur but also incest.

If Sam's psychic journey involves traversing a heterotopic space in which past and present are juxtaposed, so as to uncover the complex interests involved in his father's controversy with Charlie Wade, it also contains the countermove.[18] In the course of his investigation Sam reorders the fragments that witnesses offer him into a coherent narrative sequence, which allows him to translate the violent differences that brought about the new, hybrid Frontero into a meaningful story. At the beginning of his search Sam examines a group photograph of Sheriff Wade and his team, analyzing it with a magnifying glass, isolating certain details from the image. Several scenes later, Sayles cinematically performs the work of the pathologist sent down to Frontero by the Texas Rangers. In a shot focusing only on the pathologist's hands, we see him place the black-and-white photographs taken at the alleged crime scene, one after the other, on the table, forming a sequence that begins with a long shot of the opened grave and moves on to several close-up shots of the skull and the Masonic ring found next to it. These images eventually begin to take on a materiality of their own, as Sayles superimposes the photographs onto the actual body parts found. The camera pans from the bottom upward along the fully cleansed skeleton, whose bones have been reassembled. With the next superimposition Sayles shows us the gloved hand of the pathologist measuring one of the bones. The next cut shows us the rusty sheriff's badge being placed in cleaning fluid. After briefly returning to the pathologist as he measures the jaw and the upper part of the skull, Sayles concludes this sequence by having the pathologist lift the now fully cleaned badge from the acid with a pair of tweezers, to show us a close-up of its inscription: "Rio County." Like Sam, the pathologist is trying to reassemble the fragments of the dead body and its paraphernalia in a manner that will make it possible to file a clear report. The report he subsequently hands over to the current sheriff of Frontero supports Sam's suspicion that the corpse is that of Charlie Wade. However, the pathologist's findings do not lead to a coherent narrative that offers an unequivocal explanation of the death that occurred, because after such a long period of decomposition he can no longer determine the cause of death.

Sayles offers another visualization of the assembling of fragments, having that exercise function as an attempt to inhabit the past. This runs parallel to the stories of the witnesses that Sam questions. One night he sits at his office desk, flipping through the death certificates of people whom Wade had killed, claiming they had resisted arrest. Next to these official papers from the Texas Department of Health lie copies of the sheriff's payroll, contracts for the sale of property around Frontero, and Sam's notes of the witnesses' reports, where he has recorded the dates and the names of the central characters involved in the events that occurred in the last years of Charlie Wade's term as sheriff. Sayles has the camera pan over these documents, cutting together diverse bits and pieces, focusing only on details, to emphasize that Sam is as yet able only to recognize fragments rather than any ordering principle. These documents also represent a geography that he can't inhabit. To make visible the point that Sam is far less able to move fluently in this material than in the stories told to him by the witnesses, Sayles pits the representation of these official documents, rendered cinematically as brief closeups of fragments and superimposed images, against the smooth transition with which he marks the lack of a boundary between past and present when it comes to personal memory, narrated orally to a witness of the next generation. At one point in this sequence, Sayles actually holds a superimposition for several seconds, displaying how Sam's face, searching for some revelation, dissolves with the signs on the official documents that he is unable to decipher. The camera then pans from the top down to Sam's notes. Once more we see only brief excerpts, so that we are forced to wander through the material presented on the screen without actually finding any coherent image. Sayles concludes the uncanny visual juxtapositions of documents and notes with a close-up of Sam's right hand, which, having reached the bottom of a page of notes, places three question marks next to the date "4/'57." This presentation of individual dates, representing Charlie Wade's dubious activities, is as incapable of producing a meaningful version of past events as the war dates that Pilar wrote on the blackboard during her history lesson. In contrast to her student Chet Payne, however, Sam is not willing to content himself with a simple formula for his confusion: "Some kill, others profit." Instead, he realizes that it isn't enough to reconstruct the causal sequence between the fragmentary events people have been telling him about. Finding out who did what to whom will not produce a plausible story with which to explain the woundings, psychic and physical, of the past.

The further Sam goes into the past, the more blurred become the boundaries between right and wrong actions, between a heroic figure and an obscene figure of paternal authority. He becomes increasingly aware that he will have to give up his desire to see in his father a simple opponent, whose code of moral behavior is clearly distinct from his own, and instead accept the enmeshment of jurisdiction and transgression that his father embodies. Indeed, at the end of Sam's search, Buddy Deeds will appear far more flawed than the legend has it, guilty not only of adultery but also of theft and complicity in manslaughter. Yet he is not the ruthless judge and executioner that his melancholic son had imagined him to be. During one of his interviews, Sam speaks to an Anglo bar owner, who confesses his fear that the white part of Frontero is in a state of crisis. The line of demarcation, he proclaims, has gotten fuzzy, and yet "to run a successful civilization you got to have lines of demarcation between right and wrong, between this one and that one." As Sam smiles ironically, Cody assures him that his father had understood the danger involved in questioning Anglo supremacy and allowing for racial mixture: "He was . . . the referee for this damn menudo we got down here. He understood how most people don't want their sugar and salt in the same jar." The longer the critical son continues his search, the more his initial suspicion is confirmed, namely that the line of demarcation between ethnic groups in Frontero was already fuzzy in the 1950s. He also finds evidence for his premonition that his father was anything but the referee in the official law of segregation; he was clandestinely one of the most radical practitioners of miscegenation.

The central point about the sharing of secrets, which held together the parents' generation, is that there had always been clandestine arrangements between the leading political figures of the different ethnic groups, even though to the public eye Frontero seemed clearly divided along ethnic and moral lines. Indeed, it was the officially sanctioned lines of demarcation that had made possible the peaceful cultural hybridity they entertained in private, whether it was business or romantic alliances. Challenged by his son, Delmore (Joe Morton), who has returned home to Frontero after many years of absence to assume command of Fort McKenzie, the old Otis Payne articulates the rationale behind the murky moral that both he and Buddy Deeds practiced. Like Sam, Delmore seeks to determine a clear boundary between right and wrong, for he has carried a grudge against his father all his life for having left his wife and children in favor of another woman. As he now confronts his father about making his bar off-limits because one of Delmore's soldiers got in a fight there, Otis tries to explain that the line between ethically correct and incorrect behavior is a fuzzy one. His bar, he explains, has over the years been the one place in town where blacks feel welcome; there he loans money, settles arguments, offers a place to spend the night to those who can't go home. "There's not enough of us to run anything in this town—the white people are mostly out on the lake now and the Mexicans hire each other. There's the Holiness Church and there's Big O's place." In response to his son's cynical comment that surely people make their choice, he replies: "A lot of 'em choose both. There's not like a borderline between the good people and the bad people—you're not either on one side or the other." Although the phantomatic emergence of Charlie Wade's corpse has given rise to both Sam's and Delmore's hopes that an investigation into the past will allow them to find their fathers unequivocally guilty, they end up receiving a different message. The blurring of the boundary between the legal and the illegal, on which the shared secrets of the parents' generation are based, leads to a viable hybridity.

As one of the last stops in his search, Sam finally crosses the border into Mexico to speak to the used-car dealer Chucho, the only surviving witness to Charlie Wade's killing of Mercedes's husband, Eladio Cruz, whom the sheriff had caught smuggling wetbacks into Texas. On his return home he stops off at a drive-in where one night twenty-three years earlier his father's men had forcibly separated him from his beloved Pilar as they were watching a film. After this incident, she spent the rest of her adolescence in a church school. He tarries in front of the enormous movie screen, now boarded over with wooden planks, before going back to Pilar and renewing his amorous relationship with her. In the final scene of the film they meet in front of the movie screen, where in a few places the rotten planks have fallen off, showing pieces of blue sky, as if framing them. Sayles shows Sam from behind, sitting on the hood of his car and staring at the white screen before him while waiting for Pilar. After she joins him, Sam shows her a black-and-white photograph he has discovered among his father's papers. Here, like a second phantom, is a visualization of the fissure in knowledge on which their own origins are based. The photo shows Sheriff Buddy Deeds and Mercedes Cruz, both dressed in bathing clothes and standing arm in arm in the hip-deep water of a river, smiling into the camera. Pilar at last finds visual proof of something that she has long suspected—that she is not only the product of miscegenation but also the half sister of the man she has loved all her life.

Sam and Pilar are thus forced to accept the kernel of illegality that had always inhabited Buddy Deeds's jurisdiction as sheriff as well as his paternal authority. If *The Man Who Shot Liberty Valance* traces the slow disillusionment of Ransom Stoddard, *Lone Star* traces Sam's re-illusionment. Having awakened from his dream of finding a murderous father, much like Ethan relinquished his racist hatred of Debbie, Sam is now able to accept the interpellation of the dead Buddy Deeds. As the logical consequence of his realization that the boundary between the law and its rotten fissures is always already an indistinct one, he can now draw the one boundary necessary for the family romance he has devised for himself and Pilar. He throws off the burden of the past, even while accepting that it has had and continues to have an effect on his emotional life in the present. In contrast to the nostalgic sadness with which John Ford commemorates the death of his lone hero, Sayles emphasizes the sense of liberation that goes along with turning one's back not on home but on the heterotopic space of memory.

The discreet declaration of love between Sam and Pilar successfully sublates their secret knowledge of the transgression of the law against incest that they will continue to commit. As Sam begins to caress Pilar's arm, she says in anticipation, "We start from scratch?" Only too willing to stop fleeing the internal trouble waiting for him in his new home, he nods to her, and she continues, relieved, "Everything that went before, all that stuff, history—the hell with it, right?" He doesn't interrupt, just stares at her pensively as she begins to focus on the boarded-up screen before them. "Forget the

Alamo!" exclaims the history teacher who had tried to teach her students the complexity of this border region. As he continues to stroke her arm, Sam remains silent but turns his head to look at the boarded-up screen. For a few seconds Sayles captures the two lovers in a shot from the back as they sit silently on the hood of Sam's car. Then he cuts to a panorama shot of the landscape; in the left side of the frame we can still see the enormous screen, standing in contrast to the blue sky, while the two cars are reduced to small points and the lovers no longer visible. Then the screen turns black and the credits roll.

Concerning this final scene, John Sayles has explained: "I wanted both the sense that they are going to go forward, something could be projected on that thing. But they're not the fourteen-year-old kids that they were. They've had some damage. Things have fallen away. They're different people. But that doesn't mean that their love is dead."[19] Like Ford, Sayles will not show us how these two will live with the gender and race trouble inscribed at the heart of their new family and home romance. In contrast to the last scene in *The Searchers*, however, they do not disappear into a dark interior, nor do they separate from each other so that the hero might return to the unlimited imaginary landscape of the western legend. Any view of this wide-open space, though framed as in Ford's film, is invariably boarded over. Sam and Pilar inhabit instead the liminality between the dark interior of the homestead and the wild prairie—a desert landscape that is no longer the scene of a contested line of demarcation between different ethnic groups but rather a space of accommodation, the place where, twenty years earlier, film legends were projected against the sky. There the lovers tarry, turning their backs not only on us but also on the stories of the past that have haunted them throughout their adult lives. In contrast to the situation of Hitchcock's unnamed heroine in *Rebecca*, here the dream of a mutual future emerges from the blurred interface between movie screen and the real living conditions of this particular region of America. In this hybrid space the irresolvable complexity of real living conditions juxtaposed with a wish for legends can be enmeshed— as a framed segment on the huge white screen that inevitably points to the one we, as the audience, are facing. It refers to a different level of reality, one that represents neither a return to the past nor a flight into cinematic images. The dream of America, of "how the West was won," emerges as a boarded-over cinema screen, but also as a fissured screen, whose enormous white surface rises like a monument against the landscape. From the master of the western genre, Sayles borrows the optimism that the hybrid inhabitants of the West find it possible to return to a home and to a family that they have left in order to make a journey for truth and justice. The sly transformation of the original Ford script consists in the way that, against the grain of the genre, Sayles gets us to dream about these successful homecomers.

Secret Beyond the Door—The forbidden room

Chapter 5

The Enigma of Homecoming
Secret Beyond the Door

Film Noir's Celebration of Domestic Anxiety

As Vivian Sobchack astutely notes, "It is now a commonplace to regard film noir during the peak years of its production as a pessimistic cinematic response to volatile social and economic conditions of the decade immediately following World War II." While the plot of the classic war film generally concludes with the allegedly happy return of the war hero to the home for which he fought abroad, film noir highlights how precarious the veteran's homecoming can be. Sobchack argues that film noir can be seen as "playing out negative dramas of post-war masculine trauma and gender anxiety brought on by wartime destabilization of the culture's domestic economy and a consequent 'deregulation' of the institutionalized and patriarchally informed relationship between men and women."[1] Indeed, the heroes of film noir repeatedly find themselves penetrating the dark world of an urban war zone and venturing into a disorienting, fascinating, and at the same time threatening counterworld of corruption, intrigue, betrayal, and decadence from which—in contrast to the war front they left behind—they can escape only through death. Thus the sense of a paranoid universe that film noir transmitted—that its protagonists were fatefully trapped in a disempowering world that denied them all agency—must be seen in the context of the transitional and politically unstable historical period from 1941, when America entered the Second World War, to the late 1950s postwar and Cold War era.

As Paul Schrader points out, the psychological and social anxieties portrayed by film noir articulate a war and postwar disillusionment that was a response in part to the false optimism of war propaganda and in part to the suspicions and conspiracy theories that emerged as a result of the new international enmity called the Cold War. Schrader also suggests, however, that film noir responds to the demand for postwar realism, for a more honest and harsh view of the social antagonisms subtending the troubled domestic economy of the period.[2] Particularly central to noir's sober view of American culture's efforts to reassert the lost social order of peacetime are, of course, the veterans returning to the workplace and the family life they had left behind. Not only did they find themselves confronted with women as the "internal enemy," which, according to Hegel's notes on war, they had initially sought to escape by going into battle. Rather, in contrast to the classic war film as well as the western, the bleak image of homecoming painted by film noir cinematically refigures the fact that the women to whom the war heroes were returning had become economically independent during the war. Called upon by American politicians to "Give your job to GI Joe," the women were compelled, often unwillingly, to return to the hearth. Because they were often dissatisfied about their removal from the workplace, the idealized home front, which war propaganda had installed as an ideology in the name of which the battle against the Axis powers was fought, proved to be merely a mythic construct. In fact, this allegedly felicitous home became a new site of contention, no longer between two cultures but now between American men and women.

Two fundamental issues thus emerged as culturally relevant in response to this return to the home: the veterans' reclamation of their position as head of the family and dominant breadwinner and the working women's dissatisfaction at being displaced from the workplace and once more confined to the domestic sphere. In what Vivian Sobchack calls scenarios of "domestic anxiety," feeding off the tension between attempts to "settle down," to reclaim an idealized situation of prewar "stability," "security," and "loyalty" and the social reality of the insecurity, instability, and social incoherence that characterized postwar America, we find the character of the femme fatale emerging as a cinematic negotiation of the fears invoked by the successful, empowered, and independent working woman.[3] As Billy Wilder depicts in *Double Indemnity* (1944), this woman, forced to confine herself to the home, will turn this allegedly felicitous space of safety into a war zone, rendering actual death the only way to achieve a successful homecoming. Yet in film noir we also find the counterparanoia: the fantasy of a postwar bluebeard, punishing the confident woman for her independence and forcing her once more into a subordinate and obedient position at the price of her life.

In addition to provoking issues of gender trouble within the home, the return of the disoriented and disconnected veteran to a troubled domestic economy brought another unresolvable antagonism—the veterans' traumatic war neurosis. Those who had remained at home did not want to confront this problem, privileging instead the image of the valiant war hero over that of the wounded and psychically vulnerable soldier who had horror stories of violence and destruction to tell. As Richard Maltby notes, in many late 1940s noir films, war trauma finds an oblique articulation in which the heroes are haunted by a violent past, mentally disturbed, maladjusted, and driven by a forlorn hope, even though they are often only implicitly marked as war veterans.[4] One might speculate that what was staged as a battle between the sexes served to cover up another scenario that was too dangerous to be enacted in Hollywood mainstream cinema in a world of alleged peace and prosperity, namely the persistent psychic trauma that was part of the war's collateral damage.

Film noir thus engages not only the domestic anxieties arising from the changed social position of the independent working woman but also the equally threatening anxieties surrounding the psychic aftereffects of war. While public discourse after World War I privileged physical over psychic wounds of war, Hollywood willingly addressed the psychic difficulties involved in coming home and in readjusting to times of peace.[5]

Astonishingly, as Dana Polan illustrates, a seminal aspect of postwar ideology had to do with the dangers emanating from the homecoming veterans. While war propaganda films had fed off the image of the American soldier whose physical prowess and psychic strength made him fit to conquer all his enemies and return home intact, a concern emerged in the postwar period that this violence, necessary in battle, could seamlessly become an unbridled destructive obsession that would threaten domestic peace. Uncertainty about whether soldiers trained to kill could successfully be reintegrated into the everyday reality of postwar America led to a paranoid refiguration of the valiant soldier as a dangerous psychopath. In his book *The Veteran Comes Home*, meant to educate the American public about what to expect from the returning veteran, William Waller explains: "The hand that does not know how to earn its owner's bread, knows how to take your

bread, knows very well how to kill you, if need be, in the process. That eye
that has looked at death will not quail at the sight of a policeman." Indeed,
as Dana Polan documents, journalists were eager to make the connection
between crime in postwar America and the military past of suspected criminals, while manuals like one titled *When He Comes Back* were distributed
to help families adjust to the soldiers' return home. Such texts tended to
argue that there was no need to fear any lasting effects of war neurosis,
owing to the radical difference between psychic disturbances introduced in
an extreme situation like war and normal family problems emerging from
trouble at home. Yet as Dana Polan points out, "Discourse on the postwar
neurotic man ends by instituting a gap between what it accepts as the awful
facts and what it desires as the best alternative." While Benjamin Bowker's
Out of Uniform begins by suggesting that over time the psychically wounded veterans will come to remember their traumatic battle experiences with
pride and satisfaction, all resentment having faded to leave a "memory of
full, intense years." He ends up admitting that the battleground has simply
shifted from a foreign to a domestic venue, and thus any imagination that
the vet and his family would once more be unequivocal masters of their
home the way they allegedly were before the war began was erroneous: "It
was only after victory that the invasion of America [by the neurotic vet] became a reality."[6]

Film noir, as I claim in the following reading of Fritz Lang's *Secret Beyond
the Door*, offers a bleak spin on Fleming's dictum "There's no place like
home." The world that the noir hero and heroine inhabit is radically dislocated, the fissures impossible to overlook, all efforts at happy endings inevitably thwarted. *Place* as a category plays such a crucial role in these cinematic scenarios precisely because what is at stake is the recognition that one
can never be at home in the postwar world. As Dana Polan notes, the precarious homecoming of the war veteran, fraught with ambivalence and anxiety, is connected in the image repertoire of film noir with the way the im-
peratives of war have invested themselves "in a particular representation of
home. At the extreme, the forties home is not simply a haven against the
outside world but a separate world of its own, a vast act of the imagination."
It becomes a self-enclosed environment, working rigorously "to close out
the world of ambiguous interaction, of ambivalent meanings," even while
proving to be "no more than a representation," grounded in nothing that
assures its permanence or its invulnerability, "often only an unstable fantasy."[7] In film noir, home thus emerges as a fragile and threatened entity, be-

cause, as Vivian Sobchack concludes, while these somber film scenarios insist that "the intimacy and security of home and the integrity and solidity of the home front are lost to wartime and postwar America," they also celebrate the uncanny transience of the dispossessed and the displaced: "a perverse and dark response, on the one hand, to the loss of home and a felicitous, carefree, ahistoricity and, on the other, to an inability to imagine being at home in history, in capitalist democracy, at this time."[8]

Lang's Postwar Bluebeard: War Neurosis or Childhood Trauma?

As I will argue for Fritz Lang's *Secret Beyond the Door*, while film noir rarely depicts homes, concentrating instead on empty streets, bars, hotel rooms, and diners, the domestic space proves here to be a particularly resonant stage for the portrayal of the anxiety provoked by the double issues that emerged from the veterans' precarious homecoming: the psychic effects of the violence that they had experienced and the onset of the battle of the sexes on the domestic front, which, in its most benign form, involves the strife-ridden transition between celibacy and marriage.[9] Lang explicitly deploys paranoia, claustrophobia, and home anxiety to visually perform how both his war veteran, Mark Lamphere (Michael Redgrave), and his wife, Celia (Joan Bennett), must come to accept that they can never be the masters of the Lampheres' family estate, Blade's Creek in Lavender Falls, New York—partly because Mark has been displaced by his sister, Caroline (Anne Revere), who has taken possession of his symbolic mandate during his absence and serves as a constant reminder of his impotent dependence on his dead mother, and partly because a traumatic neurosis renders any happy home romance impossible.

What is significant about Fritz Lang's choice of the family home as the site where these two agents of dislocation—feminine power and psychic disturbance—are negotiated is that the affective pressure left by the traumatic experience of war, of which mainstream Hollywood would allow only oblique representations, was cinematically refigured in the guise of a lethal battle of fatal love, played out in the most intimate part of the home, the bedroom. Like the manuals written to alleviate the anxieties of family members waiting for the veterans to come home, this narrative thrives on a rhetoric of ambivalence, undercutting the very optimism it seeks to present. While representations of the threat of domestic violence may have seemed less disturbing to Hollywood than those of the lasting effects of war neurosis, the implications are perhaps more insidious, for they place the danger at the very heart and hearth of the home for which wars are fought. In Lang's film noir, the psychically disturbed hero, Mark, can begin to be cured of the traumatic reminiscences that threaten to turn him into a murderous psychopath only at the expense of losing his family estate. In this reading, actual homelessness emerges as the only viable condition for psychic health. Fritz Lang implicitly follows here the psychoanalytic dictum invoked by Gaston Bachelard when he suggests, "There is a ground for taking the house as a tool for analysis of the human soul" because it is both our memories and the things we have forgotten or sought to repress that are "housed": "Our soul is an abode. And by remembering 'houses' and 'rooms' we learn to 'abide' within ourselves."[10]

Yet Fritz Lang does not subscribe to Bachelard's optimistic conception of topophilia as the imaginative engagement that provides a means of psychically retrieving emotionally charged places of abode as felicitous spaces of love, fascination, and security. Rather, Lang's journey through the paranoid hallucinations of his two protagonists implicitly renders visual the proximity between film noir's obsession with homelessness and Freud's own sober claim that psychoanalysis can only turn unbearable anguish into everyday unhappiness. Lang's film illustrates that in the noir world of postwar America, the ability to abide in one's soul is crucially coupled with the loss of home, indeed to the recognition that there can be no place like home.[11] For Fritz Lang's neurotic war veteran is ultimately able to find happiness in marriage and thus relocate himself in a world that had grown dangerously strange to him, but he manages to do so only because his wife, Celia, is willing to risk her life by cathartically reenacting what she deems to be the primal scene of his disturbance, appropriating the hybrid role of detective, psychoanalyst, and mother.

This tale about a rich New York heiress who marries a stranger she happens to meet in Mexico, only to discover that he is a murderous psychopath trying to kill her, is a twofold enactment of the mutual implications of psychic dislocation and literally being a stranger in one's own home. The war is mentioned only twice during the film, both times to note that it was after Mark's return from the battlefield that his relation to his first wife became troubled, leading to her mysterious illness and early death. Lang leaves no doubt in the audience's mind, however, that it was Mark's absence from home during the war that allowed his sister, Caroline, to usurp his place as the head of the family estate. By way of explaining this vexed sibling rivalry, to which Mark must succumb because he has repressed all knowledge of its origin, the film's narrative ultimately reveals a traumatic childhood scene that allows Celia to explain to her disturbed husband how his sense of being a foreigner in his own home is directly correlated with the murderous impulses that have deprived him of feeling that he is master of his psychic apparatus.

At the same time, Mark isn't alone in his sense of psychic and literal displacement. Upon her arrival at Blade's Creek, Celia discovers that she cannot be master of the house either. It is not, however, Caroline's skillful management of the house that stands in her way; it is her husband's murderous desires, which have rendered her new home dangerously uncanny to her. Here it is useful to recall Michael Wood's claim that in Hollywood films of the 1940s and 1950s the all-American, ideal home is actually a site of death for the hero. In *Secret Beyond the Door*, it is the heroine for whom confrontation of her home romance and death come to be coterminous.

In contrast to a western like *The Searchers*, Lang's noir bluebeard fairy tale presents a scenario in which the Lamphere couple, married in Mexico very quickly after having met there, can neither turn their backs on home nor have a phantasmatic alter ego destroy it and thereby spare them direct confrontation with its potential fatalities, namely that Mark's estate was a site of death, a museum of murder rooms. Instead, they are forced to play out the death scenario represented by the Lamphere mansion as the abode for their troubled marriage, a scenario that takes the form of a lethal duel involving clandestine surveillance and trespassing in forbidden places, all staged in the various intimate rooms of Blade's Creek. This turn toward home as the battleground implies that the repressed traces of Mark's war neurosis, which is never directly named but is associated with a scene of early childhood trauma—which Celia reconstructs from stories Caroline tells her, rendering it highly subjective at best—can be negotiated and resolved as a battle between the sexes and the generations. Lang thus performs the following chiasma: the fatal quality of the home, encoded as a feminine space in which the hero feels alienated because of the unbearable proximity of the maternal (or sororal) authority, is transformed into the site of death for the woman (Celia), who is seeking to take on the maternal position, and thereby completely occludes the other significant scene of trauma, the literal battleground.

From the start Lang positions *Secret Beyond the Door* as his heroine's story, told primarily from the point of view of the disoriented wife rather than that of the psychically disturbed veteran. Initially her voice-over calls upon us to indulge in the mysterious dangers brought by her sudden marriage, as it is her voice that ultimately posits a coherent pattern for the uncanny events that befall her at Blade's Creek. Indeed, Lang is also very clear that it is her desire for death which finds its abode in the Lamphere mansion. The childhood scene of trauma, with which she finally cures her husband of his murderous urges, serves as a protective fiction that not only obscures the war neurosis, allowing it to remain undiscussed, but also masks the way death and the home of marriage were, from the start, conflated in her romance with Mark Lamphere. Celia proves to be a feminine refiguration of the classic Hollywood hero insofar as home to her is also a site of death, but in contrast to Ethan Edwards, she wants to penetrate it, because it will allow her to work through her ambivalent feelings about marriage and her unequivocal fascination with lethal self-expenditure. Happiness for her ultimately involves turning her back on a home that, as an architectural embodiment of both her and Mark's violently consumptive desire, has literally been consumed by flames and now resides only in the state of blissful transition that exile affords.

Yet this solution can be effected only after she has entered the noir home's heart of darkness and confronted there her own death wish, manifested in the guise of her murderous husband. To emphasize that what is to come is the heroine's tale, *Secret Beyond the Door* begins with a flashback in which Celia recounts the events that led to her sudden marriage to a man who has remained a complete stranger to her. She remembers that as long as her brother, Rick, was still alive, she had resiliently turned down all offers of marriage. After his death, which left her the sole heir of their family fortune, she decided to take a trip to Mexico with her friend Edith Potter (Natalie Schafer), to take her mind off her grief but also to spend some time away from her fiancé, Bob, who had been her brother's lawyer and had started wooing her after Rick's death. Once in Mexico, she meets her dead brother's double—a mysterious older man who is the publisher of an architectural magazine in New York City. Within a few hours Mark succeeds in taking the affective place left vacant by the death of her brother, and she decides to marry the stranger who has made such an irresistible impression on her. But when Mark abruptly breaks off their honeymoon and leaves his wife alone in Mexico while he returns to New York without any explanation, Celia realizes how little she actually knows about her husband. Then, on the morning of her arrival at Blade's Creek, her paranoia begins to be fed by Mark's son, David, who is convinced that his father was responsible for the sudden death of his mother. To her surprise, she discovers that none of the rooms in the upper part of Blade's Creek have locks, while the special "felicitous" rooms that Mark has been reconstructing in the cellar of the house are replicas of historical murder sites—and the one room he keeps locked from everyone is a perfect reproduction of Celia's own bedroom.

The psychic excavation work that follows, supported by Celia's ceaseless exploration of the corridors and rooms of the Lamphere mansion, could be viewed as an ironic take on the gesture of cathartic reenactment that underwrites Freud's talking cure. As Celia penetrates ever deeper both into Mark's psyche and into the innermost chambers of his home—as though, in line with Bachelard's claim, not just his memories but also the things he has chosen to forget were obliquely "housed" in the wife's bedroom that he has reconstructed—she uncovers past events that allow her to reconstruct a primal scene of early narcissistic wounding, having to do with an enforced and utterly painful separation from the mother he adored. What she surmises, even though she has only Caroline's hearsay and her own intuition to support it, is that because the young boy encoded being locked in his bedroom, and thus severed from his mother, as a traumatic form of abandonment, he developed a pathological hatred of both his own mother and her surrogates—his first wife, Eleanor, and now his second wife, Celia. Working with the analogy between Mark's past, locked away in his unconscious, and the last of his "felicitous" rooms, which he keeps locked from her, and with the analogy between the wife's body and the maternal bedroom, Celia is able to break his amnesia, or at least his murderous fantasies about having to destroy his new wife, in which he hopes to turn a scene of utter vulnerability (being abandoned by his mother) into a scene of empowerment (rendering the woman he has married because she reminds him of his mother utterly vulnerable by threatening her with death). As Celia slyly surmises, in the logic of Mark's paranoid delusions, killing his wife in her bedroom would function as an antidote to having been locked out of his mother's bedroom. One might, of course, offer the counter speculation that killing the woman, who by virtue of her gender is foreign to him, might also be an apotropaic collateral of a different scene of trauma, the situation of having been threatened by alien soldiers, which he now refigures in the act of overcoming an equally alien internal enemy.

Without ever fully discrediting the possibility that Celia may be off the mark in her reconstruction of the violent urges driving her husband, Fritz Lang foregrounds the trauma at the heart of the mother-child bond by referring to the scenario Freud invoked in *Beyond the Pleasure Principle* to illustrate how the death drive works. Like the little boy's game with a wooden spool, in which he gleefully throws it away and then retrieves it by pulling on a string attached to it, so as to imitate his fantasy of control over the absent mother, Mark's murderous hallucination also involves a game of *fort-da*. Freud suggests that the little boy's game was a form of compensation for having been forced to accept that the mother he so greatly adored would leave him alone in his room for many hours. "By himself staging the disappearance and return of the objects within his reach," Freud claims, he was able to gain control over an unpleasant event. At the same time Freud notes the ambivalence at work: the child could not possibly have "felt his mother's departure as something agreeable," even though the throwing away of the spool, which represented the mother's departure, was "staged as a game in itself and far more frequently than the episode in its entirety, [had a] pleasurable ending." Significant, then, for the crossmapping that I am proposing between Freud's discussion of the death drive and Lang's cinematic enactment is that the emotional gain of the *fort-da* game resides in making the beloved object, which punishes one by not being ever-present, disappear.

Mark's reproduction of allegedly "felicitous" rooms of murder, culminating in the duplication of his wife's bedroom, turns his painful memories of abandonment into a scene of agency. On the one hand Mark's repetition compulsion allows him to transform a situation in which he is helpless and passive into one where he assumes an active, sadistic role. On the other hand, the act of throwing away his second wife by murdering her also satisfies his desire for revenge against his mother for having seemingly abandoned him, for as Freud notes, throwing away the object so that it was "gone" satisfied the child's "suppressed impulse to revenge himself on his mother for going away from him." Mark's insistence on being locked into his hallucinations, which veer toward murdering his wife, can be translated as a phantasmatic enactment of the statement "All right, then, keep me locked up in my fantasies. Go away! I don't need you. I'm sending you away myself."[12]

Nevertheless, Fritz Lang, in his cinematic homage to Freud's speculations on the death drive, includes a double fissure. For one thing, the *fort-da* game that Mark plays is not an example of a young child's great cultural achievement of relinquishing his drives but rather the expression of a regressive resurgence of those archaic drives. The maternal body is replaced not by a symbol (the toy) but by a second actual body (the second wife). Furthermore, even though Lang explicitly plays with Freud's conviction that in the course of psychoanalysis it is possible to discover a traumatic primal scene that explains the neurotic illness of a potential killer, he leaves open the question of the reason for the reemergence of Mark's murderous drives. Lang obliquely suggests that it might well have been Mark's experience of war that triggered the initial manifestation of his psychic alienation and that now possibly represents a different wound to Mark's narcissism, one for which no traumatic primal scene can be found. At the same time, Celia privileges a solution to Mark's mental disorder in which his murderous urges are linked to an unsuccessful emotional jettisoning of the maternal body, so that she can also claim that these violent drives have been haunting him since early childhood. As a result of the way Lang sets things up, the viewer is unable to decide whether the origin of Mark's murderous desire is really to be located in his inability to affectively separate himself from his mother or whether Celia simply resorts to this scene of unsuccessful denaveling so as to find a surrogate representation for Mark's war trauma, for which he has neither visual representations nor words.

If the latter is the workable scenario, Celia can hope to cure Mark of his proclivity toward violence, regardless of whether the primal scene she identifies is accurate or simply a screen memory for Mark. Once we view this solution as one that Celia narrates and that Mark simply passively accepts—much as the entire film scenario is shaped as her wish-fulfilling dreamscape—we might further speculate that it would clearly be more satisfying to Celia to imagine that the strange man she has married is a potential wife killer than to accept that he is a dangerously neurotic survivor of war. Nevertheless, Fritz Lang himself never resolves the question; he subsequently translates this twofold narcissistic wound into the misogynist fantasy that in order to recover his lost patriarchal position of power Mark must seek revenge on all the women in his life who take care of him. The compensation for this way of working out his neurosis, one might surmise, resides in the fact that at the heart of his home he does not have to face the contingency of death, as would be the case in the battlefield. Here, he himself can determine the conditions under which he will look death in the eye. Yet the undecidability performed by Lang is such that one would immediately have to counter any reading that privileges war neurosis by asking whether the latent trauma can't indeed be read back to a repressed hatred of the mother, activated by virtue of Mark's experience of abandonment on the battle front.

What is disturbing is that regardless of how one seeks to explain the origins of Mark's murderous desire—be it the traumatic separation from the mother or the shock of war—it is nevertheless aimed at the body of the woman who loves him and seeks to cure him. Equally disturbing is that this noir fairy tale corresponds to the wish fantasy of the endangered woman, with this postwar bluebeard serving as the hero of a scenario shaped from the start by the female narrator's desire to enjoy a situation in which her life is threatened. Elizabeth Cowie astutely distinguishes Celia from the clueless girl of the Grimm fairy tale by pointing out that she is neither young nor inexperienced but "sophisticated, self-possessed and self-assured," and thus "not yet or not sufficiently a victim of her circumstances." She is no innocent player in a murderous love scenario; instead, by emotionally endorsing a connection of desire with death, she actually takes on a role counter to that of the war veteran.[13] Indeed, this beautiful worldly wise woman wants to pit her own confrontation with death against her feeling of psychic numbness induced by her brother's death. In this noir dreamscape, Celia's fantasy of experiencing a threat to her life constitutes a feminine appropriation of the experience of war, even though it is played out as a love duel and not as a fight between political enemies.

Mary Anne Doane has suggested placing Lang's film in a cycle of Hollywood films that she calls narratives of feminine paranoia because they all revolve around the wife's suspicion that the husband she discovers to be a stranger might also be a murderer. The ambivalence of these films resides in the fact that while the protagonist gives in to her anxieties about being threatened by her husband, she is also clearly marked as the "agent of the gaze, as investigator in charge of the epistemological trajectory of the text, as the one for whom the 'secret beyond the door' is really at stake," with the mysterious husband simply an auxiliary player in a fantasy scenario that she fully commands. In these cinematic narratives it is the home, to which women in classic Hollywood cinema have a particular claim, that comes to be "yoked to dread, and to a crisis of vision." According to Doane, the uncanniness of these scenarios of feminine paranoia derives from the violence that is anticipated but that also is "precisely what is hidden from sight." The marriage, with its architectural materialization of the family home, proves to be a heterotopia of sorts: "It asserts divisions, gaps, and fields within its very structure."

Indeed, in these noir refigurations of the anxieties revolving around marriage, an external horror infiltrates the domesticity of the home, rendering visible the instability of the boundary between internal and external and thriving on a split, as Doane claims, "between the known and the unknown, the seen and the unseen."[14] Fritz Lang's noir home is shaped as a stage for the uncanny dislocation of domestic familiarity in which, significantly, the murderous fantasies of a traumatized war veteran can be interchangeable with his wife's fantasies about being pursued by an enemy. Celia, much like the unnamed heroine in *Rebecca,* discovers her own alienness mirrored in her husband's odd behavior, as though he were a phantom embodying the gap in her self-knowledge. In her desire for death she is strange to herself, and the Lamphere mansion, as an uncanny abode, functions as an architectural correspondence to the uncanniness inscribed in her psychic apparatus, itself an immaterial, spiritual abode. One can thus add a further layer to the way the psychoanalytic solution that Celia offers for both Mark's and her own delusions in *Secret Beyond the Door* superimposes a scene of early childhood trauma onto the trauma of the war veteran. Ultimately both transform into narratives that describe her own psychic ambivalence, notably the doubts that this self-possessed and independent woman harbors toward marriage as the solution to her desire to break out of her own locked room, namely her sexual inhibitions.

Fritz Lang never denied that Hitchcock's *Rebecca* was the model for his own cinematic refiguration of a psychoanalytic case study in paranoia, but he declined to locate the analogy between the two films in the mysterious death of a first wife and the presence of a jealous housekeeper who spies on the new mistress, then burns down the mansion in the end.[15] Rather, he insisted that the connection between the two was one of failed appropriation. As he explained to Peter Bogdanovich, "You remember that wonderful scene in *Rebecca* where Judith Anderson talks about Rebecca and shows Joan Fontaine the clothes and fur coats and everything? When I saw this picture (I am a very good audience), Rebecca was *there,* I *saw* her. . . . And— talking about stealing—I had the feeling that maybe I could do something similar in this picture when Redgrave talks about the different rooms. Now let's be very frank—it just didn't come through for me."[16] So it seems that Lang himself felt the inadequacy of his version of Hitchcock's dramatic mise-en-scène portraying the fascination of a secret room and the forbidden—because it is fundamentally dangerous—feminine power harbored there. Nevertheless, *Secret Beyond the Door* does refigure Hitchcock's drama revolving around the traumatic dislocations inscribed in the home romance in a revealing manner, and not least because the dangerous power emanating from the maternal figure of authority is overdetermined in Lang's appropriation of *Rebecca*. Mark is haunted not only by his dead mother but also by his dead first wife, while Celia must confront two maternal figures, who, before her arrival, occupied the position left vacant by the death of Mark's first wife. Caroline, the sister, is transformed into a benign version of Mrs. Danvers who is only too willing to hand over her duties to Celia, while the governess of Mark's son, David, Miss Robey (Barbara O'Neil), functions as the malevolent rival who, in contrast to Mrs. Danvers, does not seek to preserve the memory of her deceased mistress but rather wants to become mistress of Blade's Creek herself.

Two further transformations prove to be significant, as will be discussed in greater detail later. First, Fritz Lang appropriates the voice-over of a woman remembering the past events that led to her present situation of exile. In contrast to the voice-over in *Rebecca*, however, where the disembodied voice initiates a ghost story and then disappears when Joan Fontaine actually appears onscreen, Joan Bennett's voice-over never stops. Instead, as though it were a jettisoned part of her body, it follows the heroine's every move, superimposes questions and interpretations onto her facial expressions and movements, and forces us to read each scene as Celia's phantasmatic working through of the doubts, confusions, and anxieties called forth by her ambivalent desire. As Tom Gunning notes, Lang, wishing to emphasize the discrepancy between Celia's interior monologue and her actions, initially had someone other than Joan Bennett speak the lines, so as to stage his conviction "that the unconscious is another, 'someone' in us we perhaps don't know."[17] And second, although Lang's dreamscape is radically shaped by the somber visual style of film noir, he does, in the end, offer us an image of the restituted couple, which Hitchcock denies us in *Rebecca*. After Blade's Creek has burned down, Celia and Mark return to the hacienda in Mexico where they had begun their honeymoon. A scene at the beginning of the film showed them lying in a hammock, with Celia resting her head on Mark's chest, and in the final sequence of the film we see her sitting in a deck chair, while Mark rests his head in her lap. No longer suspended in the illusion of marital harmony and happiness, they have arrived at the ground of reality and have come to accept that traces of psychic fallibility will always haunt their marriage. But because they have awakened from the excitations of noir hallucinations into the sobriety of everyday unhappiness, they, like the couple at the end of *Lone Star*, can begin to dream of a shared future.

An Ominous Home Romance

Fritz Lang's homage to the discursive tropes of Freud's work on the vicissitudes and resilience of early narcissistic wounds does not simply come down to the fact that his heroine, as well as her women friends, are fluent in the language of psychoanalysis. More significant, perhaps, is that the premise upon which Lang's enmeshment of war trauma, fantasies of matricide, and bluebeard narrative is based recalls Freud's discussion of the work of dream representation. Dreamscapes, he wagers, function like stages for traumatic knowledge, which can find an oblique expression there, but only in a condensed and dislocated manner, under the auspices of psychic censorship. In reference to the tropic language of psychoanalysis, the title sequence of *Secret Beyond the Door* is superimposed on an expressionistic painting of a door, standing upright at a slanted angle, without any supporting walls, in an open space. Behind this door we find a wide, completely flat landscape, as well as a slightly clouded sky, on whose horizon the first beams of a rising sun can be seen. With Celia's voice-over, however, a far more troubled visual language is introduced. Indeed, the very first sentence she utters, describing the dream images that haunt her, functions as a counterpoint to the open, sunlit geography invoked by the title sequence as an allegorical representation of what lies beyond closed doors. For what she invokes, which frames the story she is about to tell, is the dark, archaic forces that draw one back into the realm of psychic delusion and confusion: "I remember long ago I read a book that told the meaning of dreams. It said that if a girl dreams of a boat or a ship, she will reach a safe harbor, but if she dreams of daffodils she is in great danger." At the same time we see drops falling into a pool of water, forming concentric ripples. Because the liquid surface is shown in a close-up, however, we have no way of determining its exact parameters. Also visible is the reflection of a multitude of sparkling spots that light up and fade, although it remains unclear whether they are indirectly reflecting the starlight of a nocturnal sky or an artificial illumination. Beneath the liquid surface we can detect the shadowy contours of flowers and stems, although it is impossible to determine exactly what kind of vegetation they are.

Once the camera has begun to slowly pan over the water's surface from the left to the right of the screen, it captures a small paper ship, folded from a newspaper. As the ship softly floats into the center of the frame, we see its contours clearly reflected on the liquid surface and watch it cross over the pernicious-looking dark figures, which now prove to be even more mysterious than at first, for upon closer examination we discover that, while this shadowy foliage initially gave the impression that it was submerged in the water, some of the dark shapes are actually on the surface, partly obscuring the reflection of light there. As the camera continues panning along the water, the ship floats out of the upper left corner of the screen and is replaced at the bottom right by white daffodils drifting on the water's surface as well as beneath it. We see them only in fragments, as they are partly overshadowed by the dark, indiscernible figures uncannily superimposed on them. Furthermore, because they are not floating above the water, but are rather partially submerged in it, they, unlike the paper boat, have no reflection on the surface.

With this first sequence, Lang thus situates the incipient noir romance in a dreamscape that recalls a world the heroine once read about in a book, so that it might help her find a name for the strange anticipation she is experiencing on what should be an utterly joyous day, namely her wedding day. At the same time he emphasizes that all three invoked representations, to which Celia will repeatedly refer in the course of her narrative as she recalls the past—the locked door, the boat entering a safe harbor, and the daffodils drifting ominously on the water—are protective fictions in the twofold sense of the term. Like all dream representations they are condensed images that protect the dreamer from the traumatic knowledge she harbors within her unconscious by allowing her to give voice to it in an encoded and thus psychically bearable manner. Yet these representations also function as intermediaries that protect the subject by blocking out and rendering impermeable this dangerous knowledge. Her strange dream rendition of the transient position that she occupies as a young woman about to marry not only combines a proleptic anticipation of the home that marriage will afford her with an analeptic recollection of the dangers that might befall her upon entering this as yet unknown territory because it reminds her of some things she used to read and dream about such that her anticipation of what her future with Mark holds for her looks like the fulfillment of a prophecy. Staging her uncertainty about her future as the false choice between the safe haven represented by the boat and the danger represented by the daffodils also introduces a further level of undecidability, for it remains unclear whether the force that causes both the boat and the daffodils to float on the surface of the dreamscape emanates from herself or from an external, foreign power. Does her dreaming self inhabit these images or do they inhabit her?

After Celia has named the two choices open to her in relation to her romantic desire, the tone of her dreamy, seductive voice suddenly changes. With a lighter and almost sharp intonation she interrupts her own ominous anticipation at exactly the same moment that Lang cuts from the murky surface of the water to an image of church bells ringing. As though she were scolding herself, Celia exclaims: "But this is no time for me to think of danger. This is my wedding day!" Given that the visual language of her dream is clearly literary, one might ask whether Celia interprets her wedding as a possible danger precisely because it allows her to give body to a piece of strange wisdom she once found in a book. Or is it that her ominous marriage to Mark allows her to confront a piece of traumatic knowledge that she has been harboring within her psyche and that is now embodied in the figure of a mysterious husband who could represent either a safe haven or danger? What presents itself as a free choice, however, uncannily collides with its opposite, a forced choice, not because Celia invokes the question of fate but because either choice involves death. Marital security, the ostensible safe harbor, could prove to be as lethal as any direct danger posed by her strange husband. To this one might add another question: if Celia can freely choose to open a door and thus escape the dark forces lurking beneath her romantic desire, wherein the origin of her death drive resides, does her dark desire represent a fate imposed upon her from outside or does it define the most intimate core of her sexuality?

As we are shown a close-up of the church bells ringing, Celia's voice-over reveals another piece of appropriated knowledge: the folk wisdom that on her wedding day the bride should have something old, something new, something borrowed, and something blue. With this seemingly benign antidote to the ominous dream imagery, Lang finally moves to the magnificently decorated interior of a Mexican cathedral. From an arched balcony at the back of the church, his camera initially shows the figures grouped around the altar, viewing them from behind a silhouetted statue of the crucified Christ, as though it were an omen of the pain overshadowing this wedding ceremony, while Celia's voice explains, "Something old is this church, four centuries old." Then the camera slowly moves from the dome, along the magnificent walls and toward the altar, while Celia calls it a "felicitous structure," built as a place where events of joy could happen. As Lang's camera finally captures the back of the groom, standing before the altar, Celia continues to explain in a confident tone, "and something new is Mark himself." With the next cut we finally see the bride, and thus the body that belongs to the voice we have been hearing, as Celia slowly emerges from the side entrance at the left of the altar, dressed in a splendid white wedding gown, her face still hidden in shadow. With a trace of romantic sentimentality in her voice she declares, "And love is new for me."

When she has finally left the liminality of this shadowy passage and has fully emerged into the candlelit open space before the altar, Celia's voice once more changes in tone. In a whisper she describes the uncertain emotions she feels as she stands frozen for a moment before approaching the altar. All confidence and self-possession seem to have abandoned her as she explains, "My heart is pounding so. The sound of it drowns out everything. It says that when you drown your whole life passes before you like a fast movie." With this ominous utterance Fritz Lang introduces a flashback that plays through the scenes that led to this sudden marriage, always accompanied by Celia's voice-over. The acme of the inserted narrative of the events leading to the wedding is, of course, Mark's proposal of marriage, which, according to Celia's comments, seems to resolve her emotional ambivalences regarding her choice of bridegroom. As Celia explains to Mark, the engagement to Bob, which she had accepted shortly before her trip to Mexico, seemed to promise her "a quite familiar room where I'll be safe, with a warm fire burning on the hearth." As she comments in her voice-over, accepting Mark meant that the door to that room of safety closed "and another opened wide and I went through and never looked behind, because wind was there and space, and sun and storm. Everything was behind that door."

One must not forget that Fritz Lang does more than introduce this flashback by having Celia compare her recollection of the proposal from Mark to the film that flashes before the eyes of someone about to drown; he also returns to this somber premonition once the kiss with which Celia seals her engagement to Mark is over. As he shows us the bride's face, smiling at Mark as he approaches her, we once more hear Celia's voice-over, anxiously stating, "Suddenly I'm afraid. I'm marrying a stranger. A man I don't know at all. I could leave, I could run away, there is still time." As she notices her friend Edith, who has remained with her in Mexico to serve as her bridesmaid, she recalls that she is a woman well aware of her social position. For a moment she reverts to the confident voice of self-criticism, reminding herself that running away from one's wedding just isn't done. But the demons of her doubt continue to haunt the performance of the wedding vows we are shown on the screen. As Celia finally reaches the altar to accept Mark's wedding ring, she maintains, "But I'm afraid," and as she adds in an ominous tone, "Maybe I should have followed the dark voice in my heart. Maybe I should have run away," her wedding ceremony ends.

Celia's Dislocated Voice-over

Deploying another implicit reference to *Rebecca*, Fritz Lang emphasizes that Mark's marriage proposal was premature, for both Mark and Celia secretly harbor doubts as to the loyalty they have pledged each other. Before they can really commit to loving each other they must traverse the hallucinatory space of their emotional ambivalence regarding marriage. By sustaining his heroine's voice-over, Lang (in contrast to Hitchcock) achieves two effects: Celia continues to thematize her discontent with the marriage promise she gave too hastily, and the doubling between screen image and sound track performs cinematically how little this bride occupies an appropriate symbolic position. While war movies of the early 1940s had come to use the voice-over to emphasize the authenticity of the represented events and procure a sympathetic identification from their audience, film noir used the technique to present a heavily subjective confession by male protagonists who were searching for the truth behind a conspiracy or intrigue. The tension resulting between narrating voice and visualized flashback, which offers partly a tautological, partly a disjunctive relation between word and image, leads Karen Hollinger to describe the structure of these cinematic scenarios as "narrative battles that extend out into the narration itself. This strategy prevents them from achieving the sense of narrative resolution and unification of point of view that the films" seek at their conclusions.[18] Fritz Lang himself had written to Lotte Eisner on February 1, 1947, about the beginning of his shooting of *Secret Beyond the Door*, "I am experimenting with using superimposed sound for the 'thought voices' of the leading characters, and I find the idea intriguing to work out." As Eisner notes, for Lang "the words of the subconscious are not like asides in a play but are somehow placed on a different plane, belong to a different dimension." Although the enmeshment between the heroine's subjective gaze and her acoustic self-commentary "tightly integrate[s] the whole structure of the action," she goes on to explain, those two elements also paradoxically "free the action from its improbabilities, reinforcing Lang's 'fantastic realism.'"[19] We not only follow events through the heroine's eyes, but the self-doubt that accompanies all her actions—whether she is simply sitting in a room, exploring the halls and rooms of Blade's Creek, or sleeping at night—allows us to identify with her voice and thus gives credence to her delusions, as well as to the solution that she will finally offer to the strange events of her marriage.

A closer examination of Lang's use of Celia's voice-over, however, reveals a far more disjunctive effect. On the one hand, owing to the voice-over, the love duel between Celia and Mark is fought through as a narrative battle that thrives on the internal coherence provided by Celia's unceasing stream of consciousness, which holds together all the visual representations of how she perceives Mark and her new home. On the other hand, her voice-over also corresponds to what Michel Chion has called an "accousmatic voice," in the sense that it is not exclusively attached to a character within the diegetic reality of the film, nor is it simply the voice of a narrator external to the story; rather, it serves as a spectral manifestation, floating in a mysterious transitional and intermediary realm that can only phantasmatically be located.[20]

That we sometimes hear her commentary without seeing her body and that the voice-over actually belongs to two women, a reminiscing Celia and an experiencing Celia, illustrate the accousmatic quality. Celia's remembering of past events constructs a narrative sequence under the auspices of a dream language that she introduces in the first moments of the film. This part of her recollection is an analeptic narration suspended between two temporal sites—the past that she has traversed and can now find a coherent explanation for and the future that is about to set in, both as a break with the past and as a continuation of it. At the same time, it is an empowered narration, indicating her triumph over her hallucinations. While the reminiscing Celia is the author of the entire story that *Secret Beyond the Door* presents to us, the voice-over at times refers to a second Celia, the one who experiences the events—a deluded player involved in the story she is narrating, as limited in her perspective and knowledge as all the other players. This second, commenting rather than analeptically narrating, voice exhibits no ability to translate contradictory fragments into a coherent narrative whole. Rather, what Celia's stream of consciousness signals is the way she, giving in unconditionally to her own doubts and delusions, is helplessly drawn into a repetition compulsion. Again and again Fritz Lang returns to the mise-en-scène that he used for the wedding ceremony, with the voice of Celia commenting on her emotional ambivalences during visualizations of her self-doubt. She is herself caught up in the act of self-analysis, incessantly playing back in thought the strange behavior of her husband, until she is finally able to come up with a satisfying subjective narrative explanation. One might thus surmise that Fritz Lang intends Celia's voice-over to be a feminine version of the death drive of her traumatized husband. Her voice-over, trying to figure out what disconcerts and alienates her, and his gesture of repeatedly reconstructing rooms where an extreme experience of vulnerability took place, juxtapose the pleasure of repeating something displeasurable, so as to overcome it, and the traumatic experience of fallibility that can be displaced, or transformed into a protective fiction, but never obliterated.

Celia's delirious voice-over makes visible that the fantasy she is indulging in, so as to organize her ambivalent desires regarding marriage, revolves around a masochistic enjoyment of the potential threat emerging from her husband. Yet one might also say that the accousmatic voice-over was so intriguing to Fritz Lang because it allowed him to explore his heroine's homelessness through the visual and acoustic rhetoric that cinematic language offered him. Owing to her search for truth, impelled by her fundamental doubts, Celia remains a restless inhabitant of all the abodes she passes through—the hacienda of her honeymoon, the Lamphere estate Blade's Creek, and in a figural sense also the home that her marriage to Mark is meant to afford her. Indeed, all she can do is pace restlessly up and down the diverse bedrooms she finds herself in, accompanied by the ceaseless readjustments she makes to her critical judgment of her situation, or wander along the dark corridors and up the somber staircases in her new home, driven by her desire to enjoy her own peril.

The unending stream of consciousness, uncannily dislocating her emotionally wherever she finds herself, forbids her to reside without premonitions in the abodes connected to her marriage and also makes it impossible for her to actually leave the place where her lethal anxieties take on hallucinatory shape. Thus the seamless transition from Celia reminiscing about the past to Celia actually experiencing the dangerous events of this past produces the exact opposite of a coherent, plausible story. Far from having an assuaging effect, Celia's voice-over forbids an identification with her in the same gesture with which it compels this; the conjunction between her visual rendition and her acoustic inquiry creates a distortion rather than a harmonious marriage between image and sound. Lang's noir heroine is clearly not at home in her present situation, nor is she at ease with her fantasies organizing her desire. Furthermore, because, starting with the depiction of her first, unhappy honeymoon, the difference between the voice of the accousmatically narrating Celia and the voice of the Celia who is involved in the hallucinatory scenario can only imperfectly be drawn, belated narration and immediate experience uncannily collapse into each other.

At the same time, Celia's repetition compulsion points out that something recedes from her epistemological imperative. Her refusal to inhabit any of the abodes available to her without self-doubt allows us to recognize to what degree the wedding vows in the Mexican cathedral thrived on covering over an inherent, but clandestine, gender trouble. The unresolvable antagonism inhabiting this marriage finds its aesthetic analogy in the disjunction that the uncanny voice-over introduces into the cinematic rendition of this noir romance. As Slavoj Žižek has noted, the accousmatic voice in cinema can be compared to a blind spot. By disturbing our commonsense notion of a "fully constituted reality, in which sight and sound harmoniously complement each other," the voice-over "cuts out a hole in the visual reality: the screen image becomes a delusive surface, a lure secretly dominated by the bodiless voice" of the one masterminding the narrative. Indeed, in the opening sequence of *Secret Beyond the Door*, we find that the feminine voice-over begins simultaneously with the drops falling on the surface of the pond, rendering it clearly a delusive surface. As a result, Celia's visualized body and her voice do not complement each other; instead, they represent an antagonistic relation, because, as Žižek further argues, the spectral autonomy of the voice-over points to the "dimension of what eludes our gaze." The relationship between voice and image "is mediated by an impossibility: ultimately, we hear things because we cannot see everything."[21] By virtue of this rhetoric of distortion, however, Lang articulates not only the illusory power of the cinematic image but also the antagonistic kernel on whose repression all psychic and social systems structurally rely, in the sense that an opacity (between voice and image, between representation and reality) must be posited and repressed at one and the same time, if a belief in the harmonious transparency of signs is to hold.

Central to Žižek's discussion of the anamorphotic quality of the voiceover is that because of this cinematic distortion of an accurate representation of reality, the non-symbolizable antagonism is articulated, and around it all psychic reality revolves, even while it is regulated by symbolic fictions that screen out this traumatic real. According to Žižek, this real of antagonism becomes available because psychic reality is split into two fictions: an officially sanctioned narrative, aimed toward stability and harmony (notably the psychoanalytic claim that a jettisoning of the omnipotent maternal body is necessary for adult psychic health), and private fantasies that celebrate destability, distortion, and difference and called publicly sanctioned symbolic fictions into question. In the case of Celia and Mark's marriage contract, an officially sanctioned symbolic fiction regulates their shared relation to reality, which, as the priest declares, unites them as a couple in a harmonious manner, even while our expectations of Hollywood narrative style are premised by another contract, namely that the diegetic reality be governed by a harmonious relation between sound and image, so as to make it a coherent fictional space. From the start, however, Fritz Lang counterbalances this drive toward stability by introducing difference, which takes the shape of an initial incompatibility between the private fantasies of his two protagonists. While Mark uses their marriage as a platform for his efforts toward self-empowerment, Celia uses it to enjoy scenarios of lethal self-expenditure. Even though these two fantasies are initially at cross-purposes, they are ultimately translated into a symbolic fiction promising harmony, but only after the antagonism they represent is literally carried out as a narrative battle in the reconstructed bedroom, where Celia wins by imposing her interpretation of the origin of Mark's murderous impulses and thus enforcing coherence over distortion.

As the element that initially signaled the twofold disjunction—between image and sound track as well as between the marriage vows and Celia's psychic privileging of danger over marital safety—the voice-over itself ultimately establishes the marriage contract instead of hallucination as the victorious symbolic fiction. As Slavoj Žižek notes, official symbolic fictions, such as marriage vows, seek to deny that disharmony and difference might lie at the heart of all conjugal bonds, even while phantomatic fictions embody this disturbing lack of harmony. However, the psychically and aesthetically satisfying oscillation between symbolic and phantomatic fiction works by virtue of an insurmountable occlusion. Even in the battle between narratives that takes place in Mark's reconstruction of Celia's bedroom, the repressed real antagonism can be represented only as another protective fiction. If Celia's voyage through her paranoid hallucinations begins with the fantasy "the man I love is keeping a secret from me, locked away in his mind," so as to give voice to her own doubts about the stability of the marriage contract, in the peripeteia of the film this delusion is merely translated into a more viable, because more empowering, fiction: "If I unlock the door to Mark's psychic crypt, nothing will recede from my grasp, neither the dark figures that haunt him nor those that have been haunting me, though I have never being able directly to name them, long before I ever met him." With this rhetorical short circuit Lang shows Celia's analysis of her strange husband to be an auto-analysis, resulting in a fiction that allegedly clears up both his and her emotional ambivalences in one fell swoop. He also signals that it is as impossible to escape a compulsion to produce interpretive narratives as it is to escape the psychic traces of traumatic kernels that are superimposed on the reflecting surface of our internal mind scene without ever taking on a decipherable shape.

Love at First Sight

Celia's voyage across the hallucinatory working through of her home romance involves two discoveries. First is her analysis of her own ambivalent feelings, negotiated as the tension between the two choices that marriage seems to confront her with—a safe room with a fire burning in the hearth or the contingency of an open space, where everything is possible. Second, her detection work cum analysis of her traumatized husband allows her to enjoy her own precarious desire for looking death in the face as well as ultimately contain her own death drive. Lang stages the first meeting of his two protagonists in Mexico in such a way that these two analytic trajectories appear, from the start, to be mutually dependent phantomatic distortions of the symbolic fiction of marriage. The flashback of Celia comparing herself to someone who is drowning begins with a scene depicting her older brother, Rick—her "mother, father, and check-signer"—warning her that she should marry because he is worried about dying from heart failure. During this scene he introduces her to the eligible young lawyer Bob, who works for him and who, in the following scene, proposes to her two months after Rick's death. He insists, however, that she take a vacation in Mexico before making her decision.

Lang then cuts to a market scene in a Mexican village, his camera panning left to right across the busy, colorful crowd of vendors, musicians, local shoppers, and tourists until it reaches Celia and her friend Edith Potter looking at the merchandise in one of the stalls. As the vendor, whom we see only from the back, offers a necklace to the taller, blond woman, Celia turns toward her, showing her the wallet she is holding and asking her whether she thinks it is too commercial. After her friend declares that it is perfect for Bob, Celia hands the leather wallet to the vendor, telling him that the initials she would like to have embossed on it are "R.D." Here Lang abruptly shifts the position of his camera to get a low-angle shot from behind. Edith has turned away from the vendor to speak to Celia and now partially faces the open square in front of the stall, but Celia still has her back fully turned to the camera. Edith begins telling Celia about a man whom she was going to marry, who was "the image of Bob," but at the very moment when she is about to disclose why he broke off his engagement with her, she is interrupted by a woman screaming. With a 180-degree pivot Celia turns away from the vendor, who was facing her, and together she and Edith look in the direction of a street cafe where two Mexicans, both holding knives, have begun to fight; a Mexican woman can be seen leaning against the wall of the cafe, calmly watching the battle being fought over her.

Horrified, Edith tries to get Celia to leave this violent scene immediately, explaining, "I don't want to be an innocent by-stander." Celia, however, remains frozen in place, as if fascinated with what she's seeing. While the camera pans slightly to the left, thus placing Edith outside the frame and presenting Celia alone in a medium shot, we hear her voice-over explaining that she was strangely held, that she had seen fights before, nightclub brawls over a cigarette girl, "but this was different. A woman and two men fighting for her with naked knives. Death was in that street." With this scene of interpellation, Lang astutely reiterates the choice his heroine faces, represented by the two conflicting fantasy images: the commercial leather wallet for Bob, a gift meant to seal a marriage engagement that promises a safe haven, and the knife fight, a random altercation that is fascinating but also dangerous. Celia begins to identify with the woman, and as Lang cuts to a close-up of her radiant face, her voice-over explains: "And I felt how proud she must be." Suddenly one of the men hurls his knife in the direction of his enemy but misses the mark, and the knife lands in the wooden counter of the stall where Celia is standing, only a few inches to the right of her black-gloved hand. Fully in line with the scenario that Althusser describes as a paradigmatic scene of interpellation, Celia, who had turned around in response to the cry signaling a death-driven expression of love, now accepts this calling as her own. She acknowledges that, being positioned directly behind one of the fighting men, she, like him, only accidentally escaped being struck by the knife. What she implicitly recognizes is that her own desire does not mirror that of the woman who proudly watches as men fight over her. Rather Celia desires to become a player in a love duel, from which she will only barely escape unharmed. Still transfixed by the scene, she gently pulls her hand away from the counter, for a moment looking longingly at the knife, now embedded in the counter amid the commercial jewelry. Only then does she seem to wake, as if from a trance, as her voice-over explains, "Suddenly I felt that someone was watching me. There was a tingling in the nape of my neck as though the air had turned cool." Initially we continue to see only Celia in a medium shot from the front, as her eyes wander over the crowd that has gathered in front of the cafe. Then, as she continues to explain, "I felt eyes touching me like fingers," Fritz Lang cuts to a close-up of Mark.

Unnoticed by anyone but these two noir lovers, a second battlefield has opened up, superimposed onto the Mexican street scene by virtue of a fantasy involving the eroticization of death that these two strangers silently share. While Fritz Lang moves back and forth twice between close-up shots of Mark gazing at Celia and Celia returning his gaze, he has her voice-over recall that there was a current flowing between them, "warm and sweet and frightening, too." She imagines that he has seen something behind her makeup that no one had ever seen—a desire to enjoy unbridled violence, a desire that she herself didn't know was there before this incident. Sighing, she finally turns toward her friend and asks her to leave the marketplace with her, leaving behind the leather wallet she had chosen for Bob. In the next scene the two women are sitting in a cafe and we hear Edith explaining to Celia that when she finally snapped out of her trance she looked as if she had seen Death himself. Celia, as though brooding, replies, "That's not how he looked," and reminds Edith, who is surprised at this cryptic remark, that she was going to call her husband, Arthur—Celia's ploy to rid herself of her friend so that she can be alone to meet the strange man whose gaze had caressed her a few minutes earlier. As Tom Gunning argues, "Celia has responded to a gaze at once deadly and desiring and it is the balancing act she will have to carry out with her own attraction to death that will drive the film."[22]

One might, indeed, speculate that Mark appears in Celia's field of vision in the shape of a psychic phantom, along the lines proposed by Nicholas Abraham and Maria Torok, embodying an aspect of Celia's sexual desires that she has, up to this moment in her life, had intimations of but never consciously acknowledged. Instead of the lethal security that marriage to her attorney, Bob, would afford her, the stranger seems to promise something that she has been harboring as a forbidden desire, the absence of all safety nets. As Mladen Dolar has argued, love has the "mechanism of forced choice always attached to it. To put it simply, one is compelled to choose love and thereby give up the freedom of choice, while by choosing freedom of choice, one loses both." The point is apt, because, while on the manifest level of his cinematic narrative, Lang pits safety against danger as the two choices open to his heroine, he implicitly shows that she actually has no choice at all. The accidental meeting between Mark and Celia proves to be the realization of their clandestine wishes. As Dolar continues in his description of the logic behind the notion of love at first sight, "What happened unintentionally and by pure chance is in the second stage recognized as the realization of innermost and immemorial wishes and desires. The contingent miraculously becomes the place of deepest truth, the sign of fate." The lovers discover that "pure chance was actually no chance at all: the intrusion of the unforeseen turned into necessity."[23] To choose love proves to involve a choice that has already been made for one—by fate or by one's unconscious—even if the two people involved become aware of this only after the event or not at all.

Much along the lines proposed by Dolar, Fritz Lang performs the uncanny enmeshment between contingency and fate in the way Celia is so suddenly drawn by Mark's gaze, believing it to contain her truth, to be an outside gaze that corresponds to a piece of intimate self-knowledge. The moment when the gazes of his two noir lovers meet, giving voice to this clandestine desire, is also the moment when her love life suddenly and unexpectedly gains total significance. Thus the narrative of fated love, caused by sight, emerges as a strategy of psychic relief. Celia's oscillation between marriage as a safe haven and marriage as danger is suddenly suspended. Precisely because her love for Mark appears to her as fate, as an unavoidable necessity, Celia can tell herself that when it comes to her desire, she has no freedom of choice. The safe haven and the danger prove to be two sides of the same coin. As Mladen Dolar concludes, "If love aims at the extimate— the intimate external kernel—it is also a protection against it, but a protection that is ambiguous and constantly failing. The other side of the extimate is the uncanny, the emergence of the object that brings about disintegration and that becomes lethal."[24]

A narrative battle is thus being waged in *Secret Beyond the Door* in yet another sense: the symbolic fiction of love at first sight is pitted against the phantomatic fiction of a desire for lethal disintegration, called forth by a traumatic near-death experience. Indeed, the trajectory of Celia's hallucinatory journey, which will end in the precarious restitution that her second honeymoon affords, could be summarized as follows: Her ambivalent feelings about marriage are endowed with an irrevocable meaning as she falls in love at first sight with a stranger who shares her fascination with danger. This contingent meeting is encoded as a love dictated by fate, because it allows her to explore the noir implications of her ambivalent desires, collapsing danger and safety even while privileging the fiction of love's necessity. This allows her to avoid the even more disturbing possibility that a desire for destruction is completely without meaning, that it is a pure lethal drive that can never be assimilated into the symbolic structure of marriage. Celia's narrative solution takes hold after she has reenacted the near-fatal encounter with death that she could only be witness to in the market scene in Mexico; her reprise of that scene takes place in her husband's replica of her bedroom, where at her body two positions collide—that of the fought-over woman and that of one of the endangered fighters—and this restabilizes the symbolic contract of declared marital harmony that had become distorted in the course of her tale. If the entire story begins with her resisting her dead brother's desire that she should finally marry, she ultimately complies with this wish, yet, significantly, she does so by reencoding it as a different type of law—that of love at first sight. Yet the satisfaction remains uncannily twofold: Celia can tell herself that since destiny had a hand in it, she could do nothing but endorse the choice already made for her, yet she can also insist upon her own agency. Her curiosity, as well as her persistence, allows her to win the narrative battle over her husband. She has given in to her dead brother's demand, by first giving it the face of death that she feared always lurked beneath it and then re-encoding this figuration yet again, into the face of a man so deeply troubled that he requires her as a maternal surrogate.

Voyage to the End of Noir Fantasies

Celia's homecoming occurs under the auspices of the core trope to which she has recourse in order to describe what accepting Mark's proposal of marriage means to her, namely the closing of one door and the opening of another, the exchange of a quiet, familiar room where she will be safe for an open space of excess, containing everything she can imagine. During their first meeting, Mark offered himself to her as a fairy-tale prince, calling her a twentieth-century Sleeping Beauty, a wealthy American girl who has lived her life wrapped in cotton wool but who now wants to wake up. He hopes that offering to marry her will unleash the turbulent desires that she has been keeping under lock and key. Once they have married, Celia takes it upon herself to open the door to Mark's repressed knowledge about a narcissistic injury, in order to help him return to a state of normalcy. The turning away from the symbolic fiction of love toward the phantomatic fiction of destructive anger is brought about by the obverse—the significant locking of a door. One evening during her honeymoon at the Mexican hacienda, Celia allows the owner to convince her that she would be wise to test her husband's patience. After the old woman has left, Celia sits in front of her mirror and brushes her hair. Suddenly she decides to lock the door so that, in contrast to what they have agreed upon, Mark cannot come to her; instead he must wait for her to come down to him.

On the manifest level this is a form of lover's test, allowing the young bride to see whether she can assert her mastery in the wedding contract that they have both agreed to—to be together for better or for worse. Pleased with her ruse, Celia sits in front of her mirror, proudly gazing at her reflection, and waits to see how her husband will respond to her assertion of feminine power. Mark, unable to enter her room, interprets her game as an effort to call into question his unrestricted access to his wife. When Celia, after waiting a few minutes, follows her husband to the garden in front of the hacienda, she finds a stranger there. Because she has locked him out of her private rooms, he has decided to lock her out of his emotional realm. He pretends that important business requires him to return to New York immediately, and he leaves her that very night, to punish her for having dared to question his superior authority over the abode they inhabit and, concomitant with this, his position within their marriage. Like the *fort-da* game that Freud describes, the sudden disruption of their honeymoon bliss allows Mark to translate a situation of passivity into one of empowerment. To prevent any further narcissistic injuries from his new wife, he prefers to lock himself out of his own accord. Their battle over the locking of a door allowed Celia to draw a boundary between an intimate space where she was mistress and a foreign body seeking to penetrate this space. Mark, however, uses her game for a different type of boundary drawing. By consciously excluding himself from the transitional abode he is sharing with his new wife during their honeymoon, he assures himself that his intimate feelings will remain locked away from her.

Left alone, Celia once more sits in front of her mirror, and now the voice of brooding sets in, playing through all the possible reasons for Mark's mysterious behavior, while her body begins to pace up and down her room, somatically enacting the painful doubts she is beginning to harbor. Although she quickly realizes that his lie and his sudden departure resulted from her having locked the door, she is as yet unable to find an explanation for their unexpected quarrel. Instead, the demon of her repetition compulsion takes hold, allowing the discord at the heart of their marriage and her doubts about Mark's love to emerge. While she had initially compared her acceptance of

Mark's marriage proposal to the opening of a door onto a wide landscape, she is now obliquely reminded that during their very first conversation she suddenly thought of daffodils. The danger that was always part of her sense of liberation from the secure but stiflingly restrictive safety of marriage now resurfaces and leads to her turning away from the open landscape that she had wanted to connect with her choice of the stranger she met in Mexico. Because she herself has closed a door on Mark, she must now open a different door, one behind which she will find neither a safe home with a fire in its hearth nor an open space; behind this door she will find the crypt in which Mark has preserved his painful memories. The murky interface between a familiar haven and an unfamiliar open space at stake in Celia's uncanny home romance indeed finds its architectural embodiment in Mark's family estate, Blade's Creek, where an economy of distortions reigns and thus renders visible the dark core at the heart of Celia's marriage.

The bride is met at the train station by Mark's sister, Caroline, who, like the old woman at the hacienda, represents a third position, uninvolved in the phantomatic game that this newlywed couple has begun to play. At the very moment that Celia crosses the threshold of her new home, however, Fritz Lang plunges her companion into shadow, as though to offer a visualization of how even her reasonable judgment has been drawn into the darkness of this house. While Caroline does everything to make the bride feel at home in her new abode, Mark's arrival at the train station the next morning allows Celia to continue to doubt that she will ever feel at ease at Blade's Creek. Upon espying a bouquet of lilacs pinned to the collar of Celia's jacket, Mark suddenly becomes cold and impersonal, whereas a moment before it had seemed as though he had completely forgotten their earlier quarrel.

After he once more abruptly leaves Celia without explaining why, she asks his driver to take her back to her new home, but during the ride an inner monologue sets in, directly articulating her homelessness: "Home, where is home? Not with Mark, not anymore. It was a gamble and I lost, period. I'm going back to New York. Back to what? To the empty life I lived before Mark. If only Rick were alive. I could go home with Rick. But what would he say? There's only one question, he'd say. Do you love him or don't you? And can that stuff about your pride and how your feelings are hurt. Do you want a man or [a] husband off the assembly line?" Unable to fashion for herself a home other than the symbolic fiction of her love for Mark, which has given her psychic support after her brother's death, she decides to return to Blade's Creek after all. In the course of the film she will repeatedly translate her unwillingness to choose a less uncanny material and psychic abode into her insistence that her love for Mark was unavoidable and thus remains an inescapable necessity. Significantly, however, she does so during this car ride by implicitly invoking her dead brother's voice of interpellation. She is able to convince herself by virtue of ventriloquizing the dead brother, who had always wanted her to commit herself to a husband, that to find a home in marriage means accepting another symbolic fiction, namely that the marriage vows are there to shield the couple from the disharmony of gender trouble that is necessarily part of this contract. Her monologue ends as she sternly reminds herself, "Those were big words you said in front of that altar. Love, honor, for better and worse, including the time when he's worried and moody. After all you're no easy dish yourself."

With this symbolic mandate intact, she is psychically equipped to return to her new home and to battle the demons locked up in her husband's mind and her own demons of doubt. The evening after their unhappy meeting at the train station, Celia waits for her husband to return, and when she hears his car she rushes out to meet him. Dressed completely in white, she stands poised in the open frame of the doorway to the house, mockingly asking him, "Do you want me to carry you over the threshold?" On this sunlit threshold, they kiss passionately for the first time since their lovers' quarrel in Mexico; they are positioned perfectly within the frame of an open door, marking the boundary between the uncanny interior of the house and the wide-open space on the other side. In response to his question of whether she is still angry with him, Celia replies, "I buttered my bread, now I have to lie on it," cleverly mixing her metaphors to indicate not just a double hunger but also her obedience to the symbolic vows of marriage that she undertook. However, she interrupts Mark, who in relief wants to kiss her again, explaining, "I choose the weapons and the battleground," bidding him to come upstairs with her to her bedroom, which, as she discovered on her first day, has no lock and key, just like all the other rooms on the upper floor of the Lamphere mansion.

They seem to have survived their first marriage crisis, even though Celia still senses that Mark is keeping significant parts of his intimate thoughts from her. During a visit to the "felicitous rooms" that Mark has collected in the cellar, Celia's bridesmaid, Edith, discovers a locked seventh door, but Mark insists that a man must have some secrets and refuses to unlock it. Significant about the architectural trope that Fritz Lang consistently uses in this noir fairy tale is that the locked door and the promise of a secret lying beyond it finally offer Celia a spatial embodiment that will allow her to translate the uncanny doubts tormenting her into a fantasy scenario of empowerment, in which she will have agency over the fated love she had previously declared unavoidable. Mark had explained to her that in architectural discourse "felicitous" doesn't mean happy, but "happy in affect, fitting, apt, an architecture that fits the events that happen in it."[25] Accepting his theory, she can tell herself that by entering the one locked room that he so diligently preserves as his secret, she will gain entrance to all the psychic material he also insists on keeping under lock and key. As in the first scene of the film, Lang offers an unequivocal symbolic language.[26] Shortly after the tour of the felicitous rooms, Caroline tells her sister-in-law the story of how Mark was once locked into his bedroom and when he emerged was beside himself with rage, while David, Mark's son, confides in her that he believes his father killed his mother. These two confessions precipitate an new string of doubts. Celia's voice-over wonders, "What goes on in his mind that he can change so suddenly?" While Fritz Lang presents a low-angle close-up shot of the seventh room, Celia continues to describe her plan of surveillance and detection: "He keeps it locked, like this door. I have to open them both, for his sake."

But just as opening the door of the forbidden room entails opening the passage to a scene of early childhood trauma, it also entails returning to another traumatic scene: the duel in Mexico, which had caused Celia to recognize her own desire for self-expenditure. As Reynold Humphries notes, because Mark is metonymically inscribed into the text by a house that represents danger, Celia's exploration of this home signals that what she wants to give herself in the guise of truth is actually death: "To discover the secret beyond the door is to discover the secret of life, namely death."[27] Two traumatic scenes are thus condensed in this room, whose common denominator is that both lovers want to use it as the hallucinatory stage on which they might play through for real a battle between life and death. Beyond the locked door, Celia is no longer an innocent bystander and Mark is not simply the collector of rooms that prove an obscure architectural theory. Serving as the scene for a horrific inversion of the notion that their love was fated, the room will harbor a different kind of fateful encounter. Here they will confront and enjoy the traumatic kernel of their marriage, the dark, indecipherable figuration that floats beneath the liquid surface of Celia's dream work, in which marriage entails the choice between boats (safe harbor) and daffodils (danger), sustaining these and at the same time exceeding the protective fictions that both tropes represent. And like the love they recognized at first sight, the romantic showdown between Celia's and Mark's gazes proves to be one in which neither has a choice. If Celia initially decided to return to Mark because she imagined her brother's call, which demanded that she accept her symbolic mandate, she now must acquiesce to the other interpellation that structures the maturation of the subject: the maternal figure of authority and the danger that emerges when her unbearable proximity has not been psychically jettisoned.

The quarrel that is instigated when Mark refuses to show her the seventh room precipitates Celia's investigation of her husband. In her conversations with the others who live at Blade's Creek she tries to reconstruct the puzzling fragments of Mark's past. Significantly, she chooses a scene, as I have already pointed out, that reveals the ambivalence connected to maternal authority, and thereby she successfully occludes two other questions that have emerged. First, why was Mark's marriage to his first wife so unhappy that Eleanor, convinced that he didn't love her, died mysteriously? And second, what caused Mark to return from the war a totally changed man? In other words, Celia's focus on the psychic anguish caused by overidentification with the maternal body is crucial because it allows her to undertake a significant reversal in the course of her detective work. She exchanges the role of pursued wife, as she had cast herself in her preferred fantasy scenario of feminine paranoia and had cultivated in relation to Mark since his strange behavior in Mexico, for the role of protecting mother. As a result of this transformation, the self-confident Celia, who threatened Mark with her insistence on determining when her room—and with it she—would be open to him and when it would not, no longer is a threat to his sexuality. At the same time, by assuming the position of the dead mother, Celia herself can relinquish the view of feminine sexuality that is inscribed by traces of the death drive. She no longer needs to choose between her two preferred notions that marriage entails either a safe but sexually lethal abode or a potentially fatal homelessness. Rather, she can now combine her poise and self-confidence with her fascination for the fallible in the shape of nurturing an infantilized, retraumatized man.

The Seventh Room

Fritz Lang significantly divides Celia's momentous entrance into the seventh room into two scenes. In the first one, she walks along the uncanny corridor leading to the cellar rooms one night, carrying a flashlight to show the way. With a copy of the key that she has clandestinely procured, she is able to open the door to the forbidden room and, when she enters, turns on the light, and pulls aside the heavy brocade curtain, she, like the young woman in the bluebeard tale, discovers what she believes to be a scene of death. Initially Celia's voice-over whispers, "It's Eleanor's room, the bed she died in." As she begins to survey the space before her, however, she realizes that this can't be so. She recognizes that the candles in front of the mirror are uneven, as the candles in her room are—because she used the wax of one of them to make an imprint of the door's key—and she finally concludes, "It's my room. It's waiting for me!" Having reached the height of her enjoyment of the possibility of imminent death, she rushes from the room and runs to her actual bedroom on the first floor of the house. She gets her coat, then once more carefully descends the stairs, intending to quietly flee this strange abode. On one of the steps, however, she finds an item from the third room—the scarf with which Don Ignazio, one of the murderers whose room Mark has reconstructed, strangled his three lovers.

As though to indicate that this is the acme of her hallucinatory enjoyment of the uncanny strangeness that inhabits both her marital home and her fantasy work, Fritz Lang signals here that the boundaries between safety and danger have fully collapsed. Blinded by the fear that she also fully enjoys, Celia runs from the house, losing her way in the fog, and as she wanders back and forth without actually getting anywhere, a male figure appears out of the dark behind her. At this point in the narrative Fritz Lang inserts the only harsh cut within the entire film, and once more we hear the accousmatic voice of his heroine. For a few seconds the screen is completely dark, accompanied by the voice-over of a woman screaming. We have returned to the initial scene of interpellation, where Celia had responded to a woman's cry by turning toward two men who were threatening to kill each other over the woman. But now it is clearly her scream.

With the next scene, a different voice-over is employed, along with a different subjective position. We see Mark leaving the bathroom where he has just shaved; as he dresses, his voice-over describes the trial scene he is inventing for himself. It is a macabre scenario in which he plays both the prosecutor and the man accused of having killed his wife, Celia. He explains that he found himself possessed by the urge to kill the woman whom he loved above all else in the world. The cause of this death drive, he argues, is that women, notably his mother and his sister, Caroline, have always controlled his life, and the impotence that this has imposed on him has resulted in an unconscious desire to destroy them. Since he is helpless against this murderous desire, he had to inflict it upon the privileged representative of feminine power who is currently tormenting him; he confesses as well that he would do so again, even though he is aware of his crime. What is crucial about this scene is less that on the manifest level of the narration it employs an extremely heavy-handed reference to Freud's theory of drives in an effort to exonerate the murderer than that the anticipation of a trial scene can't actually be Mark's fantasy. He knows that he didn't kill Celia the night before. Fritz Lang showed us in the previous scene how, from his bedroom window, he watched her flee into the fog, and shortly afterward he enters her sitting room and, astonished at finding her emerging from her bedroom, asks her why she came back. One might offer a more speculative reading for the inclusion of his voice-over. Having reached the acme of her voyage through the phantasmatic space of her marriage, Celia has appropriated Mark's fantasy, making the jury scene a part of her inner theater. Thus she is able to enjoy knowledge of her death by virtue of the traces it has left behind in the form of her husband's confession before the law.

This reading allows Fritz Lang to show how perfectly and how perfidiously Celia represents feminine omnipotence. In the scene following the inserted dream representation, when Mark has found Celia unexpectedly in her part of the house, Lang allows her to reappear in both his and our field of vision as she crosses the threshold between her bedroom and the more public sitting area. She begins to explain that she has returned because she loves him. Walking toward him, fully confident in her movements and her words, she adds that she returned because she married him for better or for worse, thus implicitly signaling to him that, unlike his mother, she will not abandon him—indeed, she will impose her presence on him even if this goes against his wishes. The brilliance of Lang's mise-en-scène resides in what her declaration of love implies. Although he believes he can kill her, she has already incorporated him into her psychic space and is thus fully in control, just as his mother was.

As Tom Gunning suggests, the first scene in the forbidden bedroom "is the culmination of both Celia's point of view and her interior monologue. In Celia's voyage of discovery . . . she has found her voice and speaks out loud her horrifying discovery." The two Celias—the one somatically enacting her doubts by wandering homeless through the many different places in Lang's dreamscape, the other endlessly brooding, her mind wandering restlessly from one image or explanation to the next—have finally come together. The cessation of her uncanny voice-over signals the beginning of her actual homecoming. Gunning concludes: "Far from losing her voice, Celia has learned to speak and located her problem no longer in her fear, or feelings of self-reproach for being an inadequate wife, but squarely in her husband." She uses this newfound voice to practice a magically effective talking cure for him, which, I would claim, begins with the last of the 180-degree turns that Lang stages for his heroine: her turning her back on the foggy woods, and the escape that they represent, and instead facing the heart of darkness lurking in the home and marriage she has symbolically vowed to be loyal to.[28]

The second scene in the forbidden room is, indeed, staged as a repetition of the peripeteia enacted in the earlier bedroom scene. This time, however, rather than walking toward her husband, Celia remains seated on the chair next to her bed, while Mark crosses the threshold into his seventh "felicitous" room and slowly approaches her, being as unable as she is to avoid this lethal confrontation that they have been anticipating. She explains to him that she would rather be dead than live without him, because that would be a slow death, for a lifetime. In so doing she repeats the formula of fated love, contacted at first sight, in which the choice between life or Mark was a false one. She can only choose Mark, even if it costs her her life. But the magic of interpellation that this noir fairy tale depends upon is that, from the moment when she consciously accepts the position her husband has designed for her—a position that she was so overwhelmed by that when she entered the forbidden chamber the first time she had to flee at the height of her *jouissance*—impotence turns into power. Much as she had during their honeymoon in Mexico, she is now waiting like a spider for her victim to get caught in the web of a fragmented narrative that she will force him to accept as his own truth. The trick that she will try to play on him, so as to cure him of his murderous desire, is to accept that his early childhood trauma, like the love he felt for her at first sight, consists of knowledge he has been carrying around with him, even though he can recognize what is still unfamiliar only by virtue of the cathartic reconstruction that she has performed for his sake.

Yet with the end of Celia's voice-over, a further reversal of her part in this dangerous game has occurred. On the manifest level of the narration, the love duel is presented as Mark's fantasy of self-empowerment, in the course of which he will seek to kill Celia in order finally to assert his power against all the women in his life who have made him aware of his fallibility. But equally manifest is that, in this final stage of their battle, Celia is no longer the one who is threatened; instead, she is the fighter who still has the knife in her hand, while her opponent has already lost his, having thrown it at her and missed. As she hurls at him the fragments of his past that she has been able to piece together—his hatred of lilacs, his anxiety about locked doors— she tells him the version of the story about the locked bedroom that she heard from Caroline, coercing him into explicitly naming his matricidal urges and only then revealing that it was his sister, not his mother, who locked him in. The cathartic power of this declaration is twofold. First, when the son learns of the innocence of the mother, he can relinquish his murderous drives, symbolized by his allowing the scarf that he holds, with which he had meant to strangle Celia, to fall to the ground. Second, Celia's declaration neutralizes the power that the phantasmatic mother has had over him since his childhood.

But although in this magic moment Mark is actually able to psychically jettison the maternal body, it is only to introduce a new phase of psychic dependence, for he now surrenders himself unconditionally to another omnipotent woman. She is not a substitute for his ever-teasing sister, nor for the first wife whom he could never emotionally accept, but rather for the mother of the family romance of his childhood, who was meant to be there only for him, nurturing and comforting him, comparable to the mothers and sisters who, as William Wyler depicted in *The Best Years of Our Lives*, transformed themselves into nurses and provided unconditional emotional support to the traumatized veterans who were coming home to them after the war. If the matricide fantasy of the paranoid veteran had come to be crossed with the bluebeard fantasy of the paranoid woman of independent means, Fritz Lang, however, requires a third antagonist for his lovers to finally quit the battlefield that defines their noir romance. As in the duel in Mexico, the battle is waged in the presence of a female onlooker. At Blade's Creek, however, she is not the object over whom two lovers fight, nor does she simply watch the duel. Rather, Miss Robey, the governess, has decided to intervene in the confrontation between the married couple, so as to bring about the demise of her rival in the hope of taking her place. Believing that Celia is alone, she locks the door to the forbidden room and then sets fire to the Lamphere mansion.

On a more cynical note, one might also surmise that, in postwar Hollywood, the psychically fallible veteran must be weaned from his urge to kill, yet he cannot be denied his masculine prowess altogether. After all, he must still be able to fight if a designated external enemy should appear again.

Startled by the smoke that has begun to fill the bedroom, Celia and Mark manage to break open the door, but they succumb to the smoke and faint in the entrance hall of the burning house as Miss Robey watches from a safe position among the trees in the garden outside. With the demise of the traumatized child, the veteran in Mark reawakens. Slowly rising to his feet in the smoke-filled space he is able to make his way to the glass door leading to the veranda, crash it open, take a few breaths of fresh air and return to the burning hall to save Celia from the flames. As Tom Gunning notes, the "melodramatic rescue . . . remasculinises Mark and has him now break through the locked door," even while it refeminizes Celia.[29] Lying unconscious in the arms of her husband, she can finally turn her back forever on the uncanny home, where she had come to enjoy the murky interplay between safe haven and danger. The symbolic fiction of love, with which Lang's film closes, requires a twofold rescue. After Celia has saved her husband from the glowing ashes of his dormant desire to kill, he rescues her from her burning desire for self-expenditure.

Beyond the death waiting for them both in the fateful bedroom, they magically find another door leading back to life and to the restitution of their marriage contract. In the final scene we see the couple returned to the hacienda of their honeymoon, far from their New York home. Celia is leaning back in her hammock chair, while Mark, sitting on the ground next to her, rests his head in her lap. While she gently strokes his hair, he declares, "That night you killed the root of the evil in me, but I still have a long way to go." She immediately counters with a narrative of her own: "*We* have a long way to go." Mark takes her hand and kisses it, as she continues to beam down at him mildly.[30] One might conjecture that, like Sam and Pilar at the end of *Lone Star*, they know that they will never be completely free of the traumatic events of the past, and for that reason they bet with full confidence on the symbolic fiction of love.

As Mladen Dolar insists, at the end of any psychoanalytic cure the law of love persists, even if the subject has recognized the contingent accident on which romance is based, as well as the delusions it can induce, and the lack that the beloved will never be able to fill: "For that alien extimate kernel that love has to deal with and which lies at the bottom of its paradoxes is the only precarious and evasive hold for the subject, and at the same time what makes its impossibility." At the end of *Secret Beyond the Door* the voice-over has finally stopped and with it, the cinematic convention that image and word correspond has been restored, so that the mode of representation supports the marital love contract whose restoration we have just witnessed. Distortion is no longer required, because the lovers have accepted the fiction of home that their mutual embrace affords them. Homeless in a cultural-geographic sense, they know that the safe haven of marital happiness, like the paper boat representing it in Celia's dream, floats on the surface of a pond that is inhabited by dark figures. Home can only be a precarious and transient state for them, but one they might sustain as such, a shield against real antagonism for a long time. Then, too, perhaps at the end of this noir fairy tale no further distortions are necessary, since the murderous drives of the husband have clandestinely become part of the wife. Celia's insistence that "*we* have a long way to go" could well also mean that the phantoms haunting this marriage lost their power not only because Celia and Mark were able to fit them into a shared narrative about the past but also because the wife has incorporated her husband's strangeness, making it part of her own psychic abode.

Imitation of Life—Between the black mother and the white one

Chapter 6

Sustaining Dislocation
Imitation of Life

A Director with Two Names

Douglas Sirk, in his interview with Jon Halliday, insists that in all his melodramas he was concerned with irony as a form of social criticism. He repeatedly foregrounded moments when dreams of success and happiness no longer hold because his protagonists realize that they can never escape the constraints of the cultural laws imposed on their desire for self-fulfillment. Consistently at stake in his appropriation of this cinematic genre, therefore, was an exploration of the fissures within the Hollywood convention of the happy ending, as well as a focus on the irradicable traces of the impossible dream of untainted happiness that remain even after the desire for its fulfillment has been curtailed in order for one to be content with an actual home and a symbolic place in the world. Indeed, Sirk, dubbed by film critics "master of the unhappy happy-end," always insisted that one can live with everyday unhappiness only by successfully containing any passionate desire to break out of the conventions that bourgeois culture imposes on its subjects. Apodictically put, for Sirk the concept of hope always threatened to collapse with its uncanny double, despair.[1] Discussing the analogies between Sirk's German career and his American one, Halliday at one point during the interview remarks that the closing sequence on the steamboat in *La Habanera* (the last film Sirk made under his German name, Detlev Sierck, for the UFA in Berlin) bears a striking resemblance to the

closing sequence of *Imitation of Life*. In the former, his heroine Astrée
(Zarah Leander) leaves Puerto Rico behind, taking her son, Juan, whose
Latin American father, Don Pedro (Ferdinand Marian), has just died, back
to her home in Sweden. As she stands at the ship's railing, looking back at
the island where she has spent the last ten years of her life, she explains to
the man who has been instrumental in her returning home, "You know, ten
years ago I thought the island was paradise. Later I thought it was hell, and
now—I regret nothing." A part of the desire that initially compelled her to
stay in Puerto Rico after her first visit, rather than returning home, will remain even after she finally does end her exile. In *Imitation of Life*, Sarah Jane
(Susan Kohner), the daughter of the African American Annie Johnson
(Juanita Moore), who had been passing as a white showgirl in Hollywood,
also finally returns home, in her case for the funeral of her mother. In the
final sequence of this film, she sits in the car of the white actress Lora
Meredith (Lana Turner), for whom her mother has been working as a live-
in maid for many years, saying farewell to both her mother and the African
American community that she never wanted to be part of and now realizes
she can never belong to. In response to Halliday's comment about the similarity between these two scenes, Sirk explained, "Well, Zarah Leander's
feelings on that boat are not entirely linear. She has been in the place ten
years, the ten best years of her life. As she looks back she is aware that she
is getting out of rotten—*but definitely interesting*—circumstances. Her feelings are most ambiguous. I think in the end of *Imitation of Life* the ambi-
guity is more external: the irony is in the eye of the audience."[2]

In the last film Sirk made for the UFA, he thus implicitly evokes the
tragedy of the *Mischling*, which he will fully explore in his last film for Universal Studios. As an ironic reflection on the ideology of racial segregation,
so typical of the American obsession with miscegenation in the 1950s, the
biracial child returns twenty-five years later in the form of Sarah Jane Johnson, who, as her mother explains, "favors her daddy. He was practically
white. He left before she was born." Her ambiguous skin color allows her
to move back and forth between two symbolic worlds, the one she was born
into by virtue of her mother's race and the one she has fantasized belonging
to because its color is valorized in the world she lives in. However, in this
film, which was to become a blockbuster in 1959, Sirk's heroine is not like
Astrée, who knows precisely where home is but doesn't want to be mistress
there. For Sarah Jane, the notion of being at home in any untroubled manner is no longer viable. Her only options are to decide in favor of one of the

two incompatible cultural interpellations informing her or to sustain the insoluble antagonism emerging from her cultural hybridity. Having to choose between two symbolic worlds means that she is forced to repress one of the alternatives and, further, the one she chooses is also curtailed.[3] In his films Sirk had consistently highlighted that by choosing a symbolic home, one inevitably encounters the unfulfilled desire that is part and parcel of any romance—be it with a place or a person. Such a forced choice between possible homes takes on a new significance, however, if the person involved can no longer distinguish unequivocally between what is home and what is foreign because her very body forms the line of demarcation between the two.

Significant about the fact that the final sequence of Sirk's picture for Universal resembles the final sequence of his last UFA film is not merely the emotional sympathy that he ascribes to the protagonists who find themselves sustaining the antagonism of two conflicting cultural interpellations. Rather, the affective intensity of these two final scenes resonates so poignantly because both reflect aspects of the director's own biography. Obliquely inscribing his own circumstances onto Astrée's story, Detlev Sierck gives voice to the forced choice open to him as a filmmaker working in Nazi Germany but married to a Jewish woman and thus desperate to get out of circumstances that he, like the heroine of *La Habanera*, felt had become rotten, even though UFA had been a great attraction for him since the mid-1930s, when he had begun making films there.[4] When in the final sequence of *La Habanera*, Astrée returns to a home that has become foreign to her, she is also taking leave of a place she can no longer bear, much as Detlev Sierck sought to leave Berlin for a foreign but hugely desired new home. One might further speculate that, as he was editing this final scene and waiting for the passport that would allow him to join his wife in Rome and emigrate to the United States, he came to realize, like his heroine, that choosing to leave his "rotten circumstances" behind would mean embracing cultural dislocation as the definition of his subjectivity.

Then, at the end of his successful Hollywood career, when he was about to return to Europe, he once again found a cipher for his own sense of being split between two identities—an American one and a European one—in a female protagonist. Like Sarah Jane, he had discovered that the loss that goes along with a move from a familiar culture to a foreign one always haunts you. His agent had encouraged him to change his name from Detlev Sierck to the more American Douglas Sirk. Thus the director who was to become a master in employing mirrors as a trope for the illusion of untroubled happiness driving his protagonists in their search for love and success created his own double. At the end of his life, when he was already quite ill and his mind, according to Jon Halliday, sometimes wandered, he confided to his friend, "There are two Douglas Sirks. The trouble started when I changed my name."[5]

Living Imitations of Life

Since the reappraisal of Sirk in the late 1960s, culminating in Rainer Werner Fassbinder's declaration that among his films "were the most beautiful in the world,"[6] critics have repeatedly noted that he chose melodrama as the privileged genre for his aesthetics of contradiction not simply for thematic reasons but also because it encourages the gesture of double articulation that was so dear to him. While telling stories about women and men caught in emotional impasses, Sirk, as Christine Gledhill notes, always had recourse to ironizing devices such as aporia and peripeteia, "deployed to undercut what are described as the hollow sentimentalities derived from a feminized consumerist culture."[7] In her collection of essays, significantly titled *Home Is Where the Heart Is*, Gledhill argues that Sirk is known for the way he visualizes the contradictions inherent in bourgeois ideology, even though he appropriates the same ideological values that he also seeks to disclose and displace.[8] Produced under the auspices of ironic distance, these films became successful because they supported the very desire for escapism that they also obliquely sought to subvert. As Tag Gallagher recalls about watching Sirk's melodramas years before film critics rediscovered them as paradigms of cultural critique, "We might not have used words like 'distanced,' 'subverted,' or 'irony' . . . but we felt all of it in *Imitation of Life*: the searing paradox and despair of racism in America, the ambivalence that made it worse, and yes! we felt the 'distancing': we knew we were experiencing a movie . . . yet we saw ourselves in each of the characters. That's why we were crying."[9]

An acceptance of 1950s Hollywood melodrama as oblique social critique, however, raises the question of what is the object of this ideological debunking. Sirk offers his audiences fantasy scenarios that satisfy a desire to escape the unbearable contradictions inherent in their everyday lives, while, at the same time, in the cinematic world—so clearly staged as an artificial, illusory film—they find themselves confronted with situations that they readily recognize as ciphers for the familiar impasses of their own psychic and social reality—the very issues that they seek to escape by going to the movies. Claiming that "no ideology can ever pretend to totality; it must provide an outlet for its own inconsistencies," Laura Mulvey insists that fissures are actually inscribed into the seemingly coherent worlds emerging from an ideological film genre like the Hollywood melodrama. For her, "ideological contradiction is the overt mainspring and specific content of melodrama, not a hidden, unconscious thread to be picked up." She therefore suggests viewing the melodrama genre in general as "a safety valve for ideological contradictions centered on sex and the family"[10]—and one might well add centered on notions of home and cultural emplacement as well. Along these lines Geoffrey Nowell-Smith suggests that if one thinks of the melodrama genre as "a contradictory nexus," then the importance of films such as Sirk's *Imitation of Life* "lies precisely in its ideological failure." Because the melodrama genre "cannot accommodate its problems, either in a real present or in an ideal future, but lays them open in their shameless contradictoriness, it opens a space which most Hollywood forms have studiously closed off."[11] For Thomas Elsaesser the true pathos of Sirk's films lies in the discrepancy between the ambitions of his characters, seeking to live exalted family or home romances, and their reality—"living out the impossible contradictions that have turned the American dream into its proverbial nightmare."[12] On a more optimistic note, Linda Williams locates the utopian moment of modernism in the double articulation of melodrama, structured as it is upon the "dual recognition of how things are and how they should be," which ultimately contains a moral, wish-fulfilling impulse toward the achievement of justice that is typical of American popular culture.[13]

In all cases, however, this critical debate highlights that the typical Sirk protagonist, far from being at home in her world, can carve out a viable place for herself only by accepting dislocation. Indeed, it was Sirk's declared aesthetic aim to deploy characters who were torn between their desires and the laws defining their social position, even while he refused to depict a successful triumph over this indelible contradiction between personal happiness and public restrictions. This concern with the hopelessness of his protagonists' lives finds its aesthetic correspondence in what has come to be considered his trademark—the enmeshment between cool, rational calculation and unrestrained enjoyment of excessive sentimentality. On the one hand, Sirk was able to inhabit the melodrama genre with such mastery because that was where he found the perfect combination of kitsch, craziness, and trashiness that he sought in order to illustrate that grand emotions find their most adequate aesthetic representation in stories about human confusion and conflict.[14] On the other hand, his was always a didactic project, for he compels his audience to identify unconditionally with the exaggerated passions performed while at the same time rationally enjoying his visual figurations of the contradictions inscribed in human passion. Just as the conditions of life that torment his protagonists have no cure, the logic of the melodrama genre that Sirk employs has no simple solution. Indeed, his hybrid cinematic strategy calls upon us to believe in the happiness of love or the intact home even though it forces us to recognize how fragile these fictions are. Sirk's films thus dislocate us not only because we are asked to identify ourselves with protagonists who are tormented by conflicting desires but also because we find ourselves torn between two contradictory aesthetic effects. We are moved, and at the same time we recognize that our affective response is the result of an ideological interpellation. In this contradiction, transmitted on the level of the aesthetic process, a remainder emerges that exceeds both the ideological message and its explicitly performed disclosure.

As we watch the opening credits of *Imitation of Life*, we hear Earl Grant's voice on the sound track, assuring us that "without love you're only living a false creation, an imitation of life." Yet at the same time we see diamonds falling down one by one from the upper part of the image until they have filled the entire screen. Against the background of this iridescently magnificent but illusory glamour, Sirk tells the story of four women, each of whom is inextricably caught up in life's imitations. The contradiction to which each of these women falls prey revolves around the conflict between the desire to fashion herself according to her dreams and ambitions and the claim that she can overcome and even repress all conflicts in life that curtail these dreams.[15] The film begins with two women meeting accidentally on a crowded beach on Coney Island. The actress Lora Meredith (Lana Turner) is desperately looking for her daughter, Susie (Terry Bernham), and finds her playing happily with Sarah Jane (Karin Dicker), the daughter of the unemployed Annie Johnson. The two women decide to live together and raise their daughters together, in an imitation of the American nuclear family of the postwar period, though—significantly—without fathers. While Lora, in the course of the next ten years, becomes a successful Broadway star, Annie emerges as the clandestine master of the Meredith home. She organizes the housekeeping and generates the human goodness and warmth that holds the four women together as a family. In fact, the friendship between these two women is the only conflict-free aspect of an otherwise strife-ridden plot, subtended in part by Lora's blindness toward race difference but supported also by an implicit clandestine homoerotic miscegenation.

Yet this lack of tension between the two mothers is hardly perceptible given the troubled relationship between them and their daughters. For Lora, driven by fantasies of success, life occurs almost exclusively onstage. She is proud of the home she has been able to finance as a result of her successful career, yet she remains to a degree foreign there, for she can never fully exchange her role as actress for that of mother and housekeeper. When she is not actually onstage, she performs for her friends and family the role of the star, constantly receiving better offers that she can't turn down. At the same time she is aware that her success is nothing more than a protective fiction, because her zealous pursuit of new roles revolves around an indefinable void. In a poignant scene that takes place in her dressing room after a premiere, she explains to Annie, who is helping her change for a party to be held in her honor, that she knows if she were to give up her ambitions she would find herself confronted with a fundamental sense of lack: "You make it . . . then you find out it doesn't seem worth it . . . something's missing." It is, however, impossible for her not to give in to her urge for public recognition, so that, while she repeatedly promises her daughter that she will end her career, her most dominant imaginary relation toward her real living conditions remains to the end the role of the radiant actress. In contrast to Lora, who feels estranged from her home and, implicitly, from her daughter, Annie sees her position in the Meredith household as the fulfillment of her family romance. In this home she can enjoy a lifestyle that would otherwise be denied to her as a black woman living in a world prejudiced against miscegenation, even though she is restricted to fulfilling the stereotype of the black servant.[16] At the same time, she is able to secure for herself a viable position within the black community of the New York suburb. Yet on account of her race she, too, to some degree lives only an imitation of life. Excluded from the white world of the theater, she waits in the back rooms of the various residences she shares with her employer, who, unlike herself, can earn money with her public appearances. She comforts Lora in her despair, looks after her daughter during her absences, and vicariously enjoys her successes, as the privileged maternal spectator. Thus, in Annie's fashioning of herself as the infallible mother of the Meredith home, illusion plays as central a role as it does in Lora's fashioning of herself as the successful Broadway actress. Annie fills the maternal position that has remained empty because of Lora's career, and imagines her one moment of glory to be her magnificent burial, which she has planned as minutely as Lora has engineered her public fame on earth.

While the two mothers can live with the contradictions that inhabit their mutual home, the two daughters openly acknowledge that they feel like strangers there. Although the sixteen-year-old Susie (Sandra Dee) goes to a good private high school and is showered with gifts from her mother, she feels wounded by her mother's constant absences. In order to compensate for this lack of maternal love, she falls in love with Steve Archer (John Gavin), who had been rejected by Lora as a husband while he was still a struggling photographer. After ten years, he has returned and is now running a successful advertising agency. He renews his courtship, only to discover that the daughter desires him as well. Susie's romantic passion is, of course, nothing other than her imitation of life. By appropriating her mother's gestures and clothes, she turns into a collateral figure; she enjoys Lora's romance by proxy, much as the audience enjoys Lora's many theatrical roles. In one scene Sirk actually shows mother and daughter sitting on a sofa, wearing similar clothes, their hairstyles practically the same, holding a telephone receiver between them, from which we can faintly hear the voice of the man they both love.

Although her reasons are far more concrete than Susie's wounded narcissism, Annie's daughter, Sarah Jane, also feels that she cannot belong to the Meredith household. White enough to pass, she literally embodies Sirk's concern with ambivalent protagonists, split in their personalities and restlessly driven by an insatiable desire. She is unwilling to assume the subordinate position her mother has adopted, and so she creates for herself a family romance that obliquely reflects the unsolvable conflict of her ethnic background: she denies being the daughter of the unequivocally black Annie. Like Dorothy in *The Wizard of Oz*, she dreams of a place beyond the New York suburbs, a place where she can escape all the race trouble that vexes her and that reduces her either to the role of servant or to a life exclusively in the black community. After several attempts at refashioning herself as a white woman in the New York area—initially in hopes of marrying a young white man from the suburb where she lives, then in working as a dancer in a New York nightclub—she finally escapes to the West Coast. This she sees as her only chance, for as long as she lives close to her mother, her appropriation of whiteness is disrupted because Annie, checking up on Sarah Jane at school or at work, insists on telling everyone that she is her mother and thus repeatedly recalls her daughter to the place of her ethnic origins.

Sarah Jane's case is the most radical in Sirk's film, because her solution to making it in the white world requires a choice between an imitation of white life and the loss of existence itself. She resolutely explains to her peers that she would rather be dead than allow herself to be fixed exclusively in her black identity.[17] Her flight from maternal interpellation, however, seems to succeed only with her move to Hollywood. When Annie visits her there, she is finally willing to promise Sarah Jane that she will never again disturb her performance of whiteness, yet she returns home with a broken heart and dies shortly after this last confrontation with her daughter. Consequently, Sarah Jane is irrevocably recalled to the home and the ethnic background that she had sought so furiously to escape. Deeply humiliated by the cruel demand she made on her mother, Sarah Jane finally publicly acknowledges Annie as her mother at the funeral, only to find that she is rejected by the black community. Thus she is once more returned to her uncanny position in the Meredith family.[18] Sitting between Lora and Susie in their car, with Steve looking on from the front seat, she can only watch, grief-stricken but silent, the spectacle that excludes her. What remains is merely the imitation of emotional understanding between the deceased and her surrogate family, because Sarah Jane's public confession comes too late for any real affective restitution to take place. Emphasizing the underlying element of hopelessness, Sirk claims for the final scene of *Imitation of Life*, "You don't believe the happy end, and you're not really supposed to. What remains in your memory is the funeral. The pomp of the dead."[19] Instead he celebrates the inevitability of human unhappiness, the failure of both symbolic interpellation and the magical belief in the power of love. At the same time, Sirk's bleak claim is that there is no escape from ideology, even if it is shown to be nothing but imitation; there can be only a recognition of its failure. As Joan Copjec notes, "It is not primarily the characters (the small others), but rather the big Other who is charged in melodrama with inauthenticity, in the sense that it is incapable of supplying the grounding or validation for any character's existence."[20]

Sirk's last Hollywood melodrama highlights one of the central concerns of the genre: that these cinematic scenarios fail to construct a world for their characters to inhabit and thus point to the fundamental homelessness that underlies human existence. All four women live imitations of life: Lora, the fiction of being a successful actress; Annie, the fiction of being a surrogate mother to a white daughter and mistress of a white suburban home; Susie, the fiction of being in love with her mother's lover; and Sarah Jane, the fiction of becoming a successful white showgirl. At the same time, these fantasies are inevitably hybrid, haunted by the very contradictions that their imitations are meant to screen out. Lora knows about the emptiness of her success, Annie recognizes that her daughter will never be happy, Susie is forced to accept that she cannot steal her mother's lover, and Sarah Jane must acknowledge that even the most successful performance of whiteness will not resolve the racial difference she embodies. Indeed, to seek freedom from contradictions by fleeing into an imaginary refiguration of their actual living conditions must fail. The ambivalence in feeling, which drives each of the women to live an imitation in the first place, recalls the psychic material that has been repressed. Whenever one of the four must choose between her ambition and the fate of love, Sirk visually performs the impossibility of resolving the contradiction between an imitation of life and an authenticity won through love by inserting a mirror reflection of one of his protagonists as she seeks to claim her right to self-definition.

For example, in staging the scene in which Lora calls her family after the premiere of her first stage appearance to tell them about her success, he places her in front of a mirror, with the telephone attached to the wall on the right side of the mirror. As she tells her family about the overwhelming applause she received for her performance, we see her "opposite" (as Sirk called the mirror images of his protagonists), framed by the mirror in such a way that the doubling of mother and actress leads the viewer to speculate that there is something uncanny about her public success, straddling two interpellations—the demands of her theater audience and those of her family. In a parallel scene we find her sitting in front of a mirror when she confesses to Annie that after all her struggles to make it as a Broadway actress she has discovered that something fundamental is missing from her life. Once more Sirk shows his protagonist split in two—the persona of the glamorous actress, framed by the mirror and thus arrested as an illusory image, and the woman facing the self-creation she chose to privilege over wifedom and motherhood. By visually performing his protagonist's self-fashionings as mere illusory reflections, Sirk repeatedly foregrounds the idea that, in contrast to the theme song of his film, an authentic life and its imitation are uncanny mirror images of each other, both constantly threatening to collapse.

As Sirk explained, "*Imitation of Life* is more than just a good title, it is a wonderful title. I would have made the picture just for the title, because it is all there."[21] The radical contradiction posed by life cannot be resolved into a happy ending, because life and imitation are welded together, just as the subject is welded both to the symbolic codes whose interpellation wounds its narcissism and to the imaginary relations it must entertain so as to make real living conditions bearable. In his conversations with Jon Halliday, Sirk explains further: "Here is a wonderful expression: seeing through a glass darkly. Everything, even life, is inevitably removed from you. You can't reach, or touch, the real. You just see reflections. If you try to grasp happiness itself your fingers only meet glass. It is hopeless."[22]

As critics have repeatedly noted, the cinematic signature that is typical of Sirk's American melodramas can be located in the way he employs mirrors and framings to obliquely point to the real, which can be evoked only in its absence, but never reached. These mirrors and frames render visible the way in which Sirk's characters are caught in conventions and prejudices that distort all authentic feeling and agency; they also point to the way that these women, owing to their cultivation of illusory fantasies, are caught in a hopeless ambivalence. Yet what ultimately fascinated Sirk about the use of mirror reflections was the way they allowed him to represent most poignantly the uncanniness of human existence: "What is interesting about a mirror is that it does not show you yourself as you are, it shows you your own opposite."[23] We recognize ourselves only through reflections, notably the images we fashion for ourselves, or the way we see ourselves reflected in the eyes of others. Yet as Jacques Lacan notes in his seminal essay on the mirror phase in psychic development, published some ten years before *Imitation of Life*, the act of recognizing oneself in a mirrored image is always inscribed by misrecognition, for the image we see has undergone a double fracturing. It is not only an inversion of the figure it mirrors, but it returns to the subject only by a detour through an intermediary, namely as a representation. It thus harbors the disjunction between body and image, and in so doing obliquely points to the way any narcissistic jubilation, meant to be supported by the mirror image, is always already troubled.[24]

If one accepts that the work of fantasy is located beyond cultural interpellation because fantasy brings to light the residues of psychic material that must be relinquished if the subject is to take on an unequivocal position in relation to the cultural laws determining her, then Sirk's last Hollywood melodrama can be called a celebration of the crisis of interpellation. Even while he shows how each of the four women hopes to find a harmonious solution to her conflicted desires by accepting a fixed position within her given symbolic community—whether on a public stage or in a private home—he also explores the opposite desire. Each of the women harbors the fantasy that she might not have to accommodate herself to the cultural codes that curtail her ambitions. While each finally recognizes the impossibility of realizing this dream, something persists in the fantasy life of Sirk's protagonists that will not fit into the clear symbolic position prescribed by interpellation.

Indeed, the choice between two incompatible cultural interpellations proves to be not just a forced choice but an impossible one. All Sirk's protagonists can do is to recognize that they have no choice. Each choice brings with it a real loss. If the title song claims that love is the emotional state located beyond interpellation, promising to cure the contingencies of everyday life ("without love you're only living an imitation of life"), it does so in order to illustrate how all notions of love itself are inscribed by ideology. One might well imagine the lover proclaiming, "I occupy the place allocated to me by the law, but I know that I exceed the symbolic position ascribed to me, because I also occupy another place—the place my beloved has chosen for me."

At the same time, if ideology resembles a dream, as was discussed in the chapter on *The Wizard of Oz*, so does love. Like ideological interpellation, love is nourished by a desire for unity and harmony and is unwilling to acknowledge the impossibility of a state untroubled by contradictions; it, too, seeks to avoid the radical antagonism that is inextricably inscribed in human existence as an extimate core within subjectivity. Yet if we follow Mladen Dolar, who suggests that the birth of the subject occurs when it recognizes the irreversible cut between its real living conditions and any imaginary refiguration of these circumstances, we also recognize that the failure of interpellation is constitutive of the subject's desire. Because interpellation to a degree is never complete, because in our identity we are more than the symbolic position ascribed to us, we desire in the sense of imagining for ourselves identities other than the one ascribed to us. Indeed, the protagonists in Sirk's late melodrama can no longer articulate the radical contradiction of their desire in a simple opposition between "being at home/returning home or being foreign." Instead, their only choice is to cover up their sense of psychic and geocultural dislocation by assuming a culturally codified, yet also illusory, role.

The *Mischling's* Crisis in Interpellation

As already discussed in the introduction, Freud coined a trope for the work of fantasy, which ascribes its power to the ambivalent position it takes on in the psychic apparatus. In his article "The Unconscious" he notes that fantasies are "highly organized, free from self-contradiction . . . and would hardly be distinguished in our judgement" from the formations of the consciousness. On the other hand, he adds, "they are unconscious and are incapable of becoming conscious, thus qualitatively belonging to the preconscious, while factually belonging to the conscious system." The seminal point he makes about fantasies, however, is the following analogy: "Their origin is what decides their fate. We may compare them with individuals of mixed race who, taken all round, resemble white men, but who betray their colored descent by some striking feature or other, and on that account are excluded from society and enjoy none of the privileges of white people."[25] Fantasies represent hybrid figurations that uncannily embody the threshold between two radically separate areas of the psychic apparatus—the conscious and the unconscious—but because of this alleged "mixed race nature" also threaten to become the uncanny site where uncontradictory expressions normally allocated to consciousness collapse with their opposites. In so doing, they transform into a highly contradictory expression of the remains of the real, which, according to Sirk, we can never directly reach. Fantasies can never fully become conscious; they recede from our judgment because they never fully jettison the unrepresentable affects and drives of the unconscious. Their power thus resides in their deep and irresolvable duplicity. They may be able to conceal their actual consistency—the traumatic core on which the antagonism between unconscious knowledge and all belated representations relies—yet this repressed knowledge inevitably returns to prohibit fantasies from inhabiting the conscious in any untroubled way. Although fantasy work, as protective fiction, seeks to resolve contingency into coherent stories, the transference never fully succeeds; by seeking to occlude their internal antagonism—the kernel of extimacy, both intimate and external, so basic to the human psyche—they only reintroduce contradiction.

The analogy between the work of fantasy and the *Mischling* is significant for my own reading of *Imitation of Life* because of the fatality of the logic proposed by Freud. In the same manner that fantasies try to jettison their origin but only find themselves drawn back to the repressed other scene from which they emerged, so, too, Sirk's Sarah Jane cannot escape from her place of origin. Instead she relentlessly carries her legacy with her, even when she hides it behind a brilliant performance of whiteness. At the same time, Freud's definition of fantasy also evokes the anxiety that the *Mischling* elicits in her peers. Sarah Jane's ability to appropriate an appearance that, if one essentializes ethnicity, is in fact foreign to her, evokes an anxiety about the situation, from which she seeks to shield herself and others. Precisely because the *Mischling* cannot be assigned to any one particular group, her presence elicits the disturbing recognition that our notions of inhabiting our symbolic communities in a simple and unconflicted manner are more troubled and fragile than we wish to admit. Linking fantasy work to the *Mischling*, Freud supports his more general claim that fantasies radically trouble any unequivocal cultural interpellation, even though one could see the *Mischling* as a paradigmatic example of such a crisis in representation. What, after all, does a *Mischling* do, if not appropriate the foreign appearance that she does not factually own so she can answer to the interpellation of the duped others: "Yes, that is me"? At the same time, however, the *Mischling* also proclaims the opposite of such an unconflicted self-definition, albeit not always of her own volition. She seems, after all, also to make the claim to her peers, "No, that is not me. I am an illusion, a reflection of the symbolic position allocated to me according to my circumstances—a symbolic position I am expected to take in relation to your cultural codes." As D. N. Rodowick puts it, Sarah Jane's problem of identity points to "the difficulty which the individual character finds in their attempts to accept or conform to the set of symbolic positions around which the network of social relations adheres and where they can both be 'themselves' and 'at home.'"[26] Sarah Jane radically troubles any notion that one could ever really be at home—in a public role, in a community, or in a material abode.

It is, then, only logical that Sirk, concerned with rendering visible the uncanny fissure inscribed in the work of fantasy, should have chosen a young woman who can pass for white as the pivotal figure of his film. As he explains to Jon Halliday, "The only interesting thing is the Negro angle: the Negro girl trying to escape her condition, sacrificing to her status in society her bonds of friendship, family, etc., and rather trying to vanish into the imitation world of vaudeville. The imitation of life is not the real. . . . The girl [Susan Kohner] is choosing the imitation of life instead of being a Negro. The picture is a piece of social criticism—of both white and black. You can't escape what you are. . . . I tried to make it into a picture of social consciousness—not only of a white social consciousness, but of a Negro one, too. Both white and black are leading imitated lives."[27] Indeed, the story of Sarah Jane can be read as a *mise en abyme* of the entire narrative, given that it forms the dark kernel around which all the other embodiments of imaginary refigurations revolve.[28] Sarah Jane, who, removed from her mother, appears to inhabit the white world with impunity while her mother's interpellation continually recalls her to the black world she leaves behind, is a character who most perfectly represents the oscillation that Freud attributes to the vicissitudes of fantasy. If one is willing to follow Freud's cue and see in the work of fantasy a form of passing, with unconscious knowledge passing for uncontradictory conscious material, then the hybrid Sarah Jane emerges in Sirk's film as a representation of fantasy par excellence.

What is significant about the analogy I am proposing, however, is that the boundary transgression performed in the act of passing consists, as Werner Sollors notes, in a cultural invention. Far from touching on any real social conditions, passing concerns an imaginary relationship. The sanctions against it, imposed by both ethnic sides, presuppose that one part of the racial heritage—the black side—is more real, essential, and determining, while the other side—the allegedly appropriated white side—is contingent, comparable to a masquerade, and thus insignificant or fraudulent. From this, Sollors concludes that stories about passing satisfy both a modern fascination with the undecidability of identity and the desire to anchor social identity as related to the legacy of one's race in a world where such lines of demarcation constantly threaten to fall apart.[29]

The disturbing aspect of the interracial subject consists, however, in the idea that she or he has no essential ethnic kernel but is instead split in her or his biological heritage—an ideology to which Freud also falls prey when he presupposes a simple opposition between a real identity kernel and an appropriation of a second identity. The act of passing is troublesome because the seamless appropriation of an allegedly foreign identity works only if that identity is actually as much a part of the heritage of the passer as the racial identity to which her peers seek to reduce her. Functioning as an uncanny foreign body who exceeds both of her ethnic origins, the *Mischling* forbids all untroubled drawings of boundaries and all unequivocal allocations of identity. In the same way that a spectator cannot determine the difference between an allegedly originary cultural identity and an appropriated one based only on the appearance of someone passing for white, a person like Sarah Jane also cannot hierarchize the racial and cultural differences written into her body—unless she submits herself to an external interpellation, in her case the law of the mother, which would require her to decide exclusively in favor of her black heritage. One might then say that the act of passing embodies a crisis in interpellation, because what we find literally reemerging at the body of the passer is a trace of what remains after symbolic interpellation has taken place. For the *Mischling* the choice of belonging to a particular geocultural place can only be a forced choice. What is precarious about the act of successful passing, then, is that the appropriated unconflicted identity is threatened not only by the biological hybridity of the subject but also by a second instance of interpellation—the desired (but forbidden) other side, which is just as resilient as the culturally privileged interpellation.

In order to develop the proposed analogy between the work of fantasy in general and the story of the woman who, like fantasy work, finds herself oscillating between two callings, I will concentrate in the following reading only on those scenes that revolve around the uncanny figure of Sarah Jane, since these illustrate so well how Sirk's protagonists can never be "themselves" in an untroubled way, as they can never be "at home." In the first scene of the film, after Lora has found her lost daughter in the care of Annie and has introduced herself to the black woman, Sirk shows us the young Sarah Jane casting her scrutinizing gaze twice over her mother's body. In the face of the visual contrast of her mother to the figure of Lora Meredith, who seems to correspond far more closely to her ideal of the maternal body, she appears to gain a critical distance with respect to her own mother. Her rejection of Annie's acceptance of the subordinate position that culture ascribes to her is forcefully articulated as they accept Lora's invitation to share her home. Sarah Jane had already burst into tears on the beach, when Susie asked her where she lived and she had to respond, "No place." Then, after Lora and Susie had turned around and begun to walk away from the beach, she addressed her mother for the first time tenderly, crying out, "I wanna go home, too!" Once Lora has taken them home with her, however, Sarah Jane wants to determine her place within this new abode on her own. She rejects the present of the black doll Susie gives her and instead grabs for the white one, which she is willing to exchange for the black one only when Annie forces her to. Annie then asks her daughter to follow her to their new living quarters behind the kitchen. On the threshold between the two spaces that have now come to be clearly differentiated along color lines, Sarah Jane retaliates, cruelly taunting her mother with the question "Why do we always have to live in the back?" Even though she ultimately follows her mother, she throws the black doll away just before entering her new home. Sirk's camera, significantly, tarries with the image of the doll lying on the floor, as though it were a materialization of the residue that remains after Sarah Jane has been forced to choose the black one of two possible maternal figures, and with her, the room in the back. Yet the marked rejection of the black doll takes on a second meaning. Representing the body of the black girl by proxy, it articulates the fact that Sarah Jane also has a place on the other side of the now closed-off back room. As Susie's companion and as Annie's daughter, she can inhabit both sides of the threshold, yet she also remains alien to both.

From the moment Lora enters Sarah Jane's field of vision, she represents the cultural law that the young girl seeks to appropriate for herself. She tries to relate to her as though she were her daughter. She imitates Susie falling into Lora's arms when she returns in the evening, and, like Susie, asks for a good-night kiss. As part of her rejection of Annie's insistence that she be content with her back-room existence, she also feels inspired by Lora's ambition to seek happiness in a public display of appropriated roles. Nevertheless, Sirk insists on a significant difference between these two feminine destinies. Lora's decision against domesticity and in favor of her career as an actress is based on a simple opposition, embodied by the two men who are wooing her. Sirk poignantly stages this opposition in the proposal scene, having Steve declare his love to Lora in the narrow corridor in front of her apartment door. One has the sense that she is being boxed in, cornered with his demand that she be loyal only to him, for his offer of marriage is dependent on her resigning from the theater. Having declared his romantic feelings for her, he asks her whether she, too, loves him. Although she hesitatingly replies, "I think I do," the kiss with which Steve hopes to seal their romance is interrupted by the ringing of the telephone in Lora's apartment. Through the closed door we hear Annie talking to Lora's agent, Allen Loomis (Robert Alda). Caught between Steve's proposal of domestic happiness and Loomis's proposal of fame, Lora immediately recognizes where her desire lies. She forces herself out of Steve's embrace and rushes in to accept Loomis's call—and with it his offer for her to appear in a new play by the successful Broadway writer David Edwards. Although Steve tries to warn her that the life she is about to pursue isn't real, she responds, "At least I'm after something!"

Sirk's relentless irony emerges in the fact that choosing the theater is staged as a descent for her. Having decided that she will go immediately to her agent's office and pick up the manuscript of the play, she hurries down the stairs of her apartment building—as though descending to Hades—with Steve following her, offering reasons why she should not pursue this path. Once they have reached the entrance of her building, she assures him that she would rather break off all relations with him than have him tarnish her dreams of success. Although she will pay dearly for this choice, she will never actually regret having made it, because it was never inscribed by the same contradictions as Sarah Jane's decision to choose the life of the stage instead of her mother's proposition of home.

This peripeteia, in which Lora chooses the theater over marriage, is, however, significantly framed by two scenes that allow Sirk to render visible the analogy between the white actress and the showgirl who passes for white. It is introduced and succeeded by scenes in which Sarah Jane comes to recognize that for her to pursue her ambition to inhabit what she perceives to be a world not troubled by race is a false choice that she can only regret. Each attempt on her part to jettison her black heritage results in the appearance of her mother and her insistence on a response to her maternal interpellation. Sirk includes a scene just before Steve's proposal to Lora in which Annie catches Sarah Jane passing in school. Her daughter flees the classroom upon seeing her mother, only to be confronted by her in front of the school building. The dialogue between them illustrates that the violence inscribed in Sarah Jane's rejection of her mother's interpellation is aimed both at Annie and at herself. As her mother asks her to put on the coat and boots she has brought to her so that she will not catch pneumonia, she responds, "I hope I die." Then, after Annie has admonished her not to be ashamed of her heritage, because that's simply what she is, Sarah Jane directly accuses her: "Why do you have to be my mother?" The logic of the family romance she has fashioned for herself is such that if only she were able to cast off her corporeal origins she could determine for herself the position she wished to assume in her symbolic world. Annie, however, responds to this failure of her maternal law with a rhetorical turn, which corresponds to Freud's schema. Like fantasies, the *Mischling* cannot escape the destiny of her origins.

Having brought her daughter back home to the Meredith household, where the law against miscegenation plays no role, Annie confesses to Lora, while sitting at the kitchen table, that her daughter has been guilty of passing. Once more Sarah Jane resists her mother's attempt to assign to her a single cultural identity, by responding, "I am white, as white as Susie." Lora tries to arbitrate, explaining that in her home it makes no difference whether she is black or white, because she is loved. Yet this is not an acceptable compromise for Sarah Jane, who insists that the unsolvable conflict between her origins and her appearance cannot be reduced to a sentimental solution of mutual affection. Annie, in turn, sees in her daughter's passing a false ambition and pits against it her own conservative family romance. Heavily influenced by her Christian faith, she sees divine justice in the fact that one can't escape one's fate, and she declares to Lora, who is so blind to questions of race that she naively believes Sarah Jane's racial ambivalence can be explained away: "I don't know. How do you explain to your child she was born to be hurt?" Actually, both women are saying the same thing. One cannot escape from the narcissistic injury that life inflicts on the mature subject, given that once it has accepted symbolic interpellation, it can never harmonize its individual desires with the inconsistencies and constraints of real living conditions. The characters simply want to interpret this injurious knowledge in different ways. Lora selfishly seeks to pit her family romance against the codes of segregation and wishes to remain blind to their consequences outside her home, while Annie translates what Sollors calls the invention of passing into a divinely ordained fate, because that way the contingency of the injustice she and her daughter experience can be lived as a coherent story.

Sirk cuts from Annie's sentimental proposition that her child was born to be hurt to Steve's proposal scene, in which Lora refuses to accept the unjust fate of a marriage without a career. The effect of this sequence is that the real hopelessness of Sarah Jane's story reflects back on Lora's illusory hopefulness. The radical break that Lora makes with Steve, and thus with the possibility of romance in her life, is what introduces the next scene: a Christmas evening in the seemingly happy home of a family run by an interracial same-sex couple. Annie, sitting in an armchair with Susie on her lap and Sarah Jane standing behind her, leaning on the back of the chair and looking over her right shoulder, is telling the story of the birth of Christ. Lora, in turn, walks quietly past them with the script of the part she is studying in her hand. At the point where Annie describes how Mary and Joseph could find no place at the inn and chose as their abode for the night a stable among animals, Lora briefly interrupts her own reading and smiles at the two girls, who are deeply engrossed in the story Annie is telling. Then, once more lost in the part she is to perform, she paces across the room until she has reached the mirror at the other end. In its reflection we see her smiling at herself and assuming the gestures of the fictional persona she is to play. Dissatisfied with her impersonation, however, she turns away from the mirror and her double image so as to practice a different facial and vocal intonation. Both Annie and Lora are suddenly interrupted in their separate performances by the ringing of the telephone. It is Steve, calling to ask to be forgiven, but Lora refuses to speak to him, instead asking Annie to continue with her story, while she, now standing behind the armchair, returns to studying her role.

Annie is once more interrupted in the holy family romance she is narrating, this time by her daughter, who asks whether Jesus was black or white. This is an interruption Lora cannot simply ignore by returning to her script. She fully wakes up from her silent self-absorption and looks at Sarah Jane in irritation. As though a transfusion has occurred, the young woman now takes her turn at performance and presents a hybrid enmeshment of the two maternal figures. Like Lora, convinced of her ability to fashion herself according to her own desires, she appropriates Annie's tale to make it her own story. In response to Lora, who assures her that it makes no difference what skin color Jesus had, since "he's the way you imagine Him," she insists that race makes a significant difference, declaring to the family assembled around her, "He was like me . . . white." By not offering any visual resolution for the contradiction that Sarah Jane has voiced, Sirk allows us to recognize that with this performative statement she has introduced something troubling into the seemingly intact Christmas family tableau. The camera remains relentlessly fixed on the face of the young woman, so close that Lora, standing behind her, is cut off at the neck, her face outside the image, and Annie's head is visible only from behind. Fully aware of the impact of her declaration on both maternal figures, Sarah Jane, looking at neither of them, gazes smugly off into an empty off-screen space in front of her. Now she is the one who is absorbed in enjoying a persona she has dreamed up for herself.

Imitation of Whiteness

In the second half of the film Sirk presents three longer sequences that show how Sarah Jane's ability at mimicry makes the two mothers realize that they, too, are only fallible masters of the home they have set up together, even while they also show how the hybrid daughter draws violence onto herself with her wish to determine her own racial identity. The first of these scenes begins with deception. Sarah Jane, who does not want to go on the picnic that Lora has organized for Steve, pretends to be sick with a migraine. Sitting on the edge of her bed, Annie tries to give her daughter some advice, then reluctantly withdraws to join the others, who are already waiting for her in the car in front of the house. The minute she has left the room, Sarah Jane jumps out of bed, goes to her closet, and takes out a slinky silk dress. Holding it in her right hand, she looks out the window and watches with satisfaction the departure of her unwanted family members. It is not until the following scene, after the others have returned from their picnic, that we discover she has sneaked off to the village to meet her white boyfriend, Frankie. To explain to him why she can't take him home, she has been lying, telling him that her parents are very strict. Her dual duplicity—the concealment of her true background from Frankie and the concealment of her white boyfriend from the two maternal figures ruling at home—is further emphasized by an explicit representation of the liminality of her existence within this household. We see her looking through the kitchen window from the outside, waiting for her mother to leave the room. Then she quietly enters through the back door and steals upstairs to her room, hoping no one will notice her clandestine entrance.

But outside her room she meets Susie, who has been looking for her. To stop Susie from telling on her, she confesses her secret affair. In response to Susie's seemingly innocent question whether her boyfriend was "colored," she unfolds her complex imitation of being white. For one, she has recourse to the threat she uttered to her mother, after Annie had caught her passing in school: "Well, if he ever finds out about me . . . I'll kill myself . . . because I'm white, too. And if I have to be colored, then I want to die!" What Sarah Jane's ability to shift seamlessly from one racial affiliation to the other renders visible is the performative quality of racial identity. In one and the same gesture she claims to be white, while also acknowledging that this is not all that can be said about her racial origins. She must deny this troubling hybridity in order to hold on to the simple identity of "whiteness" that she has fashioned for herself. In so doing she gives voice to the fact that racial identity is nothing natural but rather the result of a symbolic allocation within a cultural community shaped by the simple opposition between black and white. From the point of biological anatomy she is, of course, black, but the symbolic meaning of this for her peers is contingent. Her mimicry of whiteness actually mirrors the imaginary relation that any given person entertains toward her, but in so doing it also feeds off the wish that, by virtue of the recognition in the other, she might find a stable, unequivocal position in the world. Sarah Jane quite explicitly conceives of her ambition to pass successfully as a performance. She proudly announces to Susie, who listens to her in amazement, "I want to have a chance in life. I don't want to have to come . . . through back doors, or feel lower than other people, . . . or apologize for my mother's color. She can't help her color . . . but I can . . . and I will!" At this point she is still unaware of the vacuity of her dream, much as she doesn't yet realize the price she will have to pay to succeed. Instead, with tears in her eyes she declares herself to be safe from detection so long as she fashions her identity exclusively in relation to this romance with whiteness: "I'm going to be everything he thinks I am. I look it. And that's all that matters."[30] The category of racial essence doesn't exist for her; she is concerned only with the question of which possible appearance she will choose for herself. Whichever way she decides, she becomes guilty of the masquerading that Annie accuses her of. She can be master of no home, whether it be a white household or a black one. In the former, what troubles is her deceptive skin color; in the latter, it's the racial heritage that cannot be seen on the skin.

In order to explore this insoluble contradiction, Sirk moves from her confession to two scenes in which Sarah Jane performs the equation she postulates between appearance and being, by virtue of her ability to mimic whiteness to perfection. In so doing, however, she also subverts stereotypes of blackness and whiteness: in the first scene it is her parody of the black plantation slave; in the second, her rendition of the unconditionally subservient white suburban wife. In both cases, however, her performance not only makes visible the failure of each particular stereotype but also uncovers the kernel of violence inherent in the restriction of a hybrid subject to simple definitions of the self. Both scenes occur on the evening of the picnic. Lora, who has invited Loomis and an Italian film agent for cocktails, asks Sarah Jane to help her mother to prepare hors d'oeuvres. Because Sarah Jane initially hesitates, Lora assumes that she wants to go out to meet a boyfriend, and assumes further that he must be black. Without clearing up the misunderstanding, Sarah Jane goes to the kitchen, where her mother confronts her with a similar expectation. She is angered by the desire of both maternal figures to reduce her to her black identity, which in the world that Sirk depicts is concomitant with belonging unequivocally to a subservient class. "Busboys, cooks, chauffeurs! No, thank you!" is her comment about the young men her mother wants her to meet.

She thus chooses to perform a parody of the black identity that they ascribe to her. After Annie has asked her to take a plate of shrimp into the living room, where Lora and her guests are drinking cocktails, she taunts her mother: "Why, certainly! Anything at all for Miss Lora and her friends." Sirk cuts to the two agents, debating with each other while Lora sits silently between them. Then suddenly the Italian stares at the figure who has just entered the room. The next shot shows Sarah Jane, balancing the plate of shrimp on her head, lasciviously swinging her hips and walking toward the people sitting on the sofa. Speaking in the stereotypical dialect of the Hollywood black plantation slave, she explains to "Miss Lora an' yo' friends" that she has brought them "a mess o' crawdads," then sets the platter on the table and leans toward the men, smiling absurdly and rolling her eyes in mimicry of another cinematic stereotype of the subservient black slave woman. Irritated by her performance, Lora asks her where she learned this "trick," and without changing her intonation the disobedient daughter replies, "Oh, no trick to totin', Miss Lora. Ah l'arned it from my mammy . . . and she l'arned it from old Massa . . . 'fo she belonged to you!" Then she smiles one last time at the Italian, with her eyes absurdly wide open, and leaves the room. Lora rushes after her into the kitchen and challenges her about her improper behavior. Sarah Jane replies by stressing how empty the identity construction is that the two maternal figures in her life impose on her: "You and my mother are so anxious for me to be colored. . . . I was going to show you I could be."

As Judith Butler notes, "Performing in excess, exaggerating the role of maid, indeed submitting it to the melodramatic requirement of hyperbole, Sara Jane deploys imitation to expose the power-differential of race and to refuse it."[31] Sarah Jane has, of course, explicitly chosen for her performance of black identity the stereotype of the subservient, always smiling servant, and in so doing has willfully misunderstood the double maternal interpellation imposed on her. By having recourse to a distortion of the black woman, she wants to render visible that for her the difference between a simple stereotype and the unequivocal reduction to one racial identity (black) insisted upon by Annie and Lora is only a question of degree. In essence the mothers' well-meaning determination of her identity fails as much to address the unresolvable contradiction of her cultural affiliation as any clichéd notion of black femininity she might choose to appropriate. For her to accept any one unequivocal identity is a form of racial cross-dressing, since it brings to light the performative construction of all geocultural definitions of identity, while at the same time pointing to the exclusion of hybridity, for which there is no room in any of the notions about black or white femininity that were culturally prevalent in the 1950s.

Following Judith Butler, one might argue that accepting the interpellation of the cultural codes relating to race, gender, and class definition is always a form of approximation, for, as she notes, "there is a cost in every identification, the loss of some other set of identifications, the forcible approximation of a norm one never chooses, a norm that chooses us, but which we occupy, reverse, resignify to the extent that the norm fails to determine us completely."[32] Yet in Sarah Jane's case, this injurious interpellation is taken to a radical extreme, for she cannot escape into the fantasy that there might be an interpellation she would feel more at home in, a social dress that would fit her better. While she tells herself that the white persona she has fashioned for herself might be this ideal, she is repeatedly forced to recognize the emptiness of her ambitious self-redefinition. To highlight his own skepticism, Sirk ends the scene with Sarah Jane recognizing the validity of the advice that Annie and Lora give her. She accepts Lora's prohibition against her ever performing the black slave again in her house, and she also falls into her mother's arms, explaining that she hadn't meant to hurt her. The one sentence that will, however, resonate in the following scene is the accusation that she nevertheless directs at Lora: "You don't know what it means to be different." The difference written onto her body can simply not be resolved by Lora's fantasy that in this hybrid household of women harmony rules and the question of racial and class distinctions plays no role. Instead, we have Sarah Jane's insistence that she can never be at home with herself or this household.

In the following scene Sirk directly addresses the race difference that is repeatedly screened out in Lora's home. In the meeting between Sarah Jane and her boyfriend, Frankie, that takes place the same evening, he stages the untenability of Annie and Lora's confidence that, with time, conflicts can be resolved. Although Sarah Jane's impersonation of the subservient white woman, willing to do whatever her husband requires of her, is far less exaggerated than that of the black servant, she is nevertheless accused of pretense. As they stand on a deserted street of the town, in front of an empty window of a store that is up for rent, Sarah Jane suggests to Frankie that they run away to New Jersey, because she is having trouble at home. She assures him that she would do anything to be with him, and he initially pretends to believe her; leaning against the window, he admits that her suggestion might not be a bad idea. To expose the distortion subtending Sarah Jane's family romance, which lets her believe that she might come to have a protecting home and a happy family existence in a white community, Sirk first gives us a front shot of Frankie. Above his head the sign "Bar" can still be seen on the window, while to his left we see a reflection of Sarah Jane's face, smiling at him in a mixture of expectation and ingratiation. The moment he asks her whether it is true what he has heard—that her mother "is a nigger"—Sirk's camera draws back to shatter what was clearly nothing but a mirrored reflection of the possibility of happiness. At first we see the two debating with each other in a close shot, their upper bodies filling the entire frame. It is now Sarah Jane's turn to test Lora's race blindness on her boyfriend by responding, "What difference does it make? You love me." Then, as Frankie persists, asking directly, "Are you black?" Sirk's camera cuts to a close-up of Sarah Jane's face as she tries to convince him of her right to determine for herself her racial definition: "No, I'm as white as you!" But like her mother, Annie, her boyfriend will not let her choose freely the position within her symbolic world that she wishes to assume. As he begins to slap her face, the camera cuts back to the reflection in the empty shop window, so that we see him beating her up only as a mirror image, a framed reflection at whose bottom edge, as though it were the subtitle of the scene of violence we are witnessing, we see the sign "For Rent."

Then the camera cuts once more to the couple, and we see Frankie continuing to beat her until she collapses in a dirty puddle between two wooden crates. He has violently shown her the position she can assume as a black woman in his world—not that of the lover, his equal, standing before him and confessing her love, but rather that of the helpless woman, the victim of his rage. The brutal irony that Sirk imposes on this scene refers to the enmeshment of gender and race trouble around which the entire plot revolves. The physical violence with which Frankie responds to Sarah Jane's independent self-fashioning echoes Steve's verbal violence in responding to Lora's insistence on fashioning her own life. Steve had, after all, threatened that if she was not willing to relinquish her dream of becoming a successful actress on her own, he would forbid her to continue acting once they were married. But Frankie's violence also gives concrete body to the warning that both maternal figures have given Sarah Jane about the dangers of passing. Indeed, this is the turning point in Sarah Jane's relation to Annie, for here she has been physically compelled to accept the consequences of her mother's interpellation. The forced choice she now makes is to put as much distance between them as possible so that she might live her fantasy of being white with impunity, even though she knows full well that it is an imitation. In other words, even while she rejects Annie's dictate that she should go to a black college and integrate herself in the black community, she does accept its jurisdiction. But acknowledging the legitimacy of the maternal law remains tantamount to breaking it, to radically denying both her heritage and the black identity it proposes for her.

It is, then, only logical that the unresolvable contradiction at the heart of Sarah Jane's symbolic existence culminates in a direct confrontation between daughter and mother. Annie visits her daughter in the nightclub near

Hollywood where she seems to be successfully pursuing her career. Performing a different stereotype, that of the white showgirl, she is wearing a low-cut gold lamé dress with a slit skirt, paste earrings and choker, and half-length turquoise gloves. Sitting in a turquoise armchair that rocks backward, she floats past the audience on a conveyor belt, striking the seductive poses typical of the pinup—pouring herself champagne, setting the glass aside, exhibiting her alluring body—until her seat has been conveyed to the back of the stage. In this exclusively white world of show business she exceeds the other girls with her performance. Even more radiant than they, she proudly displays her seemingly immaculate "white" body to the audience, even winks at one of the two men sitting at a table directly in front of a spot on the stage where the conveyor pauses for a moment. They smile back, confirming to her the success of her performance.

Annie follows Sarah Jane to her room in a hotel and assures her that no one saw her come in. She didn't come to bother her, she explains, but simply to see her one last time. This time Annie does not challenge her daughter's passing; rather than questioning the position Sarah Jane has chosen to assume in her symbolic world, she asks her whether this choice has brought happiness. In response to the question of whether she has found what she really wants, Sarah Jane abruptly turns away from her mother, and looking into the mirror above her dresser, she defers both her mother's gaze and her question, performatively declaring: "I'm somebody else! I'm white! White! White!" For a moment Sirk shows us the mirror's reflection, which now places Sarah Jane, defiantly regarding her white counterpart, next to Annie in the same frame. The visual framing that Sirk has chosen allows us to see Sarah Jane from behind as well as her mirror double, while Annie can be seen only as a reflection in an image we are asked to read as her daughter's imaginary refiguration of her relationship with her mother. Yet as was the case with Lora, practicing her first Broadway role the Christmas after she broke up with Steve, the mirror reflection brings no satisfaction to Sarah Jane. Rather, as she looks at her "new" persona, standing next to her black mother, she recognizes the failure written into her imitation of whiteness. She keeps reiterating, as though it is her magic ritual of interpellation, that she is now white. Yet Sirk has her break into tears and then turn around to face her mother directly, signaling the perseverance of the maternal interpellation.

A second peripeteia has occurred here. Sirk, who enjoyed cutting his actors' monologues, arguing that the camera sees everything even without words, suddenly stages a tacit understanding between mother and daughter.

It is as though Sarah Jane, having seen the unseverable bond between herself and her mother reflected in the mirror, is proclaiming, "I am white here. In this world I answer to a symbolic identity that casts me as white. But at the same time I know that that identity isn't me. I am assuming this position only in a reflection, as an imitation. Not in the real." At the same time, her tears silently bespeak a different truth, namely the recognition that "this, too, isn't happiness, because I know that the part of myself I have cast off remains, the trace of a different calling—you calling me back to your affection—and that means that I remain alien here as well." Precisely because in this moment of confrontation Sarah Jane recognizes for the first time that she is no more able to relinquish her mother than Annie is capable of relinquishing her, she can articulate the terrible law that will ultimately result in Annie's death: "Mama, if by accident we should ever pass on the street, please don't recognize me!" Although Annie is willing to accept this prohibition, she sets against it the indelible power of her maternal love. Taking her daughter into her arms one last time, she seduces Sarah Jane into accepting her law of the heart, as though to proclaim, "I love you so much, nothing you do can keep me from loving you."

The irresistible emotional outburst that this scene provokes in the audience has as its basis the tragic irony that Sarah Jane can accept her mother's love unconditionally only after she has irrevocably rejected her mother's declaration that she is unequivocally black. The tears she sheds, the passion with which she embraces her, while repeatedly sobbing "Mama" in response to Annie's sentimental maternal interpellation, testify one last time that for Sarah Jane the choice between being the daughter of a black woman and appearing as a white showgirl in defiance of her heritage is not simply a forced choice but an impossible one. In this conflict between mother and daughter what is at stake is not the question of who is right and who is wrong but the question of negotiating two equally legitimate, yet utterly incompatible, imaginary refigurations of the real.

The only solution to the aporia, as Sirk shows in the subsequent narrative resolution of the scene, is for mother and daughter to bond over a mutually shared secret. Their sentimental anagnorisis is interrupted by the appearance of Sarah Jane's roommate, who has come to fetch her. Now Annie herself performs an act of cultural cross-dressing. Before the eyes of her astonished daughter she seamlessly slips into the role of the classic "Mammy," the other figuration of black femininity that Hollywood stereotyping allowed in the 1940s and 1950s. The motel room is suddenly transformed into a stage, as

Annie proves to her daughter that, in return for Sarah Jane's recognition of her maternal law of love she will acknowledge her law of passing. Calling her daughter by the pseudonym she has assumed in Hollywood, she explains to the roommate that she just happened to be in town and dropped in to see "Miss Linda." As she had assured her daughter several moments earlier, in the presence of another white person she no longer claims Sarah Jane as her daughter. Yet it is precisely because they now share the same gesture of simulation, and only because of this shared secret, that an authentic declaration of love can pass from mother to daughter. It is as though Annie is saying, "Because I love you, I accept your forbiddance. But I can do so only because I am sure of your love, even if it is a love you forbid both me and yourself." This love is not beyond interpellation, but rather includes a parodic appropriation of the law imposed by her maternal interpellation. For their peers, the love between mother and daughter has become invisible, yet for us—the audience—it is perfectly clear, albeit as an authentic expression hidden beneath an imitation. With the roommate's presence fully in mind, Annie takes leave of her daughter, still calling her Miss Linda, while Sarah Jane, having turned her back on her roommate to make sure she can't see her face, mouths the word "Mama" without uttering a sound. Then, after the black woman has gone, the roommate, imitating a Southern accent, voices her surprise that Sarah Jane had a mammy. Supporting the misunderstanding, Sarah Jane can, for the first time, acknowledge her mother to a white person. With tears in her eyes, she leans against the door through which her mother has just left and responds obliquely, such that her roommate will not understand: "Yes—all my life."

The inevitable unhappiness that Sirk seeks to celebrate here has two aspects: Sarah Jane will recognize Annie as her mother only if it is part of her passing scenario, and Annie no longer hears her daughter's confession, because the door separating them has closed. She returns home, confesses to Lora her conviction that she has failed as a mother, and breaks down emotionally. In what follows, Sirk adopts the iconography of the deathbed scene, so often employed by the bourgeois novel to ritually enact family solidarity in moments of crisis. The sentimentality evoked by the anticipation of death allows the extended family to reconfirm their alliances with each other, while the dying woman employs her final leave-taking not only to determine how her possessions are to be distributed but also to confirm the image of herself that she wants those who survive her to remember.[33] However, Sirk, as he does with the other paraphernalia of melodrama, appropriates the deathbed scene to disclose the way in which the authenticity of the emotions deployed here is merely a further imitation of life. Annie's doctor, her minister, Steve, and the black butler, Kenneth, have all gathered around her deathbed to pay their last respects, and Lora sits on her right side. Between Lora's head and Annie's we see, propped up against the lamp on the bedside table, a photograph of Sarah Jane smiling radiantly. Annie explains to those assembled how she wishes her possessions to be divided up, calling upon each of her grief-stricken friends individually and entrusting each with a particular concern.

The most important task is, however, entrusted to the entire group, and yet she has already turned her gaze from them before she begins to explain how she imagines her funeral. In an earlier scene she had explained to Lora that our wedding day and the day we die are the great events of our lives, and now she publicly elaborates on the dream she has been harboring as her own home romance all these years, over and against her real experience of racial and class discrimination, and in radical opposition to her daughter's passing. At stake here is her fantasy of finally reaching a more noble home than the one she has been inhabiting on earth. As Mahalia Jackson sings in the funeral scene, which immediately follows this deathbed scene, the belief of the dying woman is that "I'm going home to live with God."

This public transition is intended to belatedly perform Annie's belief in the meaningfulness of human fate, which she connects to the indisputable benevolence of God. The funeral ceremony, which she has planned down to the last detail, is the ritual meant to forcefully demonstrate to her survivors the imaginary relation that has allowed her to bear the unhappiness of her real living conditions. Lora responds to Annie's description of her funeral with indignation. But Annie retorts, "I'm just tired, Miss Lora, awfully tired," then leans back on her pillow and quietly closes her eyes. According to Sirk, the "No" with which Lora responds to her friend's demise, is the one good line Lana Turner has in the entire film, the only moment in which her performance appears real. "All her life is tied up with this negro woman, about whom she really knows nothing; and so when the negro woman dies, Lana is left completely empty."[34] Indeed, Sirk lets Lora call out in vain twice to the deceased, then fall forward onto the bed in distress, thus lying next to the dead Annie. All that remains on the screen at the end of this scene is the face of Sarah Jane in the photograph, now framed by two mother figures who have both turned away from her. With this mise-en-scène, which restores contradiction to the field of vision, Sirk undermines the grand emotions that Annie's speech aroused in the spectators, because the daughter on whom her entire emotional life had depended is not merely absent. Rather, her radiant smile is nothing but an image. Annie's conviction that her funeral will represent her proud transition into God's glory in worldly terms is as much a protective fiction as her boundless love for her daughter, which she proclaimed on her deathbed.

Sirk's staging of the funeral begins with an image of one of the stained-glass windows in the church, in front of which Mahalia Jackson stands on a raised platform, singing down to the congregation about the trouble of the world. As the camera pans down, we see for the first time the earthly congregation among whom Annie had found a home, parallel to, yet also fully apart from, the Meredith household—a black community at whose center is the Baptist church, about which Lora never asked her and to which Sarah Jane never wanted to belong. In their mutual grief over the loss of the woman who had been so successful at separating the two worlds she lived in without—in contrast to her daughter—experiencing this difference as a conflict, we find realized the interracial mix that Lora had evoked whenever she tried to convince Sarah Jane that race makes no difference when it comes to questions of the heart. Amid the crowd we recognize the faces of Annie's white friends and acquaintances—Lora, Steve, Susie, Lora's agent Loomis and the playwright David Edwards—and as the camera pans across the crowd to the back of the church, it becomes hard to distinguish between black and white faces.[35] When Mahalia Jackson has finished her song, several members of the congregation carry out Annie's white coffin, lavishly decked with white flowers, and place it into a splendid hearse drawn by four white horses.

At this moment Sarah Jane disturbs the ceremony conceived by her mother, just as she had once interrupted Annie's story about the birth of Christ. Then, she was seeking to set her own fantasy of being white against the fact of her mother's race; now, she seeks to acknowledge this maternal heritage. In despair she explains to a policeman who is trying to hold her back, "But it's my mother." Breaking away from him, she throws herself onto the coffin. Her first, private admission of her maternal affiliation in the motel room in Hollywood was uttered behind a closed door, but now her public admission, in which she begs Annie's forgiveness and proclaims her love for her mother to everyone, is uttered over her mother's dead body. Thus the fissure inscribed in all worldly happiness remains to the end in Sirk's mise-en-scène. In the hotel room in Hollywood Sarah Jane could not assure her mother that she was finally happy in her new symbolic home as a white showgirl but could only performatively declare her whiteness, and now she will never be able to utter the sentence her mother had passionately wanted to hear: "I am coming home to you." She is forever arrested in the state of having wanted to return but having come too late.

Lora, however, insists on tailoring one's desires to the codes of propriety. When she notices Sarah Jane's arrival, she gets out of her car and walks rapidly toward her. By calling to her, "Oh, Sarah Jane, don't," she wakes the grieving girl from her senseless and excessive public display. She leads the distraught Sarah Jane back to her car while the coffin bearers, who had watched this unexpected emotional outburst in silent disbelief, finally close the door of the hearse. Sarah Jane's attempt to become part of the black community with this public acknowledgment of her mother fails. In the eyes of the public she is now in exactly the position she'd always wanted: with her white surrogate family and cut off from the predominantly African American crowd who are paying their respects to a member of their community. In silence, Lora Meredith and her family look out the window of their car as the hearse passes them. Sirk's camera pans back twice into the interior of one of the houses next to the street along which Annie's hearse passes on its way to the cemetery, so that we see the funeral procession through a wood-framed window. Then he cuts to a direct close shot of the magnificent spectacle—the grieving spectators, the laden coffin, and finally Lora and her family, still sitting in the car, which has now begun to drive away from the funeral scene. We see Sarah Jane, her head resting in exhaustion on Lora's right shoulder, while Lora has placed her left hand on her own daughter's shoulder. Apart from them, we see Steve, softly smiling at this alliance of women that has been not only restored but reconfirmed. It is as though Lora has come to occupy the position that Annie had while telling the Christmas story, while Steve now occupies her position of onlooker.[36]

Master of Unhappy Endings

The film ends with a final image of the hearse making its way down the street as onlookers line the sidewalks. Sirk himself has maintained that one is not to believe the happy end, since everything is so obviously hopeless. Even if Lora has been able to reconstitute her family alliance so that, for a brief moment, over Annie's dead body, a happy turn of events seems to have occurred, "Lana will forget about her daughter again, and go back to the theater and continue as the kind of actress she had been before. Gavin will go off with some other woman. Susan Kohner will go back to the escape world of vaudeville. Sandra Dee will marry a decent guy. You see, there is no real solution of the predicament the people are in, just the deus ex machina, which is now called 'the happy end.'" To this he adds, "It makes the crowd happy. To the few it makes the aporia more transparent."[37]

Indeed, given the distortion Sirk has built into his representation of the funeral by including the shots through a window frame, he explicitly renders visible how fractured is the image that we get of the real anguish of his characters and, by implication, how murky their own view of this traumatic event of death inevitably is, clouded by their respective fantasies, from which the real continues to recede. The reconstituted family at the end is as much a protective fiction as Annie's orchestration of her own funeral. As a result, it is not just the four white mourners gazing at the funeral procession through the window of Lora Meredith's car who are excluded from the celebration that is literally passing them by. The audience also occupies a liminal position, compelled to oscillate between an unreflected sentimental identification and a self-critical distance. The interpellation of an ideology, based on the law of racial segregation, fails for us just as it does for Sirk's hybrid protagonist, which is why we are willing to indulge in protective fictions, be they the family romance that unites mothers and daughters or the home romance of a Christian woman who believes her death to be a homecoming to the realm of God.

At the same time, Sirk forces us to recognize that these fantasies fail as well, because they are nothing other than imaginary distortions of real circumstances, which will always exceed and thus trouble the self-fashionings that each of the protagonists undergoes, even though these are necessary as stories by which they—and implicitly we—can go on living. If in Ford's *The Searchers* we, as the audience, found ourselves in a position analogous to that of Mose Harper, forever in his rocking chair on the porch between the prairie and the interior of the homestead, at the end of *Imitation of Life* we find ourselves in a liminal position as well, though less topologically specific. Sirk compels us to recognize that we have been presented with nothing but representations, seen through a glass darkly, and thus he implicitly leaves us with a forced choice. We are called upon ultimately to choose an ironic gaze, which allows us to steer a course between the Charybdis of symbolic laws that are injurious to narcissistic images of the self and the Scylla of love. As he himself pointed out to Jon Halliday: "The irony is in the eye of the audience." We can, however, choose not to choose, not to accept the ironic stance he seeks to impose on us—and therein lies the final turn of the screw.

In his conversations with Douglas Sirk, Jon Halliday suggests that the funeral scene could also be read as Sirk's cinematic performance of his own leave-taking of Hollywood. Sirk not only agrees with this analogy but also readily discusses his own biography in terms of the typical melodrama plot. Late in life, he explains, he came to recognize that his escape from Nazi Germany brought with it the unsolvable conflict of cultural dislocation, which took material shape in the juxtaposition of his new American name and his old German one. If the ending of *La Habanera* had initially mirrored his desire to escape the decidedly rotten circumstances of his life in Berlin, this scenario of compelled leave-taking came to haunt him again when, after having completed *Imitation of Life*, he chose once again to go into exile. Though he returned to Europe, he did not return to the home he had left in the late 1930s. Rather, having decided to make no more melodramas, he went on to live the melodrama plot that he had so successfully filmed for both the German UFA and the American Paramount studios. As he explains to Jon Halliday, he had been tempted to return to Hollywood and complete a promising career, because "there is an undeniable lure of this rotten place." The choice that he actually made, about which he was never entirely happy, arose from his decision to take the illness that had befallen him during his last Hollywood years seriously. By way of describing the emotional confusion that resulted in his decision to return to the European home he had once left, he explains: "I had no roots any more in Europe, and I don't think I wanted to sink new roots into ground that had become foreign to me. In the meanwhile I had become much more at home in America." Realizing that if he did return he would not be able to resist being drawn back into filmmaking and would end like Lora or Sarah Jane, caught up in imitations of life, he decided in favor of a different kind of unhappiness. "I stayed in Switzerland, where I am not at home either, and sometimes, thinking about myself, it seems to me I am looking at one of those goddam split characters out of my pictures."[38]

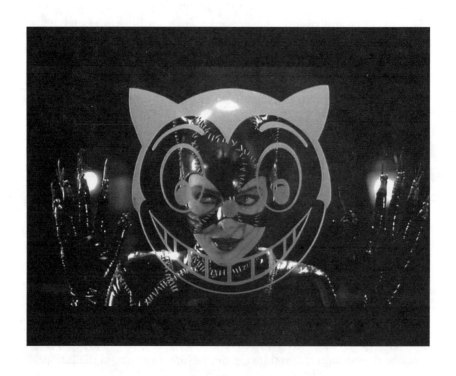

Batman Returns—Catwoman strikes back

Chapter 7

The Homeless Strike Back

Batman Returns

A Monster Is Born

Tim Burton announces his own return to the comic figure Batman, whom Bob Kane invented in 1939, with a forceful fanfare.[1] At first his camera, which in the course of the film will repeatedly imitate the unimpeded movement of flight that its protagonist is famous for, captures the heavy neo-Gothic iron gate at whose apex is welded the name "C. Cobblepot." Then, without interrupting its trajectory, the camera flies over the blocked entry, climbing up along the facade of this stately old mansion, only to stop at an enormous top-floor window, behind which we discern the silhouette of a man standing and waiting in apprehension. Burton immediately cuts to the illuminated interior of the magnificent room to show us a close-up of the master of the house, who—lost in thought while smoking a long, thin cigarette—gazes outside at the snow-covered nocturnal landscape. On the sound track we suddenly hear the moans and screams of a female voice, at which the master of the house turns away from the window, clearly disturbed. While the camera follows his gaze as it takes in the grandeur of this living room—the gold brocade curtains lining the windows, the wooden paneling along the ceiling, the marble floor, and the festively lit fireplace— the high door at the farthest end of the room opens suddenly. A nurse, followed almost immediately by a physician, comes running in; the master, deeply perturbed, silently passes them and enters the room they have just fled. We begin to hear the strange, croaking scream of a newborn child. The doctor, who has covered his mouth with his hand in disgust, once more turns toward the half-opened door behind which the master of the house disappeared, while on the sound track the horrified scream of the father replaces the other voices. A traumatic birth has taken place on this wintry evening, yet we are shown only the affective traces of it on those who have witnessed it. The actual horror, as well as the monstrous body emerging from it, belongs exclusively to the uncanny offscreen space. Indeed, because the monstrosity remains invisible, it retains its horror.

With a fade-out that, like the beginning of the scene, is accompanied by a musical fanfare—this time featuring sweet bells along with the dark violins and trumpets—Tim Burton cuts to an image of the parents. Now the master of the house no longer stands alone next to the window of his magnificent mansion. His wife has joined him, standing to his right. Elegantly dressed, they hold martini glasses as they look thoughtfully out at the snow-covered evening landscape. As in the first scene, they suddenly turn away from the window, and again the camera follows their gaze, panning along the walls of their living room, which is festively lit. We see a lavishly decorated Christmas tree and the warmly glowing fire in the fireplace, casting the scene in a homey light. Once it has reached a wooden cage standing on the floor, the camera arrests its movement. The inhabitant of this other home, appearing like a heterotopic countersite to the stately walls surrounding it, is pounding at its walls from within, as though seeking to escape; a white cat stands in front of the cage, blocking our view of the strange creature within and regarding it with curiosity.

With a clearly visible cut, Burton suddenly changes the perspective of his camera and places us inside the wooden cage, close to the figure of the uncanny infant. Though we can hardly make out the contours, we see the infant's arm reaching through the bars of the cage for the cat, which disappears inside the dark interior of this little home, leaving us with only its distressed cries. Because Burton has, once more, changed to an external perspective, we see the struggle taking place within the cage only indexically, as the continual shaking of its wooden bars. Disgusted at the monstrous creature that has come to trouble their stately home, the two parents look at each other in silence and simultaneously empty their martini glasses, as though to seal the tacit decision they have already reached.

With the next cut, Burton changes location, showing us the Cobblepot parents pushing a basketlike perambulator along a snow-covered path in a park. Once they are quite alone, they stop on a stone bridge and thrust the basket into the river flowing beneath them, close to the city's zoo. Without hesitation or regret they thus abject the body whose monstrous hybridity has rendered visible the traumatic kernel of their parentage. On this Christmas evening the birth that has tainted the peace of the stately Cobblepot home is allegedly undone by a violent act of exclusion. At the same time, however, as though he sought from the beginning to set the Old Testament against the New in his noir Christmas tale, Tim Burton superimposes the title sequence onto a depiction of the subaltern route that his postmodern Moses takes. Sure of its way, as though its arrival on a foreign shore were predetermined by fate, the basket containing the alien creature floats along the walls of the cloaca subtending Gotham City, into the deepest interior of this cavelike geography, where it finally comes to rest.

As in the biblical text, upon arrival at its new home, the basket containing the ostracized infant is discovered by the indigenous population of this foreign land. In his noir comic world, Tim Burton has transformed the Egyptian princess and her ladies-in-waiting into penguins who will raise the foundling as though he were one of their own, making their dark, foul-smelling animal world his new home. The site of Oswald Cobblepot's exile thus significantly resembles a crypt, because the sewer emerges as a site of residue, where all the trash of the city's inhabitants is thrown away and preserved, even if vanished from the city's surface. The title "Gotham City, thirty-three years later" serves as a narrative transition between the previous scene of abjection and the world of everyday normalcy and foreshadows the return of the monstrous creature, which, owing to its journey down the sewer on its first Christmas Eve, was thrust into oblivion, only to reappear as the city's phantasmatic inversion of Christ. Seeking revenge for his rejection by his parents, the monstrous first son of the prestigious Cobblepot lineage will return home to claim the symbolic name of his father, having spent his first thirty-three years in the world of refuse and garbage, entertaining what Freud called the classic family romance. As an orphan raised by surrogate parents, he will seek to exchange the ersatz home of the cloaca, as well as his extended surrogate penguin family, for his true home and his socially more noble real parents.

This homecoming is, however, not simply played through as the violent inversion of the symbolic fiction of a harmonious family home; it is sustained by an equally violent act, that of filial abjection. Burton's noir comic, like the classic western plot, addresses the question of which hybrid creatures are allowed to return home and which must remain in a hetero-topic community—like the sewer, which though it runs beneath Gotham City is hidden from its normal citizens. Burton thus enmeshes a personal story with a collective one. Oswald Cobblepot (Danny DeVito) has hired the terrorist Red Triangle Gang to pave the way for his homecoming by turning Gotham City into an urban war zone of crime and destruction, so that the repudiated son can miraculously appear in the guise of a comic book savior. Part of what the occupation of the city by malign foreign bod-ies renders visible is the clandestine act of violence on which the symbolic fiction of the Cobblepots' happy family life was founded—the ostracism of the firstborn son. This urban street violence also, however, renders visible the criminal economic corruption that underlies the wealth of one of Gotham City's most powerful citizens, Max Shreck (Christopher Walken), for Oswald Cobblepot enters into an alliance with the unscrupulous busi-nessman.[2] Here another symbolic fiction is exposed, namely that the po-litical and economic interests of the city can be regulated exclusively in a legal manner.

To visually foreground that the frame for the return of both Batman (Michael Keaton) and his opponent the Penguin is that of the subject in exile, Burton's establishing shot for the actual story, thirty-three years later, depicts a seemingly happy and wholesome scene of urban Christmas festiv-ities. On a snow-covered square in the center of Gotham City, an actress, costumed as the Ice Princess in a seductive, sleeveless gown, presses a red lever on an ignition box and lights up the monumental Christmas tree, while Christmas songs simultaneously emerge from enormous loudspeakers that have been placed strategically around the square. Only a few blocks away, a newspaper boy calls out the headlines of the paper he is trying to sell, featuring a story about the uncanny Penguin, who has made his home in the city's sewer system.

Having thus introduced his protagonist as a figure of journalistic jingo-ism, Tim Burton shifts the position of his camera to show the festivities from the perspective of the hybrid foundling, as though the voice of the newspaper boy has called him to the scene. Through the bars covering the gully that separates the sewer from the city, he watches the lit Christmas tree, and, as he did that first Christmas in the living room of his noble par-ents, he pushes his fin-shaped hands through the bars. But now he is not preying on any one individual whom he could drag through the bars into his dark home. Rather, his bodily gestures indicate that he has turned the entire city into his prey. Burton once more shifts his location and has his camera pan up the walls of a skyscraper whose red neon sign—"Shreck's"— immediately indicates to us the name of the owner of the building, analogous to the cast-iron nameplate on the gate of the Cobblepot mansion. We see the gigantic cat head, revolving around its own axis on the rooftop of the department store, before Burton's camera enters the inner office of Max Shreck and moves toward the round table where the owner of the department store is trying to sell his plan for a new power plant to the mayor of the city and his associates.

While the politicians assure Shreck that all their studies show that Gotham City has enough power to get it into the next century, his secretary, Selina Kyle (Michelle Pfeiffer), who has come to refill their coffee cups, offers another suggestion. In this battle between powerful men, her voice sounds like that of an alien creature. The politicians simply stare at her in dismay, while she, losing courage, begins to stutter, and then her boss humiliates her further by turning her into the butt of a joke: "I'm afraid we haven't properly housebroken Miss Kyle," he apologizes, and, winking at the mayor, he adds, "but she makes a hell of a cup of coffee." When it comes to a battle between the sexes, all the men present unite and, by responding to Shreck's comment with mute laughter, assure him of their allegiance. Shreck's oldest son interrupts the men, now enjoying the camaraderie of a merry laugh, to remind them that it is time to go down "and bring joy to the masses." Selina remains alone in the room, still holding the coffeepot in her right hand, the tray with milk and sugar in her left. Deeply shamed by what just happened, she scolds herself for her inappropriate intervention, calling herself a "stupid corn dog." She identifies with the symbolic position, assigned to her by her boss, of the untrained animal who has not yet learned her place in the world of business, where powerful men make pacts. As such, she has, however, also accepted the role of the non-integratable other, over whose exclusion—even if in joke— the symbolic fiction can be reinstalled to proclaim that politicians and businessmen can deal with each other harmoniously, even if they have differences, because they share the same gender.

With the following sequence, however, phantasmatic figures strike back and with their performance of social unrest and violence make visible the unsolvable antagonism that inhabits all notions of the harmonious regulation of social communities. After the mayor steps onto the platform erected in front of the Christmas tree and calls upon Max Shreck, "Gotham's own

Santa Claus," to join him onstage, Shreck tosses presents into the crowd, then goes to the microphone to give his Christmas address. Although he has left his speech in his office, he nevertheless ritualistically invokes the spirit of Christmas: "I wish I could hand out world peace and unconditional world love, wrapped in a big bow." As the crowd begins to applaud enthusiastically, a monstrous present, wrapped in red foil and tied with a green ribbon, suddenly appears at the far end of the square, as though it is an uncanny materialization of the wish proclaimed by the wealthy businessman. The mayor ecstatically whispers into Shreck's ear what a great idea this is, yet as the latter admits that it isn't his, the gigantic present bursts open. A horde of motorcyclists wearing skull masks emerges and drives right into the crowd, which immediately begins to flee from the violence that has suddenly come upon them. At the same time a hurdy-gurdy man with a monkey on his shoulder steps in front of the platform and opens the front of his barrel organ to reveal the machine gun inside. With this he shoots at the Christmas tree until all the lights have been extinguished. The Christmas spirit of harmonious peace and love has been transformed into an obscene spectacle of carnivalesque violence.

While the mayor and the businessman have no choice but to throw themselves on the platform in front of the extinguished Christmas tree, in hopes of escaping unscathed from the violence, the police chief who has been called to the scene of the crime remembers the signal Batman gave to Gotham City as a token of his commitment to fighting crime. Indeed, Batman has come to occupy the position of the western hero, though rather than roaming the prairie he lives in isolation on the periphery of the city. He has vowed that should the internal unrest of the community once more erupt, he will reclaim his symbolic mandate as savior of the city and turn the urban geography into a scene of battle, where he can challenge those who inflict violence in a fight based on a simple, clearly demarcated opposition between good and evil.

With the next scene Tim Burton cuts to Bruce Wayne's stately mansion. We find the master of this house sitting alone in a big leather chair in his unlit library, his head propped motionlessly on his right arm, his unfocused eyes gazing as if lost in melancholy. Suddenly the light signal of the Batman emblem appears in the nocturnal sky, projected from the center of the city by a police searchlight. This signal is picked up by a swiveling mirror that has been placed on the roof of Bruce Wayne's mansion specifically for this purpose, and it is sent, as a refraction, into the dark interior of his home. As

though waking from a trance, Wayne immediately responds to the interpellation, turns his head 180 degrees, discards the posture of melancholic
dreamer, gets up from his chair, and walks toward the window. Burton thus
visually underscores through Wayne's actions that the projection of the Batman signal means the beginning of a fantasy scenario that Bruce Wayne will
experience in the real. We now recognize that the swiveling mirror has re-
produced a reflection of his emblem and projected it onto the wall of the library; it is under the auspices of this insignia appearing in the dark center
of his home, duplicating the one that all the citizens of Gotham City can
see projected on the sky, that Bruce Wayne can once more enter the comic
book scenario of heroism he has been dreaming about.

Analogous to the way in which Martha Edwards opens her door in *The
Searchers* to a heterotopic prairie landscape out of which the man she has
been clandestinely yearning for rides toward her, the intrusion of this light
signal into Bruce Wayne's library opens up a heterotopic countersite in
the multimillionaire's home. He will don his Batman uniform to arm
himself for his fight with the representatives of evil. He, too, enters the
realm of illusion, and Tim Burton, like John Ford, indicates this by including a self-reflexive reference to his own cinematic medium. The two
shots in which he illustrates the relationship between his hero and the signal interpellating him as Gotham City's savior appear like a *mise en abyme*
of the entire film. The first shows us the reawakened hero from the front
in a low-angle shot. His face, radiant with anticipation, is framed by an
oval halo in whose center the Batman emblem rises like an all-powerful
black figure over the head of Bruce Wayne, as though it is his crown. This
signal has also illuminated the previously darkened library, so that now we
can discern tall bookshelves lining the walls, a reference to the fictional
quality of the battle about to unfold. The second shot shows Bruce Wayne
from the right side, in a long view that reduces him to a tiny masculine
figure who faces the window through which his Batman signal is being
projected. He seems to stand at attention before this symbol, as though
on a stage. Only his face is lit by the beam of the searchlight falling
through the window, while behind him the projection of his larger-than-
life emblem rises majestically above him. Fully in line with Althusser's
scene of interpellation, Tim Burton thus stages how his protagonist Bruce
Wayne can be confirmed in his identity as a hero only if he is called by
the people of Gotham City. The possibility of answering, "Yes, it is I
whom you appeal to. Yes, I will take on the position of savior, which you

have designated for me," represents the resuscitating force that alone can call him back to the world of the living from his crypt, where he stores his alter ego, Batman, after each victory over his adversaries—much as the Cobblepot son has been residing in a subaltern crypt as his alter ego, the Penguin. The tragic irony of this interpellation, however, consists in the following conundrum: because his role as savior of Gotham City is tied to the incursion of violent foreign bodies, his desire for this symbolic mandate is inevitably coupled with a desire for a renewed outbreak of violence.

How Bruce Wayne Became Batman

In Tim Burton's *Batman*, released three years earlier, we can find the traumatic primal scene of violence that turned the son of a successful physician into a hybrid man-beast. One night when young Bruce was walking home with his parents from a movie theater, they were accosted by two criminals. Before the eyes of the young boy, one of the robbers shot both adults, leaving the boy unharmed only because his partner advised him to do so. This dual narcissistic injury—the loss of his family coupled with the experience of having to watch helplessly while his parents were killed—produces a personality split in Bruce Wayne—the birth of a seemingly invincible Batman in the body of a boy abandoned by his parents. Within the logic of Bob Kane's comic world, this uncanny masquerade allows Bruce Wayne to mitigate the psychic homelessness that the loss of his parents and, concomitant with it, the recognition of a fissure introduced into his home called forth in him. In the guise of his double, the masked hero protecting all the upright citizens of Gotham City from criminals, he can psychically surmount that traumatic childhood experience. In his fantasy scenario he is no longer reduced to the role of helpless witness; he has fashioned himself as the powerful defender of the helpless. Significantly, however, this transformation requires the appropriation of precisely the alien power that has irrevocably tainted the symbolic fiction of a harmoniously regulated family and home life that he had imagined for himself before the fatal event of his parents' death. In the guise of Batman he thus renders visible the antagonism that, in the sense of an incalculable contingency, articulates the precariousness of all situations of happiness. Like the hero in the classic western, he defends the citizens of Gotham City as a way of compensating for his own traumatic dislocation within the Wayne family.

In contrast to the Penguin, Bruce Wayne does not resolve his family romance in the traditional sense, because, as an orphan, he carries the name of a noble family and lives in the stately mansion bequeathed to him. Rather, in the course of *Batman*, he is able to find the man responsible for the death of his parents, Jack Napier (Jack Nicholson), and is thus also able to give a name to his trauma. Confronting this man who now calls himself the Joker, he throws his adversary from a church tower into the dark abyss of Gotham City, and Jack Napier dies on the same cobblestones where he once left the corpses of Bruce Wayne's parents. However, even though the enigma of Bruce Wayne's personality split is solved at the end of *Batman*, the fissure in his psychic apparatus remains, and his home becomes quite literally the abode for his two selves. He continues to be haunted by his desire to protect the citizens of Gotham City from crime and insists that he be ritually recognized as the savior of the city. For this reason he bestows upon Gotham City the searchlight fitted with his emblem, so that the city's citizens can call him "whenever the forces of evil cast their shadow on the heart of the city." In so doing, he ensures that he will be able to repeatedly transform his own childhood scene of trauma into a dream of omnipotence. Like all other neurotics possessed by a repetition compulsion (notably Lang's noir hero, Mark), the hero of Tim Burton's comic saga can mitigate the fundamental knowledge of his own fallibility by refiguring it as a scenario of battle in which he is never the one threatened but always the one who is superior in strength and intelligence. Two disturbances are, however, inscribed into his strategy of self-empowerment, counterbalancing the pleasure of the fantasy. The traumatic knowledge of his own fallibility is ultimately reactivated in tandem with his enjoyment of a battle for life and death. At the same time his desire to return to a site of undisturbed happiness can be articulated only by virtue of an enactment of his own insurmountable personality split, leaving him uncannily suspended between the persona of fallible millionaire and the figure of invincible heroic savior.

Bruce Wayne, who at the beginning of *Batman Returns* is shown in his castlelike mansion on the periphery of Gotham City, is quite literally not master of the house bequeathed to him by his parents, because the two symbolic mandates that he claims as his own have also caused a split in his place of abode. The official part of the house consists of magnificent halls and rooms that he is willing to show off to the prominent citizens of Gotham

City who attend his lavish festivities. Here he can publicly demonstrate the skill with which the orphaned son has turned the inheritance left to him by his father into boundless prosperity. The unofficial, secret part of his place of abode, tellingly called the bat cave, contains a complex surveillance system of the entire house, an arsenal of costumes and weapons, a workshop to repair and construct his battle machinery, and a multimedia workstation. What is significant about the architectural uncanniness that he inhabits physically is not only the correspondence it has to the split in his psychic apparatus. It also visualizes how difficult it is to draw a clear line between the violence performed in the name of the symbolic fiction of a harmoniously regulated community and the violence that is articulated in an unresolvable antagonism subtending all social communities, even though these communities seek to repress it in order to function in everyday reality.

At the same time, this physical and psychic split illustrates that the line between the mythic hero whose hybridity can be integrated into the symbolic community and those freaks whose violence and otherness cannot be integrated is, at best, a murky one. To emphasize the blurring of this boundary, Tim Burton offers us an additional view of the Batman signal projected onto the nocturnal sky during the exposition of *Batman Returns*. Having initially shown us how its light beam magically draws Bruce Wayne out of his melancholic trance, and only then showing the signal from the perspective of the citizens of Gotham City, who hope that their hero will return to save them from this new incursion of violence, Burton ends the sequence with a low-angle shot. Through the iron bars of the gully, we see the signal towering above the skyscrapers in the night sky as though for a few seconds we have taken on the position of the Penguin, who as yet remains invisible. Burton thus calls forth the speculation that this orphaned split personality, like Batman, has chosen to respond to Gotham City's call for help, even if only by identifying with his rival in an opposite way: "Yes, I am the threat that lives beneath your streets. Yes, I accept the challenge of ascending to your world. I, too, who was once abandoned, know the plight of utter vulnerability and want to be your savior!"

Dual of the Hybrids

With this exposition Tim Burton offers a visual connection between the two fantasy scenarios that will struggle against each other throughout the film, each following Freud's dictum that only the unhappy person fantasizes, never the happy one. Though in different ways, both Bruce Wayne's savior romance and Oswald Cobblepot's homecoming romance represent an imaginary correction of their dissatisfying realities. Both are the orphaned single first sons of wealthy parents and both, though for different reasons, enact the fact that they are no longer fully master of their symbolic mandate by way of a split in their personality, in which they appear as hybrid human-beast figures. If Bruce Wayne assumes the persona of Batman to fulfill his ambition to cleanse Gotham City of all criminalistic foreign bodies, and in so doing to compensate for the narcissistic wound inflicted upon him by the violent death of his parents, the Penguin, having been violently cast away by his parents, harbors the ambition of reclaiming the name his father gave him, Oswald Cobblepot, so that he might return to the symbolic home of his parents and in so doing be recognized by the community of humans. At the same time, Tim Burton emphasizes the failure that is irrevocably inscribed in fantasies revolving around an imaginary replacement of an allegedly harmonious home. He does more than demonstrate how illusory any attempt at regaining the abode of childhood necessarily is, given that the unqualified protection of a home, as well as the unconditional love of one's parents, can only be a fantasy scene for the adult subject. Burton also explores the dark core at the heart of the home romance by reenacting what it means to return to this site when the site of the dreaming subject's origins actually coincides with the site of violence and thus collides with the very condition that brought about the subject's sense of alienation in the first place. It is significant that for both daydreamers, the question of reclaiming a lost home will ultimately be negotiated not at the scene of a new home but on the nocturnal streets of the city. Furthermore, their return to the city, meant to confirm their symbolic recognition, will result not in a peaceful regulation of social disagreements but in the outbreak of open warfare.

The location for this violent confrontation is, from the start, semantically encoded as an allegorical fantasy geography, much as was the case in Fleming's Oz, Ford's Monument Valley, and Hitchcock's Manderley. In contrast to the other films discussed in this book, however, Gotham City is never presented as the heterotopic countersite to a so-called normal world, as is the case when Dorothy crosses the threshold of her homestead and discovers she is no longer in Kansas; or when Martha Edwards walks out onto her veranda, shielding her eyes against the bright light of the mythic western landscape; or when the movement of the windshield wiper lays bare the view of Manderley for Hitchcock's unnamed heroine. Instead, the geography of *Batman Returns* is designed from the start as a clearly marked illusory refiguration of New York City. While David Fincher's unnamed city represents the gloom of an allegorical purgatory, Tim Burton's Gotham City represents an ideologically infused fictional comic world, divided into an urban center regulated by a minimal symbolic consistency and its phantasmatic countersites—the places from which the homeless hybrid creatures return, rendering the entire city uncanny.

If, in previous chapters, I have repeatedly discussed the films in the context of fantasy work, as this represents an ambivalent appropriation of an external law that reveals itself to be the externalization of an intimate kernel of the symbolic identity that this law affords, I have done so to insist on the way this results in a significant bifurcation. The official law defining the subject produces both a symbolic protective fiction and its uncanny, phantomatic counternarrative, the latter aimed toward dissolution. For *Batman Returns*, this bifurcation can be traced in the crisis of interpellation that Tim Burton places at the heart of his film. The double names of the two rivals, each explicitly naming the *Mischling* status of the two heroes, point to the unstable boundary between the official interpellation, which supports the symbolic community at large, and its phantasmatic counterpart. Yet the two rivals are significantly conceived by Tim Burton as inversions of each other. While the Penguin openly admits to being a monstrous body, whose fantasy of self-aggrandizement promises him that he will be able to abject the animal part in favor of the human part of his being, Bruce Wayne has recourse to the mask of the freak belatedly. His hybridity serves to embody his psychic dislocation, even while its fancied improvement consists in shielding his human vulnerability and, instead, privileging the alleged invincibility of his animal part.[3]

At the same time, the result of the crisis in interpellation, called forth by virtue of the *Mischling* status of the two heroes, is that, because the two rivals inhabit two bodies, and thus two psychic identities, they must also engage in a double strife. On the one hand, they challenge each other as to who will be the savior of Gotham City, and on the other hand, their combat calls forth the question of which symbolic interpellation will be privileged—that of the socially adapted firstborn son, negotiated over the name of the father (Wayne, Cobblepot), or that of the phantasmatic combatant, negotiated symbolically by virtue of naming the hybridity between human and beast. The dark powers of fate, which place Burton's comic book scenario closer to film noir than to the western,[4] can perhaps best be described if we return once again to the trope that Freud coins to describe the proximity between the work of fantasy and the racial *Mischling*. As we have already discussed in the chapter on Sirk's melodramas, Freud argues that for all fantasy scenarios "their origin is what decides their fate. We may compare them with individuals of mixed race who, taken all round, resemble white men, but who betray their colored descent by some striking feature or other, and on that account are excluded from society and enjoy none of the privileges of white people."[5] The two rivals for power over Gotham City, whom Tim Burton expressly conceives as *Mischlinge*, represent in an ambivalent manner why the act of fantasizing is equated with a crisis in interpellation, much as the act of falling in love is. They do more than embody the altogether common daydream of returning home. Their desire to force themselves, by virtue of their homecoming, upon the exact official community from which they must be excluded if this symbolic order is to function represents the fate of fantasy work itself. Like these hybrid creatures suspended between being humans and being freakish or monstrous beasts, fantasy work may push forward into the realm of consciousness, but because it originates within the unconscious it will always remain excluded from fully belonging to conscious psychic processes.

Yet Tim Burton privileges what Freud merely gestures to: the dark core inscribed within all fantasy work, which explains why daydreams are so intimately connected with dislocation and homelessness. For both Bruce Wayne/Batman and his adversary Oswald Cobblepot/the Penguin, their "origin" is, indeed, "decisive" for their "fate." The hero who masquerades as the invincible savior can never forget that this role was born from the traumatic experience of unconditional helplessness, even though the compensation it affords inevitably also points to the fissure thus ineluctably inscribed in all hopes of family happiness. The rejected son who returns to the city of his parents can shed neither the smell of the sewer he grew up in nor the memory of the traumatic experience of having been abandoned by his parents. These two hybrid creatures both enact a particular wish scenario, as well as tracing the gesture of fantasy work par excellence. Fantasy work, after all, never arrives where it hopes to, since its hybridity dictates that it can never shed its origin in the unconscious, a site we might readily call the sewer and the scene of primary traumatisms within the psychic apparatus of the subject. While the figures of fantasies can to a certain degree be assimilated by consciousness, they must nevertheless be repelled, because parts of this psychic material are too dangerous for the ego to confront directly. In the same manner, Burton's phantasmatic *Mischlinge* can be only partially integrated into the social community of Gotham City: Bruce Wayne, because of his patronage of projects involving the welfare of the city, and Oswald Cobblepot, as will be discussed in detail further on, because he will seek to run for mayor. Both, however, ultimately find themselves excluded from the city, because their origins preclude their ever being able to fully shed the enjoyment of violence, which is too dangerous for the stability of the community to allow for any direct confrontation with it. The aporia of fantasy work that Tim Burton's *Mischlinge* so compellingly play through is that what their desire is aimed at, namely an untainted, harmonious abode in the world, is both a transfiguration of a past childhood that never existed and a structural impossibility, for fantasy work always returns to the traumatic kernel it is meant to shield. It preserves this traumatic kernel as much as it protects the conscious ego from it. Fantasy work can never fully belong to consciousness, but it can also never avoid returning there, where it can have only a provisional, limited home.

Violent Homecoming of the Banished Son

The plot of *Batman Returns* plays through a twofold short circuit of returns to the place one has been abjected from or voluntarily left, which organize and regulate fantasy work. On the one hand is the recognition that an antagonistic foreign body inhabiting the subject thwarts any untainted self-identity, forcing it to return to the origins of its desires in the unconscious; on the other hand is the counterdirectional recognition that unconscious psychic material continually strives for a displaced articulation and thus returns to the consciousness in the guise of phantasmatic figurations of the repressed. What is significant about Tim Burton's appropriation of psychoanalytic tropes is that the insoluble antagonism inherent to fantasy work is played out as the wish fantasy of a social antagonism. With this battle scenario, each of the two *Mischlinge* perceives his rival as the materialized embodiment of the foreign body that prohibits an untroubled self-identity. The trick of this wish fantasy consists in the illusion that the destruction of the representative of an antagonistic social power promises not only peace for the community at large but, more important, the restitution of the split subject's mastery over his own house. This conflation of psychic and social antagonism, however, requires the inclusion of a third player, namely Max Shreck. After Bruce Wayne has been awakened from his reverie by the Batman signal, he immediately puts on his costume and in his armored car drives to the scene of violence that has emerged in the center of Gotham City. Once there, he manages to disperse the Penguin's Red Triangle Gang. As Batman arrives, Max Shreck tries to flee the scene of battle, yet as he traverses a gully in the lonely alley that he has chosen as his flight route, the grid suddenly gives way beneath his feet and he falls into the heterotopic countersite from which the plague that has descended upon the city emerged.

Once more Burton's camera undertakes a flight movement, which, as in the previous scenes, traverses the architectural structure of a site of power. As Max Shreck descends into the sewer, the camera moves upward, flying toward the iron gate whose crest bears the designation "Zoo." This time the camera doesn't fly over the closed gate, but rather moves smoothly through the open space between the spiked bars and the oval frame in which are fixed the letters of the name of the place that lies behind it (recalling Hitchcock's camera at the very beginning of *Rebecca*). In contrast to the opening sequence, the camera doesn't pan along the wall of a mansion but rather flies over the architectural structures of the zoo, which are now covered in ice and snow. As it moves closer to ground level, the camera captures the bridge from which the infant Oswald Cobblepot had been discarded by his parents. Then it continues its flight through the structure of a steel statue until it has reached the inner part of the zoo, a small mound carrying the name "Arctic World." Only then does Burton, as in the previous sequences, cut to the interior of this building. We discover that Max Shreck has landed in the subaltern cave at the end of the sewer canal where the Penguin and his court, the Red Triangle Gang, masquerading as clowns and ladies-in-waiting, are enjoying a festive meal. In his surrogate home, the vindictive outcast son explains to Max Shreck that they share the experience of being perceived as monsters, adding, "but somehow, you're a respected monster and I am, to date, not." He then continues by proposing a pact to the unscrupulous businessman. He feels that he has already spent too long in the sewer with his penguin family and that the time has come for him to ascend. Like Max Shreck, he explains, he wasn't born in the sewer, and like him, he wants some respect: "a recognition of my basic humanity." Above all, however, he wants to discover "who I am." By finding his parents, he wants to reclaim the name of his father, calling his demand "simple stuff that the good people of Gotham take for granted."

Max Shreck is to help him realize this wish, and the businessman initially seems to agree to this pact because the Penguin shows him that the cloaca is the toxic underbelly of Shreck's prosperity. After all, the Penguin had begun his speech by declaring, "What you hide, I discover. What you put in your toilet I place on my mantel. You flush it, I flaunt it." He proves this to Max Shreck by extracting from his special Christmas stocking three gifts—a thermos bottle filled with a batch of toxic waste from Shreck's allegedly clean textile plant, which has flown into the sewer canal; the restored documents Shreck had had shredded, proving that he owns half the firetraps in Gotham City; and finally the hand of Fred Atkins, his old partner, whom he had had killed. Max Shreck's willingness to orchestrate a "welcome home scenario" for the Penguin, however, derives less from the outcast son's intimidation than from his realization that he can profit from the freak's fanaticism. An intrigue is born in Shreck's mind, in which the Penguin is not only recognized by the good people of Gotham City for his humanity but also proclaimed as their savior in times of need. Shreck thus proves to have something else in common with the monstrous Penguin— everything that he does serves his ambition and his self-aggrandizement. He wants to become the clandestine master of Gotham City and needs to recruit a partner in crime, who will be the official mayor. The Penguin's ascent from the sewer, staged as a scenario of the son returning home, is meant to function as a protective fiction, hiding the obscene underbelly— the corruption and fantasies of omnipotence of Max Shreck, the mastermind behind it.

To visually emphasize this pact, Tim Burton stages the Penguin's ascent explicitly as a mirror inversion of Max Shreck's descent into the subaltern realm in which repressed material has been contained, so that it might at some point return to the world aboveground. Once again, the mayor appears before the citizens of Gotham City to give a speech. This time he shares the platform that has been erected on the steps of the town hall with some of his associates, including Max Shreck, as well as with his wife, who holds their younger son on her lap. As the mayor begins to denounce the urban chaos that the citizens of Gotham City have been forced to live with, declaring that the violence is going to stop, the grate from one of the gullies is slowly removed from inside the sewer canal. Burton then cuts to a medium shot of the mayor, who gestures toward his wife, sitting next to him, as he intones the pathos of Christmas. This should be a time of healing, he declares. At the very moment, however, when he promises his constituents that last night's violence won't happen again, it emerges like a phantom from the open gully. A clown has suddenly appeared, somersaulting from the top of the stairs toward the mayor. Upon reaching the platform, he steals the mayor's child from the arms of his wife, briefly whispers into the microphone that he isn't really one for speeches, and then proceeds to somersault down the remaining stairs, disappearing into the opened gully with the stolen baby clasped to his chest.

On the sound track we hear the exchange between the thief and the Penguin, which has been staged for the benefit of the horrified crowd that has gathered around the opening in the ground. While the clown vocally mimes a violent tussle, in the course of which the Penguin is able to liberate the mayor's son from his captor, Burton actually shows us what is happening behind the scenes. The clown hands over the baby so that the Penguin can ascend from the gully, the mayor's son safely in his arms, thus allowing him to be celebrated, according to plan, by an enthusiastic crowd. The mother gratefully retrieves her son while the Penguin, with Max Shreck at his right side and the mayor at his left, poses before the flashbulbs of the photographers. The "welcome home scenario" designed by Max Shreck has succeeded. The outcast son has returned the stolen son, thus reuniting the family of the mayor. As the Penguin explains to the press, he hopes that Christmas may be a time of healing for him as well. With the studied gestures of deep emotional involvement, he declares in front of the cameras positioned at Gotham Plaza, "All I want in return is a chance to find my Mom and Dad. A chance to find out who they are and thusly who I am. And then, with my parents, try to understand why they did what I guess they felt they had to do to a child who was born a little different. A child who spent his first Christmas, and many since, in a sewer."

Tim Burton shows us the television broadcast of this speech from inside a festively decorated living room in Bruce Wayne's home. While his butler, Alfred, is putting the final touches on the Christmas tree, the master of the house is deeply touched by what he sees on his TV screen. Yet even as Bruce Wayne comments, "I hope he finds them," sympathy turns to rivalry. The intrigue, orchestrated by Max Shreck, will soon become a competition between the beast man Batman, whom the citizens of the city have declared to be their privileged savior, and his imitator, the Penguin, for the return of the cast-off son only initially runs peacefully. Alfred is justified in pointing out to his master that his wish to prove that the Penguin is not what he seems may have more to do with his own wish for self-aggrandizement than with the welfare of the city. He astutely notes, "Must you be the only lonely man-beast in town?"

Bruce Wayne continues to track the development of the Penguin's fame from within his own radically split home. On the television screen in his bat cave he watches the Penguin successfully reclaiming his family name, Cobblepot, and with it the symbolic position attached to it by Gotham City's society. Once more Burton's camera flies over a locked iron gate, in front of which a crowd has assembled, but now it hovers at the tip of the gate that bears no name, and, in a high-angle long shot, it depicts the Penguin slowly approaching a grave at the far end of a cemetery. Then Burton cuts to a medium shot, so as to move in closer on the pathos-laden performance of the son, who has finally returned home, placing roses on his parents' grave, then turning his back on their final resting place to face the crowd that is waiting for him on the other side of the gate. He will no longer allow anyone to call him the Penguin, he declares: "I am a man. I have a name—Oswald Cobblepot." In answer to a journalist who points out to him that he can now no longer settle his difference with his parents, the Penguin once more mimics the spirit of Christmas that the mayor had invoked in his speech before town hall: "I forgive them"—a declaration that is immediately turned into the headline of all the major papers of Gotham City, so as to further ritually confirm the symbolic fiction of communal healing.

The mutual implication that Tim Burton detects between homecoming and a return to psychic as well as corporeal exile, however, requires the traversal of both a phantomatic fiction and a symbolic one on the part of his two hybrid heroes, which articulates the dark kernel underlying all notions of communal and personal self-identity. This uncanny force, veering toward the dissolution of all protective fictions, is manifested as a social antagonism, primarily as the political battle between Max Shreck and Bruce Wayne, who opposes Shreck's project for a new power plant. At the same time the ambivalent rivalry between the Penguin and Batman comes to the fore over this political disagreement, serving in part to help decide which man-beast will be allowed to carry the title of official savior of Gotham City; it also, however, serves Max Shreck's clandestine plan to take over the power of the city in the figural as well as the literal sense. At the body of Oswald Cobblepot, these two contentions overlap once Bruce Wayne discovers that Max Shreck's new protégé is the leader of the Red Triangle Gang. His disagreement with the businessman over the construction of the power plant proves to be the official side of a coin whose obscene counterpart is the battles he fights, dressed as Batman, with the terrorist clowns on the nocturnal streets of Gotham City. Indeed, one might well speculate that his resilient opposition to Max Shreck's project calls forth the next wave of violence, which will allow the corrupt entrepreneur to push forward his business interests against the resistance of the multimillionaire by enmeshing his political ambition with Oswald Cobblepot's desire to reclaim his symbolic heritage—for the last phase of the "welcome home scenario" orchestrated by Max Shreck consists in the campaign to get Cobblepot nominated as mayor. In order for him to become the father of the city, however, there must be a political platform and a catalyst for recalling the current mayor. Shreck claims he can supply the signatures that will overturn the ballot, yet he declares that they need something more, an incident like "the Reichstag fire."[6] Standing amid the posters advertising his nomination for mayor in the office that Shreck has set up as the campaign office, Oswald Cobblepot initially hesitates, believing that this intrigue will sidetrack him from his actual interests. But after Max assures him that this is his chance to fulfill his destiny, he is overcome by anticipation of the obscene enjoyment of the violence that he will unleash to promote his manager's clandestine interests. Calling out "Burn, baby, burn," he introduces the next night of violence, at the end of which he will emerge as the only man able to replace an utterly fallible mayor and restore peace to Gotham City.

Enter Selina Kyle

This uncanny "welcome home scenario" is, however, troubled by the intrusion of another combatant, Selina Kyle. After being humiliated by her boss, she leaves Shreck's department store, but soon finds herself in a different kind of trouble: the first wave of violence the Penguin has unleashed on Gotham City to prepare his ascent. In the turmoil of the crowd, running away from the square where the shooting began, she loses her glasses. Before she can retrieve them, Batman's armored car stops directly in front of her. For the second time that day she unwittingly becomes the helpless object in a battle between men. One of the members of the Red Triangle Gang, who has also noticed the approach of the car, attacks her from behind and threatens her with a stun gun, only, however, in order to provoke Batman. Batman accepts the challenge and slays his foe, while Selina, who kicks the man in the clown suit once he has fallen to the ground, is forced to accept the role of damsel in distress who is saved by the valiant hero.

Her attempt to strike up a conversation with her savior fails. Batman merely looks at her in silence for a moment, then turns his back on her. Once alone with the fallen man, who had shown her how vulnerable she is, she can resort only to an ironic self-deprecation. "Well, that was very brief," she notes about her encounter with the savior of the city, "just like all the men in my life." As she begins to pick up the objects that she had dropped during the attack, she adds, "What men?" As she turns once more to the clown figure lying at her feet and notes, "Then again, there's you. But you need therapy," she discovers that the Penguin has, in fact, sent her a Christmas present, even if it wasn't intended for her. From the clown's outstretched hand she takes the stun gun and tests it surreptitiously on the slain man, giggling to herself as she watches his body jerk with the electric shock. At this point in the story, her act remains a gesture illustrating how she is unable to assert herself in a battle fought between men. She can inflict pain only belatedly. But the pleasure that lights up her face as she realizes the results of this insignificant act of violence foreshadows the change of character that is about to take place.

Burton moves to his plagued heroine's scene of homecoming by cutting to the interior of a partially lit kitchen. The door slowly opens, Selina briefly looks across the threshold, turns on the light, and before closing the door behind her, calls out cheerfully, "Honey, I'm home." Only once she has actually entered her abode does she explain: "Oh, I forgot. I'm not married." Exhausted, she drops her coat, shawl, and purse on a chair on her way to the refrigerator, where she fetches some milk for her cat, which, like herself, has just returned home, jumping in through the window above the kitchen sink. Selina immediately relates the cat's miaow ironically to her own condition, ascribing to it a comment about her own low self-esteem: "What?" she asks. "How can anyone be so pathetic?" Then, walking slowly toward her bedroom, she stops to check the answering machine, which is strategically placed on a table between the kitchen and the bedroom, and adds, "Yes, to you I seem pathetic. But I'm a working girl. Gotta pay the rent." As she crosses the threshold into her bedroom—the most intimate part of her home—she passes a pink neon sign on the wall that says, "Hello there." Accompanied by the disembodied voice of her mother on the answering machine, reprimanding her for not coming home for Christmas, she opens her Murphy bed, while the mother adds a second degrading comment, attributing her absence to the fact that she is languishing in Gotham City as a lowly secretary.

The mise-en-scène that Burton has chosen is significant, working as it does with contradictions. Even while the neon sign on the wall promises a scene of welcome and the bed Selina is about to make suggests the comfort and safety of home, the maternal voice contradicts all illusions about her daughter's happy inhabitation of either her position as a working girl or the actual abode where she lives. Although Selina talks back to her mother's voice as she defiantly places the pillows on her bed, she is also complicit in the evaluation of her own failure. She agrees, after all, that her situation is lowly, and indeed lonely. At the same time one can surmise that she, though not an orphan like the other two protagonists of *Batman Returns*, has no parental home where she feels welcome enough to go for the holidays. The next message illustrates just how impossible is any hope of escaping her present dreary existence. A male voice excuses himself for having to cancel the Christmas getaway they had planned together—his therapist says he shouldn't act as someone else's appendage. Selina, whose face lit up at hearing his voice, initially ran toward her telephone in happy anticipation. Now, however, she deletes his message in anger, and, having slumped onto the sofa and cast off her shoes, more weary than before, she listens to the next message, an advertisement for new Gotham Lady Perfume, telling her that "it makes women feel like women and the men have no complaints either." Angered at this further reference to the unsolvable contradiction that inhabits her life as a working girl, namely her inability to assert herself as a professional while also pleasing men, she moves on to the next message.

Yet we should note that all the while she was listening to the advertisement she was fondly turning the stun gun in her hand and musing on the difference between the idea of feminine seduction promised by Gotham Lady Perfume and the violent power afforded by the object that she held. Upon hearing the next message, however, she is forced to interrupt this brief reverie. Her own voice now reminds her that she has left the Bruce Wayne file in the office and that she must return there to get it for the meeting the next morning. This message destroys all sense of comfort she thought she might have in being at home, yet she is now emotionally armed for her return to the nocturnal world outside, which will end with a significant transformation of her life. In lieu of the warm bed for which she had longed, she can comfort herself with a lethal weapon.

Upon hearing her own voice calling her back to Max Shreck's office, she casts the stun gun away and jumps up from the sofa, puts on her shoes and coat, and turns her back on the home that can neither offer her any real comfort nor protect her from external voices imposing their desires on her and forcing her to recognize how fallible her emotional and professional life actual is. The sentence with which this scene began—"Honey, I'm home"—is incorrect not only because there is no beloved waiting for her at home. This sentence that since the 1930s has been spoken by the husband returning home from the office also indicates for her a second scene of homelessness. She has not successfully appropriated a position in the professional world for herself either. She is at home nowhere—not in the symbolic world of work and not in the private world of the family.

The homelessness of the street at night is thus the adequate scene for the twofold disillusionment—the thwarted romance and the humiliation by her boss—that she experiences while everyone else is propagating Christmas cheer. Once more we see the "Shreck's" sign rising in red letters over the entrance of the building she has been compelled to return to. A moment after Selina arrives, the master of this empire, having crept up the unlit staircase leading to his office, discovers her standing in front of an open file cabinet, engrossed in reading the material she has found in one of the files. Acting on his conjecture that she should be treated like an animal that hasn't yet been properly housebroken, he creeps up to her quietly from behind and whispers into her ear, "Working late?" Selina, who has been too perturbed by what she has found in the file to notice his approach, is startled by his sudden appearance and looks up at him in shock.

Then, as though she no longer wants to suppress her dissatisfaction with her role as his assistant, she begins to perform an inversion of her ambition to please. She seems to unconsciously desire the fatal embrace that this confrontation will provoke, for she confesses to Max Shreck that, in preparation for tomorrow's meeting with Bruce Wayne, she has pulled all the files on the proposed power plant and even opened the protected files. At Shreck's ironic comment, "How industrious," she smiles proudly and relates how she figured out what his password was. She takes this dangerous cat-and-mouse game one step further by sitting down in his chair at his desk, even while still mimicking the shy, docile secretary. As he sits at the other end of the desk, she confides that what she found in these protected files was very interesting, playing back to him in the language of the allegedly clueless secretary his diabolical plan and pretending not to understand the intrigue she has discovered, saying it's "a bit on the technical side." She describes her discovery that the power plant is a power plant in name only, that in fact it is going to be a giant capacitor that, instead of generating power, will be sucking power out of Gotham City and stockpiling it. Looking at him demurely, she offers her assessment of the project: "A very novel approach, I'd say." In response to his question "And who would you say this to?" she replies quietly, "Nobody," indicating by the expression on her face that she is willing to enter into a pact with him. Max Shreck takes up the challenge by invoking the insignia of his department store, the grinning cat's head. As he approaches her, as though to threaten her physically, she suddenly rises from her chair, realizing that perhaps she has taken her challenge too far. In response to his question "What did curiosity do to the cat?" she once more admits her own vulnerability: "I'm no cat. I'm just an assistant. A secretary."

In a film in which all three hybrid players are continually confronted with the question of which designation they want to respond to—their given name or the name of an assumed animal persona—Selina Kyle replies with what Freud calls the gesture of denial. Less than an hour earlier, at her home, she had attributed to her cat, which is able to roam the urban streets without care or inhibition, the very freedom and sexual satisfaction she finds lacking in her own life. One might thus surmise that it is precisely this animal that has come, in her psychic reality, to represent an answer to the narcissistic injuries she experiences in her professional and personal life. To be a cat would mean to be omnipotent, independent, and empowered. Max Shreck thus merely serves as the catalyst for the metamorphosis that has already taken place in Selina Kyle's unconscious, allowing this clandestine desire to take material shape. Selina, who has begun to walk slowly backward toward the window behind her, seeking to flee from her boss, who is moving toward her and once more threatening to do violence, assures him that her discovery will remain their secret. Once she has reached the windowsill, the unscrupulous businessman explains to her that this power plant is his legacy to his son and nothing must interfere with that. At this, Selina's unconscious desire again articulates itself in an encrypted statement. As in the earlier scenes—before her boss's associates in his office and then on the street during the attack—she is literally standing with her back against the wall, and once more she ironically invokes her own helplessness as the one strength she has: "Go ahead. Intimidate me. Bully me, if it makes you feel big. It's not like you can kill me!" Max seems to have won the first round of this verbal battle, because with the retort "Actually, it's a lot like that," he leans toward her, then moves back slightly, to feign that this was all a joke. As she begins to laugh in relief, he lunges forward and pushes her out the window.

As she falls, two cat images are connected with her descent: the enormous swiveling laughing cat head on the roof of the department store and a similar laughing cat head painted on the red marquee at the front of the store, the marquee that for a moment interrupts her fall but cannot prevent the fatal impact on the snow-covered street. One gets the sense that Burton wanted to highlight the traumatic experience of her symbolic death visually by showing that not even this last protection can withstand the force of her fall. Like Oswald Cobblepot, Selina, having been violently ejected from the department store, which functions as an architectural correlative to the symbolic community she wanted to belong to, finds a more adequate home in the community of animals. The alley cats emerge in hordes, licking, pulling, and nibbling at her body, until she is resuscitated. Astonished, and smiling slightly, Selina opens her eyes. Like Oswald, she, too, will return to the place from which she has been violently expelled, to inflict on her opponent the fallibility that he imposed on her. She will insist on her own version of the Old Testament dictum—"a die for a die"—thwarting his legacy to his son and returning to him the gift of death that he bestowed on her.

Now Selina returns home again, and this second homecoming gives material shape to the fissure inscribed in her physical and psychic place of abode. As before, we see her opening the door to her apartment, but this time, as though to emphasize the transformation that has occurred in her homecoming ritual, she remains standing on the threshold and merely whispers the greeting, "Honey, I'm home," while her face remains hidden in shadow. Only then does she turn on the light and add the second part of her greeting, again in a whisper: "I forgot, I'm not married," but not before a cat has slipped in with her. This time she leaves the door open as she walks forward, as if in a trance, knocking over the lamp on the table outside her bedroom. Whereas in the earlier homecoming she had neatly placed her coat on a chair, she now lets it fall to the floor. It is as though the power of disintegration entered her old home with her. Like a sleepwalker, she goes to the refrigerator, gets the milk, and pours some in the bowls on the floor in answer to the cat's miaow, but this time she spills some of it, then drinks from the carton herself so greedily that milk sloshes over her neck and her dress. Continuing her homecoming routine, she goes to the answering machine and begins listening to her messages, but this time she does not enter her bedroom right away. Instead she continues to drink from the milk carton as she once more hears her mother's disembodied voice asking her why she hasn't returned her call. Yet what precipitates her ensuing pleasurable destruction of her home isn't the recurrence of her mother's voice in the second message, more demanding and accusing than before, but the repetition of the message advertising Gotham Lady Perfume. This time it invokes the very scene of lethal humiliation she has just left: "One whiff of this and your boss will be asking you to stay after work for a candlelight staff meeting for two."

The final bit of information that this perfume is to be had exclusively at Shreck's department store provokes Selina to throw her milk carton at the answering machine, violently knocking it and the telephone to the floor. She then grabs the stuffed animals sitting on her sofa and pushes them down the drain in her kitchen sink with a wooden spoon, where the electric disposal chops them into tiny pieces and sends them into the sewer. Radiant with pleasure for the first time, Selina surveys the feathers that are left fluttering around the sink, proud of this evidence of her successful resistance to the illusion of romance and happy homes. At this point alley cats begin to enter her transformed home through the kitchen window, and with a frying pan, she starts smashing the pictures hanging on her walls and the mirrored shelf that holds favorite knickknacks. As more cats gather in the apartment, she takes a can of black spray paint and sprays graffiti onto her pink walls and the door to her closet. Next she opens the closet door and sprays paint on a particularly homey pink T-shirt with two kittens on the front. She then rummages wildly among her clothes until she finds a patent leather coat. With this under her arm, she enters her bedroom.

While in the first scene, Burton showed her from the side as she passed the neon sign on the wall, we now see her from the front. As she passes this sign that welcomes her to the intimate part of her home this time, she hits it twice with her elbow, knocking two letters off the wall. The next cut shows a bed neatly covered with a yellow blanket in a cute attic room, being slowly covered with black paint, and only as Burton's camera moves back do we realize that Selina is destroying the object most representative of any allegedly happy childhood—her dollhouse. She breaks it apart and throws the pieces on the floor. The destruction of her toys functions as the perfect materialization for her recognition that her claims to a harmoniously regulated home and family life are only a symbolic fiction, an illusionary ideology that she must radically reject. Once more Burton illustrates why the greeting

"Honey, I'm home" is fundamentally inadequate. The position that Selina actually occupies in the world she lives in cannot even be mentioned in conjunction with the concept of home. Indeed, the psychic homelessness she has been living even though she covered it over with the pink walls, the toys, and the other trappings associated with the "home, sweet home" paradigm now erupts in full force and she destroys all the objects supporting the injurious romance of a happy home that she once had in childhood: the photographs of her loving parents, the toy reproduction of a protective home, and the first objects of her love—her dolls and stuffed animals.

She has clearly entered a fantasy scenario revolving around her own self-aggrandizement, although it is the inversion of the classic daydream. Having destroyed everything that pertains to a happy return to the homey abode of her childhood dreams, she now substitutes objects that celebrate its opposite—an unconditional homelessness. The horde of cats now gathered inside her home and just outside the window to her bedroom takes the place of her mother's disembodied voice. On the table that had held the now smashed dollhouse, she sets up her sewing machine and fashions for herself a new, uncanny home from the patent leather raincoat. Deftly she stitches a black leather cat suit, which will allow her, not unlike Bruce Wayne in his bat suit, to assume the figure of the seemingly invincible cat she had repeatedly been confronted with as the insignia of Shreck's empire. Protected by this new identity, she will be able to prowl the nocturnal streets and take up her own particular battle with her male opponents.

Once her transformation is complete, Tim Burton moves his camera outside the bedroom of the home she has destroyed and reveals to us that the neon sign, under whose auspices this metamorphosis had taken place, has changed. In the absence of the two letters that she knocked off, the message is no longer "Hello there" but rather "Hell here." We see Selina suddenly emerge in her new costume from behind the curtains of her bedroom window. Like Bruce Wayne responding to the signal that the citizens of Gotham City had sent him, she appears as though on a stage, the changed neon sign signaling the auspices under which she has refashioned herself—the self-created symbolic interpellation to which she is willing to respond. As though they were her audience, cats have gathered on her windowsill as well as on the windowsill across from her home, and she addresses them as though she wants to thank them for the resuscitation they brought about. As she begins to bend forward, her hands resting seductively on her knees, then stretches and thrusts her arms wide above her head, she calls out to them: "I don't know about you, Miss Kitty, but I feel so much yummier." Like these feline creatures who have occupied her newly transformed home, she will now begin to search for her erotic pleasure on her nightly prowls.

Thus Catwoman emerges as the apex of a triad that connects her to the other two uncanny *Mischlinge*. In the battle zone to which the Red Triangle Gang has reduced Gotham City, she assumes a position that places her in competition with the two rivals Batman and the Penguin, even though her specific agenda places her in a league of her own. If the Penguin has ascended from the sewer to reclaim the home of his parents and Batman finds himself a stranger in his own home because of his split personality, Catwoman has forged a relationship to the place one might call home that more resembles Ethan Edwards's position in *The Searchers*, willingly turning her back on home. In contrast to Ford's hero, however, she requires no opponent to destroy her home for her. She doesn't enter the arena of battle in order to defend the symbolic fiction of an ideal home that she cannot be part of; she already knows that for her there can be no happy home because her wish to be loved as a woman and recognized in her professional ambition represents an unsolvable contradiction. In contrast to the two male combatants in Burton's noir comic world, she recognizes that there can be no protection against the traumatic kernel at the heart of all identity constructions, which makes one a stranger to oneself and which makes all material, symbolic, and psychic abodes provisional at best. She willingly abandons the illusion of protection that the happy home is meant to afford because she can't bear the disillusion it invariably brings with it; she exchanges home for the homelessness of the alley cat, precisely because she can then oscillate between the open street and a temporary sojourn in an apartment that now no longer carries any claims of being an intact abode. She doesn't need to fully destroy her home, as does Ethan Edwards, nor does she have to feel imprisoned by its constrictive idyll, as do Sirk's heroines.

She has reached this point because she has transformed the fissure inherent in all symbolic, psychic, and corporeal modes of abiding into the insignia of home. No name of the master of the house is written over the entrance of her door, as on the gate to the Cobblepot mansion; no crest on the gate identifies the locale, as at the zoo. Nor do we find an emblem signifying the owner's power, as is the case with the Batman sign projected onto the wall of Bruce Wayne's library by virtue of a complex machinery of mirrors, or with Max Shreck's name, rising above the entrance to his department store.

After her transformation, Selina Kyle's home exists unequivocally not in the name of a symbolic parentage but rather under the sign of an unsolvable antagonism: "Hell here." She resembles the Penguin in that her spirit of combat is sustained by an obscene enjoyment of violence aimed at taking revenge on the man who has humiliated her and caused her to fall to her death. She also shares the desire of the rejected son: she wants to no longer be treated as an outcast by the men who determine the rules of the game; instead, she seeks to be recognized as a legitimate player in her own right. Her difference from the other two *Mischlinge* consists in the fact that, having been thrown out of a window of Shreck's department store, and thus ejected from the symbolic community at large, she wants no part in protective fictions revolving around home and other conventions such as the battle between villains and saviors. She is willing to risk everything in order to enjoy with impunity the heterotopia that has opened up for her on the nocturnal streets and rooftops of Gotham City.

Several sequences later, Burton shows us how Selina uses her masquerade to ironically undermine Batman's role as the savior of women in distress. This scene, too, is staged as a repetition, compensation for a previous scene of narcissistic injury. A young woman walking along a street is dragged into an alley by a petty thief and pushed against a wall as he tries to steal the contents of her purse. Suddenly a shadow falls on the struggling woman and her assailant. The thief turns around and walks toward the strange creature, who taunts him by saying, "I just love a big strong man who's not afraid to show it with someone half his size." As he is about to hit her, she purrs to him, "Be gentle, it's my first time," and begins to skillfully kick his face with her spike-heeled boots. Retreating until his back is against the wall, the thief is now in the same position as the woman he has just assaulted, and also the same position Selina was in when she was attacked by a member of the Red Triangle Gang. After Catwoman has scratched his face three times with the pointed knives she has inserted into her gloves in lieu of cat's claws, the thief falls to the ground. She then turns toward the young woman. She will, however, accept no word of thanks, instead accusing her: "You make it so easy, don't you? Always waiting for some Batman to save you." In contrast to the scene in which the Penguin declared to the crowd at the cemetery that, having found his parents, he was now reborn as Oswald Cobblepot, Selina Kyle uses this scene to transmit a message about her own rebirth. To the woman she saved, who is now as shocked as before, she declares, "I am Catwoman. Hear me roar."

Like Batman in the earlier scene, she abandons the saved woman, but in contrast to him, she doesn't turn her back on her. Her means of exit from a scene of violence is somersault, which allows her to keep her gaze fixed on the other person as she flips backward around her own axis. This of course, also provides a perfect corporeal analogy for the fact that from this moment on, she will never allow a man to get her into a situation where she has her back against a wall. The only space she will accept at her back is the freedom of the nocturnal street.

A Second Battle Line Is Drawn

On the second night of violence that Max Shreck inflicts on Gotham City in imitation of the Reichstag fire, these three hybrid creatures finally meet in combat. The Penguin orders the members of the Red Triangle Gang to set fire to the small stores in Gotham City (implicitly invoking the ransacking of Jewish stores during *Kristallnacht*), so that Batman is forced to return to the city to protect its citizens. In the midst of the terrorist violence that has once more taken over the streets, however, Catwoman suddenly appears. She nimbly skips along the shop windows of Shreck's, beneath its symbolic insignia, the giant swiveling head of the smirking cat. Burton cuts to a window onto which this symbol has been stenciled in white paint. Suddenly Catwoman appears behind the grinning cat face, places both of her hands, masked as spiked cat's paws, on the window glass, and looks through the stenciled image, as though this were her second mask, into the interior of the department store. But one might also say that with this mise-en-scène Burton reiterates visually that Catwoman has taken it upon herself to perform the obscenely violent underbelly of this insignia of Max Shreck's symbolic power. Superimposed onto the image painted on the glass, her face, framed by her black cat mask, appears as the dark core of this emblem, and in the following sequence she will break into the building, where she no longer wants to be "properly housebroken," so as to break down the entire house. In so doing she actually performs the return of exactly what lay at the heart of the curiosity that had cost her one of her lives—her wish to challenge her boss rather than be subservient to him. Having entered, she whips the heads off the window dummies, thus castrating these materializations of the docile femininity she has cast off. After she has managed to successfully scare away the guards by threatening them with her whip, she moves on to her actual business.

At this point Burton intersplices the two scenes of combat, moving repeatedly between Batman fighting off the bullies sent by the Penguin—indeed, blowing one up with the same stick of dynamite that the criminal had tried to throw into a shop window—and Catwoman, who discovers a canister of gas hidden behind the wall in Shreck's kitchen department and tears off the hose so that the lethal fumes fill the interior of the store. Initially the two scenes seem to be unrelated. Yet once Batman finally encounters his opponent and both man-beasts embark on a verbal sparring match in which each seeks to signal to his rival how convinced he is of his own victory, they are suddenly interrupted by Catwoman, who somersaults toward them. Because Tim Burton films her approach in a frontal long shot, we recognize that the intimate conversation between Batman and the Penguin had taken place under the symbolic auspices of Shreck's red neon sign, not directly at the entrance to the department store but on the other side of the street. At the exact moment when Catwoman reaches the curb of the sidewalk where they are standing, the building, which serves as the architectural manifestation of the bone of contention the two man-beasts are fighting over, namely Max Shreck's corrupt politics, explodes.

Here Selina Kyle, disguised as Catwoman, behaves differently from Debbie, who, in the scene at the foot of the sand hills in *The Searchers*, seeks to bring about peace between her uncle Ethan and her husband, Chief Scar, because she emotionally belongs to both of the geocultural places that these men represent. Selina actually intervenes in the verbal combat between Batman and the Penguin, so as to join the fight. She does so in order to open up a second, far more ambivalent arena of strife, in which alliances with the one or the other opponent are possible, supporting the battle that is being fought in the name of universal values such as asserting or warding off the powers of evil. But she never allows herself to be sidetracked from her own highly particular interest—the destruction of Max Shreck. In this action, she radically undermines any untroubled demarcation between legitimate and obscene violence subtending Batman's use of force, as will be shown in my discussion of the subaltern showdown at the end of the film. Because she insists, to the end, on her violent desire for vengeance, she makes it impossible for the male combatants to carry out a battle with a clear front line.

In the following scene, Burton highlights the way Catwoman introduces gender trouble into the violent conflict between men. Once the Penguin chooses to leave the other two masked creatures alone to battle each other, the boundary between an ideologically motivated fight and a love duel can no longer be sustained. After Catwoman and Batman have scrambled up the roof of a nearby building, they fight each other as they had other adversaries in the previous scene. After Batman has successfully thrown his opponent to the ground, however, Catwoman deftly shifts gears, accusing him: "How could you? I'm a woman." Suddenly Bruce Wayne's empathy breaks through the armor of his bat suit and he apologizes to her. Her verbal intervention, however, proves to be nothing but a ruse. With renewed force she jumps up from the ground, lashes her whip, and sends Batman falling backward from the rooftop. She skillfully captures his outstretched hand in the noose of her whip as he is about to plummet into the dark abyss beneath their feet. Speaking down to the man, who is now dependent on her mercy, she haughtily explains, "As I was saying, I'm a woman and can't be taken for granted." Of course, Batman strikes back, throwing acid at her shoulder, so that she once more loses her position of superiority and is in danger of falling into the abyss herself, but he saves her, pulling her up to the ledge on which he is now standing.

Once more Catwoman skillfully enmeshes the conventional techniques of war with the weapons of female seduction, and once more Batman falls prey to her shift in register. "Who are you? Who's the man behind the bat?" she whispers alluringly, only to add, "Maybe you can help me find the woman behind the cat." She begins to caress his armored body with her gloved hand, until she discovers a part about which she might claim, "Here you are." Bruce Wayne's human side once more breaks through his disguise—not his gallant politeness this time, but his romantic desire. For one moment we see flickering in the eyes behind the mask a spark of hope that he might be able to transform this scene of battle into a scene of love, where both players recognize each other truthfully for what they are. But Catwoman wants the chase, not the catch. With one unerring thrust of her fist she hits her sentimental opponent right in the middle of his stomach, whereupon he immediately falls back into his role as invincible warrior and pushes her, with an equally unerring thrust, off the ledge of the building on which the precarious interlude had taken place. This time she falls backward onto a wagon filled with sand that just happens to drive by as she is about to hit the pavement. She laughs quietly to herself as she realizes that she has been saved by kitty litter, the material that would have proved whether she was housebroken or not.

The extent to which all attempts at drawing clear front lines have been radically troubled by the appearance of Catwoman becomes clear in the course of the intrigue that unfolds as a result of this second night of violence. Having returned a second time from death, Catwoman insists on performing the obscene enjoyment of violence, subtending as its ground and vanishing point all official symbolic law; she enjoys the destruction of the very public space in which she had sought to be recognized symbolically. She also insists on blurring the boundary between a monstrous figure who troubles peace and a healing defender of peace, for she undertakes to pay back the violence that was done to her. While the Penguin emerges from the sewer in order to politically represent an obscene law, feeding off the very material that had been harbored in his surrogate home, and while Batman returns from his home on the periphery of the city to reinstall a legitimate jurisdiction to counter this obscene law, Catwoman renders visible that the violence emanating from all three *Mischlinge* may serve very different political interests. Yet it is structurally comparable in that in all the cases, regardless of the political intent, it renders visible the contingency as well as the real antagonism of destruction. Catwoman explodes Max Shreck's department store and thereby supports Bruce Wayne's interest in curtailing the power of his political adversary. But her intervention is not in support of his belief in the fiction of a consistent symbolic jurisdiction; rather, it is to disclose the rotten kernel at the heart of all symbolic law. At the same time, she has returned from her lethal fall to transmit to all three of her opponents a message about the limits to their fantasy of being invincible, thus also rendering visible the hidden core inhabiting all fantasies about self-aggrandizement and ambition. By introducing gender trouble into the conflict between men, she is able to trick her fellow players into confusing a politically motivated alliance with a love pact, even while she ultimately resists all alliances.[7]

Just how much she troubles the arrogant savior fantasies of the other two *Mischlinge*, while repeatedly recognizing her own fallibility, becomes clear in the third night of violence. On the day after Batman has thrown her off the rooftop, Catwoman enters into an alliance with the Penguin, seeking to publicly humiliate her other opponent, Batman. During a television speech, the Penguin challenges the mayor to light the Christmas tree the following evening, as a symbolic gesture to prove that law and order have been reestablished in Gotham City. Admitting that he no longer trusts the mayor's power, he sends a second, hidden challenge to Batman. Looking directly into the camera, he voices his hope that Batman will help guard the peace.

On the day of the ominous ceremony, Selina Kyle allows Bruce Wayne, who met her while she was mournfully looking at a dollhouse in a shop window, to invite her to dinner at his home. Although neither of them has seen through the masquerade of the other, both want to experience the other side of the uncanniness as some familiar but expressed emotion that they experienced in their love duel, namely the wonder of love as a moment of revelation. The battle on the rooftops of Gotham City turns into a seduction scene in front of a fireplace in Bruce Wayne's elegant living room. Bruce tries to explain to the mysterious secretary that his last romance failed because his beloved had difficulty reconciling the two truths that make up his identity. Selina recognizes in his "difficulty with duality" her own predicament and gives in to Bruce's passionate embrace because she herself is finding it hard to maintain the boundary between her unmasked appearance and her animal alter ego. Although both Selina and Bruce can oscillate between their two personas, their spirit of combat ultimately wins over the desire for romantic love. They once more break off their love game, partly because they want to hide the wounds they inflicted upon each other the night before, but also because they hear on the television news that the Ice Princess, who was to light the Christmas tree, has been abducted. Both of them quickly leave the warmth and protection of the domestic fireplace without telling each other where they are going. By the tragic logic of their love, they feel uncannily attracted to each other because they share the truth of the difficulty with duality. At the same time they also resemble each other in that they prefer to perform the phantasmatic scenario of combat inscribed into the symbolic fiction of love, rather than give in to a romantic love that would deny this traumatic truth.

They will meet again high up on a roof terrace, where the Ice Princess sits tied to a chair. While Catwoman is able to drag the vulnerable woman to the flat top of the building, apparently assuring her safety, the Penguin appears and causes her to fall into the dark abyss, literally onto the red electric box with which the Christmas tree is lit. Yet the police searchlights that scan the top of the building for her assailant find only Batman, astonished and ashamed at his own ineptitude, while the crowd is now convinced that he is the villain. The Red Triangle Gang once more attacks the populace gathered at the plaza, thus realizing the premonition Oswald Cobblepot had voiced on TV only hours earlier, namely that the mayor was not in control of the criminal elements of the city. At the same time, Catwoman and Batman continue their love duel high above the violence that has broken out on the streets of Gotham City, pinning each other to the ground and taunting each other with cruel wit, only to suddenly break off the duel, with Batman leaving the scene in silence, the winner undecided. The Penguin, who has appeared to claim Catwoman as his love prize, finds himself mocked as well, and like Batman, his response to wounded masculine pride is to toss her off the building, so that for a third time Catwoman falls backward into the nocturnal sky, this time crashing into the glass roof of a hothouse. Now she no longer smiles to herself. The cry of anguish that she emits in response to this retaliation is so shrill that the entire glass house breaks over her head. A repetition compulsion informs this nocturnal battle in which all three *Mischlinge* are involved, which, rather than supporting their respective fantasies of being invincible, highlights its traumatic counterpart—the recognition of their fallibility. Catwoman is forced to stand by and watch another woman fall to her death as the result of a feud between two men. Concomitantly, she must recognize that she has unwittingly been complicit in this lethal game. Angered at the way she has been used, she explains to the Penguin that she had merely wanted to frighten the Ice Princess. But he is unwilling to listen to her argument and forces her to experience once again the impotence of simply being disposed of rather than being taken seriously as a combatant; indeed, she is literally thrown away by her opponent.

Batman also experiences a multiple retraumatization that night. He is forced to helplessly witness the fatal fall of the Ice Princess, as he had been forced to witness the murder of his parents, without being able to intervene. In his absence the members of the Red Triangle Gang have hidden a transistor in his armored car so that, in further evidence of his fallibility, he finds he is no longer in command of the vehicle. Instead, the Penguin uses a remote control to regulate the movements of his opponent's car, turning it into a lethal war machine. Far from protecting the streets, Batman now produces massive destruction instead. Although he is able to remove the transistor just before the car would have hit a woman with a shopping cart who stood frozen in terror in the middle of the road, the traumatic core at the heart of his fantasy of omnipotence has broken through. Like Catwoman, he has been forced to recognize how fragile his masquerade as invincible savior actually is; moreover, the disempowerment staged by the Penguin has also forced him to realize how fissured the boundary is between an obscene enjoyment of violence and the conscientious deployment of violence in the name of a symbolic fiction of reestablishing law and order. Implicitly, Burton thus invokes the anxiety called forth by the return of war veterans, as discussed in relation to film noir. Batman's uncanny deployment of violence confirms the fear that a soldier may well not be able to be integrated into the peacetime community because his return can so easily shift the war zone to the home front—to the streets and homes of those he was trained to protect.

Three Kinds of Homecoming

If Bruce Wayne and Selina Kyle had initially believed that their masquerade as infallible mythic combatants would serve as an apotropaic gesture against the fissure inscribed in their psychic apparatus as well as in the symbolic position they inhabit in the world, their recognition of the fallibility of their masquerade does not lead to a withdrawal from battle. Instead, their desire for destruction is merely heightened, and they respond to this narcissistic injury with more acts of violence. The next morning the citizens of Gotham City are willing to recall their mayor. They stand in front of the platform before the town hall and applaud Oswald Cobblepot. But Bruce Wayne is able to intercept the transmission of his speech with the help of the complex media machinery in his bat cave, and in retaliation for the public degradation inflicted upon him the night before, he now humiliates his rival. Suddenly the crowd hears not the voice of Oswald Cobblepot promising them urban peace but the voice of the vindictive Penguin, which Bruce Wayne had secretly taped, articulating his obscene enjoyment in the violence he was wreaking upon Gotham City. Thus for Oswald Cobblepot the traumatic core at the heart of his returning-home fantasy comes back to haunt him. Utterly demasked, he stands before the people from whom he had wanted nothing more than human recognition and is forced to watch helplessly as they tear down his campaign posters, shout abuses, and throw food at him.

But like his rivals, he will not retreat, and also like them, he finds himself returned to the initial scene of his trauma. Fleeing toward the zoo with policemen threatening to shoot him, he jumps off the same bridge from which his parents had cast him thirty-three years earlier, compulsively repeating the abjection they had inflicted on him. He returns to his surrogate constituents in his subaltern home and admits the failure of his attempt to live a double symbolic mandate. In front of his beloved penguins and the members of the Red Triangle Gang he viciously declares, "My name is not Oswald. It's Penguin. I am not a human being. I am an animal. Cold-blooded." He, too, will strike back, with a final biblical plague. As though he had always already counted on his own failure, he now takes out the list of all firstborn sons and commands his men to abduct these children on the night of Max Shreck's annual Christmas ball and drown them in the sewer. He is, indeed, no longer an uncanny figure but the unequivocal figure of evil, whose terror had been invoked by newspaper headlines at the beginning of the film: THE PURE REVENGER.

Tim Burton's resolution of his dark Christmas tale thus consists in a merciless demontage of the symbolic fictions declaring that home, in the sense of a viable community, might be regulated in a harmonious fashion, that families are based on alliances of sympathy, and that living with duality is possible. For his three *Mischlinge*, the dream of a happy inhabitation of the world (be this in the sense of a symbolic or a romantic recognition) has traumatic consequences. Only the recognition of the foreignness in oneself offers a platform for agency. At the same time, the traumatic traces of the experience of having been treated as a foreign body by one's family or one's community, and thus excluded from it, cannot be eradicated. All attempts at transforming psychic and social homelessness into the protective fiction of infallibility and homey happiness are doomed to fail, and in addition, the ambivalent, fragile protection that love or social recognition affords always brings with it its uncanny inversion, the threat of lethal dissolution. Selina is the only one who is able to carve out for herself a position of strength from the unavoidable recognition of psychic and social dislocation. Her dream that a "honey" might be waiting for her when she comes back from work, as well as her ambition to be recognized by her boss, results in her being thrown off buildings three times, even though she trusts in the proverb that claims she has six lives left. Bruce Wayne's dream of being repeatedly ritually reinstalled as the savior of Gotham City results in his inflicting more destruction on the city than the terrorist criminals he is actually meant to protect it from. Oswald's dream of returning to the world he was once jettisoned from results in his humiliation on the very stage where he hoped to be nominated mayor. In response, he declares total war on the home that can never be his.

Down in the sewer the combatants finally meet for the first time. While dancing together at Max Shreck's Christmas ball, Selina and Bruce discover each other's true identities, but, as in the scene in front of the fireplace, they must interrupt their romantic embrace because the renewed eruption of violence forces them once more out into the winter night. The Penguin had suddenly appeared on the dance platform to claim Max Shreck's older son, only to abduct the father instead. In the next scene we find him hanging in a cage above the stinking waters of the cloaca, while the Penguin gleefully moves forward with his alternate plan for a final solution, because Batman has successfully undermined the abduction of the first sons of the city. In front of the entire assembly of his penguins, their leader asks them to march into Gotham City with rockets strapped to their backs, to assemble in the square in front of Shreck's department store so as to "liberate" Gotham City with their collective suicide bombing. Once more, however, Batman succeeds in thwarting his rival's plan by intercepting the Penguin's signal and sending his army back to the zoo. Here the Penguin, in an unconscious gesture that signals his inability to curtail his own desire for destruction, detonates the bombs himself, exploding his own army as well as his surrogate home, the zoo. With the buildings, the sculptures, and even the sign falling down, Tim Burton stages the literal collapse of the symbolic fiction of the animalistic drives in the human subject, negotiated over the question of whether animals can be domesticated and their lives regulated in a harmonious manner in this zoo geography.

As though it were a mirror image of the destruction that is taking place aboveground, a game of life and death is undertaken beneath the zoo. Catwoman, who intervenes one last time in the battle between men, captures Max, who has managed to escape from his cage, with her whip and demands his life. Batman tries to convince her to hand him over to the police so that not the law of violence but a symbolically anchored jurisdiction might put him on trial. She insists, however, that the official law applies neither to people like him nor to people like them, calling Batman naive. Yet Bruce Wayne wants to enforce both the allegedly legitimate law and the family romance that Selina has inspired in him, and he pleads with her, "Let's just take him to the police. Then we can go home together." Addressing her by her first name, he tries to appeal to his rival's empathy: "Don't you see, we're the same. Split, right down the center." At this point Catwoman is standing halfway between both men and is thus forced, whenever she looks at one of her opponents, to turn her head 180 degrees from the other opponent, as though Burton wants to render visible that she is being called upon at this moment to choose between two desires, even though it is a forced choice.

Tearing his mask off, as though to signal that he is willing to sacrifice his invincible protective armor for their amorous relationship, Bruce hopes she will decide in favor of his home romance and against Max's death. She responds by confessing to him, "Bruce, I would love to live with you in your castle, forever, just like in a fairy tale." Then, as he gently begins to caress her face, the knowledge of her irrevocable homelessness returns, forbidding the choice of the romantic protective fiction of a happy home life that he is offering her. Lashing out at him, she pushes him away, explaining, "I just couldn't live with myself. So don't pretend this is a happy ending." Forced to choose between love and death, Selina realizes that she has nothing to choose. It is, after all, as she explained to Max earlier, a question of "a die for a die." For her, in contrast to Debbie in *The Searchers*, returning to a new home is not an option, even if she were accompanied by a person who resembles her in his self-estrangement. In an act that one might call ethical, she accepts what was always her destiny and destroys the embodiment of the obscene underbelly of the official law, even though it costs her Bruce Wayne's love and also her life. As Max Shreck calls out her first name, she turns around to face her only real love object—the rival in battle. Responding to this interpellation, she rips the mask from her face, as though she is giving birth to Selina Kyle, the self-empowered subject. While Max aims to shoot her, she reminds him of the proverb about the feline emblem of his empire—not the one explaining what killed the cat but the one declaring what will keep her alive: "You killed me, the Penguin killed me, Batman killed me. That's three lives down." After taking four of his bullets, she laughs at his impotence and says, "Two lives left. I think I'll save one for next Christmas." With the stun gun in her hand, she bends toward him seductively, offering him a kiss that will be fatal to both.

Bruce Wayne once again becomes witness to a murder, as he is once more forced to relinquish his wish of using love to turn his split home into a safe and protective emotional abode. This time, however, a trace of hope remains that will allow him to cover the trauma of vulnerability with a dream about the happiness love might still have in store for him. As he walks over to the place where the deadly duel between Selina and Max has just taken place, he finds only the charred remains of the businessman. The figure of Catwoman has disappeared from the battlefield without a trace. In her place the Penguin emerges from the sewer, but before he can take revenge on his rival he falls dead. As Bruce Wayne steals away from the battlefield, the rejected son, Oswald the Penguin, is welcomed home by the only creatures on whom he could always rely. From the stone portals of the cave, the few penguins who have survived the explosion push toward him and drag him lovingly into the water from which they once received him. As he slowly begins to sink, Tim Burton focuses on the reflection on the water's surface, revealing the figures of the penguins mourning him. As in the opening sequence of Fritz Lang's *Secret Beyond the Door*, however, this remains a marred reflection. The drops of water that fall onto the surface, as well as the movement caused by the descent of the corpse, make the image murky. Returning his camera to the last survivor, Tim Burton is able to offer one viable solution for his noir fairy tale in which those who were violently ousted from their symbolic homes strike back in revenge, enacting the uncanny underbelly of the symbolic fiction that communities can be regulated in a harmonious fashion and internal antagonisms translated into solvable conflicts. Bruce Wayne, sitting in his black Mercedes, is being driven home through the snowy nocturnal landscape by the only person he can really trust. On the way, he suddenly believes he has seen Catwoman's shadow moving along the wall of one of the buildings. He immediately asks Alfred to stop the car, and following the phantom figure into an alley, he discovers instead a cat. With her in his arms, he returns to his car and they drive on. In answer to Alfred's Christmas greetings, he responds, smiling mildly to himself, "Goodwill toward men, and women." Tim Burton's camera captures the black Mercedes one last time from the back, in a high, long shot, allowing it to drive out of the frame, while panning up one of the buildings. We recognize immediately that a new dream has been born, as though finding the cat has reinvigorated Bruce Wayne's fantasy. Once the camera has arrived at the top of the building, the Batman emblem is suddenly projected against the sky, and we see the masked head of Catwoman from behind, returned to the film screen, rising to meet the challenge.

At the end of *Batman Returns*, no solution is found for the "trouble with duality" and the concomitant homelessness that the protagonists suffer. The ambition to return honorably from exile fails, as does the hope that love might offer a protection from the knowledge that the subject is never identical with itself. If I have chosen to end my discussion of the various configurations of home that Hollywood has to offer with this noir fairy tale, it is not only because, like David Fincher in *Seven*, Tim Burton explicitly invokes the visual iconography of Christian mythology, deploying it as a familiar image repertoire in which both his dislocated protagonists and we, the audience, can feel at home. I chose this closing example also because, in a way that summarizes all the cinematic narratives that have been discussed in this book, Burton offers three tropic figurations for the way the subject may use the work of dreams to shape a sense of psychic and social dislocation in relation to nostalgic representations of home.

For Oswald Cobblepot, death emerges as the only way to return to a reliable place of abode, protected from all troubling contingencies. Having tried to ascend from the subaltern world of the sewer into which his parents had thrust him, he returns once more to the location of exile, destroying the architectural structures of this world as well, so that, like Annie in *Imitation of Life*, he is left with no other choice but to cross the threshold from life into death, and in so doing to turn himself into a memory trace for the survivors who mourn him.

For Selina Kyle a different kind of self-expenditure offers itself. Mysteriously escaping from the scene of her death because she believes in the power of proverbs, she appropriates the fate of the classic western hero and tarries on the rooftops of the nocturnal city. Having irrevocably transformed her dollhouse-like home into a provisional place of abode and turned her back on all chances to find a happy home, she can now enjoy the unlimited freedom of the vagabond, wandering with impunity in the heterotopic geography of the urban night. As long as there is someone who, placed on the threshold of the home he has been forced to return to, continues to dream about her return, she will continue to have one life left.

Finally, the nostalgic Bruce Wayne returns home, knowing full well that because he and his place of abode are split right down the middle, he will never be the master of the house but will always be forced to flee his trouble with the duality at the heart of his home into the simple opposition of a battle fought on the urban streets. Yet, returning home with his butler, Alfred, and the stray cat he has picked up, he has reached a certain degree of satisfaction. Like Hitchcock's unnamed heroine, like Fleming's Dorothy, like Lang's Celia, like Sirk's Sarah Jane, he can live with the sobriety of his everyday existence and the dissatisfaction that any real, concrete inhabitation affords because he can trust that, in his dreams, he can return to the scene of adventure, excitement, and self-aggrandizement.

For all three of these figures, returning home involves returning to a heterotopic site, superimposed onto the community of Gotham City: the grave at the bottom of the sewer, the dark mansion on the periphery of the city, and the nocturnal street, where, hidden behind a mask, one can pay back old debts and fight old love duels. In these heterotopic localities each one of the three *Mischlinge* can live through the traumatic knowledge of fallibility that is inscribed into any notion of home as well as any notion of self-identity. There they can invent dreams about belonging, or about home-lessness, depending on which is more appropriate to the emotional needs of each of them.

Notes

Prologue

1. See Richard Dyer, *Seven*, 59.
2. In an interview with Laurent Vachaud, David Fincher explained that while *Seven* is set in New York City, what he was truly after was the atmosphere of any big city infested with evil, which could serve as any megapole, while at the same time intending a crossmapping onto Dante's geography of the inferno in his *Divine Comedy*. With each new crime scene, he intended the film's viewer to get the impression that the two detectives were entering a new circle of hell until, in the last sequence—under a blazing sun as it sets on a desert landscape, amid huge electric aerial masts—they (figuratively) reach the center of hell itself. Vachaud, "Entretien avec David Fincher," 84.
3. I take this concept from Michel Foucault's essay "Different Spaces," in James Faubion, ed., *Essential Works of Foucault, 1954–1984*, 2:175–86.
4. Patrice Fleck has argued that in contrast to other recent serial killer films, *Seven* "seems to ridicule the possibility of detective as gatherer of knowledge" and is thus "suggestive of the impotence rather than omnipotence of law enforcement" ("Looking in the Wrong Direction: Displacement and Literacy in the Hollywood Serial Killer Drama," 42).
5. See Stephen Greenblatt, "The Circulation of Social Energy," 1–20.
6. As Dyer astutely notes, to consider a serial killer as a pathologic person beyond the pale of normal sanity implies distancing oneself from the implication that he may be expressing impulses common to all men, not least because the relation between serial killer and society might well be one in which the killer, "far from being against or outside society, as embodied in the law, in fact over-identifies with it" (*Seven*, 47).
7. Dyer, *Seven*, 34 and 78.

Introduction: Not Master in His Own House

1. In her article "Dream/Factory," Jane M. Gaines notes that while the utopian dimension of Hollywood should not be overlooked, one problem with the fantasies this "dream factory" produces is that they are always compromised, so that the issue of exactly how they are constrained continues to be one of the most important questions for film scholars.

2. In "Fantasy and the Origins of Sexuality," Jean Laplanche and Jean-Bertrand Pontalis offer a description of the work of dreams that explains its proximity to cinematic narration. They argue that fantasies represent scripted scenes, usually visually enacted, in which the dreaming subject is always present, both in the role of observer and in the role of actor. At the same time, they postulate, in a manner crucial for my own privileging of home as a staple of fantasy work, that the origin of sexuality is integrated into the structure of the three primal fantasies that Freud isolates. All three—the primal scene, fantasies of seduction, and fantasies of castration—revolve around the question of origins: Who am I in relation to the legacy of my family? What is the origin of my drives and my desires? What is the origin of my body's fallibility and mortality? For an overview of scholarship that combines cinema and psychoanalysis, see E. Ann Kaplan, "From Plato's Cave to Freud's Screen"; Elizabeth Cowie, *Representing the Woman: Cinema and Psychoanalysis*; and the collection of essays in Janet Bergstrom, ed., *Endless Night: Cinema and Psychoanalysis, Parallel Histories*.

3. I take the term from Bruce Kawin, *Mindscreen: Bergman, Godard, and First-Person Film*, and his distinction between the subjective camera (which pertains to a particular protagonist's way of seeing) and scenes clearly marked as referring to hallucinations or fantasy scenarios.

4. See Leonard J. Leff and Jerold L. Simmons, *The Dame in the Kimono*.

5. Sigmund Freud, *Introductory Lectures on Psycho-Analysis* (1915–1916), in Freud, *Standard Edition* (hereafter *S.E.*), 16:285.

6. As Hamid Naficy notes, the question of belonging and dislocation revolves around three concepts: house as the material place in which one lives, home as a temporary and moveable place that "can be carried in memory and by acts of imagination," and homeland as an abstract, absolute, and mythical place; see his "Introduction: Framing Exile," in the collection of essays he has edited, *Home, Exile, Homeland: Film, Media, and the Politics of Place*, 5–6.

7. In proposing this analogy I am indebted to Julia Kristeva's discussion of the correlation between the cultural experience of exile and the sense of psychic dislocation. The experience of cultural foreignness, thus her provocative claim, emerges as a counter-experience to that of the alterity produced by the workings of the unconscious, with the foreigner a cipher for any foreign body inhabiting the psyche; see Kristeva, *Strangers to Ourselves*. See also Sharon Willis's discussion of Joel Schumacher's film *Falling Down*, and other contemporary Hollywood films shaped in relation to home, in her introduction to *High Contrast: Race and Gender in Contemporary Hollywood Film*.

8. Sigmund Freud, "The Uncanny" (1919), *S.E.*, 17:220.

9. Ibid., 245.

10. Ibid., 226.

11. For a discussion of the intimate quality of the uncanny, see Mladen Dolar's essay "'I Shall Be with You on Your Wedding-Night': Lacan and the Uncanny."

12. Quoted in Jonathan Rée, *Heidegger*, 28.

13. Sigmund Freud, "The Unconscious" (1915), *S.E.*, 14:191.

14. Sigmund Freud, "Creative Writers and Day-Dreaming" (1908), *S.E.*, 9:147.

15. Ibid., 148.

16. Sigmund Freud, "Family Romances" (1909), *S.E.*, 9:241.

1. Uncanny Appropriations: *Rebecca*

1. François Truffaut, *Hitchcock*, 123.

2. For a discussion of the difference between Du Maurier's novel and Hitchcock's film, see Karen Hollinger, "The Female Oedipal Drama of Rebecca from Novel to Film."

3. See also *Hitchcock's Films Revisited*, in which Robin Wood suggests that Hitchcock's first Hollywood film "establishes definitively two of the major bases of his later work: the identification with the woman's position, and the preoccupation with male sexual anxiety in the face of an actual or potential autonomous female sexuality: the central structuring tension of many of his greatest films" (231–32).

4. Alfred Hitchcock, "In the Hall of Mogul Kings," in Sidney Gottlieb, ed., *Hitchcock on Hitchcock*, 228.

5. Truffaut, *Hitchcock*, 125.

6. Leonard J. Leff, *Hitchcock and Selznick: The Rich and Strange Collaboration of Alfred Hitchcock and David O. Selznick in Hollywood*, 36–84. For a general introduction to Hitchcock, see Donald Spoto, *The Art of Alfred Hitchcock: Fifty Years of His Motion Pictures*.

7. I will discuss the actual beginning of the film, "I's" voice-over and her dream images of Manderley, later in the chapter.

8. For an in-depth reading of the home movie sequence, and the manner in which it performs "I's" paranoid anxieties about her marriage and her new home by raising the issue of who is in possession of the gaze, see Mary Anne Doane's seminal article "Female Spectatorship and Machines of Projection: *Caught* and *Rebecca*," in *The Desire to Desire: The Woman's Film of the 1940s*, 155–75, as well as Judith Mayne, *Private Novels, Public Films*, 127–42, and Ed Gallafent, "'Black Satin': Fantasy, Murder, and the Couple in *Gaslight* and *Rebecca*"; both Mayne and Gallafent have responded to Doane's discussion, with the former arguing that the obsession and paranoia performed in the film are intimately tied to the very possibility of a female gaze, while the latter offers a counter-reading that focuses on Maxim's emergence in a sadistic male fantasy.

9. See Slavoj Žižek, *The Fright of Real Tears: Krzysztof Kieslowski Between Theory and Post-Theory*, 33–35.

10. See Avril Horner and Sue Zlosnik's discussion of how in Daphne du Maurier's novel Manderley proves to be a highly complex phantasmatic site, in their *Daphne du Maurier: Writing, Identity, and the Gothic Imagination*.

11. See Jean Laplanche and Jean-Bertrand Pontalis, "Fantasy and the Origins of Sexuality," 5–34, as well as my discussion of their argument in the introduction.

12. Even though William Rothman offers no in-depth analysis of *Rebecca*, see his study *Hitchcock: The Murderous Gaze* for its discussion of the self-reflexive camera work that was to become Hitchcock's trademark.

13. It is worth noting that in the course of the film, Joan Fontaine actually grows in size not only in relation to the place she inhabits but in relation to her husband as well. She initially seems to be much shorter than he, but she has almost attained his height in the scene where he notes that she has become the thirty-year-old adult he never wanted her to be, wearing a dark satin dress and a pearl necklace.

14. As Laura Mulvey notes in the chapter "Pandora's Box: Topographies of Curiosity," in *Fetishism and Curiosity*, this scene can be read in conjunction with the Pandora myth as it refigures feminine curiosity with enclosed, secret, and forbidden spaces into an investigation of the female body and the enigma of femininity: the transgressive desire on the part of the woman to see inside the female body as a mode of self-exploration but also as a manner of confronting the horror with which Western culture has connected the feminine body (60–61).

15. See John Fletcher's reading of *Rebecca* as a couple fantasy in "Primal Scenes and the Female Gothic: *Rebecca* and *Gaslight*," 351.

16. Judith Butler, *Bodies That Matter: On the Discursive Limits of "Sex,"* 126.

17. In an interview with J. Danvers Williams, Hitchcock explains his treatment of Daphne du Maurier's novel: "I shall treat this more or less as a horror film, building up my violent situations from incidents such as one in which the young wife innocently appears at the annual fancy-dress ball given by her husband in a frock identical with the one worn by his first wife a year previously" ("The Censor Wouldn't Pass It," in Gottlieb, *Hitchcock on Hitchcock*, 200).

18. Tania Modleski, *The Women Who Knew Too Much: Hitchcock and Feminist Theory*, 51.

19. Joan Copjec locates a further analogy between these two scenes in the fact that both Rebecca's bedroom and the beach house represent parts of Manderley that are particular sites of uncanniness, with the beach house marking a surplus and Rebecca's bedroom in turn marking an absence, a deficiency. Both, however, can be seen as extimate sites, "the most horrible part of the house—not because it is a distillation of all its horrifying features but because it is without feature, the point where the house negates itself" (*Read My Desire. Lacan Against the Historicists*, 132–33).

20. Pascal Bonitzer, "Partial Vision: Film and the Labyrinth," 58.

21. Doane, *The Desire to Desire*, 170.

22. Modleski compellingly suggests reading *Rebecca* as a classic feminine Oedipal story, in the course of which the bisexual girl must learn to relinquish her homoerotic attachment to the maternal body so as to fully accept her heterosexuality. While Hitchcock's film thus veers toward the building of the classic couple, Modleski insists that traces of the abjected maternal force remain—a reminder that the subversive feminine can never fully be assimilated into paternal law, much as traces of bisexual desire remain even after the feminine subject has been com-

pelled to choose heterosexuality, haunting her as an uncanny reminder of the cost of maturity.

23. Butler, *Bodies That Matter*, 126.

24. Thomas M. Leitch, *Find the Director and Other Hitchcock Games*, 115. He reads *Rebecca* as a seminal account of homelessness in Hitchcock's work "because of its use of the theme to link the motifs of instability, alienation, and the loss of identity" (122).

25. Truffaut, *Hitchcock*, 127.

26. See Rudy Behlmer, ed., *Memo from: David O. Selznick*, 309–10. See Leonard J. Leff's rich presentation of the battle over *Rebecca* between the American producer and his British filmmaker, in *Hitchcock and Selznick*, 36–84.

27. Julia Kristeva, *Powers of Horror: An Essay on Abjection*, trans. Leon S. Roudiez (New York: Columbia University Press, 1991).

28. Darian Leader suggests reading *Rebecca* as a feminine Oedipus story, in which "identity is elaborated in relation to the shadow of another woman," which is to say as a question of taking her place, initially by taking her costume to be exactly like her and then by emphasizing their difference. For Leader, the contrast to Danvers illustrates what the success of this story entails; he claims that to her, "one woman can never be substituted for another," thus putting her in exactly the place of the daughter whose terrible commitment to the mother makes her refuse to accept any substitution (*Promises Lovers Make When It Gets Late*, 19–31).

29. Modleski, *The Women Who Knew Too Much*, 55. My own discussion is greatly indebted to her analysis of the battle between Selznick and Hitchcock in relation to the Oedipal story performed by the film.

30. Though my own reading insists on a feminine encoding of Manderley, or rather sees Manderley as the site of contention between paternal and maternal figures of authority, Robert Samuels argues that this beginning performs that one of the ways a female voice can enter into the home of a masculine-controlled place is by detaching its voice from its body, with the heroine privileging retention of her memories over and against her husband's tendency toward repression. The insistent repetition of Rebecca's initials, especially the "R" on the case embroidered by Danvers, Samuels argues, marks both the possibility and the impossibility of memory, given that the cost of the heterosexual couple building at the end of the film requires that both the masculine mansion and the feminine desire it contained be burned down (*Hitchcock's Bi-Textuality: Lacan, Feminisms, and Queer Theory*, 45–57).

31. I take the notion of crypt from the work of Nicolas Abraham and Maria Torok, in *The Shell and the Kernel*, on transgenerational haunting, notably the secrets that are passed from one generation to the next and that thus structure the psychic reality of the successive generation, even though direct access to the content of these secrets is barred.

32. For a discussion of the gendering of the voice-over in classic Hollywood cinema, see Kaja Silverman's *The Acoustic Mirror: The Female Voice in Psychoanalysis and Cinema*.

33. Fletcher, "Primal Scenes and the Female Gothic," 354, 370.

34. Slavoj Žižek, *The Plague of Fantasies*, 10.
35. Truffaut, *Hitchcock*, 131.
36. Ibid.
37. Ibid., 133.

2. Home—There's No Place Like It: *The Wizard of Oz*

1. Ted Sennett, *The Great Hollywood Movies*, 44.
2. Reading the *Wizard of Oz* as a classic rite of passage of an adolescent girl, Inez Hedges suggests that in this tale, where Dorothy navigates between two female role models—a wicked mother and a good mother—only to seek help from a fallible father, "home, the end point toward which the fantasy moves, starts out by crushing the wicked witch of the east" (Hedges, *Breaking the Frame: Film Language and the Experience of Limits*, 113). From the point of view of gender, Fleming's musical thus offers a compromise fantasy. Initially Dorothy's frustration with the powerlessness she feels is transformed into a destructive power, with the home, once it has become unhinged, emerging literally as the instrument of her omnipotence, but later it—and the conservative dictum—are re-anchored, once more locking Dorothy into place. See also "Wearing the Red Shoes: Dorothy and the Power of the Female Imagination in *The Wizard of Oz*," in which Linda Rohrer Page suggests that as Dorothy takes the Kansas farmhouse with her to Oz, she also implicitly takes the spirit of Aunt Em, representing the classic Victorian "angel in the house." While the red slippers connect her to the wicked witches, Dorothy's use of them to return home can be read as a canny reinstallation of the patriarchal catechism for women, which requires them to stay in the domestic sphere. The magic power of the witch who was initially crushed by the flying house ultimately reinserts the adventurous girl into the familiar home from which she sought to liberate herself, transforming the liberator of Munchkinland into an imitation of her Aunt Em, into another angel of a Kansas frontier home.
3. Ted Sennett, *Hollywood Musicals*, 131.
4. As Paul Nathanson notes in his book-length study *Over the Rainbow: The Wizard of Oz as a Secular Myth of America*, the most common analytical approaches to this film are anthropological or psychoanalytical, focusing on the rite of passage undertaken by its heroine. Accordingly, he suggests that the film functions as a secular myth about how growing up as an American is tantamount to going home, even while this liturgical message about the collective identity in modern America is enhanced by *The Wizard of Oz*'s being shown on TV every Christmas. In a similar vein, Daniel Dervin suggests in *Through a Freudian Lens Deeply: A Psychoanalysis of Cinema* that Fleming's musical represents Dorothy's passage through the phallic phase, in the course of which returning home is tantamount to finding her femininity. Pamela Robertson, in turn, argues somewhat more critically in "Home and Away: Friends of Dorothy on the Road in Oz" that this rite of passage negotiates the "road movie's contradiction between the desire for home and away" in a retrogressive manner (271), for although *The Wizard of Oz* uses the yellow brick road as

an escape from the boredom of home, it privileges the road movie's potential con-
servatism, by using "the road and the encounter with others on the road to reaffirm
the benefits of staying home . . . opting for the familiarity" (283).

5. I take the concept of the *pharmakon* from Jacques Derrida's reading of the dia-
logues of Plato in *Dissemination*, in which he uses this concept to refer to certain
remedies that, depending on the dosage, can be either healing or lethal.

6. As Mladen Dolar has argued in "Beyond Interpellation," the constitution of the
subject cannot be thought of without an intimate kernel of externality, for which
Lacan coined the term "extimacy." The development of the subject from one who
dreams of belonging to a particular place in an infallible and unconstrained manner to one that recognizes the limitations imposed on its desire for self-identity,
plenitude, and infallibility by symbolic interpellation implies a cut between internal fantasies and the prohibitions experienced in external reality. Fleming visualizes this cut through the quasi-surreal intermediary sequence that links Dorothy's
departure from Oz with her reawakening in Kansas—namely, the image of the
girl, now outside the film's diegesis, floating through space like the unhinged
house in the earlier scene of transition. She continues to utter the sentence
"There's no place like home" as she also continues clicking together the heels of
her ruby slippers, while she moves through this liminal phase. As Dolar insists,
however, the constitutive cut, the break, the rupture that accompanies the emergence of the subject always produces a remainder because "there is always a part of
the individual that cannot successfully pass into the subject" and that haunts the
constituted subjectivity. Yes, this "remainder, marking that the clean cut is always
unclean, that ideology, to a certain degree fails, is neither exterior nor interior, but
not somewhere else either. It is the point of exteriority in the very kernel of interiority, the point where the innermost touches the outermost, where the materiality is in the most intimate" (78).

7. The novel by Frank Baum, on which the film is based, is a children's book in a su-
perficial sense only. One can easily make out the ideological project of the Populist Party, founded in 1891, a reform movement sustained by the agrarian sector,
which originated primarily in the western United States. The party candidate,
William Jennings Bryan—the model for the Cowardly Lion of Baum's novel—received the majority of votes at the Democratic convention in 1896 because he supported the replacement of the gold standard with the silver standard. He also supported the economic rights of farmers with respect to loans, as well as an
eight-hour day, graduated taxation, and retirement benefits. Read in relation to
the political agenda of this party, the seminal imagery of the novel can be decod-
ed as follows: "Oz" is the abbreviation for *ounce*, the unit of measurement that indicates the proportion of gold to silver in a coin; Emerald City is a representation
of Washington, D.C., capital of the green dollar bill, also referred to as the "green-
back." For Baum, the figure of the Wizard served to expose the financial wizards
of politics, the large corporations, the stock and trust companies, as swindlers.
Along the same line, the tornado represents the revolutionary movement of the silver standard, which would have offered the farmers and workers more freedom

and political power, while the yellow brick road refers to the gold standard then in place. Accordingly, the magic shoes in Baum's novel are not red but silver. The Wicked Witches of the West and the East represent the leaders of the large corporations and stock companies whose entire power was based on gold, while the members of the Populist Party, primarily from the southern and western states, are represented by the Good Witch, Glinda. The Scarecrow stands for the farmers, who may not have a university education but possess common sense; the Tin Woodsman can be read as a symbol for the industrial workers, exploited and rusty but with a heart that is, with respect to the distribution of power, in the right place. Finally, the Cowardly Lion, to whom Professor Marvel hands over the rule of Oz at the end of the story, stands for the Populist movement itself. Even the fact that the Wicked Witch of the West meets her end when Dorothy dumps a bucket of water over her head can be interpreted as a historical reference, to the drought afflicting California at the time. Since the death of the witch represents the liberation of the West from the gold standard and big-money interests, it functions within Baum's ideological dream as the long-awaited rain that would call the arid southern and western states to new life.

8. Louis Althusser, "Ideology and Ideological State Apparatuses (Notes Towards an Investigation)," 123.
9. Sigmund Freud, "Creative Writers and Day-Dreaming" (1908), *S.E.*, 9:146.
10. Dolar, "Beyond Interpellation," 92.
11. Sennett, *Hollywood Musicals*, 131. For an exhaustive presentation of the production and post-production history, as well as the merchandizing, of *The Wizard of Oz*, see also John Fricke, Jay Scartone, and William Stillman's *The Wizard of Oz: The Official 50th Anniversary Pictorial History*.
12. Analyzing the mythology that surrounds the American concept of home as the best possible place in the world, Richard F. Selcer suggests in his article "Home Sweet Movies: From Tara to Oz and Home Again" that it has become more than a place; it has become a symbol for everything good in America and a yardstick for the decline of America, and it is treated as an institution. Because the idea of home had become so much a part of Hollywood's favorite themes by the 1950s, this "ideology," this "institution," was actually enlisted as part of a massive campaign "to recapture the millions of viewers who were staying home to watch their new televisions. Coming back to the movies was made synonymous with coming home for wayward audiences." Newspapers ran nostalgic advertisements "to remind readers about how wonderful the good old days of Hollywood had been—and still were" (62).
13. Ibid., 52.
14. Michael Wood, *America in the Movies*, 10.
15. Ibid., xx.
16. Ibid., 23.
17. Ibid., 192.
18. Slavoj Žižek, "Symptom," in Elizabeth Wright, ed., *Feminism and Psychoanalysis: A Critical Dictionary*, 424–25.
19. Sigmund Freud, "Family Romances" (1909), *S.E.*, 9:241.

20. My reading of the way in which Dorothy negotiates her desire, both in relation to the harshness of symbolic laws and to the unbearable proximity of lethal self-expenditure, borrows heavily from Slavoj Žižek's presentation of a triad of desire in *Looking Awry: An Introduction to Jacques Lacan Through Popular Culture*, 125–40.

21. Žižek, "Symptom," 425.

22. Althusser, "Ideology and Ideological State Apparatuses," 133–34.

23. Ibid., 130.

24. Dolar, "Beyond Interpellation," 77.

25. Ibid., 78.

26. Salman Rushdie notes that the movie "never really made money until it became a television standard years after its original theatre release" (*The Wizard of Oz*, 11).

27. Richard F. Selcer offers a different historical reading of Fleming's musical. Situating it within the context of the American Depression and the threat to the American family and home that went along with this moment of mass migration, he reads it as a "battle cry for all the dispossessed," arguing that theater audiences of 1939 had no trouble identifying with Dorothy's peregrinations because "tens of thousands of Americans were already roaming the nation's streets and highways in search of new homes, having been displaced from their former abodes" ("Home Sweet Movies," 60). Lynette Carpenter, in turn, argues in her article "'There's No Place like Home': *The Wizard of Oz* and American Isolationism" that the film reflects the influence of world politics around 1939: as a reluctant argument against American isolationism, with the cyclone "an apt if unintentional image for the advancing threat of world war" (40). Ironically, the fame of Fleming's heroine, as Carpenter describes, took on a life of its own as the war in Europe spread. Her love of home, combined with her resilient courage to fight the witches of the world, turned her into an idol of the British people, with RAF pilots using "We're off to see the Wizard" as the "theme song for their defense of London against the German Luftwaffe, and Australians adopting the same song as their marching music in the Libyan desert" (44).

28. See also "Down the Yellow Brick Road: Two Dorothys and the Journey of Initiation in Dream and Nightmare," in which James Lindroth offers a comparative reading of *The Wizard of Oz* and David Lynch's *Blue Velvet*, arguing that Lynch takes "everybody's favorite, sun-drenched fairy tale and turns it into a nightmare" (166).

29. Rushdie, *The Wizard of Oz*, 23.

30. Ibid. It is precisely in this sense that Gary Ross in *Pleasantville* (1998) has his hero take refuge in the supposedly ideal world of a 1950s soap opera as protection against the breakdown of urban American culture at the end of the 1990s. But in this black-and-white world of Pleasantville he, like Dorothy, finds more than the simple harmony that is lacking in his real-life conditions. He also introduces the color that brings with it the contingency of the unpredictable, aimed at accident and change, because he realizes the emotionally lethal quality of the state of homely happiness that is located on the other side of the television screen. As I will discuss in further detail in the chapter on John Ford's *The Searchers*, a figure such as Gary Ross's *everyboy* chooses to return to his 1990s home not least because a world

protected from all difference is an unbearably stifling one; in so doing, he reinserts precisely the aspect of the American Dream that Fleming expulsed: the right to an articulation of difference, be it the difference of race or that of gender.

31. Rushdie, *The Wizard of Oz*, 57.

3. Seduction of Departing: *The Searchers*

1. As Joseph McBride and Michael Wilmington note in *John Ford*, the child of Irish immigrants not only repeatedly transformed the founding legend of America successfully into cinematic language but also never tired of addressing the issues confronting the immigrant with the cultural legacy of this legend. In interviews he liked to conceal or falsify the facts pertaining to his biography, such that his exact date of birth continues to be disputed. As Richard Waswo notes, "It seems more than coincidence that this poet of our precariously ambivalent civilized identity should have taken somewhat successful pains to disguise his own" (*The Founding Legend of Western Civilization: From Virgil to Vietnam*, 301).

2. McBride and Wilmington, *John Ford*, 24.

3. Edward Buscombe, *The Searchers*, 64 ff. See also Michael Coyne's discussion of *The Searchers* in *The Crowded Prairie: American National Identity in the Hollywood Western*, in which Coyne argues that Ford's late westerns contain coded representations of 1950s America's social and political tensions, notably racism and McCarthyite anti-communism, by dislocating contemporary concern into a different historical period. Discussing the two different temporalities invoked in Ford's late westerns, Richard Hutson suggests in his article "Sermons in Stone: Monument Valley in *The Searchers*" that while the classic Cold War era had a sense not only that the frontier was gone but that it had always been a myth, this period "was also marked by strong belief that these myths were necessary to hold on to a national purpose with some semblance of coherence and relationship to a national past" (in Leonard Engel, ed., *The Big Empty*, 203).

4. Michel Foucault, "Different Spaces," in James Faubion, ed., *The Essential Works of Foucault, 1954–1984*, 2:178.

5. Tag Gallagher notes in *John Ford: The Man and His Films* that Ford was always interested in reminding his audience that his own myths were based on the myths devised by others, so that while the "Texas 1868" looks nothing like the *real* Texas, it does look the way "Texas *ought* to look," with Ethan wandering in a wilderness that is a metaphorical space, in which "anything is permitted and to which civilization has yet to come" (329, 331). See also Andrew Sarris's *The John Ford Movie Mystery*, in which Sarris calls Ford's Monument Valley a "slice of stylized nature," his "greatest tone poem" (175).

6. Richard Hutson, "Sermons in Stone: Monument Valley in *The Searchers*," in Engel, *The Big Empty*, 199.

7. McBride and Wilmington, *John Ford*, 37.

8. Michael Wood, *America in the Movies*, 42. It is interesting to note that one year later, John Ford made the film *Wings of Eagles* about naval commander Frank

"Sprig" Wead, played by John Wayne, in which the lethal quality of the home that American heroes fight for was literally staged. Returning to his wife (Maureen O'Hara) after a long term of duty, nominally to finally settle down, Frank leaves the warmth of his marital bed the first night home because he hears his daughter crying, falls down the stairs, and breaks his back. He will spend many months in a naval hospital, divorce his wife in the process, and never return home again. Even when his wife finally convinces him to return to her, he is saved from the calamity of home. He is called back to duty, and the attack on Pearl Harbor takes his life, thus offering him the glorious end of a soldier. If, as Sharon Willis suggests in her reading of John Schlesinger's *Falling Down,* in *High Contrast: Race and Gender in Contemporary Hollywood Film,* part of the recurrent cinematic theme of "going home" is an appeal for a return to the way things used to be, one must always bear in mind that this "happy place of the past" is not just a nostalgic reconstruction, desirable precisely because it is lost; it is also always doubly encoding, kept at bay precisely because it is stifling and dangerous for male heroes.

9. Wood, *America in the Movies,* 50.
10. G. W. F. Hegel, *Phenomenology of Spirit,* 88.
11. Ibid., 288.
12. I am deeply indebted to Jan Freitag for the suggestion to crossmap Hegel's theory of the necessity of war onto Judith Butler's notion of gender performance in *Gender Trouble: Feminism and the Subversion of Identity,* so as to use the critical trope of gender trouble to theorize the unsolvable antagonism, which refuses to be subsumed into any simple—and thus resolvable—gender opposition, instead emerging as the unsolvable kernel of difference at the heart of all notions of community.
13. For a discussion of the versatile use to which John Ford puts the many framed doors and windows, delineating the boundary between interior and exterior spaces, see William Luhr and Peter Lehman's reading of *The Searchers* in *Authorship and Narrative in the Cinema: Issues in Contemporary Aesthetics and Criticism,* 85–135.
14. Like Dorothy, she steps across the threshold of her familiar home to find on the other side a magical world, inhabited by an array of strange and marvelous figures absent from the drudgery of her everyday existence—in this case the lonely cowboy, the revengeful Indian chief, the greedy tradesman, the powerless cavalry officer, and the dangerous outlaw.
15. As John Ford explains in his interview with Peter Bogdanovich, "Well, I thought it was pretty obvious—that his brother's wife was in love with Wayne; you couldn't hit it on the nose, but I think it's very plain to anyone with any intelligence" (Bogdanovich, *John Ford,* 35).
16. Buscombe, *The Searchers,* 69.
17. Sam Girgus suggests that this scene can be read as an example of the way John Ford deploys the Puritan jeremiad, illustrating as it does his pilgrim's messianic fanaticism to purify, avenge crime, and uphold ideals, by introducing his "new stature as a dark, menacing and alienated hero. . . . The shot of Wayne's anguished face dramatizes many layers of meaning. Fear, foreboding, grief, and horror all

play out across his frozen stare and burning eyes" (*Hollywood Renaissance: The Cinema of Democracy in the Era of Ford, Capra, and Kazan,* 45).

18. Buscombe, *The Searchers,* 21. Along the same lines, in *The Western Films of John Ford* J. A. Place suggests that Scar "becomes the agent of Ethan's unacceptable unconscious desire to invade and destroy the home of Martha and Aaron, from which he feels so excluded, and (presumably) to rape Martha" (164), while Susan Courtney, in "Looking for (Race and Gender) Trouble in Monument Valley," suggests that the doubling of Ethan and Scar allows us to read Scar's "sexual relations with Lucy and Debbie as an outlet for Ethan's oedipal desires" (112). As David Thomson notes, "Scar is not real Comanche, with a life of his own, but as much the white man's projection as Monument Valley is an absurd place to start a farm," played, furthermore, by a white actor from Germany, wearing makeup and a feather ("Open and Shut: A Fresh Look at *The Searchers,*" 29).

19. Buscombe, *The Searchers,* 21.

20. Jane Tompkins argues that the rise of the western in fiction can be read as a male flight from the feminization of culture, as an escape to a literary sphere from which women continued to be excluded even after having won public acknowledgment as writers in the period after 1880 (*West of Everything: The Inner Life of Westerns*). Offering a very similar reading of the politics of gender trouble in this late western, Susan Courtney suggests that what makes man wander is obviously woman: "For in *The Searchers* woman repeatedly confronts the traditional significance of sexual difference, as she often assumes attributes of the phallus more than men, wielding not only books and guns, but a sharply pointed look as well" ("Looking for [Race and Gender] Trouble in Monument Valley," 109).

21. Countering the argument that John Ford's own position is in line with that of his racist protagonist, Peter Lehman suggests that "*The Searchers* deals centrally with racism, and its main character is a racist. This doesn't mean, however, that the film should be simply characterized as racist. Much of the film critiques racism" ("Texas 1868/America 1956: *The Searchers,*" in Peter Lehman, ed., *Close Viewings: An Anthology of New Film Criticism,* 403).

22. Peter Wollen, *Signs and Meanings in the Cinema,* 122.

23. See Brian Henderson, "*The Searchers*: An American Dilemma," for a discussion of the kinship structures and their ideological implications, as this is played out in Debbie, who functions as an object of exchange between white and Indian culture.

24. As David Boyd notes in his article "Prisoner of the Night," in which he discusses influences of *The Searchers* on Martin Scorsese's *Taxi Driver,* one of the significant differences is that "there is no counterpart to the character of Martin Pawley, no one suggesting the possibility of reconciliation, no alternative to the suicidal nihilism of Travis himself" (30).

25. McBride and Wilmington, *John Ford,* 159. As Tag Gallagher notes, Ethan's conflict "mirrors ideally the racism of society," recalling that Brad Jorgensen was willing to give up his life, "unable to deal with the thought that his beloved died less than pure," while Laurie endorsed Ethan's desire to see Debbie dead, telling Marty

that "Debbie's mother would want Ethan to put a bullet through the girl's brain" (*John Ford*, 333). Yet the presence of Marty, and with it his insistence on preserving Debbie, also indicates that society as a whole can tolerate the essential paradoxes of racial violence, but as the reverend-captain and Mose Harper come to embody it. Peter Lehman goes a step further to argue that Ford, well aware of the highly contested subject of interracial sexuality, particularly between black men and white women, that had culturally surfaced with ferocity by the mid-1950s, displaces these tensions "into the past and onto another race," while at the same time showing himself to be increasingly critical of white culture and its racial blindness in general; see "Looking at Look's Missing Reverse Shot: Psychoanalysis and Style in John Ford's *The Searchers*," 68.

26. Thomson, "Open and Shut," 31.
27. Throughout the final homecoming scene we hear the last stanza of the title song: "What makes a man to wander? What makes a man to roam? A man will search his heart and soul, go searching way up there. His peace of mind he knows he'll find. But where, oh, Lord, Lord, where? Ride away, ride away, ride away." In contrast to the first stanza, heard at the beginning of the film, what the song now celebrates is no longer the home the hero turns his back on but rather the impossible place where he can find a spiritual affiliation.
28. McBride and Wilmington, *John Ford*, 157.
29. Andrew Sarris, *"You Ain't Heard Nothin' Yet": The American Talking Film, History and Memory, 1927–1949*, 103.
30. Roland Barthes, *Mythologies*.
31. McBride and Wilmington, *John Ford*, 163.

4. Hybrid Home: *Lone Star*

1. See Gavin Smith's volume of interviews, *Sayles on Sayles*, 232.
2. Slavoj Žižek, *The Plague of Fantasies*, 10 ff.
3. Mick Frogley and Matt Symonds. "Interview with John Sayles About *Lone Star*," 5.
4. Eric Foner and John Sayles, "A Conversation Between Eric Foner and John Sayles," in Mark L. Larnes, ed., *Past Imperfect: History According to the Movies*, 11.
5. Smith, *Sayles on Sayles*, 224.
6. Ibid., 219.
7. See also Lee Clark Mitchell's discussion of John Ford's engagement with the relation between history and myth at the heart of the western, *Westerns: Making the Man in Fiction and Film*, 23–24.
8. Peter Bogdanovich, *John Ford*, 34. As Andrew Sarris notes in *The John Ford Movie Mystery*, Ford's ambivalent iconoclasm resides in the fact that he "preferred to accept history and even legend as it was written rather than revise it in a radical or derisive spirit" (128), and it is this gesture of preservation that John Sayles refigures in *Lone Star*.
9. James McBride and Michael Wilmington, *John Ford*, 181.
10. J. A. Place, *The Western Films of John Ford*, 238.

11. Andrew Sarris goes so far as to attribute a self-reflexive turn to the impoverished and forgotten hero lying in his coffin, suggesting that we are meant to realize "that the man in the coffin is John Wayne"—more precisely, the John Wayne of the 1930s and 1940s, who had grown too old for an action plot, so that this film "can never be fully appreciated except as a memory film, the last of its kind" (*The John Ford Movie Mystery*, 178).

12. Slavoj Žižek, *The Fight of Real Tears: Krzysztof Kieslowski Between Theory and Post-Theory*, 125.

13. Nicolas Abraham and Maria Torok, "The Topography of Reality: Sketching a Metapsychology of Secrets," in *The Shell and the Kernel*, 1:158.

14. While John Sayles explicitly gestures toward Ford's play with facts and legends, a second implicit bond between the latter's late westerns and *Lone Star* is that both contain a cryptic reference to the postwar period. While Ford displaces his story into the time after the Civil War, with this earlier postwar period functioning as a trope for the Cold War, it is precisely the decade in which *The Searchers* and *The Man Who Shot Liberty Valance* were produced that functions as the historical past around which *Lone Star* revolves. The postwar period acts as the stage for the re-placement of the obscene sheriff Charlie Wade through Sam Deeds's father, which is to say, it is in this period that the shared secret, on which the culturally hybrid world of Frontero is based, emerges. This secret, furthermore, will haunt the next generation with the same force that the western legend haunted both John Sayles and his implicit teacher, John Ford.

15. Dennis West and Joan M. West, "Borders and Boundaries: Interview with John Sayles," in Diane Carson, ed., *John Sayles: Interviews*, 213–14.

16. Philip Kemp, "Lone Star," 48.

17. See Rosa Linda Fregoso's critical reading of *Lone Star*, "Recycling Colonialist Fantasies on the Texas Borderlands," in Hamid Naficy, ed., *Home, Exile, Homeland: Film, Media, and the Politics of Place*, claiming that "despite its overture to multi-culturalism, the film's narrative is, on closer inspection, driven by a deeply colonialist and phallocentric project" (180). Joan M. West and Dennis West, in turn, note in their review of *Lone Star* for *Cineaste* that Sayles's exploration of borders includes generational conflict, with accommodation as the key ingredient that holds individual lives and social groups together (15).

18. For a discussion of the visual techniques used, see Jack Ryan, *John Sayles, Film-maker: A Critical Study of the Independent Writer-Director*.

19. Smith, *Sayles on Sayles*, 228.

5. The Enigma of Homecoming: *Secret Beyond the Door*

1. Vivian Sobchack, "Lounge Time: Postwar Crises and the Chronotope of Film Noir," in Nick Browne, ed., *Refiguring American Film Genres: Theory and History*, 130. For an overall discussion of the emergence and development of film noir, see James Naremore, *More Than Night: Film Noir in Its Contexts*, as well as Phil Hardy's discussion of the change in women's economic and social power with the

onset of the war, in *The BFI Companion to Crime*. See also Michael Walker's article "Film Noir: Introduction" for a discussion of the historical context of film noir, in Ian Cameron, ed., *The Movie Book of Film Noir*, 8–37.

2. In his "Notes on Film Noir," reprinted in Alain Silver and James Ursini, eds., *Film Noir Reader*, Paul Schrader tellingly argues that a further explanation for the resilience of noir style in postwar Hollywood was the presence of immigrant actors, directors, screenplay writers, and technicians, whose own loss of home brought with it not only the cultural pessimism underwriting many of the noir scripts and whose schooling in German Expressionism inflected the visual style of distortion privileged by noir. As Schrader explains, "When in the late Forties, Hollywood decided to paint it black, there were no greater masters of chiaroscuro than the Germans" (55).

3. Sobchack, "Lounge Time," 131.

4. Richard Maltby, "The Politics of the Maladjusted Text," in Cameron, *The Movie Book of Film Noir*, 39–48.

5. It might be fruitful to crossmap William Wyler's *The Best Years of Our Lives*, a fictional cinematic refiguration of the veterans' difficult return home, onto John Ford's *Let There Be Light*, documenting the efforts—but implicitly also the failure—of the rehabilitation clinics set up after the war to treat traumatized veterans and make them fit enough to return home. The fact that Ford's documentary, commissioned by the War Department, was never released suggests that although his film was conceived as part of an ideology of reintegration, it also portrayed the impossibility of truly effacing the traces of war trauma.

6. Dana Polan, *Power and Paranoia: History, Narrative, and the American Cinema, 1940–1950*. For a discussion of film noir as a cultural negotiation of changes in images of masculinity brought about by the end of the war, see also Frank Krutnik, *In a Lonely Street: Film Noir, Genre, Masculinity*.

7. Polan, *Power and Paranoia*, 253.

8. Sobchack, "Lounge Time," 166.

9. See Deborah Thomas, "How Hollywood Deals with the Deviant Male," in Cameron, *The Movie Book of Film Noir*, 50–70.

10. Gaston Bachelard, *The Poetics of Space: The Classic Look at How We Experience Intimate Places*, xxxvii.

11. I take the crossmapping between Bachelard's equation of home and psychic abodes and the scenarios of homelessness celebrated by film noir from Sobchack's historical and cultural contextualization of film noir in "Lounge Time," even though she does not consider Fritz Lang's *Secret Beyond the Door*. For a discussion of the seminality of homelessness in film noir, see also Dean MacCannell, "Democracy's Turn: On Homeless Noir," in Joan Copjec, ed., *Shades of Noir*, 279–97.

12. Sigmund Freud, "Beyond the Pleasure Principle" (1920), *S.E.*, 18:15 ff. See also my own discussion of the conjunction between representations of feminine death and the *fort-da* game in *Over Her Dead Body: Death, Femininity, and the Aesthetic*.

13. Elizabeth Cowie, "Film Noir and Women," in Copjec, *Shades of Noir*, 148–50, highlights the proximity between *Secret Beyond the Door* and the bluebeard fairy

tale, as does Tom Gunning in *The Films of Fritz Lang: Allegories of Vision and Modernity*, who argues that Lang stages female agency uncovering male guilt.

14. Mary Ann Doane, *The Desire to Desire: The Woman's Film of the 1940s*, 134.

15. As Michael Waller notes in his overview, "Film Noir: Introduction" in Cameron, *The Movie Book of Film Noir*, 8–37, Lang's *Secret Beyond the Door* recalls not only Hitchcock's repeated appropriation of psychoanalytic tropes but also the manner in which Freudian discourse had taken hold of Hollywood's cinematic language by the 1940s, in large part because of the European psychoanalysts who had immigrated to California.

16. Peter Bogdanovich, *Fritz Lang in America*, 73. See also Tom Gunning's discussion of the way *Rebecca* served as Fritz Lang's source of inspiration, even though the appropriation and incorporation was by no means a simple gesture of plagiarism (*The Films of Fritz Lang*, 345–48).

17. Gunning, *The Films of Fritz Lang*, 350.

18. Karin Hollinger, "Film Noir, Voice-over, and the Femme Fatale," in Silver and Ursini, *Film Noir Reader*, 257. For a more general discussion of the feminine voice-over, see Kaja Silverman, *The Acoustic Mirror: The Female Voice in Psychoanalysis and Cinema*.

19. Lotte Eisner, *Fritz Lang*, 275.

20. See Michel Chion, *The Voice of Cinema*.

21. Slavoj Žižek, "I Hear You with My Eyes; or, the Invisible Master," in Renata Salecl and Slavoj Žižek, eds., *Gaze and Voice as Love Objects*, 93.

22. Gunning, *The Films of Fritz Lang*, 352.

23. Mladen Dolar, "At First Sight," 140–41.

24. Ibid., 142.

25. With Mark's architectural theory, Fritz Lang offers a noir inflection of the affective value of rooms and other modes of abode that Gaston Bachelard discusses as a topophilia concerned with felicitous space. For Bachelard, poetics of space is also concerned with determining "the human value of the sorts of space that may be grasped, that may be defended against adverse forces, the space of love," admitting, however, that, attached to its positive value, other imagined values might well become dominant. It is the force of the imagination that renders homes, conventionally perceived as eulogized spaces, uncanny, precisely because "space that has been seized upon by the imagination cannot remain indifferent space . . . it has been lived in, not in its positivity, but with all the partiality of the imagination" (xxxvi), and it is precisely this dark yet unavoidable force that Lang explores in the analogy he presents between the psychic apparatus and the uncanny home of his noir couple.

26. Reynold Humphries, *Fritz Lang: Genre and Representation in His American Films*, 150. Tom Gunning, in *The Films of Fritz Lang*, rightly notes that once *Secret Beyond the Door* is crossmapped onto *Rebecca* we notice a significant difference in the presentation of the uncanny rooms that the two films' death-possessed protagonists, Mark and Danvers, show to the respective young brides. The invisible presence invoked by Mark is not a person but rather a "past incident, a murder," the scene of violence, not "the object of death" (366).

27. Humphries, *Fritz Lang*, 155.
28. Gunning, *The Films of Fritz Lang*, 356. Here Gunning argues against the point made by Mary Ann Doane, who equates the end of Celia's voice-over with the death of female subjectivity, as well as against Stephen Jenkins's contention, in his article "Fritz Lang: Fear and Desire," that the film actually investigates Celia, solves her mystery, and ends by fixing her in her place "within the terms of its order" (in Stephen Jenkins, ed., *Fritz Lang: The Image and the Look*, 104).
29. Gunning, *The Films of Fritz Lang*, 361.
30. Michael DuPlessis, in "An Open and Shut Case: *Secret Beyond the Door*," compares this final tableau to a Pietà composition, with Celia "looking down at him with 'maternal' solicitude" (74).

6. Sustaining Dislocation: *Imitation of Life*

1. In his introduction to *Sirk on Sirk: Conversations with Jon Halliday*, Halliday reports an anecdote that Sirk's wife, Hilde, told him about how her husband, explaining to her on the telephone how to write the word *Stanhope*, had responded to her question whether *hope* was as in *hope*: "After a short pause I heard Douglas' guttural voice coming in on the extension: 'No–o,' he said slowly and firmly: 'Hope' as in 'despair'" (8).
2. Ibid., 52.
3. See Mladen Dolar's analysis of Louis Althusser's scenario of symbolic interpellation in "Beyond Interpellation." As discussed in the previous chapters, Althusser highlights as crucial for the transformation of the individual into a subject of ideology a response to being called. Turning around to reply to an actual or, more significantly, an implied figure of authority by declaring, "Yes, it is I who answers to that name," is, however, only the first phase. The second phase required by interpellation is the additional declaration: "Yes, I am in the place allocated to me by the ideologies inscribing my real living conditions."
4. As Sirk explains to Halliday, he had suggested this particular screenplay so that, because they were to film in Tenerife, he was issued travel papers. Although his wife at this point was already in Rome, he had to return home from this foreign location because the Nazi government had not issued him a passport. He was to get that for the next film, for which he again chose a foreign location. Thinking of the plot of *La Habanera* as a cipher for his own situation, one might speculate that he, like his heroine, is desperate to leave a place that has become psychically lethal for him, although his desire to get to America with his wife is diametrically opposite to Astrée's. He finds himself in a situation of permanent exile, while she experiences a final homecoming.
5. Halliday, *Sirk on Sirk*, 4.
6. Rainer Werner Fassbinder, "Six Films by Douglas Sirk," in Laura Mulvey and Jon Halliday, eds., *Douglas Sirk*, 107.
7. Christine Gledhill, "Rethinking Genre," in Christine Gledhill and Linda Williams, eds., *Reinventing Film Studies*, 236. For an overview of the debate revolving around

the melodrama genre and its problematic definition within film studies, see also Pam Cook and Mieke Bernink, eds., *The Cinema Book*, 157–71. For a discussion of the institutional, cultural, and historical conditions that produced both Sirk's films and the critical response to them, see Barbara Klinger, *Melodrama and Meaning: History, Culture, and the Films of Douglas Sirk.*

8. Christine Gledhill, ed., *Home Is Where the Heart Is: Studies in Melodrama and the Woman's Film*, 7. As Thomas Elsaesser notes in his article "Tales of Sound and Fury: Observations on the Family Melodrama," contained in Gledhill's volume, "Melodramas often use middle-class American society, its iconography and the family experience . . . as their manifest 'material,' but 'displace' it into quite different patterns . . . provoking clashes and ruptures which not only open up new associations but also redistribute the emotional energies which suspense and tensions have accumulated in disturbingly different directions" (60).

9. Tag Gallagher, "Douglas Sirk," 16.

10. Laura Mulvey, "Notes on Sirk and Melodrama," in Gledhill, *Home Is Where the Heart Is*, 75.

11. Geoffrey Nowell-Smith, "Minelli and Melodrama," in Gledhill, *Home Is Where the Heart Is*, 74.

12. Thomas Elsaesser, "Sound and Fury," in Gledhill, *Home Is Where the Heart Is*, 67.

13. Linda Williams, "Melodrama Revised," in Nick Browne, ed., *Refiguring American Film Genres: Theory and History*, 48.

14. As he explains to Halliday in *Sirk on Sirk*, "This is the dialectic—there is a very short distance between high art and trash, and trash that contains the element of craziness is by this very quality nearer to art" (110).

15. For an excellent discussion of the production as well as the cultural historical placement of Sirk's last Hollywood film, the screenplay, and a collection of seminal critical texts, see Lucy Fischer, ed., *Imitation of Life: Douglas Sirk, Director.*

16. Many critics have noted Sirk's problematic appropriation of the cultural stereotype of the black woman as paragon of maternity, given that what this excludes is any acknowledgment of either Annie's racial difference or her own unique subjectivity. For a discussion of the social conditions of women's work at the time *Imitation of Life* was made, see Lucy Fischer, "Three-Way Mirror: Imitation of Life," in Fischer, *Imitation of Life*, 3–28. For a discussion of how Sirk's depiction of this two-woman household can be read as a subtle critique of 1950s norms, suggesting that the institutional codes of postwar America, with their claim on domestic bliss, had already become troubled, see E. Ann Kaplan, *Motherhood and Representation: The Mother in Popular Culture and Melodrama.* See also Jackie Byars's discussion of race, class and gender in Sirk's last melodrama, in *All That Hollywood Allows: Re-Reading Gender in 1950s Melodrama* (Chapel Hill: University of North Carolina Press, 1991).

17. As Laura Mulvey notes in "It Will Be a Magnificent Obsession: The Melodrama's Role in the Development of Contemporary Film Theory," in Jacky Bratton, Jim Cook, and Christine Gledhill, eds., *Melodrama: Stage, Picture, Screen*, Sirk's film seems to ask why a society, obsessed by appearance and spectacle, should sudden-

ly fetishize essence when it comes to race. For Sarah Jane, the masquerade works only if she wipes out her black mother, so that "to achieve certain whiteness is to achieve the performance of white femininity, to become the product that she had witnessed her mother effacing herself to produce," in a performance of the spectacular femininity and whiteness already performed by Lora (131).

18. As Elisabeth Läufer suggests in her book *Skeptiker des Lichts: Douglas Sirk und seine Filme*, Susan Kohner's performance of Sarah Jane's ambivalence toward her ethnic background was compelling partly because it was her fate as well: on her paternal side she was Jewish, on her maternal side Mexican-Spanish, and thus she was considered "colored" at the time. She was the daughter of Sirk's agent and had already appeared in other films, impersonating figures of mixed race, such as the half-caste Jolie in Delmer Dave's film *The Last Wagon*. She received an Oscar nomination in 1959 for her performance in *Imitation of Life*. Along similar lines, Tag Gallagher notes: "The teenager who tries to pass for white resembles a Jew trying to pass in Nazi Germany: at any moment she will be found out. There *is* no solution" ("Douglas Sirk," 18).

19. Halliday, *Sirk on Sirk*, 151. As Sandy Flitterman-Lewis notes, the death of her mother causes Sarah Jane to cease her parodic performance of whiteness and to accept a definition of blackness that she finds injurious. While I would argue that Sirk leaves open whether she will really assume the position of servitude assigned to her mother, as Flitterman-Lewis suggests, she is right in noting that Sirk's ending makes it clear that there is no way to elide the racial and sexual discourses that interpellate the subject: "There is no possibility of 'passing' successfully forever" ("Imitation(s) of Life: The Black Woman's Double Determination as Troubling 'Other,'" in Fisher, *Imitation of Life*, 330). Along similar lines, Marina Heung critiques Sirk's allegedly conservative gesture at the end of the film, claiming that by having recourse to the ideology of the maternal melodrama he suppresses and displaces the issues of gender, class, and race posed by the Lora-Annie couple. The "sheer emotional power of this final scene," she claims, "finally operates to lay to rest the subversive energy of Sarah Jane and to reinstate Annie, in her death, as the emotional and ideological center of the film" ("Daughters and Mothers in Douglas Sirk's *Imitation of Life*," in Fisher, *Imitation of Life*, 320). To insist on Sirk's irony in this final scene, as I will show in detail, means that whether we privilege the ideological power of the maternal or the failure of ideology posed by the *Mischling* is something we as viewers must decide, while the film actually leaves this choice open.

20. Joan Copjec, "More! From Melodrama to Magnitude," in Janet Bergstrom, ed., *Endless Night: Cinema and Psychoanalysis, Parallel Histories*, 259 ff. As Fassbinder concludes, the cruelty with which both Sarah Jane and Annie seek to influence each other's actions is so compelling because it invites both critique and sympathy: "Both are right and no one will be able to help them. Unless we change the world" and "changing the world is so difficult" (in Fisher, *Imitation of Life*, 235).

21. Quoted in Fischer, *Imitation of Life*, 2.

22. Halliday, *Sirk on Sirk*, 151.

23. Ibid., 47.

24. Jacques Lacan, "The Mirror Stage as Formative of the Function of the I."

25. Sigmund Freud, "The Unconscious" (1915), *S.E.*, 14:191.

26. D. N. Rodowick, "Madness, Authority, and Ideology in the Domestic Melodrama of the 1950s," 43.

27. Halliday, *Sirk on Sirk,* 150 ff.

28. As Marianne Conroy notes, Sarah Jane's story becomes the place where the film comes closest to generating "a negative critique of its own vocabulary of female cultural empowerment," as well as the postwar status panic that she attributes to this gesture ("No Sin in Lookin' Prosperous," in David E. James and Rick Berg, eds., *The Hidden Foundation: Cinema and the Question of Class,* 130). Though Laura Mulvey is more interested in the question of feminine spectacle, she also places Sarah Jane in the center of the film, arguing that she "stands in the position of knowledge in the film, understanding, as it were, the full force of the accumulated metaphors. . . . Sarah Jane is pushed into performance by the racism of the society around her. She is told that she is not what she appears to be and refused the right to perform her appearance, the social status of 'whiteness' that is the passport to not being 'different'" (Mulvey and Halliday, *Douglas Sirk,* 36). In Ford's *The Searchers,* the figure of Martin was used to address the issue of miscegenation obliquely, even while he displaces the main character, Ethan, with his ability to cross over the threshold into the home of the Jorgensens, and Sarah Jane fulfills a similar function in *Imitation of Life.* She, too, decenters Lora Meredith, and, as Marina Heung notes, "is the catalytic character whose presence in the film convulses many of its unspoken themes" ("'What's the Matter with Sarah Jane?'" in Fischer, *Imitation of Life,* 324). Significant about the shift between Ford's refiguration of the theme of miscegenation and Sirk's is that while for Marty adoption did mean assimilation, Sarah Jane is forced to discover that she can never forget who and what she is. As Marina Heung concludes, "Blacks like Sarah Jane and Annie can remain as adopted members of the American family: invited, even appreciated, but intrinsically alien" (324). It is precisely because she cannot be blind to the uncanniness of her life within her symbolic community, and thus realizes that she will never be the master of a home, regardless of where and what it is, that—thus my own wager—Sirk could use her as the ethic center of his film.

29. Werner Sollors, *Neither Black Nor White, Yet Both: Thematic Explorations of Interracial Literature,* 249.

30. Sirk uncannily anticipates the gender crossings that emerged in the 1980s within the black and gay culture of cross-dressing, as this was documented by Jenny Livingston in her film *Paris Is Burning,* as a parodic enmeshment between the race and gender trouble that Judith Butler writes about in *Bodies That Matter: On the Discursive Limits of "Sex."* The young men performing their refiguration of the white fashion world at Harlem clubs make a similar claim, by speaking about realness as the ability to blend in, to look as much as possible like your counterpart and thus to become that desired Other. Thus, while the laws of racial segregation governing the world of Sirk have been suspended, and black self-identity has so

radically changed as to make Sarah Jane's desire to deny her black heritage seem unintentionally embarrassing, the notion of race crossing continues to both fascinate and raise anxieties. The cultural need to police the boundaries between the races that Sirk evokes in the sequences involving Sarah Jane gains additional resonance in relation to his own biography. After the fact, we can surmise that if he had stayed in Nazi Germany with his Jewish wife, Hilde, the nightmare that Sarah Jane talks about to Susie—"What do you think people would say where we'd live, if they knew my mother? They'd spit at me! And my children!"—would have corresponded to their actual living conditions.

31. Judith Butler, "Lana's 'Imitation': Melodramatic Repetition and the Gender Performative," 9. See also Marianne Conroy, "No Sin," in James and Berg, *The Hidden Foundation*, who argues that Sarah Jane's impersonation of a plantation servant implicitly casts Lora in the role of a plantation mistress, so that her angry parody involves a double irony. Butler names the real economic relations of servitude that the film's characters are at such pain to hide, and she names the racial privilege that makes Lora's rhetoric of a female culture of empowerment possible.

32. Butler, *Bodies That Matter*, 130.

33. See Elisabeth Bronfen, *Over Her Dead Body: Death, Femininity, and the Aesthetic*, especially the chapter "Death Bed Scenes."

34. Halliday, *Sirk on Sirk*, 153.

35. Marianne Conroy makes a similar point, arguing that Sirk's mise-en-scène "emphasizes the performance tropes that span both cultural styles"—the white theater and the black folk culture—even while the funeral sequence makes "a tentative but nonetheless significant gesture toward the representation of a genuinely heterogeneous cultural sphere" ("No Sin," in James and Berg, *Hidden Foundation*, 134). Richard Dyer, in turn, suggests that with the funeral sequence Sirk seems to want to say that "black culture is more authentic than white, materially and culturally," even while also marking the high point of grief in the film: "It is almost as if the film is saying that if there is anything other than imitation it is in suffering" ("Four Films of Lana Turner," in *Only Entertainment*, 96).

36. Critics differ widely on how this family resolution is to be read. Judith Butler, in "Lana's 'Imitation,'" holds that Sarah Jane has finally taken "her place next to Suzy as one of Lana's girls, suggesting that she finally achieves the great white mother she has always sought" (15), even though this is as phantasmatic a flight as her mother's staging of her funeral. Laura Mulvey sees a final, deeply pessimistic irony in the fact that Sarah Jane is received back into the newly constituted Meredith family, though she achieves her whiteness only through her mother's death (in Mulvey and Halliday, *Douglas Sirk*). Marina Heung, in turn, argues against privileging an ironic reading, suggesting instead that the ending supports an ideology of the melodrama, with its appeal to the inevitability of maternal resignation and suffering ("What's the Matter with Sarah Jane?" in Fischer, *Imitation of Life*). Finally, John Fletcher reads Sarah Jane's anguished declaration of love for her mother, "expressed in the very gesture that denies their relationship," not simply as characteristic of melodramatic emotionality but also as the narrativization of a laying bare and "seeing

through" of white racism and decadent bourgeois values, "performed through the intense emotions acted out by the woman, not at her expense" ("Versions of Masquerade," 48).

37. Halliday, *Sirk on Sirk*, 152.

38. Ibid., 155 ff.

7. The Homeless Strike Back: *Batman Returns*

1. The debut of the multimillionaire Bruce Wayne, who, in response to the traumatic loss of his parents, invented for himself an alter ego and in the guise of Batman, clad in a dark blue cape and bat mask, set himself the task of protecting Gotham City against crime, took place in the May 1939 issue of *Detective Comics*, the same year *The Wizard of Oz* was first released. The historical context of this birth allows one not only to locate the crossover between comic genre and film noir, which was to influence all cinematic refigurations of this story for the next sixty years, but also to read the adventures of this split hero, inspired by other comic figures such as Zorro and the Shadow, in relationship to the world war that broke out in Europe the same year, notably the *Blitzkrieg* in Poland and the German-Soviet non-aggression pact. Batman thus emerges as the fantasy figure over whom the highly debated role that the American armed forces were to take in the Second World War could be negotiated—as the mythic battle between a self-proclaimed hero and the powers of evil. See Phil Hardy, *The BFI Companion to Crime*, 43.

2. As Kim Newman notes in her *Sight and Sound* review of *Batman Returns*, Max Shreck's name is an explicit reference to the star of Murnau's *Nosferatu*. Burton also invokes the troubling conjoinment of the figure of the Jew with that of the vampire, played through in Murnau's film, connecting him, by virtue of his alliance with Penguin, to the biblical Moses but also to the paradigm of degeneration that Nazi ideology deployed in its anti-Semitic proclamations. Invoking a less vexed notion of degradation, Cory A. Reed notes in "Batman Returns: From the Comic(s) to the Grotesque" that Burton undermines "the values of official culture with his degradation of biblical traditions," such that "in degrading the mainstream culture it ambivalently affirms the possibility of regeneration and the promise of a new order emerging from the decay of the old" (38), even though this utopic gesture also resonates with the fantasy of a Third Reich, emerging from decay, as this was proclaimed by the Nazis.

3. In his conversations with Mark Salisbury in *Burton on Burton*, Tim Burton explains that although he was never a comic book fan, the figure of Batman had always fascinated him because of the split personality hidden behind the mask. He decided to turn the comic book hero into a cinematic hero once he realized that this is a story about a man who puts on a bat suit "because he needs to, because he's not this gigantic, strapping macho man," because the knowledge of his vulnerability compels him to don the masquerade of the invincible strong man he knows he is not: "It's like, if he had gotten therapy he wouldn't be putting on a bat-suit. He didn't, so this is his therapy" (72, 74).

4. As Burton points out in his discussions with Mark Salisbury, both *Batman* and *Batman Returns* are among the most successful films Warner Brothers produced at the time, even though the critics took him to task for the dark tones of the film. He states: "I've always felt that you couldn't even pull apart light and dark, they're so intertwined" (ibid., 83).

5. Sigmund Freud, "The Unconscious" (1915), *S.E.*, 14:191.

6. One of the many dark and ironic twists that Tim Burton introduces into his cinematic version of the Batman narrative, whose birth coincides with the acme of the Third Reich, is that the power-hungry businessman with the German-sounding name also recalls the Jewish department store owners who were forced into exile by the Nazi ideology, proclaiming them to be hybrid creatures, indeed vermin that needed to be extinguished. In a similar vein, the barrel organ man, who fires his machine gun at the Christmas tree, recalls fascist iconography, notably the caricatures of stereotypical Jews in Nazi magazines of the 1930s, such as *Der Stürmer*. The demonization of Max Shreck, which in the course of the film aligns him with the social freaks living in the sewer, should be seen as a self-conscious deconstruction of the fascist project of ethnic cleansing, and not as an uncritical reappropriation of this discourse, for Burton performs the wish to draw a boundary between pure and impure race as a horror scenario of violence, rendering visible the traumatic kernel inscribed in all notions of a racially untainted and untroubled community. Indeed, also revealed is that only a totalizing solution—the complete destruction of the heterotopic countersite beneath the city—can bring about the desire for obliteration of difference. For a discussion of the usage of stereotypical Jewish figures in *Batman Returns*, see Reed, "Batman Returns," 50.

7. For a reading that locates Selina Kyle/Catwoman more in relation to stereotypical notions of femininity, supporting an ultimate maintenance of patriarchal law, see Priscilla L. Walton, "A Slippage of Masks: Dis-guising Catwoman in *Batman Returns*," in Debora Cartmell, ed., *Sisterhoods: Across the Literature/Media Divide*, 183–200.

Bibliography

Abraham, Nicolas, and Maria Torok. *The Shell and the Kernel.* Translated by Nicholas T. Rand. Chicago: University of Chicago Press, 1994.

Althusser, Louis. "Ideology and Ideological State Apparatuses (Notes Towards an Investigation)." In Slavoj Žižek, ed., *Mapping Ideology,* 100–140. London: Verso, 1994.

Bachelard, Gaston. *The Poetics of Space: The Classic Look at How We Experience Intimate Places.* Translated by Martia Jolas. Boston: Beacon, 1994.

Barthes, Roland. *Mythologies.* Translated by Annette Lavers. 1957. Reprint, New York: Hill and Wang, 1972.

Behlmer, Rudy, ed. *Memo from: David O. Selznick.* New York: Avon, 1972.

Bergstrom, Janet, ed. *Endless Night: Cinema and Psychoanalysis, Parallel Histories.* Berkeley: University of California Press, 1999.

Bogdanovich, Peter. *Fritz Lang in America.* London: Studio Vista, 1967.

———. *John Ford.* London: Studio Vista, 1967.

Bonitzer, Pascal. "Partial Vision: Film and the Labyrinth." *Wide Angle* 4, no. 4 (1981): 55–64.

Boyd, David. "Prisoner of the Night." *Film Heritage* 12, no. 1 (1976–77): 24–30.

Bratton, Jacky, Jim Cook, and Christine Gledhill, eds., *Melodrama: Stage, Picture, Screen.* London: British Film Institute (hereafter BFI), 1994.

Bronfen, Elisabeth. *Over Her Dead Body: Death, Femininity, and the Aesthetic.* Manchester, Eng.: Manchester University Press, 1992.

Browne, Nick, ed. *Refiguring American Film Genres: Theory and History.* Berkeley: University of California Press, 1998.

Byars, Jackie. *All That Hollywood Allows: Re-reading Gender in 1950s Melodrama.* Chapel Hill: University of North Carolina Press, 1991.

Buscombe, Edward. *The Searchers.* London: BFI, 2000.

Butler, Judith. *Bodies That Matter: On the Discursive Limits of "Sex."* New York: Routledge, 1993.

——. *Gender Trouble: Feminism and the Subversion of Identity.* New York and London: Routledge, 1990.

——. "Lana's 'Imitation': Melodramatic Repetition and the Gender Performative." *Genders* 9 (November 1990): 1–18.

Cameron, Ian, ed. *The Movie Book of Film Noir.* London: Studio Vista, 1992.

Carpenter, Lynette. "'There's No Place Like Home': *The Wizard of Oz* and American Isolationism." *Film and History* 15, no. 2 (May 1985): 37–45.

Carson, Diane. *John Sayles: Interviews.* Jackson: University Press of Mississippi, 1999.

Cartmell, Debora, ed. *Sisterhoods: Across the Literature/Media Divide.* London: Pluto, 1998.

Cavell, Stanley. *The World Viewed. Reflections on the Ontology of Film.* Enlarged ed. Cambridge: Harvard University Press, 1979.

Chion, Michel. *The Voice of Cinema.* Translated by Claudia Gorbman. New York: Columbia University Press, 1999.

Cook, Pam, and Mieke Bernink, eds. *The Cinema Book.* 2d ed. London: BFI, 1999.

Copjec, Joan. *Read My Desire: Lacan Against the Historicists.* Cambridge, Mass.: MIT Press, 1994.

——, ed. *Shades of Noir.* New York: Verso, 1993.

Courtney, Susan. "Looking for (Race and Gender) Trouble in Monument Valley." *Qui Parle* 6, no. 2 (Spring–Summer 1993): 97–130.

Cowie, Elizabeth. *Representing the Woman: Cinema and Psychoanalysis.* London: Macmillan, 1997.

Coyne, Michael. *The Crowded Prairie: American National Identity in the Hollywood Western.* London: I. B. Tauris, 1997.

De Lauretis, Teresa. *The Practice of Love: Lesbian Sexuality and Perverse Desire.* Bloomington: Indiana University Press, 1994.

Derrida, Jacques. *Dissemination.* Translated by Barbara Johnson. Chicago: University of Chicago Press, 1981.

Dervin, Daniel. *Through a Freudian Lens Deeply: A Psychoanalysis of Cinema.* London: Lawrence Erlbaum Associates, 1985.

Doane, Mary Ann. *The Desire to Desire: The Woman's Film of the 1940s.* Bloomington: Indiana University Press, 1987.

——. *Femmes Fatales: Feminism, Film Theory, Psychoanalysis.* New York and London: Routledge, 1991.

Dolar, Mladen. "At First Sight." In Renata Salecl and Slavoj Žižek, eds., *Gaze and Voice as Love Objects,* 129–53. Durham, N.C.: Duke University Press, 1996.

——. "Beyond Interpellation." *Qui Parle* 6, no. 2 (Spring–Summer 1993): 75–98.

——. "'I Shall Be with You on Your Wedding-Night': Lacan and the Uncanny." *October* 58 (Fall 1991): 5–23.

DuPlessis, Michael. "An Open and Shut Case: *Secret Beyond the Door." Spectator* 19, no. 2 (Spring 1990): 58–77.

Dyer, Richard. "Four Films of Lana Turner." In *Only Entertainment,* 96. New York: Routledge, 1992.

——. "Kill and Kill Again." *Sight and Sound* 7, no. 9 (September 1997): 14–17.

——. *Seven.* London: BFI, 1999.

Eisner, Lotte. *Fritz Lang.* New York: Da Capo, 1976.

Elsaesser, Thomas. "Ethnicity, Authenticity, and Exile: A Counterfeit Trade? German Filmmakers and Hollywood. In Hamid Naficy, ed., *Home, Exile, Homeland: Film, Media, and the Politics of Place.* New York and London: Routledge, 1999.

——. "Tales of Sound and Fury: Observations on the Family Melodrama." In Hamid Naficy, ed., *Home, Exile, Homeland: Film, Media, and the Politics of Place.* New York and London: Routledge, 1999.

Engel, Leonard. *The Big Empty.* Albuquerque: University of New Mexico Press, 1994.

Fischer, Lucy, ed. *Imitation of Life: Douglas Sirk, Director.* New Brunswick, N.J.: Rutgers University Press, 1991.

Fleck, Patrice. "Looking in the Wrong Direction: Displacement and Literacy in the Hollywood Serial Killer Drama." *Postscript* 16, no. 2 (Winter–Spring 1997): 35–43.

Fletcher, John. "Primal Scenes and the Female Gothic: *Rebecca* and *Gaslight.*" *Screen* 36, no. 4 (Winter 1995): 341–70.

——. "Versions of Masquerade." *Screen* 29, no. 3 (Summer 1988): 43–69.

Foucault, Michel. "Different Spaces." In James Faubion, ed., *Essential Works of Foucault, 1954–1984,* 2:175–86. London: Penguin, 1998.

Freud, Sigmund. "Beyond the Pleasure Principle" (1920). In Freud, *Standard Edition* (hereafter *S.E.*), 18:1–64. London: Hogarth, 1955.

——. "A Child Is Being Beaten" (1919). In Freud, *S.E.,* 17:179–204. London: Hogarth, 1955.

——. "Creative Writers and Day-Dreaming" (1908). In Freud, *S.E.,* 9:141–53. London: Hogarth, 1959.

——. "Family Romances" (1909). In Freud, *S.E.,* 9:235–41. London: Hogarth, 1959.

——. *Introductory Lectures on Psycho-Analysis* (1915–17). In Freud, *S.E.,* 16. London: Hogarth, 1963.

——. "The Uncanny" (1919). In Freud, *S.E.,* 17:217–56. London: Hogarth, 1955.

——. "The Unconscious" (1915). In Freud, *S.E.,* 14:159–215. London: Hogarth, 1957.

Fricke, John, Jay Scartone, and William Stillman. *The Wizard of Oz: The Official 50th Anniversary Pictorial History.* New York: Warner Brothers, 1989.

Friedberg, Anne. "A Denial of Difference: Theories of Cinematic Identification." In E. Ann Kaplan, ed., *Psychoanalysis and Cinema,* 36–45. New York and London: Routledge, 1990.

Frogley, Mick, and Matt Symonds. "Interview with John Sayles About *Lone Star.*" *Sprocket* (1997): 4–6.

Gaines, Jane M. "Dream/Factory." In Christine Gledhill and Linda Williams, eds., *Reinventing Film Studies,* 100–113. London: Arnold, 2000.

Gallafent, Ed. "'Black Satin': Fantasy, Murder, and the Couple in *Gaslight* and *Rebecca.*" *Screen* 29, no. 3 (1988): 84–105.

Gallagher, Tag. "Douglas Sirk." *Film Comment* 34, no. 6 (November–December 1998): 16–27.

——. *John Ford: The Man and His Films.* Berkeley: University of California Press, 1986.

Gledhill, Christine, ed. *Home Is Where the Heart Is: Studies in Melodrama and the Woman's Film.* London: BFI, 1987.

Gledhill, Christine, and Linda Williams, eds. *Reinventing Film Studies.* London: Arnold, 2000.

Gottlieb, Sidney, ed. *Hitchcock on Hitchcock.* London: Faber and Faber, 1995.

Greenblatt, Stephen. "The Circulation of Social Energy." In *Shakespearean Negotiations,* 1–20. Berkeley: University of California Press, 1988.

Girgus, Sam. *Hollywood Renaissance: The Cinema of Democracy in the Era of Ford, Capra, and Kazan.* Cambridge, Eng.: Cambridge University Press, 1998.

Gunning, Tom. *The Films of Fritz Lang: Allegories of Vision and Modernity.* London: BFI, 2000.

Halliday, Jon. *Sirk on Sirk: Conversations with Jon Halliday.* New and rev. ed. London: Faber and Faber, 1997.

Hardy, Phil, ed. *The BFI Companion to Crime.* London: Cassell, 1997.

Hedges, Inez. *Breaking the Frame: Film Language and the Experience of Limits.* Bloomington: Indiana University Press, 1991.

Hegel, G. W. *Phenomenology of Spirit* (1920). Translated by A. V. Miller. Oxford: Oxford University Press, 1977.

Henderson, Brian. "*The Searchers*: An American Dilemma." *Film Quarterly* 34, no. 2 (Winter 1980–81): 2–23.

Hollinger, Karen. "The Female Oedipal Drama of *Rebecca* from Novel to Film." *Quarterly Review of Film and Video* 14, no. 4 (August 1993): 17–30.

Horner, Avril, and Sue Zlosnik. *Daphne du Maurier: Writing, Identity, and the Gothic Imagination.* London: Macmillan, 1998.

Humm, Maggie. *Feminism and Film.* Bloomington: Indiana University Press, 1997.

Humphries, Reynold. *Fritz Lang: Genre and Representation in His American Films.* Baltimore: Johns Hopkins University Press, 1989.

James, David E., and Rick Berg, eds. *The Hidden Foundation: Cinema and the Question of Class.* Minneapolis: University of Minnesota Press, 1996.

Jenkins, Stephen, ed. *Fritz Lang: The Image and the Look.* London: BFI, 1981.

Kaplan, E. Ann. "From Plato's Cave to Freud's Screen." In E. Ann Kaplan, ed., *Psychoanalysis and Cinema,* 1–23. New York and London: Routledge, 1990.

———. *Motherhood and Representation; The Mother in Popular Culture and Melodrama.* New York: Routledge, 1992.

Kawin, Bruce F. *Mindscreen: Bergman, Godard, and First-Person Film.* Princeton, N.J.: Princeton University Press, 1978.

Kemp, Philip. "Lone Star." *Sight and Sound* 10 (1997): 47–48.

Klinger, Barbara. *Melodrama and Meaning: History, Culture, and the Films of Douglas Sirk.* Bloomington: Indiana University Press, 1994.

Kristeva, Julia. *Powers of Horror: An Essay on Abjection.* Translated by Leon S. Roudiez. New York: Columbia University Press, 1984.

———. *Strangers to Ourselves.* Translated by Leon S. Roudiez. New York: Columbia University Press, 1994.

Krutnik, Frank. *In a Lonely Street: Film Noir, Genre, Masculinity.* New York and London: Routledge, 1991.

Kuhn, Annette. *Women's Pictures: Feminism and Cinema.* London: Verso, 1994.

Lacan, Jacques. *The Four Fundamental Concepts of Psychoanalysis* (1973). Edited by Jacques Alain Miller. Translated by Alan Sheridan. New York: Norton, 1977.

———. "The Mirror Stage as Formative of the Function of the I." In *Ecrits: A Selection,* 1–7. Translated by Alan Sheridan. New York: Norton, 1977.

Laplanche, Jean, and Jean-Bertrand Pontalis. "Fantasy and the Origins of Sexuality." In Victor Burgin, James Donald, and Cora Kaplan, eds., *Formations of Fantasy,* 5–34. London: Routledge, 1986.

Larnes, Mark L., ed. *Past Imperfect: History According to the Movies.* New York: Henry Holt, 1995.

Läufer, Elisabeth. *Skeptiker des Lichts: Douglas Sirk und seine Filme.* Frankfurt: S. Fischer, 1987.

Leader, Darian. *Promises Lovers Make When It Gets Late.* London: Faber and Faber, 1997.

Leff, Leonard J. *Hitchcock and Selznick: The Rich and Strange Collaboration of Alfred Hitchcock and David O. Selznick in Hollywood.* Berkeley: University of California Press, 1987.

Leff, Leonard J., and Jerold L. Simmons. *The Dame in the Kimono.* New York: Doubleday, 1990.

Lehman, Peter. "Looking at Look's Missing Reverse Shot: Psychoanalysis and Style in John Ford's *The Searchers.*" *Wide Angle* 4, no. 4 (1981): 65–70.

———, ed. *Close Viewings: An Anthology of New Film Criticism.* Tallahassee: Florida State University Press, 1990.

Leitch, Thomas M. *Find the Director and Other Hitchcock Games.* Athens: University of Georgia Press, 1991.

Lindroth, James. "Down the Yellow Brick Road: Two Dorothys and the Journey of Initiation in Dream and Nightmare." *Film Literature Quarterly* 18, no. 3 (1990): 160–66.

Luhr, William, and Peter Lehman. *Authorship and Narrative in the Cinema: Issues in Contemporary Aesthetics and Criticism.* New York: Putnam, 1977.

Mayne, Judith. *Cinema and Spectatorship.* New York and London: Routledge, 1993.

———. *Private Novels, Public Films.* Athens: University of Georgia Press, 1988.

McBride, James, and Michael Wilmington. *John Ford.* London: Secker and Warburg, 1974.

Mitchell, Lee Clark. *Westerns: Making the Man in Fiction and Film.* Chicago: University of Chicago Press, 1994.

Modleski, Tania. *The Women Who Knew Too Much: Hitchcock and Feminist Theory.* New York and London: Routledge, 1988.

Mulvey, Laura. *Fetishism and Curiosity.* Bloomington: Indiana University Press, 1996.

Mulvey, Laura, and Jon Halliday, eds. *Douglas Sirk.* Edinburgh: Edinburgh Film Festival, 1972.

Naficy, Hamid, ed. *Home, Exile, Homeland: Film, Media, and the Politics of Place.* New York and London: Routledge, 1999.

Naremore, James. *More Than Night: Film Noir in Its Contexts.* Berkeley: University of California Press, 1998.

Nathanson, Paul. *Over the Rainbow: The Wizard of Oz as a Secular Myth of America.* Albany: State University of New York Press, 1991.

Newman, Kim. "Seven." *Sight and Sound* 11, no. 4 (August 1993): 48–49.

Page, Linda Rohrer. "Wearing the Red Shoes: Dorothy and the Power of the Female Imagination in *The Wizard of Oz*." *Journal of Popular Film and Television* 23, no. 4 (Winter 1996): 146–53.

Place, J. A. *The Western Films of John Ford*. Secaucus, N.J.: Citadel, 1974.

Polan, Dana. *Power and Paranoia: History, Narrative, and the American Cinema, 1940–1950*. New York: Columbia University Press, 1986.

Rée, Jonathan. *Heidegger*. London: Phoenix, 1998.

Reed, Cory A. "Batman Returns: From the Comic(s) to the Grotesque." *Post Script* 14, no. 3 (Summer 1995): 37–50.

Robertson, Pamela. "Home and Away: Friends of Dorothy on the Road in Oz." In Steven Cohan and Ina Rae Hark, eds., *The Road Movie Book*. New York and London: Routledge, 1997.

Rodowick, D. N. "Madness, Authority, and Ideology in the Domestic Melodrama of the 1950s." *Velvet Light Trap* 19 (1982): 41–48.

Rothman, William. *Hitchcock: The Murderous Gaze*. Cambridge: Harvard University Press, 1982.

Rushdie, Salman. *The Wizard of Oz*. London: BFI, 1992.

Ryan, Jack. *John Sayles, Filmmaker: A Critical Study of the Independent Writer-Director*. Jefferson: McFarland, 1988.

Salisbury, Mark. *Burton on Burton*. London: Faber and Faber, 1995.

Samuels, Robert. *Hitchcock's Bi-Textuality: Lacan, Feminisms, and Queer Theory*. Albany: State University of New York Press, 1998.

Santner, Eric L. *My Own Private German: Daniel Paul Schreber's Secret History of Modernity*. Princeton, N.J.: Princeton University Press, 1996.

Sarris, Andrew. *The John Ford Movie Mystery*. Bloomington: Indiana University Press, 1975.

——. *"You Ain't Heard Nothin' Yet": The American Talking Film, History and Memory, 1927–1949*. Oxford: Oxford University Press, 1998.

Selcer, Richard F. "Home Sweet Movies: From Tara to Oz and Home Again." *Journal of Popular Film and Television* 18, no. 2 (Summer 1990): 52–63.

Sennett, Ted. *The Great Hollywood Movies*. New York: Harry N. Abrams, 1983.

——. *Hollywood Musicals*. New York: Harry N. Abrams, 1981.

Silver, Alain, and James Ursini, eds. *Film Noir Reader*. New York: Limelight Editions, 1996.

Silverman, Kaja. *The Acoustic Mirror: The Female Voice in Psychoanalysis and Cinema*. Bloomington: Indiana University Press, 1988.

Smith, Gavin. *Sayles on Sayles*. London: Faber and Faber, 1998.

Sollors, Werner. *Neither Black nor White, Yet Both: Thematic Explorations of Interracial Literature*. New York: Oxford University Press, 1997.

Spoto, Donald. *The Art of Alfred Hitchcock: Fifty Years of His Motion Pictures*. New York: Doubleday, 1976.

Thomas, Deborah. "How Hollywood Deals with the Deviant Male." In Ian Cameron, ed., *The Movie Book of Film Noir*, 50–70. London: Studio Vista, 1992.

Thomson, David. "Open and Shut: A Fresh Look at *The Searchers.*" *Film Comment* 33, no. 4 (July–August 1997): 28–31.

Tompkins, Jane. *West of Everything: The Inner Life of Westerns.* New York: Oxford University Press, 1992.

Truffaut, François. *Hitchcock.* New York: Simon and Schuster, 1984.

Vachaud, Laurent. "Entretien avec David Fincher." *Positif* 420 (February 1996): 83–86.

Waswo, Richard. *The Founding Legend of Western Civilization: From Virgil to Vietnam.* Hanover, N.H.: Wesleyan University Press, 1997.

West, Joan M., and Dennis West. "*Lone Star.*" *Cineaste* 23 (December 1996): 14–17.

Williams, Linda. *Viewing Positions: Ways of Seeing.* New Brunswick, N.J.: Rutgers University Press, 1997.

Willis, Sharon. *High Contrast: Race and Gender in Contemporary Hollywood Film.* Durham: Duke University Press, 1997.

Wollen, Peter. *Signs and Meanings in the Cinema.* Bloomington: Indiana University Press, 1969.

Wood, Michael. *America in the Movies.* New York: Columbia University Press, 1975.

Wood, Robin. *Hitchcock's Films Revisited.* London: Faber and Faber, 1989.

Žižek, Slavoj. *The Fright of Real Tears: Krzysztof Kieslowski Between Theory and Post-Theory.* London: BFI, 2001.

——. "I Hear You with My Eyes; or, the Invisible Master." In Renata Salecl and Slavoj Žižek, eds., *Gaze and Voice as Love Objects*, 90–126. Durham: Duke University Press, 1996.

——. *Looking Awry: An Introduction to Jacques Lacan Through Popular Culture.* Cambridge, Mass.: MIT Press, 1991.

——. *The Plague of Fantasies.* London, Verso, 1998.

——. "Symptom." In Elizabeth Wright, ed., *Feminism and Psychoanalysis: A Critical Dictionary.* Oxford: Blackwell, 1992.

Index